D1283495

T. E. Lawrence
TO HIS BIOGRAPHERS
ROBERT GRAVES
AND
LIDDELL HART

T. E. Lawrence
TO HIS BIOGRAPHERS

Robert Graves

AND

Liddell Hart

DOUBLEDAY & COMPANY, INC.

GARDEN CITY, NEW YORK, 1963

WINGATE COLLEGE LIBRARY
WINGATE, N. C.

The publishers are grateful to Messrs. Johnathan Cape, Ltd., for permission to include copyright material.

Library of Congress Catalog Card Number 63-11220
T. E. LAWRENCE TO HIS BIOGRAPHER, Robert Graves
Copyright 1938 by International Authors N.V.
T. E. LAWRENCE TO HIS BIOGRAPHER, Liddell Hart
Copyright 1938 by Doubleday & Company, Inc.
All Rights Reserved
Printed in the United States of America

T. E. Lawrence
TO HIS BIOGRAPHER
ROBERT GRAVES

Information about himself, in the form of letters, notes and answers to questions, edited with a critical commentary.

24210

PUBLISHER'S NOTE

Unless they are specifically attributed to T. E. Lawrence, all footnotes throughout this section are by Robert Graves. The letters L.H. before page references indicate the companion work by Liddell Hart.

FOREWORD

My thanks are due to the Lawrence Trustees for permission
to publish material of which they hold the copyright: they
have here relaxed their rule against allowing the use of copyright material by editors other than those whom they may
themselves officially appoint. This book and Liddell Hart's
companion volume to it are being published simultaneously
and in the same format, not merely because of the obvious
advantages of the juxtaposition but because the Trustees wish
to make a single occasion of these two exceptions to the copyright rule. (Lawrence, who authorized and contributed to my
biography of him in 1927, later authorized and contributed
to Liddell Hart's biography, published in 1934.) In deference to the Trustees' wishes, however, no popular edition of
these books will appear until six months after the publication of the official *Letters*, which are to be edited by Mr.
David Garnett.

My thanks are also due to Messrs Jonathan Cape, Ltd., for
permission to quote passages from my *Lawrence and the Arabs*,
published by them in 1927, and to Doubleday, Doran & Co.,
Inc., who published the book in the United States in 1928
under the title, *Lawrence and the Arabian Adventure*.

I have shortened some of the letters quoted here, either
because they contain trivial matter or matter that only con-
cerns myself, or because they cannot be printed in full during
the lifetime of the persons to whom they refer. As much as

possible has been retained that illuminates Lawrence's thoughts, feelings and actions. Omission marks, which have a distracting effect on the reader, have been sparingly used. The frontispiece is from an original pen-and-ink sketch which I recently bought, framed, on a stall in the Caledonian Market. I have asked a number of Lawrence's friends who were with him in Egypt or Arabia during the War to identify it; but none can. It is done on the back of a photogravure of a Byzantine work of art. On the back of the frame is written in Arabic by someone who did not know how to indicate the vowels properly: "Lawrence of Arabia." It gives a most interesting contemporary impression of Lawrence with the Arab look in his eyes and was probably done during one of his flying visits to Egypt in 1918.

R. G.

1938

CONTENTS

PART I

1920–1926

PART I

1920-1926

T. E. LAWRENCE TO HIS BIOGRAPHER,
ROBERT GRAVES

I have written, in a contribution to *T. E. Lawrence by His Friends*, about my first meeting with Lawrence at Oxford, where he had a research fellowship at All Souls College, early in 1920; and about our friendship there, which was based on a common interest in poetry and a common enjoyment of Oxford as an almost-too-good-to-be-true relaxation after our recent war experiences. Through me Lawrence came to know several contemporary poets in whose work he was interested: including Siegfried Sassoon, who had served in the same regiment as myself, the present Poet Laureate, who was my landlord, and Robert Nichols and Edmund Blunden, who were my neighbours on Boar's Hill. Lawrence was not a poet himself and frankly envied poets. He felt that they had some sort of secret which he might be able to learn for his own spiritual profit. This secret he envisaged as a technical mastery of words rather than as a particular mode of living and thinking. I had not yet learned enough about poetry to be able to dispute this. And when I did begin to learn some years later he was not to be convinced. To him painting, sculpture, music and poetry were parallel activities, differing only in the medium used. He had asked Charles Doughty, the poet, his chief hero, why he had taken the journey commemorated in *Arabia Deserta;* and Doughty had replied that he had gone there "to redeem the English language from the slough into

3

which it had fallen since the time of Spenser." I think that these words of Doughty's made a great impression on Lawrence and largely account for his furious keying-up of style in the *Seven Pillars*.

Lawrence always thought of me as a poet, whatever side activities I may have had to engage in from time to time to earn a living, and for years he was very serious about my work. Because of this he stood as a sort of guardian angel over me: if anything went wrong he was always at hand to help. Naturally, I did what I could to square things up. All this has to be said or it will not be clear why his letters to me are in so different a vein from those he wrote to Captain Liddell Hart, whom he seems to have thought of as "historian—military and general". I pointed out in 1927, in *Lawrence and the Arabs*, my biography of Lawrence—and it has since become a commonplace—that Lawrence presented a different facet of himself to each of his many friends according to their activities and characters. To me he presented an unusually wide facet, because poetry is an unusually wide subject—as later he did to Captain Liddell Hart (whom for brevity I shall henceforth refer to as L.H.), because history is also a wide subject. But there was a difference in kind between the relationships. Lawrence's most original contribution to civilization was, perhaps, his refinement of the theory of war, demonstrated practically in Arabia, and L.H. was the first to appreciate this fully; whereas I did not look to Lawrence for any practical demonstrations of how poetry should be written—he expected these from me and even asked me to keep the successive drafts of my poems, as I wrote them, for him to see how they had developed. I seldom discussed war with Lawrence, and never war as a science.

Lawrence did not mention L.H.'s biography of him to me either in 1929 when it was projected, nor between 1932 and

1933 while it was being written, nor in 1934 when it appeared. In fact L.H.'s name occurs in no letter of this series until the last. Lawrence's friendships were separated by bulkheads. His helping L.H. was, however, consistent with what he had written about the critical shortcomings of my book. He wanted a practised and sane military historian to give an account of the Arab Revolt in which he would himself figure only incidentally. This was the book that L.H. set out to write. Lawrence had said (see p. 142, l. 1) that he would give no biographer but myself any assistance in writing about him; and L.H.'s book did not seem likely to come under the heading of biography. Lawrence encouraged him in an attempt to write a wholly new book, and gave him again much of the information he had given me, concealing from him the great part he had played in the composition of *Lawrence and the Arabs*. L.H. found, as he went on, that Lawrence *was*, in a manner of speaking, the Arab Revolt; the book became a biography after all, and there is little discrepancy between it and mine, though they were written from different points of view and published with seven years' interval between them, and though L.H. was far more thorough in his checking of Lawrence's facts than I was.

The painters and sculptors also seemed to Lawrence to have a secret, and already at Paris, during the Peace Conference, he was getting in touch with them. While he was living at Oxford and in London he came to know several more. He used to offer himself as a model to see what they made of him. Nobody painted the same man. One day in 1921 I was at Paddington Station with him waiting for the Oxford train. We met (Sir) William Rothenstein: he had tea with us in a refreshment room. Rothenstein said that he had just been doing a portrait of Lawrence. "Oh," I said, "which Lawrence?" Lawrence kicked me under the table. It is only recently that I have seen Sir William Orpen's version, or rather a photograph of it. It is a curious, almost libellous magnification of a seldom-seen element in Lawrence's character—a sort of street-urchin furtiveness—and a counter-balance to John's too sentimentally heroic portrait.

Then he also cultivated the prose writers. (See p. 116, l. 10.)

As Lawrence and I saw each other frequently at Oxford there are few letters surviving from this period, and those that do were written mostly to fix appointments. The first letter is dated 15th April 1920. Nearly all the others are undated: it was only in 1922 that the dating habit became regular with him. What was probably the fifth of the series was in answer to my sending him a manuscript book of poems, which in 1921 appeared, with additions, as *The Pier-Glass*. His attitude to my work, his enthusiasms, his self-depreciation and his subjective critical method clearly appear in this letter.

July 21, 1920

Dear R.G.

You have fairly got me now: I have the *Gnat* volume and have read it many times, and frankly I don't know about it. I like it so much: it is so masculine, so much deeper than the others write—and yet there seems a conflict in it, as though you were not sure yourself which sort they ought to be. That's where the rhymed ones score, for the music is an end in itself, and thought follows it. I am not in the least qualified to talk like this, but it won't do any harm, because you will take no notice (or at least no polite notice).

Incubus—splendid: isn't "Smiles for freedom, blinks an eye" too earthly an exit from such a night? It seems to me to jerk us rather violently down from the general to the private. Also "nothing wrong" grates on my degraded ear.

Return—not "blank" thirst: surely. Thirst is an agony, tearing distracting pain that gapes a man's black mouth open, and makes him stagger drunkenly. You are all shredded out of your balance with horror. Also stone doesn't go ragged with heat, but with rain.

Heat polishes, splits, blackens it, often warps it crooked. These are pettifogging points, which would only occur to one who had nearly died of thirst. Don't attend to them.

Drinking Song—That is yours. I don't get loud with other people, and loudness in them makes me shut up. No doubt it is a good poem: but I'd rather be a prig than be sociable.

The Gnat—Of course this is the crux of the whole matter, and I feel myself hopelessly unable to pick a hole in it. Only isn't it a sort of criticism to say that I feel there is a flaw somewhere? The stuff should, I think, be fused once more before you publish it. It seems to me again a conflict between the frankly dream-stuff and the realist school. There are legends—introduced scientifically as quotes from Josephus. A mystic beast—which bumps the furniture after flying out of his mouth. Of course its strangeness, and the little fear it puts in you when you read it, may come from this very mixture of world and other-world. I'm not a poet, or I'd know how you get effects. Let's get back to verbal details. I don't like "Prepare: be ready". They are very close together. The standard of style for minor voices should be high: surely. I don't like "tyrants use": it's become a phrase now: not crisp enough: also the rhyme of "fare" and "hair" is rather wanton, I think. Your blank verse is strong, irregular and musical enough without endings of this sort. I don't also know if I like the isolated "agony", though I haven't the least idea if any change could be made. It's the hardest word to put in the whole poem, I suspect, for it must be a climax of the previous very fast-moving, high coloured verse—and you have gone up so high in the picture of the beast straining itself to get out, that a climax has to be some climax. I pity you here. The end strikes me as the goods: though I'd like something less exact than the catalogue of the new shepherd and his dog: one line or three perhaps: it does seem to me you show a perverse pleasure in using the common adjective, where one a little less usual would maintain the illusion which to me is the power of the poem.

The Magical Picture is fancy, not vision of course, and like the drinking song is not my sort.

The Pier-Glass. This is metaphysic, and your music and happy words only look out of place, about this thought. (I mean "magic" curtain, "dismal" bellrope, "sullen" pier-glass.) The last two sections do entirely without subjective furniture: couldn't you show the mood of the mind that came in on its problem-pilgrimage, less directly? A suggestion that it saw sullenness and dismality in the mouldering place, without point-blank catalogue of adjectives? I think the last two sections right up to level again, and the second, as I said, in a different key. But it's impertinence in me to discuss what only you can do.

Distant Smoke. I'll go through it to the bitter end, for perhaps you feel annoyed with a baby or something, and this will be a counter irritant. "Yesterday" to "Adam" is splendid: but I don't like "Summoned . . . up": and "Defining . . . journey" strikes me as your nearest approach to a bad line. Please remember "A Mr. Wilkinson, a clergyman" produced in a moment of absorption by a great man. I don't like "God's curse" and "Father's blessing" side by side later on. However it's only an association. The wit of the thing is simply great: but "pity" seems to me hardly the note to end on. After all these were primitive men, and pity is too soft a motive for the desert.

Look here: It's a shame to treat you this way, for my babblings are only the meannesses of a Philistine. I have enjoyed the booklet immensely. Must I send it back? Many thanks also for S.S. letter. He seems alive still, but only just. When he gets back he will go about like a sagging water-skin for weeks. Salute Nancy and the babes from me.

E.L.

"Masculine" is the key-word to this letter. Lawrence idealized masculinity, partly perhaps because he knew that he was not conventionally masculine himself, in spite of his great physical strength and habitual knight-errantry. I do not mean that he was homosexual—he was not. But he could never squarely face the fact of the existence of women; he placed them in general on a romantic plane remote from reality, in which their actual presence made him rather uncomfortable. He seems to have felt at home only with practical not-very-young women of the good-wife-and-mother type; and had a peculiar sympathy for childless married women: He was afraid of women who thought for themselves. He once wrote to me about someone: "If she proves to be one of these whet-stone women, I shall keep a film of oil between us. I prefer bluntness to sharpness." His uncertainty about women corresponded closely with his uncertainty about himself—he alternated between romantic elevation and disgust. He also told me once at Oxford that women were, historically, incapable of writing or painting anything first-class. He had little opinion of Emily Brontë, and held that there was not enough of Sappho's poetry extant to warrant his revising his opinion on her account. (The single exception he made, to my personal knowledge, was Laura Riding, but this was by a spasmodic and unnatural intellectual effort.) What he wanted from his literary and artistic experience was the sense of finding other selves of his own; and I can now see that much of his interest in my work was of this curious self-duplicating quality. These other selves were, naturally, all men, and chiefly men whom he felt to be more compromised, spiritually, than he would allow himself to be. The word "great" was often on his lips: but I think that, except when applied to soldiers or other men of action, greatness was, with him, too often a synonym for manly self-mystification. So the name of only one other woman writer occurs in any letter of his that I have seen, and that is Mrs. Clifton's (see p. 173, l. 13), whose *Book of Talbot* is written with an oriental submissiveness of wife towards her Lord and Master which most English readers of either sex will have found odd, if not unpleasant. The poem of Christina Rossetti's for which, according to Mr. Vyvyan Richards, Lawrence always had a great feeling has the same female abasement clothed in religious language: *A Martyr—the Vigil of the Feast*, an ecstatically masochistic poem which is worth looking up in this context.

Lawrence was for years the only person to whom I could turn for practical criticism of my poems. He had a keen eye for surface faults, and though I did not always adopt his amendments, it was rarely that I did not agree that something was wrong at the point indicated.

"S.S." is Siegfried Sassoon, who was then on a lecture tour in the United States.

Eric Kennington was a friend of mine. Towards the end of the War, I had got special permission from the Camp Commandant at Kinmel Park, near Rhyl, where I was stationed, for him to do portrait studies of the soldiers there. And I had also written the introduction to the catalogue of his subsequent exhibition of War pictures at the Leicester Galleries (June–July 1918). Lawrence now had the idea of taking Kennington, to whom I had introduced him, out to Arabia with him to do illustrations for the *Seven Pillars*. He said that Kennington was the only man capable of drawing Arabs as they should be drawn. Kennington was excited by the plan. At the last moment, however, Lawrence could not go, so Kennington bravely went out alone. Lawrence wrote to me (undated):

Saturday

My Lord,

I'd just got as keen as mustard on going out with Kennington when Winston Churchill in his third effort to get me to join his new Middle Eastern Department used arguments which I could not resist.

So I'm a Government servant from yesterday: and Palestine goes fut (or phut?)—— —— —— —— ——

Kennington is going all the same: (that man is a great man) and as an official I'll be able to help him even more than ever: but what a beastly mess.—— —— —— —— ——

They let me fix my own terms: so I said a temporary billet, and £1000: out of evil comes good for ——

I had meant to publish the enclosed muck in USA, to raise £1000: and now I've written to say that I've made other arrangements. Will you read them now they are born to blush unseen? They are literal extracts from a book I wrote: but all the personal (subjective) part is left out for dignity's sake. It's bloody cheek asking you to read such muck: but the intrinsic interest may atone for the lack of technique: and as an artist you should be glad to peep behind the scenes of another's affair.

You say the shop is over: but perhaps I'll see you tomorrow and ask about that: *Pier-Glass* just come: not yet cut or read: you will gather from this note that I don't feel either lyrical, pastoral, or dramatic just now.

More tomorrow, if I can't get away by 4 P.M. this afternoon.

E.L.

He enclosed four chapters of the *Seven Pillars*. The shop reference is to a general shop I was helping to run on Boar's Hill. It failed, and I was left in considerable debt.

When I wrote to tell him that I liked the chapters very much he replied:

Colonial Office
9.1.[21]

Thanks for what you said about my chapters. You know me, so I don't trust your judgment. What judge in blazes is there for the man who doesn't believe himself?

E.L.

He added:

Have you read any Joyce?   Portrait of Artist
                            Dubliners
                            Exiles
                            Poems

They should be in All Souls, if not borrowed from me. He's the yet-unfollowed master of what will be the next school.

? 16th.

Dear R.G.

I can't come now: since Feb. 28. I've been in the Colonial Office all day: every day: first Mesopotamia: now Palestine: last night Turkey. It's hopeless. I'll let you know when, if ever, I get away. . . .

> 2, Smith Square
> Wed. night

Dear R.G.

This is a scribble at 11.45 P.M. We sit late at the office, and so I've only just got your note. I'm exceedingly sorry your kids are ill: and hope you'll send me better news of them.

You say you may get to town this week. On Saturday I go to Oxford in the evening, for Sunday. Back on Monday morning. If you can, call at 2 Smith Sq. or ring it up Victoria 5960: or ring me up in the Colonial Office: room 9: and we'll feed or meet somehow.

We are making a most ambitious design for the Middle East: a new page in the loosening of the Empire tradition: and are working like beavers to end it by Wednesday. This will explain distraction of note.

Yesterday one, but to-day three members of the Colonial Office staff came to the office without hats. It is said that the permanent under-secretary has placed his resignation in the hands of the S. of S.

This change fills me with money:[1] your change will exhaust you. Will you let me know at once if I can be any help to you? I wouldn't have written it, but I'll be leaving so soon.

> E.L.

The change was a move I made with my family from Boar's Hill to the village of Islip, on the other side of Oxford. When later I explained to him about the shop debts he sent me £50 in cash and gave me the *Seven Pillars* chapters mentioned to sell in America. One of them he recalled, to print in the *Army Quarterly* in April 1921. The remainder fetched £200, which saved me.

The hat joke was that I had told him that if he went to

[1]But see p. 54, seventh line from bottom.

the Colonial Office without a hat, in the Oxford manner, it would soon set a fashion in Whitehall. Nobody really liked wearing hats, I said.

> Grand Continental Hotel
> Cairo
> Ap. 22 [1921]

Dear R.G.

A filthy pen, but a godsend since it excuses me writing much. I've just seen a review by Squire in the *Mercury* of your last book: but it's rot. I know you won't care much, but things people say about one generally stick in a little, in spite of denials: and the man has the face to call the book "promise". You know it isn't: it's fruit, ripe and splendid and as good as you can do. And while of course it isn't your last, yet it's easily your best to date, and something whose line you won't pass, as with time you'll change, and this earlier feeling will be out of your reach, backwards; so please don't try to be dramatic,[1] or anything else: all's well.

> 14, Barton St., S.W.1
> 21.5.21

Dear R.G.

I'm back in the Colonial Office, and hating it: I wrote the date on this letter without having to think: i.e.: I'm a Government Official. Don't rub it in.

I promised you £100: and gave 50: meaning to send the other 50 from London. In the rush of my going I forgot it: and to be quite straightforward I'd rather not pay it till the end of this month. I spent a lot, travelling, and my pay here is not yet put through properly, so that for the moment I'm a hundred overdrawn. This is my limit, except in cases of necessity. If the extra £50 (or more) is urgently needed, write me and I'll send it: if not, please excuse me for another ten days. There must be no risk anyhow of your going bankrupt. I'm very sorry I muddled it: it was a clean forget.

1. Now to get back to news: shop—I'm very sorry. It sounds very hard luck.

[1] Sir John Squire had suggested that I should try the drama instead.

WINGATE COLLEGE LIBRARY
WINGATE, N. C.

2. I think it's good to be out of your cottage: Mrs. H. and Mrs. M. and the Laureate[1] were three overpowering neighbours.

3. . . . [2]

4. Those articles: yes, they didn't bring much. A good reason for selling only 4 of them; I had hoped they would have been £500.[3] The lesser sum gratifies my vanity more than the big one: but I'm very sorry for your sake. However, there it is. Writing, as you once said, is a badly paid business. If any wild American writes to Watt,[4] and offers more for more things from me, please hand it on; because I've got a lot of muck in my cupboard; yet:

5. I'm very sorry you've got to chuck Oxford. Have you any idea what next: nothing at present, of course, but after that?

6. Shakespeare was constantly in debt: and then when older was able to lend money, which is the more blessed state. Rothenstein quoted to me once a saying of Gerhardt Hauptmann, that "one should take as freely as one gives": a good remark, but difficult to swallow: because it's very hard to take things.

7. . . . [5]

8. You were quite right to carry on and risk piracy.[6] If they pirate we'll rook them for damages: so hope to God they will.

9. Your great fit of writing sounds exciting: I'll look forward greatly to seeing it: you have improved the *Unicorn:* good: you've written something about General Elliot: I always wanted to know which Elliot: ? the old red thing who defended Gibraltar, or was it some Hinksey hero. I'm glad the "Tangled in Thought" has gone forward: army captains are fruitful things (why not full colonels: still fruitier?)[7] metaphysics, songs, dreams, sleeps, and royalties: it sounds a new volume: and all in rhyme, and all in editors' offices. I hope the said editors will do their part. Some day you should

---

[1]Dr. Bridges.

[2]About my health.

[3]He had priced them originally at £1300–£1500.

[4]Mr. A. P. Watt, the literary agent.

[5]About Mrs. Rosita Forbes who had just returned from a secret journey to the Senoussi country disguised as a native woman, in the company of an Egyptian explorer. Lawrence was asked to attend the banquet in her honour. He here refers to her as "a very fresh and sporting person" and praises her trip as "the best a woman has done—ever at all I think". Nevertheless he had not gone to the banquet.

[6]Piracy of the *World's Work* chapters in England.

[7]A reference to our respective Army ranks.

write a poem about an editor: (or rather you shouldn't, but Pope should have: it doesn't matter what Pope writes about).

I can't live at home: I don't know why: the place makes me utterly intolerable.

Our schemes for the betterment of the Middle East race are doing nicely: thanks. I wish I hadn't gone out there: the Arabs are like a page I have turned over: and sequels are rotten things: do you want to make a happy ending to a tragedy? On paper it isn't virtuous, but in flesh and blood? I wish I knew.

Meanwhile I'm locked up here: office every day, and much of it, and another trip E. (this time to Jeddah to see the Sherif) looming: and all the time poor Kennington is sitting in Trans Jordan, drawing, and if I was there I could help him, and make things so much easier for him: —— —— ——

Send me another dollop of news when you have patience: but don't expect wonders in return. I'm not a writer: and this life is foul.

E.L.

In the winter of 1921–1922 Lawrence was in a very nervous condition, did not eat or sleep enough, and worked over the *Seven Pillars* again, destroying the second text which I had seen on his table at All Souls. He wrote by night; his days were largely spent in work at the Colonial Office. Late in January he came to see me at Islip, and looked so bad that I told him that he must take himself in hand. I asked why he didn't try to find some appropriate woman who would help him to a settled life; because if he went on experimenting with solitariness like this there would be a collapse. He said that he had never been able to fall in love: and the hysterical pursuit of him by women who, after listening to Lowell Thomas's lectures, had fallen in love with his fame had made him avoid the society of women even more than he usually did. As a boy he had never had much to do with women, having had no sisters, only brothers, and the habit had stuck. He said, jokingly, that the only settling down he could contemplate was enlistment in the Army or Air Force, where he would be compelled to eat and sleep normally, and have no time to think. ("Sometimes we wish for chains as a variety," as he had recently written, about civilised freedom, in his preface to the catalogue of Kennington's Exhibition of Arab Portraits). A few days later he wrote me the following (undated) letter:

Sunday

Lord,

What I told you last week about my likes was not altogether true. There was an exception who provided a disproportionate share of the motive for the Arabian adventure, and who after it was over dictated the enclosed as preface to the story of it.

I turned it out a day ago when preparing for a printer: and I don't know—— It's hardly a literary question of good or bad (nearer the address to a letter) but is it prose or verse?

à toi
Jourdain.

Will you return the outburst?

L.

This letter and the one that follows are in minute handwriting—about the size of Charlotte Brontë's. When Lawrence was feeling low his handwriting shrank; when he was pleased it sometimes grew enormous. The enclosure was the dedication to "S.A." which appears at the beginning of the *Seven Pillars*. I did not take the word "dictated" literally, for he seemed to regard the thing as his own.

Who "S.A." was I do not know, and the dedication affords no help; though it suggests that S.A. was someone who would have benefited by Arab freedom and who had indeed inspired Lawrence to his leadership of the Arab Revolt. (See also the last page of *Seven Pillars*.) One of his oldest friends told me, in 1927, that he believed S.A. to have been a certain Sheikh

Achmed, an Arab with whom Lawrence had a sort of blood-brotherhood before the War; and that Sheikh Achmed died of typhus in 1918. I hinted at this in the first draft of my biography: "Shortly before he captured Damascus there came news of a death by typhus, and this is one explanation, I believe, of his coming immediately away from the scene of his triumph and of much that has happened to him since." But Lawrence commented in the margin:

You have taken me too literally. S.A. still exists: but out of my reach, because I have changed.

This is difficult to square with the words of the dedication:

... ours for the moment
Before earth's soft hand explored your shape, and the blind
worms grew fat upon
Your substance.

and with his remark to L.H. on May 27, 1933, that S.A. "croaked" in 1918. See L.H., pp. 68, l. 15, and 156, l. 8.[1]

My impression is that S.A. was a woman; else the foregoing letter was unnecessarily misleading. Lawrence had told me that he had never been in love with a *woman*, not that he had never loved anyone; and the confession that he had not been frank with me about his "likes" meant to me, at the time, that S.A. was a woman, as it does still. It is likely, in view of his temperament, to have been ideal love in the mediaeval poetic tradition of knightly love for some impossibly removed lady; and it is likely too that the news that came to him shortly before the capture of Damascus spelt not the death of S.A. herself, but the death of the idea she had represented. "The marred shadow of your gift" suggests disillusion rather than physical loss. I cannot agree with Mr. Vyvyan Richards' suggestion that S.A. was a lay figure of literary passion. S.A.

[1]The letters L.H. before any page reference indicate the companion volume by Liddell Hart.

was clearly of outstanding personal importance to Lawrence during the Revolt; the over-laborious artistry of *Seven Pillars* is another matter altogether.[1]

In my answer to the letter I said that part of the dedication was, potentially, a poem, but the rest was probably prose; and that I could show him what I meant, if he would forgive me, by isolating what I thought was the poem part. I sent him the following:

A CRUSADER

Death, eager always to pretend
    Himself my servant in the land of spears,
Humble allegiance at the end
    Broke where the homeward track your castle nears,
Let his white steed before my red steed press
And rapt you from me into quietness.

I didn't recognise "Jourdain". I thought it might be his real name, for he had told me that Lawrence was not. I asked him what it meant.

That week my third child was born (Feb. 4th), and Lawrence wrote:

> [Undated]
> Colonial Office

Dear R.G.

I'm very glad it's over: for it struck me when I got your reply that it was singularly tactless of me to send you my own muck at such a moment.

You did a magical thing to my laboured paragraph, turning it into a most exquisite verse: one of your cleanest and most beautiful. The last couplet about the horses is a miracle.

What is to be done with it? I feel like a new whoever it was, whose middle finger has been suddenly tipped with gold. The rest look idiotic, and yet one can't eat with one finger.

[1] See also L.H., p. 143, l. 3.

After Rottingdean by all means come and see me here. You don't at present know when it will be? Because I shift about somewhat. However, any time, any day can be arranged. Give me a few hours' warning: especially if you want a night. Write to Colonial Office for speed's sake.

Congratulate Nancy from me.

Jourdain was a person in Molière who was puzzled about prose and verse.

E.L.

That summer I was literary editor of a miscellany called *The Owl*. I asked whether I might publish in it an isolated *Seven Pillars* chapter which he had sent me as an alternative, should any one of the three offered to the *World's Work* be refused. I also asked his opinion on a poem of mine which was later added to and became *The Marmosite's Miscellany*, published under a pseudonym. He replied in pencil:

[Undated, without address]

Yes, that introducing part makes it clear enough. Good egg. Good poem too. As I get old I fail to distinguish between what is serious in expression, and what is comic. It's a sign of age, to read things for the meaning rather than the form. Astonishing how quickly I have got old lately. I feel too tired to go on with it. You know my book proved dud at last.

Glad you have some Melville verses. I believe Oxford is going to republish all of them. Constable is doing his prose, including *Mardi*.

About me and the *Owl*. It sounds ridiculous, because I'm not a writer. Also, isn't it too long? What is it all about? Do let me know: and when you look it up, please rack your memory to tell me what was published in the *World's Work*. I want to mark it against my MS. I have heard comment, apparently,

   (i) On my second visit to Feisal, and his camp life, and a related battle in which the Juheina ran away to drink coffee.

   (ii) On a camel charge in which I shot my camel.

   (iii) On a lot of killing round Tafas, when Talal died.

Was there more? Were there these? If my book was finished (it's binding—4 copies) I'd send you the mass of it to choose a smaller gobbet from. Your taste out of such a midden might pick something not wholly putrid. When does the *Owl* come to a head: or be hatched, or lay itself: isn't it really a Phoenix? Query—write a debate in bird-land on the point.

Do you see old Hudson (*Purple Land*) is dead? In his sleep. He was such a great man.

Books are reported all safely arrived in Chingford.

What is the perversity which makes me, capable of doing many things in the world, wish only to do one thing, book-writing; and gives me no skill at it?

E.L.

The book that had "proved dud at last" was the *Seven Pillars*. Chingford was where he had bought a plot of land to build a cottage on. Meanwhile some sort of a hut was put there and housed his possessions.

His Colonial Office engagement was drawing to a close. The next letter is in very small and very tortured handwriting on a torn quarter-sheet of note paper.

2.7.22

This is my usual quarter-minute scrawl. Came back from Cornwall on Friday. Found your Poetry. V. many thanks. Have glanced at it only, which isn't yet worth telling you. V. busy. Saw Winston yesterday. He will let me go after Tuesday which is his speech-night in the House on the Colonial Office vote. I'll be kept here some time after that: because my Mother has been ill abroad and is coming here, perhaps on Thursday, to see a doctor. I must take their rooms and meet them. Otherwise I'd have liked to go down W. with you. As I'm almost a free-agent (waiting for the last batch of sheets of my Arab book) we'll be able to meet now. Thank the Lord for Winston coming round at last. I did so want not to quarrel with him. He's a most decent person.

E.L.

On August 17th came an unimportant note about a poem I had sent him, then nothing until the end of September.

The writing was larger and more regular again. He had just enlisted in the Royal Air Force and was doing a recruits' course at Uxbridge.

Sunday, 24th Sept.

Dear R.G.

I went to 14 Barton St. on Friday last and found your *Feather Bed*. . . .[1] I wish everyone had calmness after their storms, perhaps because I hate noise more than any other thing in the world—and fear animal spirits most. So some day do write a sunset poem for my benefit. Did I ever show you my private anthology? *Minorities*, I called it. You are not in it yet, because you haven't done that special note which runs through it.

About myself. I came to a milestone, or rather to a crossroad, and turned off the old one. The Arab thing is finished, and is passionately unwholesome in my own eyes, and I wanted a fresh direction. So I enlisted, as once I laughed to you that I would, and am peaceful for the moment, a passenger in a recruits' squad. It's an odd line for me—physical activity and manual labour—but the pilgrimage is made up of such curiosities and I don't suppose that I'm going to be permanently affected by anything I don't want. It makes me no longer master of my body and I can't do or write, or even read, much now-a-days.

As for address: when I'm fixed up anywhere I'll give it you. Meanwhile 14 Barton St. but it may take very long to reach me. People think I've gone abroad, and of course I'm glad they do, for the papers would make a laugh out of this job if they heard of it.

L.

By the way James Thomson's *Sunday up the River* is most excellent, isn't it?

I never saw *Minorities*, but it seems to have been an anthology of poems in each of which the shadow of defeat hung over an individual will in conflict with a more powerful force. In the word "minorities" lurks the word "freedom" which Lawrence held in sentimental though somewhat shamefaced

[1] He comments on the poem.

esteem. He wrote to me in April 1923 of a new collection of poems I had sent him:

> *Whipperginny* fell like a star into the darkness of this camp and I have been reading it in gobbets ever since. There's a Minority in it —*A Forced Music*—you'll be astonished at my sweet tooth, if ever you see that discreditable collection.

And here I may quote an illuminating critical paragraph from another letter, written two years later:

> . . . the only place where I cavilled was your treatment of *The Tempest*. God knows we each of us have our fancy pictures of W.S. . . . and my fancy is to have no picture of him. There was a man who hid behind his works, with great pains and consistency. *Ergo*, he had something to hide: some privy reason for hiding. He being a most admirable fellow, I hope he hides successfully.

Naturally I asked him his reasons for enlisting, and quoted the case of Coleridge, who in an erratic moment in 1793 had joined the 15th Dragoons under the name of Silas Tomkyn Comberback—and made a very bad soldier. But his comrades cleaned his arms and equipment, curried his horse and did other jobs for him, and in return he wrote their letters home for them. I asked Lawrence whether it was like that with him? And would he end, like Coleridge, by being bought out by his brothers?

12.XI.22

I can't get up to London at present. It's out of bounds, because of a rumoured small-pox epidemic. What truth lies in that, I don't know. The streets of Farnborough are more full of election-posters than of newsboys: and it feels mean, somehow, to buy a paper, after one has run away in this obscurity, to escape politics . . . if it was to escape politics. I wasn't like Coleridge: I haven't written any letters home (by the way, Comberback was a self-comment on his riding: odd creature he was!) for anyone: and the routine would be beastly, if there was any: but each day brings its breathless order and each night its breathless cancellation: so that I live in a whirl. It's an animal whirl, though, and my nerves have quieted under it, in a healthy way. I nearly went off my head in London this spring, heaving at that beastly book of mine. My conscience always pricks me for not sending it you: and yet I'm proud of having had enough strength of mind to keep it to myself. It makes me miserable and angry, and I feel it a thing unfit to show to honourable or happy people.

Honestly I couldn't tell you exactly why I joined up: though the night before I did (a very wonderful night by the way: I felt like a criminal waiting for daylight) I sat up and wrote out all the reasons I could see or feel in myself for it. But they came to little more than that it was a necessary step, forced on me by an inclination towards ground-level: by a despairing hope that I'd find myself on common ground with men: by a little wish to make myself a little more human than I had become in Barton Street: by an itch to make myself ordinary in a mob of likes: also I'm broke, so far as money goes, by an unexpected event. All these are reasons: but unless they are cumulative they are miserably inadequate. I wanted to join up, that's all: and I am still glad, sometimes, that I did. It's going to be a brain-sleep, and I'll come out of it less odd than I went in: or at least less odd in other men's eyes.

I'm stuck in Farnborough nearly indefinitely: unless small-pox ends. If it does I'll come to London or to All Souls', at Xmas for a week. Send me the *Sybil* poem, please.

E.L.

I was troubled about his life in the ranks and felt that he ought to be rescued. Then I, and my family, had an invitation from the Foreign Minister of a certain remote Eastern principality to go there and live at the Government's expense: the invitation was extended to Lawrence. If he went, we would. He replied:

18.1.23

Dear R.G.

I've delayed thinking about it: and thinking is slow in B. block because people talk more readily. Now there is a sort of riot happening over by the fire: and so writing is made difficult.

The conclusion is that probably I won't. The escape from what is nearly squalor here was attractive: and ——[1] is out of the world (by the way passports won't be difficult: the I.O. will do that much for my sake. Lord Winterton was "one of us" in Hejaz): but partly I came in here to eat dirt, till its taste is normal to me: and partly to avoid the current of other men's thinking: and in your hill-court there will be high thinking. My brain nearly went in Barton St. with the weariness of writing and re-writing that horrible book of mine: and I still am nervous and easily made frantic.

So I think I'm going to stay on in the R.A.F. which has the one great merit of showing me humanity very clear and clean. I've never lived commonly before, and I think to run away from the stress of it would be a failing.

I owe you a word about that book. It may be printed privately, in a limited subscription edition, next year. A sort of 15 guinea book, almost unprocurable. I hovered for a while this year with the notion of a censored version: but that seems dishonest, until the whole story is available.

I'm glad you're feeling easier. In mechanical jargon you've been "revving" yourself too high for the last eighteen months. Such forced running means a very heavy fuel consumption, and it is not true economy.

Many thanks to ——[2] I very nearly came, but I wanted to too much for it to be a wholesome wish.

E.L.

So we did not go either.

Lawrence was recognised by an officer whom he had known during the War, and the story was sold to the press. (See L.H., p. 180, l. 10.) Reporters buzzed round the camp. It was not only that he had concealed his previous service and given misleading particulars about himself, but that his social position became impossible. The officers felt embarrassed by his fame and by his former rank, and the men thought that he was a spy sent down from the Air Ministry to report on training conditions

[1]The Eastern principality's.
[2]The Foreign Minister.

at the camp. Lawrence decided to stick it out, but a Labour M.P. gave notice of a question that he proposed to ask in the House at the next question-time as to what Colonel Lawrence was doing masquerading as an aircraftman at Uxbridge. It was decided to get rid of him.

He wrote two months later from Dorset, but giving his London address:

14, Barton St.
20.3.23

Dear R.G.

I've been some while wanting to write, and your note (which came to hand yesterday) is the last straw to weigh down my mind.

Sorry to have missed you in London: but my movings have been eccentric of late. The R.A.F. threw me out, eventually. Crime of too great publicity. Stainless character. I took the latter to the W.O. and persuaded them to let me enlist with them. So I'm now a recruit in the Tank Corps. Conditions rough too. However, there is a certainty and a contentment in bed-rock.

I wanted to ask you . . . we are near Dorchester and I run about Dorset on wheels (when they take their eyes off us) . . . do you think old Hardy would let me look at him? He's a proper poet and a fair novelist, in my judgment, and it would give me a feeling of another milestone passed if I might meet him. Yet to blow in upon him in khaki would not be an introduction. You know the old thing, don't you? What are my hopes?

youuuuuuuurs

T.E. ?[1]

I wrote to Thomas Hardy, who replied that Lawrence would be very welcome. I felt that the two would get on well together, and they did. He wrote some months later:

8.IX.23

Peccavi: but always that happens. Look upon me as a habitual incorrigible sinner: and blame upon yourself part of this last silence:

[1][Sic.]

for in your letter to me (that which caused the silence) you said "Tell me about Max Gate"—and I can't!

The truth seems to be that Max Gate is very difficult to seize upon. I go there as often as I decently can, and hope to go on going there so long as it is within reach: (sundry prices I've paid in Coy [Company] Office for these undefended absences) but description isn't possible. Hardy is so pale, so quiet, so refined into an essence: and camp is such a hurly-burly. When I come back I feel as if I'd woken up from a sleep: not an exciting sleep, but a restful one. There is an unbelievable dignity and ripeness about Hardy: he is waiting so tranquilly for death, without a desire or ambition left in his spirit, as far as I can feel it: and yet he entertains so many illusions, and hopes for the world, things which I, in my disillusioned middle-age, feel to be illusory. They used to call this man a pessimist. While really he is full of fancy expectations.

Then he is so far-away. Napoleon is a real man to him, and the country of Dorsetshire echoes that name everywhere in Hardy's ears. He lives in his period, and thinks of it as the great war: whereas to me that nightmare through the fringe of which I passed has dwarfed all memories of other wars, so that they seem trivial, half-amusing incidents.

Also he is so assured. I said something a little reflecting on Homer: and he took me up at once, saying that it was not to be despised: that it was very kin to *Marmion* . . . saying this not with a grimace, as I would say it, a feeling smart and original and modern, but with the most tolerant kindness in the world. Conceive a man to whom Homer and Scott are companions: who feels easy in such presences.

And the standards of the man! He feels interest in everyone, and veneration for no-one. I've not found in him any bowing-down, moral or material or spiritual.

Any little man finds this detachment of Hardy's a vast compliment and comfort. He takes me as soberly as he would take John Milton (how sober that name is), considers me as carefully, is as interested in me: for to him every person starts scratch in the life-race, and Hardy has no preferences: and I think no dislikes, except for the people who betray his confidence and publish him to the world.

Perhaps that's partly the secret of that strange house hidden behind its thicket of trees. It's because there are no strangers there. Anyone who does pierce through is accepted by Hardy and Mrs. Hardy as one whom they have known always and from whom nothing need be hid.

For the ticket which gained me access to T.H. I'm grateful to you —probably will be grateful always. Max Gate is a place apart: and I feel it all the more poignantly for the contrast of life in this squalid camp. It is strange to pass from the noise and thoughtlessness of sergeants' company into a peace so secure that in it not even Mrs. Hardy's tea-cups rattle on the tray: and from a barrack of hollow senseless bustle to the cheerful calm of T.H. thinking aloud about life to two or three of us. If I were in his place I would never wish to die: or even to wish other men dead. The peace which passeth all understanding;—but it can be felt, and is nearly unbearable. How envious such an old age is.

However, here is enough of trying to write about something which is so precious that I grudge writing about it. T.H. is an experience that a man must keep to himself.

I hope your writing goes: that your household goes: that your peace of mind grows. I'm afraid that last does not. Yet I have achieved it in the ranks at the price of stagnancy and beastliness: and I don't know, yet, if it is worth it.

E.L.

The handwriting in this letter bears a curious resemblance to Thomas Hardy's own and, unlike any other letter of his to me, contains a number of crossed-out words, with others substituted as an improvement of the style.

He took a cottage at Clouds[1] Hill, Moreton, not far from the camp. It was the one that he was living in at the time of his death. He told me once that it was the cottage where Eustacia Vye lived with her father, the Captain, in Hardy's novel *The Return of the Native*. Clouds Hill is called "Mistover Knap" there.

[1]Sometimes he spelt it Clouds, sometimes Cloud's, sometimes Clouds'.

Clouds Hill
Moreton
Dorset
9.V.24

Dear R.G.

Months since I felt moved to write to anyone: and now I think it's only because I ought to write elsewhere. And I haven't any paper.

The others in the hut are singing about Loch Lomond. It makes an undertone to the letter, without which you won't understand its horridness.

We live here in a suspension of mental activity, in a passivity of life which produces, for me, an impression of intense stillness . . . the hush in which one can hear time ticking away, outside, helplessly. I've cured myself of every wish to do anything or see anyone; unless the thing is ordered, it slides, so far as I am concerned. Nirvana perhaps: but there isn't a desire for nescience . . . it's just a letting slide off all of myself except the physical.

The other fellows are, as animals, so hugely more active and vital than myself, that my self-estimation justifies its lowly instinct. There are few animal spirits in me: and I'd not willingly have more.

How do your ways lie? You are writing more than usual: reviews, articles, all sorts of prose. It seems to me a good arm to put forth. The poems were getting too tight to breathe easily; and the exercise of *ad hoc* prose will loosen your spiritual arms.

Did you ever think of writing an official history? I've just explained to the powers that they would waste paper in suggesting me as the continuator of Raleigh's History of the Royal Air Force in the War. I'm so homesick to be back in it that the writing of it would be one misery. They don't know whom to ask. Hogarth did a little and then threw it up. It's a three year job, worth £600–800 a year. See Hogarth if you are tempted. He would tell you how to put in for it. My aim is to prevent, at all costs, its becoming an "official" history: and the Air Ministry are on the same side.

                                                              T.E.L.

But he seems to have made a few good friends in the ranks of the Tank Corps, though it was recruited from a less-educated class of men than the R.A.F. He used to invite them to Clouds

Hill occasionally. One of them, Private Palmer, supplied material later for my biography. Lawrence sent me the following, sometime in 1924 or 1925. It is the only poem of his that I have seen, apart from the S.A. dedication:

DIVERSIONS

"That little beast is playing Bach!"
He said, trying to find the beans
Amid the wreckage of an early feast.
"Posh!—this is too much—give me the toast
And make some tea."
They moved like khaki ghosts
About the house,
While Harry thought of staff-parades—
Duty, divinely dodged.
Presently I found the "Westminster":
Sitting upon the floor
In green, commercial state—
A columned, print-stained page bearing
The exuberance of Tomlinson,
Who chattered paragraphically
Of limited editions.
And then I laughed because
I knew he meant Sassoon.
And then we spoke of Forster
And something in the "Calendar"—
Advising decent citizens to beware of Sidney Lee.
"This book is dead," it went.
I laughed, imaging E.M.
Choking with resentment
Penning that review.

I think it came with a letter dated April 24, 1925, which did not contain much of interest except at the end:

If ever you see Edgell Rickwood, tell him please that for days I struggled to put on paper my recollections of [James Elroy] Flecker

in Syria: a theme which I thought fitting for the *Calendar* . . . but
my rotten little engine conked out.

E.S.

The rest was criticism of a story of mine, called *My Head,
My Head.*

The next letter is chiefly taken up with a detailed criticism
of some poems I had sent him, which he now returned. One
was called *The Presence*, the other *A Letter to S.S.* and referred
to my friendship with Siegfried Sassoon in the Royal Welch
Fusiliers during the War. While Lawrence was in the Tank
Corps he retained his interest in contemporary poetry, and
this survived during his service in the R.A.F. until 1929 or
1930. It was only in his speed-boat designing days that he
claimed to have lost all his critical sense and to be a mere
simple mechanic.

[Undated]

These came too late to return with *My Head, My Head*, and so
I took the liberty of laying them aside for second reading, which is
just ended, in my cottage, with the Kreutzer sonata going on the
gramophone. My Head isn't at its best this morning, owing to my
having been in trouble lately (run up for insulting a corporal, and
used the company office to purge all the draafe of my mind upon
him . . . a hot and horrible scene, which scared our ladylike O.C. out
of his manners. Case dismissed), and because there are more worries
to come next week. Court of inquiry.

However. *The Presence*. Very moving. It reads like a first draft,
too charged with passion for its form. The metre isn't common,
and does not always fit the thought perfectly. I've underlined two
phrases. The first didn't please me: and you repeat it (its grammatical
form is what I'm talking about) four lines lower.

Also "abuse" and "use" feel as if brought in just to match one
another. I may be wrong. They seem like bubbles in the mixture.
"Accusingly enforcing her too sharp identity". That strikes me as a
bit mannered. Bad-mannered, like the Sitwells' over-punctilious
ceremony of phrase. Pernickety: Max-beerbombish.

I'd like to transpose some of the opening lines: the "of whom" etc.
down to "on memory" aren't, intellectually, greater, louder, or in
complement of "dead is gone . . . underground": indeed I fancy
they come before it: and I'm old-fashioned in liking my climax last
. . . or in liking the poem to open crescendo and not diminuendo.

This is not to be taken as a denigration of *The Presence*. The power
of the whole comes through its parts . . . transcends its parts: so
that you wonder after having come down that uneven stairway of
rhymes, to find yourself possessed of a place entirely new.

On third thoughts I wouldn't alter it. The spontaneity is one of
its strengths.

What's the cause that you, and S.S. and I (from the S.S. to the
ridiculous!) can't get away from the War? Here are you riddled
with thought like any old table-leg with worms: S.S. yawing about
like a ship aback: me in the ranks, finding squalor and maltreatment
the only permitted existence: what's the matter with us all? It's like
the malarial bugs in the blood, coming out months and years after
in recurrent attacks. Have you leisure? I'd like to send you the book
I tried to write those years ago. S.S. read it, and grew kind to me,
afterwards: which was a good comment: and if your mind is now
accustomed to living, perhaps you would read it for me.

My motive is the selfish one, of wanting criticism. The margins
are blank to write upon in pencil. The print is eye-destroying, the
length of the book appalling: . . . its sincerity, I fancy, absolute,
except once where I funked the distinct truth, and wrote it ob-
liquely. I was afraid of saying something, even to myself. The thing
was not written for anyone to read. Only as I get further from the
strain of that moment, confession seems a relief rather than a risk.

T.E.S.

Private Palmer, who worked with Lawrence in the Quarter-
master's office, wrote to me about the corporal incident some
years later:

"The corporal was a Scotsman of the old school, an ex-
officer, overbearing, with a wonderful idea of his own importance. T.E. used to rag him unmercifully. The corporal had

a habit of laying the dust in the hut with a bowl of water sprinkled on the floor. This performance annoyed T.E. and everybody else, so one day T.E. got up early and swamped the hut with I forget now how many bowls of water. We all paddled. Later a man in the hut received a few days 'Confined to Barracks' unfairly, through the corporal. T.E. simply slung the corporal's suit-case into the sanitary bin."

I wrote a fanciful poem called *The Clipped Stater*. It was intended to cheer him up. It described how Alexander the Great, after his deification and apparent death, found himself caught up by spirits and conveyed to China, where his name was not known; how he was enrolled in the frontier guard on the Great Wall, and how he welcomed the experience of being a nobody; and how he felt when one day advancing to the pay desk he was given a clipped and defaced silver piece, which turned out to be a stater with his own head on it coined from the bullion that he had once captured from the Persians at the battle of Arbela. One verse ran:

> He will not dream Olympicly, nor stir
> To enlarge himself with comforts or promotion,
> Nor evade punishment when, sour of temper,
> He has pulled the corporal's nose and called him "cur".

He wrote back, in enormous handwriting:

> Cloud's Hill
> Moreton
> Dorset
> 5.XII.24

Dear R.G.

Alexander, God bless him, is V.V.V.V.G. Of course I laughed, laughed enormously, as I read him in bed in the hut. The troops

stared. I showed one excellent one (my "half-section") the MS.
cause-of-laughter, and he laughed as loudly, and has called me
Alexander sometimes since.

It isn't the whole story, though. There was an old Alexander
which survived in part, and a bit of an actor, and a sorry fellow,
and many other fellows: all of which I tried to tell of in that book
I tried to write. I wish I'd thrown it at you two or three years ago,
when its matter was still fluid. I suppose you are right now in not
wanting to read it, since it's fixed and done with and for. Saw S.S.
at Max Gate the other day. You can't imagine what a delight the
Hardys are to me. Your doing, that.

Tried to fetch Islip a fortnight ago . . . but failed.

Yours ever
T.E.S.

For Lawrence's opinion of Alexander, see L.H., p. 8, seventh
line from bottom.

For the sequel to the corporal incident, see p. 121, bottom.

He was working at the *Seven Pillars* still. "By 1924 I had
learned my first lessons in writing, and was often able to combine two or three of my 1921 phrases into one," he wrote later
in *Some Notes on the Writing of the Seven Pillars of Wisdom*.

The remark about my not wanting to see the book was in
reply to my writing that he had promised it so often, and held
it back so often for further "heaving" at it, that it probably
wasn't worth reading now, like the book of poems mentioned
by Juvenal, *octavum pressus in annum*—"worked over [or con-
densed] until the eighth year". I now wrote back to say that
I hadn't meant that seriously. But he still withheld the book,
condensing all the time, until the eighth year (1926), when
I was sent my gift copy, not previously having seen of it more
than the *World's Work* chapters, and the chapter published in
the *Army Quarterly* in 1921.

In August 1925 he was re-transferred to the R.A.F.

338171 A.C.II Shaw
Hut 105
R.A.F. Cadets College
Cranwell
Lincs.
29.VIII.25

What a long address. I begin the letter exhausted.

No, I have not seen the *Marmosite:* have not seen it yet: for I write as soon as it arrives to let you know that I am no longer an inhabitant of Dorset. The R.A.F. had its arms prized open unwillingly again for my entry: and thanks be to all the Gods I'm now in a flight, my ambition of seven years. I pull aeroplanes into and out from their stables.

Dorsetshire was a very good two years. Max Gate, Clouds Hill, and the perfection of English country round them.

I'm very sorry that your life has been ragged of late months. Illness of one's own is exasperating, because humiliating . . . and I get angry at the downfall of others when I see them as I would despise myself.

However . . .

I'm very glad to hear that S.S. is all right. He is rather like a Miltonic archangel: no doubt all right in the archangels' mess: but rather terrifying to the rank and file.

But are we even rank and file angels? Most of the R.A.F. are not angelic, except in the faculty of flight.

au revoir
T.E.S.

In October 1925 Arnold Bennett, whom the Foreign Office (apparently at Lawrence's instigation) had asked to approach me, wrote to know whether I would care to apply for the position of Professor of English Literature at the newly founded Egyptian University at Cairo. I asked Lawrence for his advice. He answered:

21.X.25

Dear R.G.

Your letter about Cairo has broken the slow digestion of your new book: whose work is far and away your poetic best. Yet it gives me a feeling that you have nearly seen through this form of self-expression.

More on this subject later. I had meant to write you about a month hence.

The Cairo job . . . Yes, I'm partly responsible for that. Chance and the War made George Lloyd a friend of mine. I hope, if you go, that you will like him. Like the man in the Psalms "He enlargeth his mouth over his enemies": and there is a snarl in it. Yet underneath he is diffident, kindly, considerate, generous, cultivated, careful. He reads: not always well and wisely, (few of us do) but is grateful for news of a good book. A very English Welshman.

I know nothing about the job. Egypt, being so near Europe, is not a savage country. The Egyptians[1] are very bestial, very savage: but you need not dwell among them. Indeed it will be a miracle if an Englishman can get to know them. The bureaucrat society is exclusive, and lives smilingly unaware of the people. Partly because so many foreigners come there for pleasure, in the winter; and the other women, who live there, must be butterflies too, if they would consort with the visitors.

I thought the salary attractive. It has just been raised. The work may be interesting, or may be terrible, according to whether you get keen on it, like Hearn, or hate it like Nichols. Even if you hate it, there will be no harm done. The climate is good, the country beautiful, the things admirable, the beings curious: and you are stable enough not to be caught broadside by a mere dislike for your job. Execute it decently, so long as you draw the pay, and enjoy your free hours (plentiful in Egypt, God's laziest country) more fully. Roam about.* Yet possibly you will not dislike the job. I think the coin spins evenly. And you can get away by choosing a successor, and persuading Lloyd that he is better than yourself.

So altogether I hope that you will take it. The harm to you is little, for the family will benefit by a stay in the warm (Cairo isn't

[1] I was asking him about the Egyptian fellahin.

*Palestine: the Saharan oases. The Red Sea province. Sinai (a jolly desert). Sudan (not bad in parts). The Delta swamps. E. M. Forster's guide book to Alexandria, published there by Whitehead Morris Co., is great literature, and a good guide. Boost it. Wilfrid Jennings Bramley's buildings in the Western Desert, near Alexandria. The Divine Mosque architecture of Cairo town. All the above are good things. [Footnote by T.E.]

warm, in winter) and the job won't drive you into frantic excesses of rage.

And the money will be useful. You should save a good bit of your pay after the expense of the first six months. And George Lloyd, if you like him, will be a good help to the family.

And so my blessing.

God help you about the assistant. I never heard of such a one. "Knows Arabic and English" forsooth. God help you again. I couldn't recommend even myself on those grounds. Even myself. Even: . . .

Oh Lord.

T.E.S.

"George Lloyd" is, of course, Lord Lloyd, who had been with Lawrence in Egypt and in Arabia. Lafcadio Hearn and Robert Nichols held university appointments in Japan.

I applied for and was given the job. I then wrote to Lawrence asking whether he thought I should try to get the assistant professorship (which was vacant) for a poet of my acquaintance who had a rather poor teaching job elsewhere at the time and was interested in Egyptology. And, if so, could he mention the matter in the right quarter. He wired back from Cranwell:

Can do but not knowing —— weakens my case and doubt if assistant job good enough for him so suggest your asking authorities keep appointment open till you arrive Cairo and investigate conditions personally Shaw.

I don't remember what I wrote back, but the next letter says:

[Undated]

You didn't quite "get" my hesitation: not that —— isn't an excellent poet, and most worthy person: but clearly he is sensitive (that poem about the old homestead) and the consequences of taking an assistant-ship might worry him. Englishmen in these small colonies abroad are snobbish to a degree: the smallness of their colony makes them smaller. I don't know what it's like in Cairo now: but in the

Sudan people with pay below £500 join a junior club, and above £500 a senior club—and God hath put them asunder. Anyway they can't meet ever, except at official places: and probably even then the lawn is roped off into Senior and Junior pens.

Let it comfort you that I spent three magnificent years in Cairo, and only went twice into a club—and then as some fellow's guest. Try the clubs: and if they are mess-like places—then do without 'em.

The important thing is GROPPI's, the Tea-garden shop: and the drink is iced coffee. Straws the process. 2 piastres the means. The children will love Groppi's. Chocolates all right, too: but not in summer.

You will, I think, really enjoy Egypt. Nancy too, I hope: but she is more difficult. You want a sense of the past to enjoy fully: and she is rather bleak upon ancestors.

The mouth organ[1] amused me: and went further and mightily amused the R.A.F. God knows where it is now.

The very best wishes for that show out East. I think you have been very wise. The Morris-Oxford also is suitable, until the children swell: and then a char-a-banc (obtainable locally) will succeed it.

If I can I'll come down the next week. But can't promise. They have made me char-man in the accounts section over the holiday, and the job holds me tightly here.

I would like to have your second impression of Cairo, after you have got over the first idea of squalor.

I went to Egypt and did not like it: I resigned at the end of the academic year. The letters I had from Lawrence while I was there have since gone astray. The only letter I have of 1926 is about a private matter which does not affect the story. It is dated September 16th, and in it occurs the phrase: "We are all intact and intangible and separate in the end." It ends:

I'm looking forward to letting go all the possessions I have before going aboard the *Assaye* about the middle of November. The advantage of a solitary man is his completeness. This should have been a

[1]Which I had sent him as a Christmas joke.

reply to your glorious letter: but I can't do it. You know you have my help and fellowship whenever you need it, in any direction I can reach.

Yours ever
T.E.S.

There was a little more before he sailed:

[Undated]

I've had the L.R. book. It puzzles me. Either she is very deep or very different-minded—another way for saying that her poems slide out of my grip. I cannot remember them, after I have read them. This is not criticism, but a personal statement. Your work affects some people that way: whereas my mind seems tuned exactly to them, so that what you say is what I'd say, if I had your power.

Off to India, or to Uxbridge for India, tomorrow. The leaving England is a very bitter thing. I wish I could stay always here in London.

Don't fail to send me word of yourself, and of how things, even material things, are with you. There needn't be any reserve between us. I'm going to ask you for help any time I need it!

Yours
T.E.S.

The L.R. book was Laura Riding's *Close Chaplet*. But he wrote, in 1930, of her *Twenty Poems Less:*[1]

I liked "*The Earth*". "*And I*" was v.g. so far as *I* was concerned: (queer how one gets contact with one poem and rejects another). "*Then Follows*" has a superb first page and sustains itself all through. I suspect it of being a big thing. . . .

Not long before his death he wrote in reference to her view of him:

The bar between Laura and me is not her artistry, but her self and mine: and quite likely her sex and mine. *You* could (*mutatis mutandis*) have done as I have done. Whereas Laura and I could never have changed places.

<hr>

[1]Out of print. But the three poems referred to are published in her *Collected Poems*, 1938.

The day after he sailed came my gift copy of the *Seven Pillars* in heavy morocco binding. In it was a tiny card:

Please sell when read.

I was in money difficulties again and, after reading the book and writing at length to Lawrence about it, finally sold it for £330: once more my fortunes were restored.

In his first letter from Karachi, there is a note about the *Clipped Stater:* identifying himself with Alexander again.

Edwin Muir in his new book of criticism is very good on the prose-writers: very weak on the poets. He falls foul of the *Clipped Stater* as an unreal only half-baked intellectual, non-imaginatively true extravagance. I laughed and laughed and laughed, knowing it was an essay in reality.

(*Essay in Reality* was the title of another of my poems.)

PART II

1927

338171 A.C.2 Shaw
Room 2 E.R.S.
R.A.F. Depôt
Drigh Road
Karachi
India
3.5.27

Dear R.G.

Your letter stares up at me from the top of my box, each time I open it. I say to it "Patience", and show it all the dozens of other letters underneath it and beside it—however it does not work. I feel a sense of grievance, for surely I wrote to you very lately? You are getting more than your share of my stamps, which are now 16 a week. The rest of my cash goes on gramophone records. We amateurs of potted music get wise in potted music. We can tell the flavour of one brand from another: and the reality is so far behind our backs that we have not even a memory of it to challenge the truthfulness of the pots.

Your broadcast did not come to Karachi. I think there is no wireless in India: and if stations do sit up to catch up England then they must sit to all hours: for we are five hours or so after your time: or is it five hours before? ("Consult any small atlas", as I wired to Petrograd during the War, when they asked me where was Kamaran.[1])

However, I've read your text, so I know as much as your 3,000,000 hearers. *Revolt in the Desert* sells, they say, like ripe apples at a fair.

[1]An island off the Yemen coast, in southern Arabia.

43

If I'd kept an interest I'd have been in the Rolls Royce class by now.

I rejoice to think of you selling your *Seven Pillars*. I hope your practice of the last seven lean years has made you a hard-hearted adept in salesmanship. Otherwise the other fellow will persuade you that you're doing him out of his living and draining his pocket, and breaking his heart. Get all you can for it. I wish I were there to write highly-spiced notes and comments over its margins. That would be £10 extra, wouldn't it?

Your poems were not many: but they were poems: and they were not repeats of earlier R.G. work. . . .[1]

I'm sorry about it, sorrier than I sound. These women wound one another more cruelly than they can wound us or we each other. But let's hope. What did Browning say? (Too much usually. So did Swinburne. I am in good company.)

Who is Gerald Bullett? Ever hear of him? Wrote a decent review of *Revolt*. Such things are rare apparently. Mostly slobber assails me. Do you refuse to know best sellers? It's a proof, I fancy, of their artistic worthlessness.

Ha Ha

T.E.S.

The broadcast was one I gave of *Revolt in the Desert* from Savoy Hill, on April 4, 1927.

I had left Oxfordshire and was living in London. In June 1927 Messrs. Jonathan Cape and Messrs. Doubleday, Doran of New York deduced from the interest in Lawrence created by *Revolt in the Desert* among adults that a *Lawrence's Adventures* for boys could profitably be published as a Christmas book. Because of the broadcast talk, they asked me to write this, allowing me until the end of July to complete it. The terms were generous, and I replied that I would undertake the job if Lawrence gave his consent.

I cabled to Karachi and back came the single word, "Yes", followed by the following letter:

[1]He writes about the poems and discusses the family difficulties of some mutual friends of ours.

338171 AC Shaw
Room 2 ERS
R.A.F.
Drigh Road
Karachi
9.VI.27.

Dear R.G.

Your cable came, and I answered it the same day, by deferred cable, sending you the word "yes". That cost 5 rupees and a half, and I had just six. In happier circumstances you would have received a more literary effort.

Great minds appear to jump together, like spawning frogs. The week before I'd heard from Hogarth of Doran's effort to get a plain life of me written: and I'd sent off a letter to Savage (an agent: my agent) telling him that if Doran couldn't be headed off, the best person to fulfil his desire was you, if you would agree to accept the commission. There may be money in it: which is my reason for wishing you to get it. From all other points of view I'm sorry. Doran should have had more sense.

As you are doing it for him, you'll have to study his interests first. Write everything you feel inclined, from whatever source it comes, or whatever angle. The time to censor is after the thing is written, not before or during. However, I needn't fear that you will let any scruple or personal motive hinder you. Butter of the Lowell Thomas sort does not keep very well: and its quotation at tenth hand is painfully rancid. Your stuff will be a gratification; only you must, without my help, find the puckers and creases and holes in my armour.

I would like to see your text, if time admits, before it goes to press: preferably in typescript. There are certain things which must not be said. Not that I care, but other people have such odd views. And politically about Arabia, there may be a touch or two which I'd suggest your adding. Your book quite likely won't be just a school-edition: and if so I may try and persuade you to act as vehicle in correcting some mistakes the public have made about the direction of my hopes.

Any questions you want answered I'll answer, either for publication or not for publication, as the case may be.

Don't send me registered letters. Their delivery is subject to great delay, and is always uncertain: for it is carried out by Indian post-men, who accept anybody's signature: whereas ordinary mail is sorted by ourselves, and is safe.

T.E.S.

By the way: I believe the U.S.A. copyright of the *Seven Pillars* is as sure as it can be made. The profits of piracy would be so great that no precautions are really adequate. Doran set up and printed the main text, in New York: and on Dec. 1, 1926, the day of publication in England, registered his edition, and presented the statutory copies to Congress Library. I gave him four copies, to let him have scope for a private flutter: took six myself: and left 10, on sale: the first at 20,000 dollars: the survivors to double, upon the sale of any one. That gives me legal copyright in U.S.A. and I could insist on Doran's supporting my rights by prosecution of any pirate publisher: but a single foreigner, and a poor one, would not be very fortunate perhaps in the State courts.

Good luck to you.

I've just remembered the Air Mail. If you post by that from London it reaches here on a Friday, and I can reply the same Friday evening, thus saving a week on the double journey. Not much: but Doran may push you for time.

When I got this letter I naturally told Mr. Cape, asking him to relay this to Mr. Doran, that it would not be a book for boys merely, but one putting the fragmentary *Revolt in the Desert* into proper relation with the Arab Revolt as a whole, and also with Lawrence's pre- and post-War life. But I undertook to write the book with such suavity and simplicity that it could also be read and enjoyed by the young.

The drawback was that I only had six weeks to collect the material and write the book, and I could see that it would be a book of nearly twice the length of an ordinary novel. And as I was no good at dictating work or typewriting it myself it had to be all done by pen-pushing. An impossible task, it seemed. I rushed round and saw as many people as were within reach and wrote to as many as were not and consulted all the documentary sources available. I worked from the 1922 Oxford text of the *Seven Pillars* (borrowed from Eric Kennington). I found it pleasanter reading than the 1926 edition, and it contained a few incidents of great interest which Lawrence cut out of the final version. I told him later of this preference and said jokingly that I hoped the lost 1919 version would turn up, because it would probably be better than the 1922 one. He did not like this very much (see p. 116, bot.), and when we met again in 1929, and the subject arose, said that he hoped to goodness the 1919 version would *not* turn up, because it was written from notes which he had destroyed after writing the book, and the subsequent versions were based largely on memory.

Lawrence helped me greatly: I sent him the typescript of several chapters at a time, as they were completed, and he returned them covered with comments. The publishers gave me a prolongation on my time until the middle of August, and Lawrence was very quick in sending back the stuff. It was all in time to be incorporated in the final proof. It must be understood that I did not intend *Lawrence and the Arabs* as "literature". It was a journalistic job, done quickly and, I hoped, inoffensively, and the writing was as subdued and matter-of-fact as I could make it. Two-thirds of the book was a mere condensation of *Seven Pillars* material. As the *Seven Pillars*, however, would not be published during Lawrence's lifetime, nobody complained about this. Moreover, in *Revolt in the Desert*, which was extracts from the *Seven Pillars* hurriedly thrown together by Lawrence before going out to India, the sequence of events was hard to follow; and I set myself the task of getting this sequence as clear as possible in my own book.

When I told him of my hurry he wrote:

28.VI.27

Your remark that Doran has given you only till late July shows me that you'll not have time to send me your script. And as you say you'll pick up facts anywhere, I'll send you some. Not knowing the scope of your book, I'll miss the target generally: and therefore I'll take no pains to put them well.

1) Family. My father's family were Co. Meath in Ireland. A Leicester squire-root, which got a huge grant from Q. Elizabeth, by favour of W. Raleigh, their cousin. Lived thenceforward in Ireland, always particular to marry non-Irish women. My father took name of Lawrence (not even my mother's name) when he left Ireland.

2) Five of us brothers. 1, 2 and 5 still alive. 3 and 4 killed in War. I born in Wales (Carnarvon Co. Tremadoc Parish) August 1888. Thence went Scotland, Isle of Man, Jersey, France, Hampshire: before settling in Oxford 1896. Where attended City of Oxford School (day) till I went to Jesus Coll. as exhibitioner in history. At school, never played games. Spare time spent books: and studying mediaeval art, especially sculpture. Later collected mediaeval pottery. At 18, specialised mediaeval military architecture: visited every XIIth Cent. castle England and France.

3) Oxford. At Jesus read history, officially: actually spent nearly three years reading Provençal poetry, and Mediaeval French chansons de geste. When time came for degree wasn't prepared for exam. Went private coach, and was advised submit special thesis to supplement papers. So went Syria in last long vacation (4 months) tramped from Haifa to Urfa, seeing 50 Crusader castles. European dress, alone, afoot, carrying only camera. Only 80 words Arabic. Guested every night in native villages, when off beaten track. Came back Oxford sketch plans photos of every mediaeval fortress in Syria, and wrote thesis "Influence of Crusades on Mediaeval Military Architecture of Europe." Got 1st Class Honours degree Modern History. Sat All Souls Fellowship and failed. Promoted Scholar Jesus. Later elected Senior Demy of Magdalen College. At University never played or looked on at any game, or sport. Lived only 1 term in college. Read all night, and slept in mornings. Vegetarian, non-

smoker. T.T. Never dined in Hall. Took no part College life. Acquired lively admiration for R. L. Poole, my history tutor. "Cut" him once: wrote apologising. Reply "Don't worry yourself at having failed come me last Tuesday. Your absence gave me opportunity to do an hour's useful work." Attended practically no lectures.

4) Carchemish. In first tour of Syria bought collection Hittite seals in Aintab (AINTAB) region for D. G. Hogarth. He just about open excavation Carchemish for British Museum. He thought I'd be useful, since I'd picked up some practical Arabic and idea of country people, and also my study of English mediaeval pottery had shown him I had archaeological sense. So offered me 15/- a day assistant. Worked Carchemish off and on (generally spring and autumn) till 1914. My special jobs there photography; pottery; sculpture. To get other hints I worked one winter Flinders Petrie, digging in Egypt. Between seasons at Carchemish I explored Syria, gaining intimate knowledge all its provinces, intending write history of Crusades. Did one season for the Palestine Exploration Fund, in Sinai (publication "Wilderness of Zin", Woolley and Lawrence) to complete survey of country between Suez Canal and Palestine, visiting Akaba, Petra, Maan, etc. Wrote travel book (later destroyed in MS.) called "The Seven Pillars of Wisdom", about Cairo, Smyrna, Constantinople, Beyrout, Aleppo, Damascus, Medina.

5) War. Outbreak of War was in Oxford. Owing glut recruits unable enlist (story physical rejection ill-health absurd: was pre-war strong as horse. Even after War submitted 1922 1923 1925 medical examination recruiting offices and each time wreckage of my body was passed fit general service). So Hogarth got me into Geographical Section General Staff (Intelligence) War Office. Worked there under Col. Hedley for 4 months, maps Sinai, Belgium, France. Then sent out Egypt upon entry of Turkey into war, "Four musketeers": Aubrey Herbert (M.P.), dead, George Lloyd (M.P.) now Lord Lloyd, British Museum Woolley, and T.E.L. under Capt. Newcombe, R.E. to do Intelligence work on Staff General Maxwell, G.O.C. Egypt. Came under Col. Clayton. Director of Intelligence, Egyptian Army. Worked at G.H.Q. Cairo till 1916, except for visits to Canal, Senussi Desert, Athens, and Mesopotamia (for surrender of Kut). Graded as Staff Capt. General List (actually 2nd Lieut.) Captain

about 1916. Major 1917. Lt. Col 1918. Promoted Major in order to be given C.B. for capture of Akaba. Finally graded G.S.O.1. Left Damascus Oct. 4, 1918. Home leave. Arrived London 11 Nov. 1918.

6) Armistice period. First escorted Feisal round England: then Paris for Peace Conference on British Delegation (F.O.) till end June 1919. Then flew out to Egypt collect diaries and photographs of war periods for Cairo. Returned Paris August 1919. Demobbed, July 31, 1919. Lived London for a while, then at All Souls after election research fellowship Nov. 1919. London all 1920. In March 1921 accepted post Colonial Office under Winston. Cairo—Jerusalem April May. London end May. Thence Cairo, Jidda, Aden, Amman, Jerusalem, till Dec. 1921 (London). Worked Colonial Office 1922 till July, when Winston accepted resignation.

7) Modern period. Enlisted R.A.F. August 1922. Daily Express published facts five months later: was (kicked out) discharged by Air Ministry Order Feb. 1923. In hope eventual reinstatement in RAF enlisted Tank Corps March 1923: and was transferred thence to RAF in August 1925, through kindly offices of John Buchan.[1]

So much for facts.

You talk about sources for these periods.

1 and 2) Nil.

3) My private tutor L. Cecil Jane of Aberystwyth University in Wales, Assistant in Faculty of History there. I used to go to him nearly every day, and discuss every possible point of all history. He could, and probably would, give you some good stuff: for he is a quite abnormal and fully-charged personality.

Also V. W. Richards . . .[2] At Jesus with me, the keeper of my books, and guardian of my patch of Epping Forest. A Welsh metaphysician who has just written a book on God, published by Pike.

4) D. G. Hogarth to whom I owe every good job (except the R.A.F.) I've ever had in my life.

Mrs Fontana. Wife of former British Consul, Aleppo. The only person who would do justice to Carchemish, which was the jolliest place I've ever seen. A marvellous, unreal, pictured pageant of a life. Do write and call on her. A very special person, with the gift of feeling.

[1]Now Lord Tweedsmuir.

[2]I have omitted the private addresses which Lawrence gave in each case.

C. L. Woolley. Wrote a book on Carchemish. . . . Carchemish was a miracle, and he turns it into a play.

5) D. G. Hogarth: and his assistant E. T. Leeds, Ashmolean Museum. Col. Alan Dawnay. Dawnay is very good. Not a bit like an officer.

Francis Rodd, a modern incarnation of Cesare Borgia. A first rate fellow. Was in Foreign Office, and knows a great deal. In Cairo all war.[1]

6) Arnold Toynbee for Peace Conference.

Sir Herbert Baker for period while I wrote *Seven Pillars:* (none of which was written at Oxford: the only thing done in All Souls was the introduction to Doughty's Arabia Deserta).

Lionel Curtis (now probably in Honolulu: See Mrs. Curtis) saw me very often during this time. I used to feed off him: for I was practically starving.

For Colonial Office period refer to Eddie Marsh.

7) For Modern Period only useful sources might be Lionel Curtis and Mrs. Bernard Shaw. Letters.

Pte. Palmer (for the Royal Tank Corps). Sgt. Pugh for RAF period.

A lot of people will give you yarns: but the above are reasonable truthful people, and not dullards. You'll have to persuade them I've given you their names.

Some special points.

My object with the Arabs: to make them stand on their own feet. To do this it was necessary to check centralising policy of King Hussein, who envisaged a united Arab world under himself at Mecca. Mecca was a hotbed of religion, quite impossible as the capital of any sort of state: the worst town in the Arab world. Yet for the war we had to pretend that he led, since unity is necessary in a movement. So we put up with Hussein till the Armistice, and then tried to put him quietly into his place.

This proved difficult. Feisal's only right at Paris was as representing the recognised "ally", King Hussein of Hejaz. All official business had to be in Hussein's name, though actually no Hejaz business came

---

[1]The Hon. Francis Rodd writes: "T.E. was not always accurate in his statements. I was in the Near East only in 1917 and 1918 and in Cairo itself only in 1918."

before Conference at Paris. All discussion was limited to Syria, and Mesopotamia.

In official "case" written by me, (a tiny document, well worth reprinting,* which Toynbee would show you: only a dozen lines long) Feisal pleaded for an eventual Arab Confederation, some generations hence, when communications by road, rail and air had drawn together the more civilised Arab provinces. We meant Mespot. and Syria. There was never any idea of a confederation, a United States of Arabia, in our time.

The case was difficult to argue, as England was booming, and meant to turn Mespot. into a great British administered province. Lloyd George couldn't dare to promise any wide measure of native self-government there. Consequently France was very stiff in her corresponding sphere of Syria. Secret treaties (see Toynbee and D. G. Hogarth) conflicted the issue.

Eventually Feisal and Clemenceau came to a working private agreement. A year later (after Clemenceau had gone) the French Govt. tore this up, on pretext that Feisal broke it, and turned Feisal out of Damascus. He withdrew to Palestine, in spite of an attempt at resistance by some of his army, and thence to Italy, and England. Later to Mecca, where he received an invitation to visit Mespot. with view to assuming its Crown.

[Here follows a passage of ten paragraphs which is printed on pages 110–14, "Events in England . . ." as far as ". . . War-promises and my hopes." It there contains additions and corrections subsequently made by Lawrence when he read the letter in my typescript; so I omit it here, to avoid duplication.]

Will you, finally, make clear that I like the R.A.F.? The being cared for, the rails of conduct, the impossibility of doing irregular things, are easements. The companionship, the interesting labour, the occasional leisures are actively pleasant. While my health lasts

---

*This official "case" of Feisal's was printed by the British Delegation press in English two days before the session of the Council of Ten, in which he pleaded his cause. Present: Clemenceau, Pichon, Wilson, Lansing, Lloyd George, Montagu, Sonnino, etc. Lord Riddell might give you the yarn of it. I spoke in English, Arabic and French! Pichon got up, and quoted St. Louis, and France's claim on Syria during the Crusades. Feisal replied: "But, pardon me, which of us won the Crusades?" [Footnote by T.E.]

I'll keep in it. I did not like the Army: but the RAF is as different from the Army as the air is from the earth. In the Army the person is at a discount: the combined movement, the body of men, is the ideal. In the RAF there are no combined movements: its drill is a joke, except when some selected squad is specially trained for a tattoo or ceremony. Our ideal is the skilled individual mechanic at his bench or machine. We grudge every routine duty, and perform our parades deliberately ill, lest we lose our edges, and become degraded into parts of a machine. In the Army the men belong to the machine. In the RAF the machines (upon earth) belong to the men, and in the air to the officers. So the men have the more of them. Whenever the public see a detachment of airmen on a ceremonial (bull-shit) parade, they should realise that these their very expensive servants are being temporarily misemployed:—as though Cabinet Ministers should hump coal in Office hours.

Some of this last page might make a good quote.

T.E.S.

Written records:

  i) Carchemish. Woolley's book.

 ii) The Palestine Exploration Fund Annual for 1914. "The Wilderness of Zin".

iii) War Period: *Mespot*. Aubrey Herbert's "Mons, Gallipoli, Kut".

   Arabia. The Arab Bulletin (Hogarth has copy).

   Lord Winterton's four articles in *Blackwood's Magazine*, about 1920.

   Major Young's articles in *Cornhill* in 1926 and 1927.

   Hogarth in *Century Magazine* U.S.A. about 1922.[1]

 iv) Post-War Period. Toynbee in annual digest of politics for the British Institute of International Affairs.

  v) I have not seen this:— An Australian, David Roseler "Lawrence, Prince of Mecca" published by Angus and Robertson (? Melbourne or Sidney)

I keep on trying to think of useful things to tell you. It is not easy.

I took the name of Shaw because it was the first one-syllabled one which turned up in the Army List index; the Adjutant General's

[1] July 1920.

secretary told me I mustn't use my former name: so I consulted the *sortes*. Later a deed-poll was made out, so the change is legal. Don't mention any of the other names (Ross etc.) which I've held temporarily.

Don't forget to say that the title Prince of Mecca was conferred on me by Lowell Thomas. From the Arabs I had no honours. The rank and file used to call me Emir Dinamit—the Dynamite King! That was a joke.

Oh yes: about those English decorations. During the war the C.B. and D.S.O. were conferred on me, in the Gazette. When I came back to London I had an opportunity of explaining, to the responsible authorities (it was George V, of course, but it wasn't [his] fault) that in my judgment the part I had played in the Arab Revolt was dishonourable to me, personally, and to the country and government which they represented. I explained that I was probably going to fight them by fair or foul means, till they had conceded to the Arabs what in my opinion was a proper settlement of their claims (the Winston solution passed my hopes: I'd have retired with less): and that I'd face the situation more easily if I had not their rewards. The King saw the point, and relieved me of them. So actually I have no English decorations: and as soon as I'd been let off the English ones I sent back my foreign ones with an account of the circumstances. There are many stories of my having had rows with the King. Not true: though of course he was worried. I had a row with Lord Curzon.

For Winston I have respect and liking. He treated me so well, and I like his courage and honesty. Also he's very kindly to everyone.

I expect you will not have to go into the question of money. During the campaign I put my pay into the show's expenses. I felt that I might be a cat's paw or a crook, but would keep my amateur status; likewise I felt, when serving for Winston, that I couldn't personally profit in any way by the salary (£1000 a year and bonus of about £300) he paid me: I had to accept the salary, for his peace of mind, but put it to official purposes. And so with the profits of my book on the campaign. Consistency makes me refuse them too. In most publishing the prime consideration is financial: but in the *Seven Pillars* it wasn't. That accounts for most of the oddnesses in its publication. Ditto with *Revolt in the Desert*.

Revolt, by the way, having paid off my debt, will, I hope, shortly be withdrawn from the U.K. market. My trustees agree to this, and I have written to Cape to determine our contract, after stock in hand has been sold. Doran will go on for ever, if he wishes. I don't care what happens in U.S.A. but in England, within a day's march of London, that hub of all delight, it is my ambition to live permanently.

Please don't mention Clouds Hill. I think of that magically beautiful place as a country home, some day. Small, cheap, retired, colourful.

As a bookman you may be amused to know that I carried with me during the desert war, 1) a *Morte d'Arthur*, 2) Aristophanes, 3) *Oxford Book of English Verse*. And no other books. They say I carried Doughty, but it's not true.

Mrs. Shaw has the two diaries from which I reconstructed my itinerary, in 1919, after the other notes were lost. There are also, in my hands, some other route-sheets, with descriptive notes of what happened on the march, daily, and rough compass-bearings and march-hours. The Wejh-Akaba notes are amongst them, and the Wejh-Wadi Ais-Aba el Naam and back. These are detailed. They contain e.g. the full text of the tribal feast chapter almost verbatim. It was with them, and with the reports in the *Arab Bulletin*, that I reinforced and pegged down my memory. I've sent round lately a three-page leaflet to all subscribers giving the genesis of the *Seven Pillars*. Do make clear that for years I did my very best to write it decently. The chapters were afterthoughts: it was written in Books. The present Chap. I (of *Seven Pillars*) was written in the air, in six hours in a Handley Page. Its rhythm is unlike the rest. I liken it to the munch, munch, munch of the synchronised Rolls Royce engines!

The names of the "unhistorical" people, the small fry, English, Arab and Turk in the *Seven Pillars* were fictitious in the MS. and were again changed for the printed text. So they are doubly unrecognisable.

S.A., the subject of the dedication, is rather an idea than a person.[1]

The subscribers' copies were all bound differently, so that any subscriber who cared for good bindings could have his or her copy rebound to taste without reducing the bibliophilic value of the book.

[1]See L.H., p. 143, l. 3.

The plates were massed at the end of the book so as to be appendices or précis justificatives, rather than illustrations.

The cost of the *Seven Pillars* was about £13,000. Reproducing the plates alone cost more than the subscriptions.

The abridgement, *Revolt in the Desert*, was made entirely at Cranwell, in two evenings' work, by myself with the help of two airmen, Miller and Knowles.

Put in a good word for Boanerges, my Brough bike. I had five of them in four years, and rode 100,000 miles on them, making only two insurance claims (for superficial damage to machine after skids), and hurting nobody. The greatest pleasure of my recent life has been speed on the road. The bike would do 100 m.p.h. but I'm not a racing man. It was my satisfaction to purr along gently between 60 and 70 m.p.h. and drink in the air and the general view. I lose detail at even moderate speeds, but gain comprehension. When I used to cross Salisbury Plain at 50 or so, I'd feel the earth moulding herself under me. It was *me* piling up this hill, hollowing this valley, stretching out this level place: almost the earth came alive, heaving and tossing on each side like a sea. That's a thing the slow coach will never feel. It is the reward of Speed. I could write for hours on the lustfulness of moving swiftly.[1]

One of the fellows here has a little book of confessions:

Favourite	colour	scarlet
"	dish	bread and water
"	musician	Mozart
"	author	William Morris
"	character in history	Nil
"	place	London
Greatest	pleasure	Sleep
"	pain	noise
"	fear	animal spirits.

(Piffle)

If Winston would tell you (or E.M.)[2] something about the 1921-1922 period, of which I'm proudest, it would be good for you. "A rare beast: will not breed in captivity" said he one day. Your brother

[1] See L.H., p. 160, l. 16.

[2] Sir Edward Marsh, then Mr. Churchill's private secretary.

Philip knows the 1914–1916 period very well, and something of the '17 and '18.

Also there is General Bartholomew, now at the War Office.

Two other small things.

My knowledge of Arabic. In Oxford I picked up a little colloquial grammar, before I first went out. In the next four years I added a considerable (4,000 word) vocabulary to this skeleton of grammar; words useful in archaeological research mainly.

Then for two war years I spoke hardly a word of it: and as I've never learned the letters, to read or write, naturally almost it all passed from me. So when I joined Feisal I had to take it all up again from the beginning, in a fresh and very different dialect. As the campaign grew it carried me from dialect to dialect, so that I never settled down to learn one properly. Also I learned by ear (not knowing the written language) and therefore incorrectly: and my teachers were my servants, who were too respectful to go on reporting my mistakes to me. They found it easier to learn my Arabic than to teach me theirs.

In the end I had control of some 12,000 words: a good vocabulary for English, but not enough for Arabic which is a very wide language: and I used to fit these words together with a grammar and syntax of my own invention. Feisal called my Arabic "a perpetual adventure" and used to provoke me to speak to him so that he could enjoy it. I fancy it must have been like Balieff's English.

I've never heard an Englishman speak Arabic well enough to be taken for a native of any part of the Arabic-speaking world, for five minutes.

Another yarn, which perhaps you know. General —— (a monocled little dapper cinema-general of the strutting type) began rowing me in the hall of the Majestic in Paris, during the Peace Conference. I replied in kind. He barked: "Don't dare to speak to me in that tone. You're not a professional officer." "No," said I, "perhaps I'm not: but if you had a division (his then rank) and I had a division, I know which of us would be taken prisoner!"

That, and my "Many happy returns" to the persistent old lady who gasped out "97" to me, fanning herself in the hall of the Continental in Cairo, are the only two times I've been smart-tongued in my life.

I say, do you know E. M. Forster? He's all right, and might tell you a yarn or two.

I don't feel that there's anything here to help you. Best of luck.

T.E.S.

I hope you haven't broken yourself on Stravinsky records. They will be a delight. Our room has a decent gramophone. Don't be too sure of a best-seller. Lowell Thomas's book may please the hero-loving public more than yours. He is first in the field, too: and I doubt your yet reaching the popular ear. I'm rather a complicated person, and that's bad for a simple biography.

Congrats. all the same on raising [that advance]. It should keep you for a year: and a year is a goodish step forward. Congs. also to Kennington,[1] on making a few pounds out of the Arab show at last. He has lain (and still lies) on my conscience. I exploited him shamefully (only him, too, I think) and morally owe him thousands: which I can never begin to pay. A rotten parasite trick.

[1]Kennington was commissioned by the publishers to illustrate my book.

I sent Lawrence the typescript of the first eleven chapters.
They came back with marginal comments on almost every
page. Some were simple amendments of my English, some
were jokes, some minor corrections of fact. The more important ones now follow with the passages to which they refer;
in some cases it will appear that I had been grotesquely mis-
informed about him. It must be made clear that Lawrence
read and passed every word of the book, though he asked me
to put a sentence in my introduction making it seem that he
had not. Except on such occasions, therefore, as the Damascus
ride, where he writes, "I prefer a wrong account", it may be
assumed that the biographical facts given in *Lawrence and the
Arabs* are not far out. Lawrence told me the factual truth
(and had an extraordinary memory for facts) whenever he
could afford to do so. In cases where he later gave a more
explicit account to Captain Liddell Hart, I have omitted his
comments, to avoid duplication. Several anecdotes told me
by friends of his are here included with his amendments. The
amendments, which are printed in smaller type—or, where
they are given interlinearly, in italic type within square
brackets—are not so important as the fact of amendment,
which amounts to acknowledgment of the truth of the anecdote. The cancellation of words is in every case his.

[1]The title of the book as published in the United States was *Lawrence and the Arabian
Adventure.*

59

"He has lately taken the name of 'Shaw' while serving as a mechanic in the Royal Air Force."

No. In 1923, when he enlisted in the Royal Tank Corps, he called himself "Shaw", and he has continued to call himself Shaw since 1925, when he was transferred to the Royal Air Force. His first enlistment after the war, in 1922, was in the name of Ross: and these two are not his only efforts to label himself suitably.

". . . hero worship seems not only to annoy Lawrence but to make him feel physically ill, [? *unclean*]"

You see, I know how false the praise is: how little the reality compared with the legend: how much luck: how little merit. Praise makes a man sick, if it is ignorant praise.

"He was born in 1888 in North Wales, of mixed blood, none of it Welsh; it is Irish, Spanish, Isle of Skye [*Hebridean*], Dutch and Swedish [*Norse*]. Mixed blood has meant for Lawrence a natural gift for learning foreign languages, a respect for the manners and customs of strange people, and, more than this, the power of actually entering a foreign community and being accepted after a time as a member of it."

I have no sense of superiority, of English over foreigners: because I have no respect for humanity. It is so small a fraction of being. English, Arabs, French, Sheep, Clouds and Moonshine!

". . . he was brought up to do without female society and the habit has remained with him."

I try and talk to a woman as I would talk to another man, or to myself: and if she does not return the compliment, I leave her.

"At the age of thirteen he went on a [*began a series of*] bicycle tour[*s*] round England by himself and [, *in pursuit of a study of mediaeval armour*,] made a large collection of brass-rubbings from old monuments in country churches."

"He made one or more [*eight*] tours round Northern [*of*] France in his school vacations, studying the [*Castles and*]

Cathedrals, and living on practically nothing. When he was sixteen he broke a leg while he was wrestling with another boy at the Oxford City School. He said nothing ~~but began to walk back home with the broken leg.~~ [*till school ended for the day, and then returned home, hardly able to walk, on a borrowed bicycle*] ~~and after a time fainted~~ [*not quite true! It takes a lot to put me out*] (he has never grown since that date). He took no interest in organised games, ~~which were too tame for him, and has never done so since.~~ [*because they were organised, because they had rules, because they had results. He will never compete—in anything*]. He went to Syria and was away for four months, returning to Oxford late for the next term. He had been on foot in ~~native dress and barefoot~~ [*European dress and brown boots!*] from ~~Beersheba~~ [*Say Haifa, or Galilee: both are accurate*] in Syria [*Palestine*] to the Taurus mountains ~~in~~ [*and across to North*] Mesopotamia, having had two bouts of fever [*I got malaria in France, when I was sixteen: and have had it so often since that it's hardly worth mentioning. Malta fever at 18. Dysentery, typhoid, blackwater, smallpox etc. since*] and once been nearly murdered."

"[The murder story.] Lawrence on his way to Syria had bought a copper watch at ~~the~~ Paris ~~Exhibition~~ for ten francs. By constant use the case had been polished till it shone. In a [*Turkman*] village ~~of Kurds on~~ [*near*] the banks of the Euphrates where he was collecting Hittite antiquities he took out this watch one morning: the villagers murmured 'Gold'. A ~~Kurdish~~ [*he was a Turkoman*] villager stalked Lawrence all day as he went out on his journey and towards evening ran ahead and met him, as if accidentally. Lawrence asked the way to a certain village. The ~~Kurd~~ showed him a short cut ~~between some rocks~~ [*across country*]; where he sprang upon Lawrence, knocked him down, snatched his revolver, put it to his head and pulled the trigger. Though loaded it did not go off: the ~~Kurd~~ did not understand the mechanism of the safety catch, which was raised. He tried the trigger again and then in anger battered Lawrence about the head with ~~the butt~~ [*stones*] and left him ~~for dead. Some shepherds had seen this happening and when the Kurd was gone took Lawrence up and did what they could for him.~~ [*damaged, but not badly. The appearance of a shepherd had frightened him off.*]"

You give the impression I was badly hurt. I did 5 miles the same evening, to the next village.

"~~When he was able to walk~~ [*Next day*] he crossed the Euphrates to the nearest village [*town of Birejik*] where he could find Turkish policemen and collected a hundred and ten men. With this force, whose ferry-fare he had to pay across the river, he reentered the ~~Kurdish~~ village and there collapsed. When he came to himself he found the village in ruins; the Turkish police and riff-raff were making merry round a camp fire; and his copper watch, his money, his revolver and his Hittite antiquities were arranged in a neat pile beside him."

Lord Curzon had got for me orders from the Turkish Ministry of the Interior to all local governors, to afford me every help. So this was easy. We drove over in 3 carriages. I had a heavy go of fever on me. The usual day-long argument happened. I went to sleep: and in the night the village elders gave up the thief and the stolen property! There was no violence on either side, and no damage done. The man afterwards worked at Carchemish: not too well, but I was easy with him.

"During this walk he ~~lived~~ [*lodged every night in the nearest village, taking advantage of the hospitality which poor Syrians always show towards other poor. So he gained acquaintance*] with Arabs of the poorer class and began his ~~study of~~ [*familiarity with*] Arabic dialects. Lawrence is not a[*n*] ~~great~~ Arabic scholar—he has ~~not been able to spare the twenty years' study which are needed before anyone can call himself an Arabic scholar—~~

[*never sat down to study it, nor learnt its letters*] but he is fluent in conversational Arabic, and can tell by a man's accent and the expressions he uses from exactly what tribe or district of Arabia, Syria, Mesopotamia or Palestine he comes. ~~And he reads the Classical Arabic of the Koran without difficulty.~~"

Not a blinking word.

"The Bedouin turns his back on luxuries and the bustling business of towns, because in the desert he is without doubt free: he has lost houses, gardens, superfluous possessions and has won instead a personal liberty in the shadow of starvation and death. This was an attitude that moved Lawrence greatly, so that his nature has ever since been divided into two conflicting selves, the Bedouin self always longing for the bareness, simplicity, harshness of the desert—that state of mind of which the desert is a symbol—and the over-civilised European self."

The two selves, you see, are mutually destructive. So I fall between them into the nihilism which cannot find, in being, even a false god in which to believe.

"The only personal recollection I heard from Lawrence about this digging in Egypt was that in the evening often when the sun suddenly sank and it got very cold he and his fellow-workers used to wrap themselves round and round for warmth in [*the*] white ~~mummy-wrappings~~ [*linen cloth which had been buried with these pre-dynastic Egyptians for their next-world use*] and ~~ride~~ [*walk*] home that way smelling of spices."

It was pre-mummy period we were digging. 4000 B.C.

"As an archaeologist Lawrence soon won reputation. He has a curious gift for reading ancient inscriptions, if given only the smallest clue to the language."

?I don't agree.

"His memory for details is extraordinary, almost morbid."

I have the faculty of putting out of memory useless knowledge, (like higher mathematics), and of correlating what I do know. So a small knowledge seems uncanny to those whose facts don't hold together and help each other.

"Lawrence has a vast well-ordered store of accurate technical knowledge on every conceivable subject and does not like to hear amateurs talk inaccurately when he is about."

You might perhaps help the outside public, by basing my knowledge on my really wide reading: I read every book which interested me in the Library of the Oxford Union (best part of 50,000 vols. I expect) in 6 years. My father used to get me the books while I was at School: afterwards I borrowed always 6 vols. a day, in his name and my own. For 3 years I read day and night, on a hearthrug which was a mattress, so that I could fall asleep as I read. Often 18 hours reading in a day, and so good at the job, by practice, that I could tear the heart out of the soberest book in half an hour.

"Lawrence has been known to give information, when ~~asked~~ [*provoked*], even where it could hardly be expected to be appreciated. 'What are you grinning at, Private ~~Ross~~? [*Shaw*]' shouted a sergeant-instructor to him one day about four years ago, when he was in the Tank Corps."

R.T.C. always Shaw. I gave up Ross in 1923, when I left the R.A.F. I'd be glad if you said little about Ross. It is a name I may use after I leave the R.A.F. My land and money are in it. This story is twisted a bit. No matter.

" 'Do you really want to know, Serjeant?' said ~~Ross~~ [*Shaw*] and then elaborately explained a joke in a late-Greek ~~comedy~~ [*dialogue*] that he had been turning over in his mind during arms-drill."

Lucian, I think.

"He ~~lectured~~ [*quoted*] for a quarter of an hour and the sergeant and squad listened without interruption in the greatest interest. Again, in a hut in the Air Force a comrade once asked him, 'Excuse me, Shaw, but what does "iconoclast" mean?' "

I acted as a handy X-word dictionary.

"and then Shaw outlined a brief history of the religious politics in fifth-century Constantinople which first gave rise to the word. But this is merely a ~~sour~~ joke on himself: he despises mere knowledge,"

because it is all imperfect. What we call knowledge is the opposite of "wisdom".

"though he accumulates it and stores it carefully from old habit."

? Am I sour? I laugh at it and at myself. My knowledge does not help me now. When I got to Uxbridge the Education Officer said to me: "And you, Ross, what is the subject in which you feel particularly weak?" "Polishing boots, Sir" said I. The others had babbled of French and geography and sums.

"This is getting too far ahead of the story, which is still about Lawrence as an archaeologist before the war. In 1911, the Turks giving consent, he went out to the Euphrates with Dr. Hogarth and Mr. Leonard Woolley, and the expedition set about uncovering the remains of the ancient Hittite city Carchemish under the modern village of Jerablus."

I was there in 1910, too.

"Lawrence himself, as Dr. Hogarth tells me, preferred sleeping outside the hut on a knoll near the diggings."

The attraction of sleeping on the acropolis was that the Euphrates, a most noble river, lapped its eastern edge.

"Here would gather ~~all~~ [*God forbid!*] the diggers and amuse him with stories, many of them scandalous, about the old

Sheik of Jerablus and his young wife, and about the Germans in their camp a quarter of a mile away."

I was not, like Woolley, a trained archaeologist. So I made it my main duty to keep the workmen happy. As smaller jobs, I had the photography, the pottery, the piecing together broken sculptures, and engineering work in laying or lifting our light railway. But the gangs came first. While they were happy the work was sure to go well. I knew them all by name, and their home affairs. Only I never knew any one of them by sight!

"With the Germans there was at first good feeling. But the chief engineer, Contzen, was a difficult man to remain friendly with."

The back of his neck was too thick. It lapped over his collar.

[Lawrence demanded a public apology to Achmed, Lawrence's house-servant, whom one of Contzen's engineers had flogged]

" 'Nonsense. The incident is closed', and Contzen turned his back.

" 'On the contrary', said Lawrence, 'if you don't do as I ask, I shall take the matter into my own hands.'

"Contzen turned round again.

" 'I shall take your engineer to the village and there *flog him*.'

" 'You couldn't and you daren't do such a thing', cried Contzen, scandalised; but then he looked at Lawrence again. In the end the engineer came to make his public apology, to the vast ~~amusement~~ [*satisfaction*] of the village."

This is a Woolley yarn. I hadn't an idea of it. Merely said I'd take him to the village and compel him.

[An armed battle between the Germans and some Kurdish workmen, in which Lawrence acted as peace-maker]: "Lawrence has a gesture which he uses in emergencies of this kind.

He lazily raises both hands, clasps them behind his head and remains silent and apparently wrapped in thought."

I try to bring the local noise into relation with the light-year distance of the lesser nebulae. A soothing exercise.

"This [ex-] brigand chief ~~Mahoudi~~ [*Hamoudi*] and a younger man called Dahoum, who was trained by Lawrence as a photographer, came on a visit with him to England. They enjoyed Oxford, particularly the sport of bicycle riding, which was new to them."

They stood in the public lavatories and stroked the white glazed walls: "beautiful, beautiful bricks".

"Among the women for whom Lawrence has had the greatest respect was the late Miss Gertrude Bell, one of the ~~three~~ great English travellers in Arabia before Lawrence: ~~The other two, according to Lawrence, were Doughty and Blunt.~~"

I mentioned Gertrude, the Blunts, and Palgrave when considering the Nefud district only. Otherwise I'd have had to put in Burckhardt, Niebuhr and others, who were yet greater.

"He does not think very highly of Sir Richard Burton, who did not travel ~~openly~~ [*single-mindedly*] as the others did and ~~gave misleading accounts of where he had been and what he had done~~ [*wrote so difficult an English style as to be unreadable. Also he was pretentious and vulgar*]. Gertrude Bell visited the Carchemish camp one morning in 1911 and, since news of her coming had arrived before her, the village was in a great state of excitement. At the time there were only three Englishmen in the camp, Dr. Hogarth who was married, Mr. Campbell-Thompson who was [*widely*] known to be engaged, and Lawrence who wore the red-tasselled belt to his flannel ~~trousers~~ which marked the bachelor in those parts."

"Shorts": and it was the belt, not the shorts which marked the young blood.

"It was decided by the diggers that Gertrude Bell was coming to marry Lawrence and all preparations were made for a festival. When, therefore, she said good-bye the same evening and prepared to go off there was a great clamour. It was thought that she had refused Lawrence and so insulted the village. Lawrence managed to quiet them down ~~somehow~~ [*by an ungallant but expedient lie*] before stones were thrown, and Gertrude Bell, who had been puzzled by the demonstration, never learned the truth until Dr. Hogarth told her some years later: it amused her greatly.

"There were two digging seasons in [*Northern*] Mesopotamia: between June and September ~~it was too hot to work~~ [*the local harvest claimed the workmen*] and between November and March the [*rains rained and the snows snowed and the*] Euphrates flooded ~~and turned everything~~ [*the lowlands*] into a marsh."

"He had repeatedly warned the British Foreign Office of the complications that would follow—the French had ambitions for the control of Syria too—but ~~no notice had been taken~~ [*Sir Edward Grey's pacific policy allowed no alternative*]. Kitchener's final words to Lawrence were that within ~~two~~ [*three*] years there would be a world war ~~but neither he nor Lawrence could stop it.~~ [*which would adjust this lesser question with the greater*]. 'So run along, young man, and ~~sell your papers~~' [*dig before it rains.*]"

"Lawrence's way of calling public attention in Europe to the concealed threat to world-peace in the building of the railway that linked Berlin with Bagdad, was to load sections of drainage pipe on mules and transport them by night to the hills which commanded the bridge."

We had no drainage pipes. This is silly. I did nothing of the sort. It's time somebody stamped on the yarn.

"Then he mounted them on piles of sand to resemble cannon. As he expected, the Germans observed them through field-glasses, got excited and wired to Berlin and Constantinople that the British were fortifying the hills. The European press was excited for days."

All untrue! So far as I know. The better Germans used to visit our digs regularly to dine with us. We kept open house. There was no enmity, except with Contzen, who was a rough drinking fellow, son of a Cologne chemist.

"In the winter of 1913 Dr. Hogarth was asked to suggest two archaeologists who might join the surveying party in the peninsula of Sinai and wired to Woolley and Lawrence to go. They came down angrily because they thought that the telegram was an order and not a request, but soon were glad to have come."

It was a Kitchener survey, for military reasons. The Palestine Exploration Fund got permission from Turkey, saying it was archaeology: and the job of Woolley and myself was to put an archaeological face on Newcombe's activity.

"They got on well with the surveyor [*Captain*] Newcombe, [*R.E.*], and made important discoveries of ancient remains. They mapped out [*not too seriously, perhaps,*] the probable route of the Israelites' marches and found the place which may have been Kadesh Barnea where Moses struck the rock and water gushed out."

"He is short, [5'5½''] with his body long in proportion to his legs so that he is more impressive seated than standing."[1]

I take your word for it: but the R.A.F. ready-made 5'6'' clothes fit me like a glove. So I must be pretty normal height and width.

"He has a big head of a Norse type, rising steeply at the back. His hair is fair (not blonde) and rather fine: his complexion

[1] Cf. Homer's description of Ulysses, man of many wiles.

is fair and his face hairless [*after shaving*]. The upper part of his face is kindly, almost maternal; the lower part is severe, almost cruel. His eyes are blue-grey and constantly in motion. His hands and feet are small. He is~~is~~ [*? was*] of great physical strength: he has been seen to raise up a rifle at arm's length, holding it by the barrel-end, until it was parallel with the ground—yet no one would suspect him of being more than tough."

"A little man with a red face, like a butcher" (Tanks Corp).
"Face like a cheap writing pad" (R.A.F.).
"A proper swede-looking chap" (R.A.F.).
"A comical little f—" (R.T.C.).
"Face & figure of a Circassian dancing girl" (Lowell Thomas).

"He has a trick of holding his hands loosely folded below his breast, the elbows to his sides, and carries his head a little tilted, his eyes on the ground. He can sit or stand for hours at a stretch without moving a muscle. He talks in short sentences, deliberately and quietly without accenting his words strongly. He grins a lot and laughs seldom. He is a dead shot [*with a pistol*]."

Will you do me the favour of saying that I never look at a man's face, and never recognise a face? This is inherited. My father one day stepped on my toe in the street, and passed on, with an apology, not knowing me. Long practice has made me able to talk to whoever accosts me, for 20 minutes at a time, without betraying that I haven't a notion who he is. Yet I remember names, and details of taste and character, & words & opinions and places vividly, and at great length.

As an instance: when I read the first para. on this page I got up and looked at my eyes in a glass. It had never occurred to me that they had a colour.[1] I haven't an idea what your eyes, or my mother's are like: and wouldn't recognise either of you, if I met you without

[1]Yet in *Seven Pillars* he tells of an old woman who found his blue eyes horrible, like sky seen through the eye-sockets of a skull.

warning. I get into great trouble in camp for "cutting" the officers when they are in plain clothes. Yet I do my best to see people. If you print the truth I'll be able to put your book in as evidence next time I'm up for office.

"When he first joined the Royal Air Force he was sent one day to nail down carpets under the direction of an Air Mar-shal's wife. She had known him well but Lawrence ~~was in hiding and~~ [*to avoid general embarrassment*] did not wish to be recognised. He went dull and stupid and she did not ~~recognise~~ [*notice anything*] ~~him.~~"

You will have to clear up this. Why should she notice anything? I was just like the others, a sweep in filthy overalls. As a matter of fact, I'm hardly ever recognised, in uniform, by people who used to know me. The tight collar and peaked cap are disguise: and there is nothing remarkable about my appearance.

At Uxbridge a fellow was showing off. He said to me "You've been east, haven't you?" "Yes," said I. "Did you ever meet Col. Lawrence there?" "No" (truthfully) "but I've heard of him". "Well, he & me were pals". I smiled all over my stomach, under my tunic.

"I have noticed that he dislikes being touched; a hand laid on his shoulder or knee is an offence; he can understand the ori-ental notion that virtue goes out of a man when so touched."

Not so much virtue goes out: as a loss of integrity.

"He will never shake hands if he can avoid doing so. [*Nor will he ever fight hand to hand*]. He does not drink or smoke. This is not due to [*principle, or to*] deliberate teetotal conviction or because he regards these things as poison, but because he has no occasion to drink or smoke. Most people begin drinking and smoking out of mere sociability: Lawrence always avoids sociability of [*any sort*] ~~this sort.~~"

I am uncomfortable with strangers: it is what the books call shyness.

I find myself hard to control anyhow. If I let in drink or love or gluttony or wine or gaming or sport it would be too much. These things, stimulants, are for the years when one is flat.

"He even avoids eating with other people.[1] Regular meal-times are not to his liking. He eats, when he does eat, which is seldom, in a casual abstracted way. He came to visit me one breakfast-time on his racing motor-bicycle: he had come about two hundred miles [*in five hours*]. He would eat no breakfast. I asked him later what the food was like in the camp. 'I seldom eat it: it's good enough. I am now a storeman in the Quarter-master's stores so I don't need much.' "

I hate waiting more than 2 minutes for a meal: or spending more than 5 minutes on a meal. That's why I live mainly on bread & butter. And I like water better than any other drink. Remember I live a very sedentary life, and needn't eat as much as a worker. Also eating should be done in a closet, behind locked doors.

" 'When did you last have a meal?' I asked. 'On Wednesday.' Since [*when, apparently,*] ~~then I have had two pieces of~~ [*he had had some*] chocolate, an orange and a cup of tea. This was Saturday."

Did I know so exactly? It's my occasional habit to knock off proper feeding for three days (rarely five) just to make sure I can do it without feeling worried or strained. One's sense of things gets very keen, so, and it's good practice for hard times. My life has been full of hard times.

"Then I think I put some apples near him, and after a while he reached for one."

I'd eat fruit all day till I burst.

"Lawrence also [*when his own master*] avoids regular hours of sleep. He has found that his brain works better if he sleeps as irregularly as he eats."

[1]See L.H., p. 210, thirteenth line from bottom.

In the R.A.F. I am in bed always at lights out: and sleep till after midnight. Then I doze, thinking more or less till reveille. At night others' minds are switched off, and that gives my thoughts longer range.

"He avoids as far as possible all social relationships, all public events. He joins no clubs, societies, groups. He answers no letters but the immediately pressing ones and not always those."

None addressed "Lawrence" anyhow! A name I heartily reject.[1] It might be a good thing to warn people not to waste stamps on the wrong name. "He will however always use the reply form of a pre-paid telegram, though not necessarily to the sender."

"He is one of the rare people who have a sensible attitude towards money. He neither loves it nor fears it [*for he has found it useless to help on the two or three occasions he has greatly desired things worth while*]. He can be a financier if and when it pleases him: for the most part he is not bothered about his bank balance. At the moment he has no bank balance at all, and has taken great care not to make a penny out of any of his writings [*upon the Arab Revolt. Apart from this he has done his best to earn money with his pen: and has made £35 in four years anonymous effort. Jam, he calls these little earnings, upon his Air Force bread and butter. He writes with great difficulty, and corrects much; and takes no pride or pleasure in anything he has written.*] "I believe that the one thing that he likes is to find someone who knows more than himself or can do something better than himself. To such a person he will attach himself and learn all that is to be learned."

All very well: but you know I've never met a man who isn't better than myself at all points except the matter actually in hand. I keep so much to myself partly because I have a crawling knowledge of my own insufficiency, and a fear lest other people see this clearly enough to leave me out.

[1]But see L.H., p. 177, l. 17.

"He has never been dogmatic about any creed or political conviction. He clearly dislikes crowds or any person whose only strength is that he is a member of some society or creed. He clearly also expects people to find themselves and be true to themselves, and to leave their neighbours to do the same."

I'd wish every man to be an everlasting question-mark.

"Lawrence does not like children [*or dogs, or elephants in mass*] in the usual sentimental way. [*He likes some children, some dogs, some elephants.*] ~~On the contrary, he dislikes and~~ [*From the rest he*] shrinks ~~from them.~~"

I am afraid of them, and sorry for them. They remind me of the shame of our existence. I am sure life is not good enough for us to invite outsiders to share it.

"This will not, however, prevent him at times from talking ~~seriously~~ [*really*] to a child, ~~if he feels that the child is~~ [*treating it as*] an independent person [*and*] not merely [*as*] a clever echo of its parents. He has, it seems, no use for the human race as such or interest in its continuance; he has no sentimentality about universal brotherhood: he despises the works of men, as Swift did."

Not despises, in first instance. I find them all parts of an illusion, like ourselves, & our ideas, & our knowledge, and our universe. There is no absolute for me.

"And has come to this view, I think, by the same road as Swift, by an overwhelming ~~love~~ [*?sense*] of personal liberty, a largeness of heart, and an intense desire for perfection ~~continually disappointed~~ [*so obviously unattainable as to be not worth starting for*]. We may conclude that when, about ~~three years ago~~" [*1922*]

You have your dates wrong, I joined the R.A.F. in Aug. 1922: R.T.C. in March 1923: and have therefore served five years, with only a fortnight's break, in 1923.

"this dislike of the crowd became too strong and he saw that it was becoming a definite limitation for him, when he found in fact after the triumph of the Arabian adventure that in avoiding becoming [*the mask of*] a popular hero he was withdrawing more and more and becoming 'unwholesomely' interested in just being himself, he took a violent course—he enlisted and bound himself to a life in which he was forced perpetually to be a member of the crowd" [*and a life as nearly physical as an animal's, in which food is provided, and drink, and a round of work in harness, and a stable afterwards till the new day calls with a repetition of the work of yesterday.*]

I have not enough resources in myself to be self-sufficient: and the services are like a lay monastery.

"What is called Lawrence's 'love of publicity' can best be explained as a burning desire to know himself, for no one can be himself except by first knowing himself."

"Love of publicity" isn't quite the phrase. Publicity is a thing I'm indifferent to, for the printed word always misses its target. I don't think I've ever been annoyed at anything I've read about myself. But it ceases to be amusing when one meets people who believe the yarns in the papers or books. One denies them. They say "How modest these great men are"—and I go out and am sick on their doorsteps.

"He is incapable of showing off ~~to the crowd~~ merely for the sake of publicity."

but I will, and often do, show off to the individual.

"If he is interested at times in what people ~~of distinction~~"

There are none such!

"may think of him this is only because their opinion may show him what sort of a man he is more clearly than any amount of self-examination can. He has been often accused of vanity because he has sat for his portrait to so many artists and sculptors: but it is the opposite of vanity. A vain man has a very clear view of himself which he tries to force on his neighbours. Lawrence sits for his portrait because he wants to discover what he is, by the effect which he produces on the artist:"

And partly because I am often asked, by the one class of human beings I'd like to belong to. I can salve the regret of not being an artist by watching artists work, & providing them with a model. I have only 4 times refused to sit.

"so far from being vain he clearly has no picture of himself at all except a rather contemptuous one. He ~~even at times, I think,~~ accepts the view that he is a complete humbug and play actor; because people who are themselves humbugs and actors see him so in their own likeness. Lawrence's curse is that he cannot stop thinking,[1] and by thinking I mean a working of the mind that is not mere calculation from any given set of facts, but a much more intense and difficult process which makes its own facts and tests them as it goes." [*and destroys them when it is over*].

It destroys its own facts, too. I go about aching to think of something, stretching my mind in every direction, & finding nothing, "lunging about" as an Arab poet said "like a blind camel in the dark". Only, the effort seems to make the mind harder and fitter.

"But the simplest conclusion about Lawrence is the best. It is not that he is a genius. This has come to be a vulgar almost meaningless word. It is not even that he is an 'erratic genius', unless 'erratic' means that Lawrence does not do the usual things that men of successful talents do: the ordinary vulgar things that are expected by the crowd."

The trouble with me often is that I am too sane: but it is not fair to expect a man who has the qualities which shine in strange weather to subdue them in calm weather.

[1]But see p. 171, l. 17.

"If Napoleon, for instance, who was a vulgar rather than an 'erratic' genius, had been in Lawrence's position at the close of the 1918 campaign he would have proclaimed himself a Mohammedan and consolidated the new Arabian Empire. Lawrence came away and left the Arabs to ~~enjoy~~ [*employ*] the freedom that he had given them, a freedom unencumbered by his rule which, however just and wise, would always have been an alien rule."

I would have contradicted myself if I had suffered all those pains to free the Arabs: and then enslaved them under myself.

"Lawrence is impish at times but never erratic; he does nothing without good reason, though his decisions may disappoint the crowd. There was nothing erratic about Lawrence when he enlisted as ~~a private soldier~~ [*an airman*] ~~three~~ [*five*] years ago."

It was a course I had decided on in 1919: and had suggested to Air Marshal Sir Geoffrey Salmond before the Armistice: but not till Winston had given the Arabs a fair deal was I free to please myself. That accounted for the delay till 1922.

Do make clear the difference between an airman's view of himself and his view of a soldier. He is brought up to despise the Army. "Soldier" is our chief insult and word of derision. Soldiers are machines or part of machines. Airmen use machines and own them. Airmen (even the little ones) are men devoted to the conquest of an element. Whereas soldiers!

"Nobody owns Lawrence or will ever own him."

"A rare animal, will not breed in captivity" (Winston).

"He is not a public Niagara that can be harnessed for any political or commercial purpose. A Colonial Governor Generalship? Imagine Lawrence [*who disbelieves in his existence and yours*] laying foundation stones and attending ceremonial parades and banquets!"

"Another suggestion has been that Lawrence should be entrusted with a mission to settle affairs in China."

I've done this sort of thing once. One does not repeat unpleasant experiences, for hire, without conviction.

"Other suggestions have been that he should edit a modern literary review,"

Silly. I'm a person entirely without literary sense.

"that he should be given an appointment in connexion with the Mesopotamian oil-fields, or a high post at the British Museum."

People do not seem to realise that I know myself very well: and that I have chosen to serve in the R.A.F. which is not a life that comes easily or naturally to me: but I find its difficulty worth coping with, and I am quietly content. If I want to do anything else I will do so, without prompting.

"The most popular suggestion has been that Lawrence should head a great religious revival."

Things can't be revived. They can be invented.

"But it is as foolish as the rest. In the first place Lawrence has read too much theology to be a simple successful revivalist;"

Nihilism is a chilly creed: whose first article is "Thou shalt not convert".

"in the second, he would have religious belief a matter for every man to settle for himself without interference from outside; in the third place . . . Mr. George Bernard Shaw made the suggestion that Lawrence should be given a government pension and chambers in some public building (he mentioned Blenheim Palace), and be allowed to spend his time exactly as it suited him."

I do not believe I'm worth anybody's paying. Also he might have aesthetic objections to Blenheim Palace. Also some one else lives there, with great difficulty.

"The only suggestion that I can make is simply this: that he should be left alone to maintain that rare personal liberty which so very few people are capable of maintaining."

I'd like it made clear that I have not written,[1] and have no intention of writing, and will not write any other book. The writing which puts the occasional jam on my bread and butter is not creative work, or original work. The rare circumstances of duty, which compelled me unwillingly to put on record a history of the Arab Revolt, are not likely to recur.

"Lawrence is a romantic. He has loved adventure for its own sake, and the weaker side because it is the weaker side, and the lost cause, and unhappiness."

I don't want to be considered, or to consider myself, as a philosophic system, or a paragon or a manual of conduct. Circumstances & my own efforts have made me free of human ties. Therefore I can dispose of myself in any market. Others cannot: they have opinions, aims, ambitions, families, wants, hopes, fears.

"Lawrence's romanticism is not incompetent, it is not unsuccessful. When a European monarch one day in 1918 greeted him with the remark, 'It [This] is a bad time for us kings. Two [Five] new republics have been [were] proclaimed today [yesterday],' Lawrence was able to answer 'Courage, your Majesty [Sir]: I [We] have just made three new kingdoms in the East.'"

We always say "Sir" to him. A good yarn.[2]

"For the real success of his romanticism he is naturally very much hated by most government officials, regular soldiers,

---

[1] This was not factually true: he had written *The Mint*, an account of his experiences at Uxbridge in 1922.

[2] See pp. 107, l. 20, and L.H., 130, last line.

and such-like: he is a disturbing element in their ordered scheme of things."

Was my "Winston" settlement of the Middle East romantic or realist? That is the big achievement of my life: of which the war was a preparation.

"Now that he is a mechanic in the Air Force, they suspect some diabolic trick for raising mutiny or revolt."

They don't understand. I want to get quit of affairs. I want to be politically and intellectually unemployable. I haven't enough money to do nothing. So I arrange a way of living which ensures these abdications—and my necessary maintenance, in an interesting life, full of the humour of incongruity, & devoted towards an object bigger than the individuals.

"He keeps his enormously wide circle of friends as much as possible in watertight compartments, each away from the other. To each friend he reveals some part of himself, but only a part."

You can hardly conceive the thousands of people I know: from tramps to Air Marshals. Don't give the idea that they are famous, all of them. I like nearly everybody: and have a special tenderness for ruffians. But I don't think I have an intimate.

"So there are a hundred or a thousand Lawrences, each one a facet of the Lawrence crystal: and whether or not the crystal is colourless and the facets merely reflect the characters of the friends whom they face, Lawrence himself has no notion. The result of this dispersion is that such of his friends as are of a possessive nature try to corner him, each believing that he alone knows the real Lawrence."

Isn't it partly, too, that I'm a person about whom it is easier to feel than to speak? The only good description of myself which I've read is the Seven Pillars. People can't put me into 3 words, because I am various, & have no single characteristic. So my friends resent

every description of me they hear: and can't give one of their own
to justify their resentment. Hence the possessive secrecy.

[At the end of Chapter II]:

From this point I have not much to say. You follow my book very
closely. I do not know if this is right, from your point of view, or
not: or if the Trustees (Eliot & Co.) will moan. Hippoclides[1] doesn't
care about copyright: and Cape will look after himself. I wish you
had not so to write against time.

There is a man—W. J. Childs, of the Foreign Office, who has
compiled, for the F.O. archives, a *real* history of the Arab Revolt.
He has all the Arab Bureau Papers. An interesting, literary fellow,
who writes well. If you have time, go and see him. But you haven't
time.

"The pilgrim road became so dangerous and difficult that
a railway was at last built (by German enterprise) from
Damascus to Medina, and the pilgrims were at last able, just
before the outbreak of the War, to set out in reasonable hope
of a safe return."

The purpose of the Rly. was political and strategic: to give Abdul
Hamid access (other than the Suez Canal) for his troops, to the Holy
Cities. The pretext was pious: the real reason strategic.

"At the outbreak of the War Lawrence had of course to give
up his excavations at Carchemish in Mesopotamia, which was
in Turkish territory. He was, at the time, in London; it was
the off-season for digging, and in any case his interest in mere
archaeology had become dulled."

Till the war swallowed up everything I wanted nothing better
then Carchemish, which was a perfect life.

[1]One of Lawrence's odd self-identifications. According to Herodotus, Hippoclides the
Athenian was the favoured suitor for the hand of a princess. One night he stood on his
head on a table and waved his legs about to dance-music. (The Greeks wore short skirts.)
When warned that he was forfeiting all respect and defeating his own plans, he remarked,
"Hippoclides does not care", and persisted in his antics. Hippoclides' not caring is wilful
illogicality, and to be distinguished from that of Gallio (see L.H., p. 194, l. 13), who
merely could not be bothered to care. Lawrence later carved the words of Hippoclides'
ΟΥΦΡΟΝΤΙΣ on the lintel of his cottage.

"At Cairo he was also engaged in getting information about the anti-British revolutionary societies in Egypt and, because the Egyptians are not as loyal in their secret societies as the Syrians and Mesopotamians, was always having visitors; one party after another came offering to betray the names of its fellow-members, until he had seen nearly the whole society. Lawrence's chief difficulty was to prevent the various parties meeting each other on the office-stairs."

In this paragraph you might work in my visit to Athens, to gain contact with the Levant group of the British Secret Service, whose Egyptian agent I was for a time, till the work grew important.

"Lawrence's official task, given him direct from the War Office at London, was to go as member of a secret mission to the Turkish Commander who was besieging Kut; to persuade him not to press the siege. It was thought that a large bribe might work, because it was known that the Turks were themselves in difficulties."

The Erzeroum capture had been "arranged" (*Greenmantle*[1] has more than a flavour of truth) and the W.O. hoped we could repeat its circs. at Kut.

"But bribes were useless, as Lawrence had told those who sent him, and only encouraged the Turks. The Turkish commander, being an ~~uncle~~ [*? nephew*] of Enver, the chief Young Turk, never needed to worry about money: so the conference developed into ~~a mere exchange of courtesies~~ [*an attempt to ransom from him, on grounds of humanity or interest, those of the garrison of Kut whose health had suffered by the siege, and whom captivity would kill.*] In these Lawrence however would not join. When the Turk said, 'After all, gentlemen, our interests as Empire builders are much the same as yours. There is nothing that need stand between us,' Lawrence replied shortly:

[1] A novel by John Buchan (Lord Tweedsmuir).

'Only a million dead Armenians', and that ended the conference."

It was Aubrey Herbert who said this.[1]

"The British Generals in Mesopotamia were not pleased with
this conference."

We got nearly 1000 of the sick exchanged for hale Turks: we
should have got 3000.

"Lawrence's private intention, which was the real reason of
his coming, was to go behind the Turkish lines and stir up the
desert tribes, whom he knew well from his Carchemish days."

No: I wanted to see if the situation in Mespot. would allow of
local co-operation on national lines between Arab & English. I found
it impossible.

[Lawrence decides to make himself a nuisance in order to get
away from Cairo. See Ch. VII of *S.P.W.*]: "The break came
in this way. The chief of staff one day rang him up on the
telephone. 'Is that Lieutenant Lawrence? Where exactly is the
Turkish Forty-first Division now stationed?' Lawrence said,
'At So and So near Aleppo. The 131st, 132nd, 133rd regiments
compose it. They are quartered in the villages So and So, So
and So, and So and So.'
   " 'Have you those villages marked on the map?'
   " 'Yes.'
   " 'Have you noted them yet on the ~~official~~ [*dislocation*] files
~~in the geography department~~?'
   " 'No.'
   " 'Why not?'

[1]Aubrey Herbert, who was dead when Lawrence made this note, had attributed the
remark to Lawrence. Since Herbert was as strongly pro-Turk as the War permitted
(gentleman against gentleman) and Lawrence was an ardent pro-Armenian, I am inclined to believe Herbert. Lawrence may have wished not to seem responsible for the
failure of the conference by having given way to private feelings.

" 'Because I prefer to keep them in my head.' [*they are better in my head till we can check the information*]

" 'Yes, but you can't send your head along to Ismailia every time.' (Ismailia was a long way from Cairo.)

" 'I wish to goodness I could', said Lawrence, and rang off."

[He is given leave and visits Arabia; on his return he advises against the sending of British troops there. See Ch. XVI of *S.P.W.*]

"Lawrence was much amused at the change in the attitude of the staff towards him. He was no longer a conceited young puppy, but a very valuable officer of great intelligence, with a pungent style of writing. All because, for a wonder, his view of the Revolt was agreeable to them."

Deedes said to Murray: "What did you think of L.?" "I was disappointed", said Sir Archibald, "he did not come in dancing pumps."

[The questions that I most wanted to ask Lawrence concerned his famous ride to Damascus, in June 1917, obscurely hinted at in Chapter XLVIII of *S.P.W.* He wrote there merely, without any geographical indications as to where he went:

I undertook this long, dangerous ride, in which to see the more important of Feisal's secret friends, and to study key-positions of our future campaigns: but the results were incommensurate with the risks. . . . When I returned it was June the sixteenth.

Lowell Thomas had heard about this ride from Lawrence's friends during his visit to Akaba in the following year; and, of the necessarily confused account that he gave of it in his book, certain details had a certain ring of truth.

I consulted Dr. Hogarth and my brother Philip Graves. Dr. Hogarth told me of Lawrence's sitting under the notice offering a reward for his head, and my brother told me of the inquisitive policemen and the cherry orchard. I believe that Lawrence was the source of these stories, and I believe that they were true, though he subsequently denied them for some obscure reason of his own.

I therefore sent him the fullest account I could put together from the various available sources, together with a map, and asked him the following questions:

"From the point of view of this map: did you go by the desert to Baalbek, and back along the railway, or *vice versa?*"

It was a zig-zag journey. If you suggest it, do it in dots.

"Other queries about the ride follow next mail. Perhaps in the interval you might put down a few notes. This is important because an obviously wrong account appears in Lowell Thomas, I find."

I prefer a wrong account, as I've said in notes.

"I send you in typescript what I have picked up, but it may be all wrong. Did you blow up the Baalbek bridge? In view of the Metawileh tribesmen? Did you visit what L.T. calls the Sandhurst at Baalbek, or try to? How many men had you with you? Did you dine with Ali Riza or Yasim, or either or both? If so, do you want it mentioned, or not? What happened at Kerak? At Rayak? Or didn't you go to Rayak? Were you disguised as a woman at any point?"]

"He decided in Bedouin style to throw himself on the mercy of fate. He would go on this ride and, so far from taking precautions, would expose himself to every possible danger."

I should qualify this para. with a perhaps or two.

"If the Turks were so foolish as to let him get back safely, they must pay the penalty of their folly, for he would ~~take it for a~~

~~sign that they were doomed and~~ carry the revolt through to a finish with no more qualms."

I am looking for a Turkish revival,[1] soon, to make Turkey a real power, as it was in XVIIth Cent.

"If they caught him, on the other hand, ~~he would not let himself be taken alive,~~"

Why not? I never had an idea of killing myself. Too much trouble.

"~~and after that~~ the revolt would get no farther than the deserts of Arabia.

"On June the 3rd. 1917, in the fifth week of the journey from Wejh, he started with a few of his bodyguard and was away a fortnight. How he reached Damascus is not known; but he went, it seems, north by way of Azrak,"

No.

"the Druse mountains and the Lebanon, where he visited his friends the Christian Syrians. He then turned down to Baalbek. At Baalbek there was a great bridge over a ravine,"

No, there is no bridge near Baalbek.

"the destruction of which would cut the one railway line between Constantinople and Palestine, Syria and Arabia for a fortnight. He went to see how much explosive was needed to destroy it. He also attempted to visit a military academy at the town but could get no further than the gate."

A training depot for Syria. No difficulty in seeing it, if one's tastes were that way.

"From Baalbek he went to Rayak, the railway junction to Beyrout, where were great railway repair shops [*No:*] and a large concentration camp of Turkish, German and Bul-

[1]But see p. 78, l. 18: "Things cannot be revived", and his bitter comments, on the rise of the Turks to power, in Ch. IV of *S.P.W.*

garian troops. He spent two days and a night in Rayak camp; a quite unnecessary visit, at his old game of finding out the disposition of the Turkish army, trusting to his command of Turkish, German and Arabic to get him through. He took one companion with him. He visited the repair-shops to get information about the rolling-stock of the railway and then went on to Damascus.

"At Damascus he visited various friends of Feisal's, including the governor of the town, and made arrangements for a rising in the city when deliverance came. While he was in the city his men encamped outside the walls in a cherry orchard: there they were disturbed by some inquisitive Turkish policemen who, however, lie buried under the cherry trees."

Not true.

"Lawrence rode into Damascus on a camel in English uniform,"

Not much!

"but nobody seemed to take any notice of that. Arabs often dressed in the spoils of the English dead. He knew the city well and went about freely, talking the Syrian dialect.

"He saw several notices pasted up offering a reward of five thousand pounds in gold for the capture alive or dead of 'El-Orens, Destroyer of Railways'. His portrait was at the top."

No such notices were ever posted, in my knowledge. Nor had they my portrait. I've never sat to a professional photographer.[1]

"He decided to put the matter to a supreme test and sat down to coffee under one of these notices: but nobody connected the man with the portrait, and after an hour or two he went

[1]Not quite true. He figured in a college group displayed in the window of an Oxford photographer throughout the War.

on. He came back then, along the line, until he reached
Deraa, where he rode across to Azrak again"

No.

"and so on to safety.

"He returned on June the sixteenth and found Nesir and
Auda still at Nebk . . ."

[After these Noes, Lawrence sent me the following notes
on a sheet torn from an R.A.F. *Workshop Record Book*. (*Job No.
Description of Work. Material used. Hours on Job. Date Started.
Date finished. Initials. Remarks.*) Perhaps it was the matter-of-
fact headings that persuaded him to be a little more explicit;
though not as explicit as he afterwards was to L.H. See L.H.,
p. 69, l. 6, L.H., p. 175, l. 16, and L.H., p. 205, l. 10.]

22.VII.27

The maps shall go back next week. It will take me more than
today to alter them, and the air mail is tonight. It comes in and out
straight away. I am writing in the shop, so that will explain paper
and pen etc.

In my report to Clayton after Akaba I gave a short account of
my excursion from Nebk northward. It was part of the truth. During
it some things happened, and I do not want the whole story to be
made traceable. So on this point I have since darkened counsel.
You'll have to say something, but you'll not be able to be right in
what you say. So hedge yourself, and me, if you can, by cautionary
phrases. Some such thing as the following:—

"From Nebk during the Akaba expedition's halt there, 'L' went
off on a solitary excursion northward. On this ride he was said to
have been convoyed by relays of local tribesmen, beginning with
the Rualla and changing them at each tribal boundary. Apparently none of his own, nor of Sherif Nasir's men completed the
journey with him. He is said to have been franked by private letters
of Emir Feisal, but nothing certain is known of his purpose, his
route, and the results of his journey.

"Casual references in the Seven Pillars point to his having visited Damascus during this trip: and probably also Ziza, where he seems to have seen Fawaz, head of the Beni Sakhr, shortly before he died. Apparently he was also at or near some of the bridges over the River Yarmuk. But he must have ridden light, and demolition work cannot have been in his programme, though an intercepted enemy report of this date mentions a bridge being damaged near Ras Baalbek, south of Hama, considerably beyond Damascus and Baalbek, the furthest points associated by rumour with his journey. The destruction of this bridge was probably a coincidence.

"On his return to Nebk . . ."

I did not dine or lunch or breakfast with Ali Riza Pasha.[1] I have never in my life set eyes on Yasim. My first war-time visit to Kerak was in 1918. Nothing happened, bar the death of a sheep, which I helped to eat. Kerak was an open town, between our force at Tafileh, and the Turk forces at Madeba.

I did not enter Rayak during the war: and was only disguised once as a woman, when I went in to Amman with Farraj and some gipsies, as mentioned in Book VIII (I think) of the Seven Pillars. "And the reference there to my ordinarily wearing British uniform when in enemy camps may refer to a practice begun during my ride northward from Nebk."

During the ride from Nebk I was never disguised: instead I put off necessary visits to dangerous places until after darkness had set in. In the dark my figure was indistinguishable from that of any other Arab of the desert fringe.

~~Once during this~~[2] . . . Lowell Thomas' account is fantastic. You will find I was only away a few days in all: and even allowing (as you might do) for two changes of camel, and a very high daily mileage not everything is possible.

You may say that "the more picturesque incidents reported of this journey are demonstrably untrue: but that L's (failure or) refusal to provide accurate details throws upon him responsibility for such fictions as are current."

[1] But see L.H., p. 69, l. 17.
[2] These words Lawrence has deleted, on the point of making a confession.

There was no "Sandhurst" at Baalbek; so far as I know: only an infantry depot, & a training camp. Many German N.C.O.'s and men. Nothing very great or very important.

You may make public if you like the fact that my reticence upon this northward raid is deliberate, and based on private reasons: and record your opinion that I have found mystification, and perhaps statements deliberately misleading or contradictory, the best way to hide the truth of what really occurred, if anything did occur.

T.E.S.

The lighter you can touch on it the better I'll be served. Sorry: on these points I can't afford to help you. T.E.S.

In retelling the story of the camel charge at Aba el Lissan where Lawrence accidentally shot his camel I naturally quoted the poem that he mentions in the *Seven Pillars* as having run through his mind during the charge. (See Ch. LIII of *S.P.W.*)

You do not copy the discretion of "Revolt" in this charge. I cut out all the tit-bits from it, so that the *Seven Pillars* should be the better book.

[The meeting of Lawrence and Allenby after the capture of Akaba]: "There was little personal intimacy between the two then or afterwards—they have not met since the capture of Damascus—but great trust and liking." (See Ch. LVI of *S.P.W.*)

We last met in 1921.

"I also asked Lawrence his opinion of Allenby. 'A great man', said Lawrence. 'For instance?' I asked. 'For instance, he once sacked the surgeon-general in charge of his Army Medical Corps, a regular, and put a Territorial colonel in his place. And surely a man who can combine armoured cars, cavalry, infantry, camel-corps, aeroplanes, warships and Bedouin irregulars in a single military operation is a great man, isn't he?' "

"persuade to combine". And I don't know whether the first line should stand. It was Allenby's business, rather. Why not say "When the Major General R.A.M.C., the surgeon-in-chief of Allenby's army had to go, he chose to replace him with ~~a temporary officer, lieutenant-colonel acting as colonel, a general practitioner, who had joined the local territorials as their medical officer.~~ the M.O. of a territorial unit."?

"When recently Lawrence published his book the one favourable opinion that he was really anxious to get was Allenby's, for he knew that Allenby would not be swayed by literary emotions."

Allenby is very strict on points of style: and loves *Comus*. He has queer sides.

Returning the first batch of typescript, Lawrence enclosed a letter:

> Karachi
> 30VII.27

Dear R.G.,

I've got your proofs finished, in four days. Not helpfully, I'm afraid. Do you know, one's reflection in a book is nearly as strange as one's face in a looking-glass? I saw a few questions of fact, where Woolley or Lowell Thomas or someone had led you astray. I put a few bright bits in the margin, in case you want to hunt the popular taste.

A bad week this for me: much extra duty, owing to a fellow's going ill: and next week will be even worse, I think. My turn for guard, which is two days wasted: and the end of the month, and God-knows-what.

I couldn't do Kennington's maps last Friday, because I was on extra duty: so I sent him or you a line. This week I have done your typescript and K's maps.

I wish you were not hurried. With time you could have written a decent *history* of the Arab Revolt, which would have put my personal contribution into the background.

> Yours
> T.E.S.

[I told, with certain decent modifications, the story of Lawrence's capture and beating at Deraa. (See Ch. LXXX of *S.P.W.*) Lawrence put it all in square brackets, for omission.]

Pp. 258–260.

As you'll readily imagine I'm dead against any of this coming out with your authority. If you say so much someone else will say a little more:—and then what will have been the use of my careful refusal to publish the Seven Pillars?

I'd have put it this way:—if I'd put anything at all—

"During this wet weather an opportunity of examining Hauran and in particular the Deraa district, inevitable scene of the next Arab advance, presented itself in the visit to Azrak of Sheikh Tallal, head man of Tafas, a small village just north of Deraa. (Enlarge upon Tallal, if you like.) Under such guidance Lawrence had a safe and comfortable trip round the vital railway junction which was to be the scene of heavy fighting in September 1918. He seems, though, to have got into trouble on the return journey, after he had parted from Tallal, for he records his arrest by the Turks (acting under the misapprehension that he was a deserter from their army) and his punishment in custody for his refusal to obey an order given him by the military governor, a Turkish major. This incident apparently did permanent damage to his nerve, coming as it did after the grave disappointments of the bridge and train failures, and the exhaustion of the last few months."

Whatever you say, let it be something which allays rather than excites attention.

"For the Akaba success Lawrence had been gazetted a C.B. ~~and D.S.O.~~, but steadfastly refused to wear the ribbons and has never accepted these or any other decorations. He did, however, accept a colonelcy the next year, but only because it enabled him to use special trains and boats 'for senior officers only'. He had ~~also~~ been recommended for the Victoria Cross ~~for his ride to Damascus,~~"

No: for Akaba.

"and was glad when this was withheld on the technical grounds that 'no senior officer had been present as witness'— the nearest senior officer having been several hundred miles away on the other side of the Turkish lines."

I was gazetted a C.B. for taking Akaba, and promoted to field rank (Maj.) from Capt. so as to be eligible for the C.B. Wingate recommended me for the V.C. instead, but it was quite properly (and much to my relief) refused. My report to Clayton admitted no individual effort of the V.C. character. It is not given for good staff work, or brainy leadership, but for courage of the fighting sort— and I am not a fighter.

My Lieut.Colonelcy came in early 1918, to put me on the level with Joyce, who was G.S.O.1 for liaison with Arab Regular Army, as I was G.S.O.1 for liaison with Bedouins—a scheme worked out by Dawnay. It isn't true to say I "accepted" it. I just went on working whatever they called me. My D.S.O. came on your p. 279.[1] Dawnay was its sponsor.

My odd pip,[2] to full Colonel, came when I wanted to return to England after Damascus. I went to G.H.Q. and asked for the promotion. They were surprised. I explained it was to get a berth on the Staff train through Italy. So they told me to put it up—special, temporary, and acting. I called it "Taranto rank".[3]

"At the base camp at Kantara in Egypt he stopped to watch a bullying officer bawling at two wretched privates, sick men from the Jerusalem fighting, who were passing on the far side of the barrack square: 'Come here, you two loungers! Take your hands out of your pockets! Why the hell didn't you salute me? Don't you know I'm a major?' The poor fellows mumbled something. 'Now stand over there,' said the major, 'and let me see you march past and salute ~~properly~~'. They obeyed and were walking off hurriedly when the major recalled them. '~~Now~~ come back and do it again [*properly*].'

[1] See p. 97, l. 5.
[2] The second star, to add to the lieutenant-colonel's crown and star.
[3] See L.H., p. 165, fourth line from bottom.

They did it again. 'One moment, [*please*], Major,' said a
voice at his elbow; ~~there is something that you have for-~~
~~gotten~~. [*No!*] The major wheeled round and saw a rather
haggard-looking [*bareheaded*] boy in a ~~dirty mackintosh~~ [*tunic*
whose shoulders were starred and crowned with badges of rank]:
Lawrence. ~~'First of all, why the hell haven't you saluted *me*?'~~
~~'Salute *you*?' said the major, with slow scorn. Lawrence took~~
~~off his Burberry and showed his badges of rank. 'Yes, me',~~
~~he said politely. 'I'm a colonel'.~~ [*No!*]. The major saluted in
confusion; the soldiers ~~grinned with delight &~~[, *happier now*,]
were shuffling off ~~again,~~ but Lawrence beckoned them to
stop. 'The thing that you have forgotten, Major,' Lawrence
went on gently, 'is that in this army the salute is paid not to
the man but to the rank, and the officer saluted is ordered
by the King whom he represents to return the salute. But of
course you know that'. The major was speechless. 'You will
therefore salute those ~~private soldiers~~ [*men*]', said Lawrence,
'whose salutes just now you failed to return.' The major
saluted, ~~then he walked away,~~ red with ~~shame and~~ rage.
But the merciless Lawrence ~~called him back~~ [*continued*].
'Major, those private soldiers saluted you twice. You will
therefore return their salutes a second time.' And the major
had to obey."

Incident did not take place at Kantara, but at a rest-camp in
Southern Europe. I have corrected other details. You have mixed
it up with an affair in Oxford St. Myself in badgeless Burberry,
head-down on a dark drizzling night, being pulled up by a Lieut.Col.
for not saluting him (he being accompanied by a lady, probably not
his wife). I peeled off the coat, slowly. He got red in the face. I said
"You can go away". The lady went a third way.

"Back in Akaba with a month to wait before the move could
begin, Lawrence decided to try the armoured cars in an experimental raid on the railway . . . The crews were all British

and there was bully-beef, biscuit and tea, with two warm blankets for each man at night. Lawrence, with no Arabs about, was content to be as English as ever he had been." (See Ch. LXXXII of *S.P.W.*)

These friendly outings with the armoured car and Air Force fellows were what persuaded me that my best future, if I survived the war, was to enlist.

[Letter enclosed with the second batch of my typescript]:

3.VIII.27

Dear R.G.

This is being written in the shop. Post should go tomorrow, but I'm on guard this afternoon, and have to finish up everything now. I finished your second batch last night: and will, I fear, have troubled you with my suggestion that you "go easy" on Seven Pillar material. But it seems to me only logical.[1] I chose not to give this to the public: my reasons may have been bad, but in any case they were my reasons, & so natural to me, whether good or bad. "Revolt" was abridged from the Seven Pillars, and contained all that I wanted the public to know. It would be no satisfaction to me if the press began to ventilate the moral dilemma in which I found myself during the Arab Revolt, and to take sides, with me or against me, in the solution which I chose. Also they cannot. The texts of the various conflicting treaties, agreements and declarations are at my disposal,[2] and not at yours or the press's. So, considering the problem on all sides I decided that a limited publication, burking the main issue, was the only one possible or expedient during the present generation.

There is a probability of "Revolt" itself being withdrawn, shortly, as you know. Only need of money compelled me to publish anything at all. And I'd like you, so far as the Arab business is concerned, to regard "Revolt" as your maximum, rather than as something to be implemented by the Seven Pillars. Please don't set the example of nibbling at its copyright!

My stuff passed because it was written by the main character.

[1]Hippoclides caring now. See p. 81, footnote.

[2]He was unable to inform L.H., however, of the precise terms of the Sykes-Picot Treaty. See L.H., p. 60, last line.

Another person writing it should have seen it with different eyes.
Had time allowed you ought to have looked at the records, and
talked with the other fellows, & written an independent history,
checking my yarn.

The Yiddisher Charleston[1] has been a great success. I have enjoyed
the Fire Bird, and Scheherazade, and the Mozart arias. It was good
of you to send them, and the financial supplement. I'm well provided
with everything now.

Yours
T.E.S.

"Lawrence engaged Abdulla the Robber as captain of his
bodyguard."

Informal rank. His pay was the same as the others.

"He paid them six pounds a month and provided them also
with their camels and rations."

Whereas the ordinary Arab in Feisal's ranks had to provide the
camel out of the same pay. So he had the pick of the countryside at
his disposal.

"The bravest individual deed of the Arab War was performed
by one of them, who at Lawrence's wish swam up the sub-
terranean water-conduit into Medina and returned with a
full report of the besieged town."

Not at my wish.

[My account of the battle of Tafileh in *Lawrence and the Arabs*
was later read by my friend, Major A. F. Becke, who asked
me for a letter of introduction to Lawrence to clear up certain
doubtful points in the battle for the official history of the
campaign for which he was making the maps. Lawrence gave
him all the information he required; and the account of the
battle which appears in the official history is based on this.

---

[1] The "Yiddisher Charleston" was a record I had sent out to him. This was for the troops.
For himself I sent the classical records. The financial supplement was money to pay for
stamps in sending the heavy batches of typescript by air mail.

Chapter LXXVI of *S.P.W.* ends with Lawrence's writing a despatch about the battle in parody of the military historians. I recorded this in my book]: "The bad joke was turned against him by the offer of another military decoration."

D.S.O. this time.

[The story of the scuttling of the Turkish Dead Sea flotilla at Kerak]: "This was one of the few occasions in military history that mounted men have fought and sunk a fleet."

One of the two occasions in British military history. I recommended myself, vainly, for a naval D.S.O. after this engagement.

[The condition of Maulud's men near Maan]: "Maulud could not get them army boots." (See Ch. LXXXII of *S.P.W.*)

The regulars got boots, most of them. The irregulars did not, though their need was as great.

[The account of Zeid's spending of the money, at Tafileh, as given in Chapter XC of *S.P.W.*]: "Zeid said nervously that he was sorry, that it was all spent. Lawrence gaped at him. Zeid explained that he had paid so much to the Beni Sakhr, so much to the Tafileh villagers, so much to the Jazih for their wages since the battle."

Zeid did admirably afterwards:—not least when he rowed in the Balliol 2nd Togger boat, and wired Sandy Lindsay apologies for coming late next term—his brother was ill, and he felt it his duty to act Regent in Irak till he recovered—and I don't want him reflected upon. Please take this seriously. I've avoided all the trouble in the Revolt version. You run upon it: perhaps you can avoid it by saying after 'He told Zeid of his plans'.

"But the Tafileh district had seen too much chopping and changing of the fortune of the Arab Revolt any longer to assume risks on its behalf. Zeid had to confess that to arrange a further advance was beyond his power.

"This was a facer for Lawrence. He had promised Allenby to fulfil a certain programme by certain dates, and had drawn special credits for the operation: and his scheme was now to break down, not for military reasons, but because of a defect in propaganda, which was the purpose for which Lawrence was attached to Feisal's headquarters. It therefore reflected personally upon him. "There was nothing for Lawrence to do" etc.

[Lawrence's attempted resignation as described in Chapter XCI of *S.P.W.*]: "He was ordered to take up the task again, and found it easier to accept than to refuse."

Not quite. I accepted the inevitable quietly.

"Colonel Dawnay was the only British officer, Lawrence writes, who learned to understand the difference between national revolt, with the irregular fighting it entailed, and modern warfare between large regular armies, and who could keep the two going together without confusion."

Surely at this point you should put in at least a word about the other officers. It may be in the omitted pages:—but I remember no references to Joyce, my superior officer throughout, and the O.C. of all British troops in Feisal's area. Joyce acted commandant at Akaba till the port work became too heavy to combine with his front line duties (remember the Arab affair was run with economy of life: we had not 5% of the Staff a formal show would have expected). Then he got a Major Scott from Egypt to command the base, and himself took over liaison duty at Feisal's H.Q. It was Joyce who ran the main lines of the Revolt, while I was off on raids, or making plans for advances. I acted as his main source of intelligence. Then there was Goslett, a Capt. who did all the supply & provision work, with the help of two or three assistant officers. Goslett, now called Mr. Raymond G., is a partner in Alfred Goslett & Co., Sanitary Engineers, with a big shop in Charing Cross Rd. and he would give you a very different aspect of the Arab Revolt to mine. The supply question covered all Feisal's adherents, and was enormous. There was also a huge trade import, for whose carriage and regulation he was responsible. Then Joyce's staff, Maynard (Maj.) and Stirling (Col.) and several other people, like Major Young, and the three Medical Officers, & the Transport officers, & the vets. . . . also the R.F.C., the Armoured Cars, the R.F.A. and lord knows what. We were some hundreds of English: but they were not for fighting, except the Armoured Car fellows. One Corpl. was accidentally killed, doing amateur police work off his own bat: no other casualty. The Arabs were the people whose duty was the fighting.

[The death of Farraj, which occurs in Chapter XCIII of the *S.P.W.* He was badly wounded, and Lawrence gave him the *coup de grace*.]

It seems to me nearly unbearable that you should publish the story of the death of Farraj. No doubt it is my fault for putting it in print, in the first case. I suggest it be cut right out. The narrative was so arranged as not to depend on it. Garnett included it in his abridgement, which is a main reason why his abridgement was superseded by my own. You could well say that in a week after the Amman visit Farraj himself was dead, being mortally wounded in a mounted raid against a Turkish Railway Patrol:—and leave it at that. These are private matters.[1]

[The taking of Amman]: "Colonel Buxton's battalion of English camel-corps had taken the town, but the Australian and New Zealand cavalry, who were to have attacked on his left and right, had been tired with their fighting at the crossing of the Jordan and a long march over the central mountain range, so had left him to carry on the battle on his own."

I hope you have Robin (Buxton's) authority for this statement. Hell to pay in Australia if you say this! They are very sensitive.

[Colonel Dawnay's organisation of the armoured car attack on the railway station of Tell Shahm—see Ch. XCIV of *S.P.W.*]: "He issued formal written operation orders with map references and accurate programme of times and objectives. This rather impressed Lawrence, whose fighting

[1]Private matters! Yet the *Seven Pillars* (in which the story appeared in full) had circulated among thousands of readers. Those who owned copies were always being pressed to lend them for a few days. And there were copies available at the Bodleian Library and the British Museum.

hitherto had all been of the careless verbal sort—("let's attack that place over there; you go round this way and I'll go round the other, and afterwards we'll blow something up if we can").

I was more amused than impressed. D's methods were suited to an army: not to a handful of men. In small work the O.C. is the thing, not the orders.

"As Dawnay knew no Arabic, Lawrence came along as interpreter to look after the tribesmen and the Egyptians."

I knew that one row would spoil the delicate balance of the Arab front: and that rows would come unless ceaseless vigilance were exercised. I was one of the very few people intimate enough with the Arabs to be ceaselessly with them without boring them into sulks. So I tried to god-father every mixed expedition. Dawnay didn't want me hanging about him.

[An account of the looting of Tell Shahm]: "Lawrence was called in to settle a dangerous dispute about loot between the Arabs and the Egyptians."

We were all within a hair's breadth of getting scragged. But don't say so.[1]

In Chapter XCV of *Seven Pillars* Lawrence had written of the Beni Sakhr fiasco: "The check taught the British to be more patient with Feisal's difficulties." I quoted it. But now he commented:

No: it made them distrust all our plans.[2]

[A story omitted from the 1926 edition of *S.P.W.* Its place is between chapters XCVIII and XCIX]: "One strange ride in July took him to Kerak, Themed and Amman, all held by Turkish troops. He was inspecting the ground for the coming Arab advance to Jericho. At Kerak, where he arrived at

[1] I cannot say why he did not want this said.
[2] But see L.H., p. 110, third line from bottom.

midnight with a party of ~~Ruwalla~~ tribesmen, the Turks were terrified and locked themselves into their barracks, expecting the worst. But nothing happened. The ~~Ruwalla~~ sheikh [*Not Rualla*] with Lawrence merely swore that he was hungry and had a sheep killed and cooked for him by the villagers. Later ~~the same night,~~

? was it? I forget.

in the pitch dark, they stumbled over some Turkish cavalry watering at a stream, and were fired on. Lawrence replied fluently with Turkish curses, and the Turks, replying bad-temperedly with a few more shots, drew off.

Everywhere he went there was Arab hospitality, coffee-fires at which he preached revolt, until he had made sure of all the clans in the ladder of his advance. On the way back, the party [*despite their making the regulation signal appointed for such cases*] was mistaken for Turks by some British aeroplanes, which, swooping low, emptied drum after drum of Lewis-gun ammunition at them.

In reporting the affair to Air-Vice-Marshal Sir Geoffrey Salmond, I recommended myself for the Distinguished Flying Cross "for presence of mind in not shooting down two Bristol Fighters, which were attempting to air-machine-gun my party". I had 20 automatics with me.

Next day, near Jurf, where Lawrence was going to inspect the ground for an attack by Arab regulars—Jurf was the only water-supply for the Turks on that part of the line—much worse happened. A party of mixed horse and foot from the railway cut off their retreat, and more troops appeared in front. There was no escape, and the Arabs, with Lawrence, taking cover, resolved to hold out to the last. Lawrence, half-glad, saw that all was over. He decided to imitate Farraj and end it quickly. He rode alone against the enemy. The mounted

Turks came forward to meet him, finger on trigger, calling out: "Testify!" He answered: "There is no god but God; and Jesus is his [a] Prophet [of God]".

"La ilaha ill'Ullah, wa Aissa rasul Ullah". A queer statement, denying the divinity of Christ; which no Christian could make, and no Moslem would make. The sort of tactless remark a nervous man might blurt out.

But they did not shoot—they gasped, stared and cried out: "Aurans!" They were friends, a party of Arab regulars, raiding the railway, but dressed in the uniforms of slain Turks and mounted on captured horses. Their rifles, too, were Turkish. They had never seen Lawrence before and had mistaken his party for members of an unfriendly Arab tribe with whom they had just been fighting.

[Lawrence's letter from Cairo on July 15, 1918, to Mr. Vyvyan Richards.]

The style of this letter is too bad for words.

[A Welsh member of Colonel Buxton's camel-corps battalion gave me an account of Lawrence's address to them before their attack on Mudowwara station: Lawrence revised this account.]

"At first sight they had not trusted Lawrence in the least, disliking his Bedouin dress and Bedouin gestures; whispering that he was a spy and would betray them. But once he began to talk: 'Men, [*Never call 'em "Men"*] we [*We*] are about to start[*ing*] on a journey [*trip*] so long and difficult that the Staff believes us incapable of performing it [*we won't manage it . . .*]' he held them with the same queer charm that he exercised over his bodyguard."

It's not queer charm: it is a logical appeal to man's vanity. Tell them there is something very difficult ahead: and they all work like blazes. Everybody on earth wants to do big things.

[Lawrence's quandary when Nuri of the Ruwalla gave him documentary proof that England and France intended to deprive the Arabs of the Arab territories which they were helping to regain]: "The truth was that after all this Lawrence did not quite know where he was, and the only relief as usual for his distress of mind was violent action and a longing for death to end his shame."

There was a particular and very horrible reason (not published) for my distress at this moment.

"Yet from actual suicide he shrank."

Suicide is to take death far too seriously: not cowardice, but flippancy, unworthy of a serious person, like myself.

[The destruction of the Turkish Fourth Army]: "It may be interesting to note the report of these operations in the official handbook *A Brief Record of the Advance of the Egyptian Expeditionary Force:*—'The Fourth Mounted Division (General Barrow's) coming up from the south with the Arab forces on its right entered Deraa unopposed on September 28th, and next day got in touch with the retreating Turks in the Dilli area. For two days the enemy was pressed and harassed, his columns were fired upon and broken up, and on September 30th the division got into touch with the other divisions of the Desert Mounted Corps and reached Zerakiye late that night.' Other references to the Arab's services are similarly ~~ungenerous~~ [*reticent*]. Of Lawrence's part in making the victory possible there is no mention discoverable beyond a ~~patronising~~ recollection of his early train-mining exploits. There are, however, plentiful references to the way that the Beni Sakhr tribe *let down* the Amman raiders some months previously."

I think you will at best only start a controversy here. It was my fault for not rendering reports to H.Q. I was busy. What mattered to me was getting the Government of Damascus. Homage in Allenby's despatches would not have gratified the Arabs.

[My account of the advance on Damascus.]

I call this section extremely good. Swift and fine in its writing and simple too. But I was on thin ice when I wrote the Damascus chapter and anyone who copies me will be through it, if he is not careful. S.P. is full of half-truth: here.

"Lawrence made Allenby the first and last request that he had ever made for himself—leave to go away. For a while Allenby would not give it, but Lawrence pointed out how much easier it would be for the Arabs if he were not present to interfere with their complete independence."

This is not quite my way of putting it. I said that the change over from war conditions to administration would go easier if my disproportionate influence were removed.

"He went off by air, and for more than a year after there were crowds always waiting at the aerodromes in hope of his return."

Car not air. Sorry: my favourite old Blue Mist.

[The Peace Conference]: "Lawrence had got himself appointed by the British Foreign Office as a member of the British Delegation."

Their idea, not mine.

"He wanted Damascus as the settled home of this new Arab independence and he wanted Feisal as the first ruler of the new Syrian state with Damascus as his capital. The French [*in exact accordance with the terms of the Sykes-Picot Treaty*] might be satisfied with Beyrout and the Lebanon and ~~part of~~ the North Syrian coast, [*for their own; and with the privilege of assisting the Damascus State with what advice its administrators required*].

"Mesopotamia would form another Arab state [*or perhaps two, even,*] and eventually some generations hence when communications by road, rail and air had drawn together the

more civilised Arab provinces there might be a ~~great~~ United
States of Arabia: ~~but not in his time.~~ [*Lawrence advised that
nothing be now done to promote early confederation: but that particularly nothing be done to hinder it*]. The Desert should be left alone
to look after itself in the old way without interference from
the settled lands [*of Arabia or the rest of the earth*].

"Lloyd George [*might have*] agreed to this, but unfortunately
~~was unable to do all that Lawrence wanted because of~~ [*the
Sykes-Picot Treaty had put Mosul into the sphere of French influence.
This did not distress Lawrence, but it threatened ruin to*] the ~~Indian
Army~~ [*Military*] occupation of Mesopotamia which the ~~Indian~~
[*Imperial*] Government, having won Baghdad at such cost,
intended to turn into a British administered province ~~like
Burma.~~ So when the case came up before the Council of
Ten—present, Clemenceau and Pichon (France), Lloyd
George (England), Montagu (Indian Government), Sonnino
(Italy) and others—the French ~~took~~ [*were allowed to take*] the
same ~~greedy~~ [*equivocal*] attitude towards Syria as the British
were taking towards Mesopotamia."

"The various contradictory pledges which Lawrence had
first been shown by the Emir Nuri were then discussed, and
finally [*after months of intrigue*] Feisal and Clemenceau
~~with Lawrence's help came~~ [*appear to have come*] to a [*secret*]
working agreement. Feisal was ~~allowed~~ [*with French help*] to
rule the greater part of [*inland*] Syria, from Damascus, and
the French took Beyrout and the Syrian coast. The Jews were
given a home in Palestine, under British protection, ~~with the
understanding that eventually Palestine should become a
partner in the United States of Arabia."~~

No: not asked for by Feisal or me.

"But the British kept Mesopotamia and ~~suppressed~~ [*discouraged*] all ~~movements~~ [*agitation*] there towards Arab inde-

pendence." [*Nothing of this agreement, if it was an agreement, was made public, during the life of the Peace Conference: but Feisal returned to Syria, and a working arrangement began to show itself.*]

"This was how matters stood at the close of the Peace Conference, and Lawrence was not at all satisfied with them. In England, at his first coming, he had refused to accept his British decorations. He explained personally to his Sovereign that the part he had played in the Arab Revolt was [, *to his judgment,*] dishonourable to himself ~~personally~~ and to ~~the~~ [*his*] country and government ~~he represented.~~ He had [*by order*] fed the Arabs with false hopes and would be obliged if he were relieved of the ~~decorations~~ [*obligation to accept honours for succeeding in his fraud*]. Lawrence now said respectfully as a subject, but firmly as an individual, that he intended to fight by ~~fair~~ [*straight*] means or ~~foul~~ [*crooked*] until the King's ministers had conceded to the Arabs ~~what in his opinion was~~ a ~~proper~~ [*fair*] settlement of their claims.

"In spite of what has been published to the contrary, there was no breach of good relations between subject and sovereign. His Majesty, though unwilling to believe that his Ministers were capable of double-dealing, sympathetically accepted Lawrence's position, and permitted him to forego ~~the~~ [*his*] decorations ~~and other honours that had been recommended for him.~~ Lawrence expressed his gratitude, . . . [*and*] returned his foreign decorations [*to their donors*] with an account of the circumstances."

This is much too blunt. You mustn't take the King's name without his permission. Show this to Cape, and let him submit your revised version for approval, to Lord Stamfordham, or someone of the Court.

[On Lawrence's advice the passage was submitted to Lord Stamfordham, and the following reply came, in time to put into the proofs of the book at the last moment:

"Balmoral Castle
"28th September, 1927.

"Dear Sir,

"With regard to the extract which you propose to publish in your book and which you have been good enough to submit for the King's approval, His Majesty does not remember that Colonel Lawrence's statement was what you have recorded: but that, in asking permission to decline the proffered decorations, Colonel Lawrence explained in a few words that he had made certain promises to King Feisal: that these promises had not been fulfilled and, consequently, it was quite possible that he might find himself fighting against the British Forces, in which case it would be obviously impossible and wrong to be wearing British Decorations. The King has no recollection of Colonel Lawrence's saying that the part he had played in the Arab Revolt was dishonourable to himself, and to his Country and Government.

"Yours very truly,
"Stamfordham."]

[According to information given me by Lawrence in 1920 and noted down not long after, it was at this visit to Buckingham Palace that Lawrence explained his difficulty in serving two masters—Feisal and King George himself; he said that if a man had to offend one of two masters it was better to offend the more powerful. The King did not at first understand his refusal of a K.C.B. and thought he was aiming higher; so offered him an O.M. When Lawrence refused even that, he sighed resignedly and said, "Well, there's one vacant: I suppose it will have to go to Foch." Lawrence made no reply but was amused at the irony of Foch being given what he refused.

The interview began with the King warming his coat tails

in front of the fire at Buckingham Palace, the *Morning Post* in his hands, and complaining: "This is a bad time for kings. Five new Republics today." Lawrence gave the King the gold-plated rifle which had belonged to Enver Pasha and then to Feisal (notched for victims). He had once had a shot at Kemal Pasha with it, but hit a staff officer at his side.]

"This explains why Lawrence at Versailles concentrated on winning over Lloyd George and Clemenceau. Whether or not it was his deliberate policy to upset Lord Curzon's dignity as he once did at ~~the Conference Table~~ [*a Cabinet meeting*] by telling him in front of all the delegates, '*My man*, you know nothing whatever about it', I cannot say. If I know Lawrence it was deliberate: but I do not know the circumstances."

This is not quite what happened. At my first meeting of the Middle Eastern Cabinet Curzon made a long allocution in my praise, introducing me. I knew most of the members, already, and naturally chafed at such patronage. So when he closed, asking me if I wished to say anything, I said, "Yes, let's get to business. You people don't understand yet the hole you have put us all into." Curzon burst promptly into tears, great drops running down his cheeks, to an accompaniment of slow sobs. It was horribly like a mediaeval miracle, a lachryma christi, happening to a Buddha. Lord Robert Cecil, hardened to such scenes, presumably, interposed roughly, "Now old man, none of that." Curzon dried up instanter.

I doubt whether I'd publish it. If you do, don't put it on my authority. Say a late member of the F.O. Staff told you.

"In July 1919 he was demobilised and at the conclusion of the Peace Conference returned to London and lived there until November 1919, when he was elected to a [*seven-year*] research fellowship at All Souls' College, Oxford. 1920 he again spent in London.

"Meanwhile things were developing politically. After

Clemenceau retired, the French Government ~~tore up the agreement between him and Feisal, on the pretext that Feisal had broken it, and~~ [*'s attitude towards Syria became stiffer, and the working agreement which had apparently existed, was replaced by a veiled state of war. This soon gave an excuse for open hostilities, and Feisal, not himself resisting, was*] turned ~~Feisal~~ out of Damascus. He withdrew to Palestine ~~in spite of an attempt at resistance by some of his army~~ and thence to Italy and England, where he pleaded to the British Government for help. Nothing could be done for him, and he returned to Mecca ~~where he was sent an invitation from the Arab freedom society in Mesopotamia to visit Baghdad with a view to assuming the crown. This meant revolt, and the British in Mesopotamia found themselves in great difficulties. Lawrence's unpopularity in certain political and military circles is due to the suspicion that he caused this revolt. It is an unfounded charge; he had repeatedly warned the British Ministers what their policy in Mesopotamia and their refusal to help Feisal would lead to. And even before Feisal's arrival the country was in an active state of revolution. On the other hand, he certainly did not dissuade Feisal from going to Baghdad.*~~'

Omit. not correct. "where he lived for some while, till he received an invitation from influential elements in Bagdad to visit Irak as their nominee for the now vacant throne of that country. He obtained assurances from the British Government that such an event would be welcome in their eyes, and was duly crowned in Bagdad with the assistance of Sir Percy Cox, British High Commissioner in 1922 (or 1921?)".[1]

"It seemed after Feisal's expulsion from Damascus that Lawrence's worst fears were realised, that having duped the Arabs with false hopes he had been unable even to win them a small degree of independence. But he did not give up hope. Finally in ~~March~~ [*Feb.*] 1921 the crisis in Mesopotamia became so

[1]See L.H., p. 144, l. 5.

acute that [*Middle Eastern affairs were transferred to the sphere of the Colonial Office and the appointment was made of*] Mr. Winston Churchill as Colonial Minister ~~came to~~ [*He sent for*] Lawrence and ~~begged~~ [*offered*] him as the only man who could do so [*the post of adviser to himself, with the promise of a fair deal if he would help*] to put things straight in the East ~~for him.~~ Lawrence consented on one condition, that the war-time pledges given to the Arabs should at last be honour~~ably~~ [*ed*] ~~fulfilled.*"*

Winston refused my condition: but offered me direct access to himself on every point, and a free hand, subject to his discretion. This was better than any condition, because I wanted the best settlement of the M.E. possible, apart from all promises and treaties.

"His '~~fair~~ [*straight*] means or ~~foul~~ [*crooked*]' are plainly given in the following ~~statement~~ [*letter*] which he ~~has permitted me to make on his behalf*"* [*wrote to me, in reply to some query as to his motives and intention during this very obscure period*]:

" 'Events in England had changed much between June 1919 when I found the Coalition Ministry very reluctant to take a liberal line in the Middle East, and March 1921 when ~~I took office under~~ [*Mr. Winston Churchill took over*]. The slump had come in the City. The Press (~~at my instigation~~) [*with help from many quarters, including mine*] was attacking the expense of our war-time commitments in Asia. Lord Curzon's lack of suppleness and subtlety had enflamed a [*situation already made difficult by*] revolt in Mesopotamia, bad feeling in Palestine, ~~revolt~~ [*disorder*] in Egypt and the continuing break with Nationalist Turkey. So the Cabinet was half persuaded to make a clean cut of our Middle East responsibilities to evacuate Mesopotamia, "Milnerise" Egypt, and perhaps give Palestine to ~~France~~ [*a third party*]. ~~Winston Churchill took office in a gallant effort to save~~

~~something from the wreck.~~' [*Mr. Churchill was determined to find ways and means of avoiding so complete a reversal of the traditional British attitude. I was at one with him in this attitude: indeed I fancy I went beyond him, in my desire to see as many 'brown' dominions in the British Empire as there are 'white'. It will be a sorry day when our estate stops growing.*]

" 'The War Office (under Sir Henry Wilson) was a strong advocate of Mesopotamian withdrawal, since the minimum cost of military occupation was twenty million pounds a year. Winston Churchill persuaded Sir Hugh Trenchard, the Air ~~Minister~~ [*Chief of Staff*], to undertake military responsibility there for [*less than*] a quarter that cost. The Royal Air Force was to be used instead of troops [*and the Senior Air Officer would command all forces in Irak. This was a new departure in Air history: but Sir Hugh Trenchard was confident in the quality of the men and officers under his command, and Lawrence, who advocated the change with all his might, believed that such early responsibility would be the making of the young Service*]: but this [*policy would only be practicable if it were*] ~~was~~ joined with a liberal ~~policy~~ [*measure*] of [*Arab*] ~~complete local independence~~ [*self-government*], controlled by a treaty between Irak (the Arabic name for Mesopotamia) and Great Britain, instead of a Mandate. ~~This~~ [*The Cabinet agreed, after an eventful discussion, and the new policy*] brought ~~instant~~ peace.' "

Do not put this last paragraph between quotation marks.

" 'British and native casualties in the five years since the treaty was made with ~~Feisal~~ [*Irak*] have only been a few tens, whereas each year before the treaty they had run to thousands. ~~Feisal's~~ [*The*] Arab Government in Irak [*while not wholly free of the diseases of childhood*] is steadily improving in competence and self-confidence. There is a progressive reduction in the British personnel there. The country has ~~complete~~ financial independence in sight. Our aim is its early admission to the League of Nations ~~as a sovereign State.~~ Our hope is that it will continue its treaty relations with Great Britain in return for the manifest advantages of intimate connection with so large a firm as the British Empire.

" 'I told Lloyd George at Paris that the centre of Arab Independence will eventually be Bagdad not Damascus, since the future of Mesopotamia is great and the possible development of Syria is small. Syria now has 5,000,000 inhabitants, Irak only 3,000,000. ~~But~~ Syria will only have 7,000,000 when Irak has 40,000,000. But I envisaged Damascus as the capital of ~~the~~ [an] Arab State for perhaps twenty years. When the French took it after two years, we had to transfer the focus of Arab nationalism at once to Bagdad; which was difficult, since during the war and armistice period British local policy had been sternly re-pressing [ive of] all nationalist feeling.

" 'I take ~~most of the~~ [to myself] credit [for some] of Mr. Churchill's pacification of the Middle East ~~upon myself. I had the knowledge and the plan.~~ [for while he was carrying it out he had the help of such knowledge and energy as I possess] ~~He had~~ [His was] the imagination and courage to ~~adopt it~~ [take a fresh departure] and ~~the~~ [enough skilled] knowledge of ~~the~~ political procedure to put ~~it~~ [his political revolution] into operation in the Middle East, and in London, peacefully. When it was in working order in March 1922 I felt that I had gained every point I wanted. The Arabs had their chance and it was up to them [if they were good enough,] to make their own mistakes and profit by them. My object with the Arabs was always to make them stand on their own feet. The period of leading-strings ~~was~~ [could] now [come to an] end~~ed~~. That's why I [*was at last able to*] abandon~~ed~~ politics and enlist~~ed~~. My job was done, as I wrote to Winston Churchill at the time [*when leaving an employer who had been for me so considerate as sometimes to seem more like a senior partner than a master*]. ~~I respect Winston's courage and honesty; he treated me very well.~~ The work I did constructively [*for him*] in 1921 and 1922 ~~was~~ [*seems to me, in retrospect,*] the best I ~~have~~ ever ~~done~~ [*did*]. It [*somewhat*] redresses to my mind the [*immoral and unwarrantable*] risks I took with others' lives and happiness in 1917–1918.

" 'Of course Irak was the main point, since there could not be more than one centre of Arab national feeling; or rather need not be: and ~~I meant it to be~~ [*it was fit it should be*] in the British and not in the French area. But ~~Winston Churchill and myself~~ [*during those years we*] also [*decided to*] stop~~ped~~ the subsidies to the Arabian chiefs and put a ring-wall around Arabia, a country which [*must be*] ~~I want~~ reserved as an area of Arabic individualism. So long as our fleet keeps its coasts, Arabia should be ~~able~~ [*at leisure*] to fight out its own [*complex and fatal*] destiny.

" 'Incidentally, of course, we sealed the doom of [*King*] Hussein. We offered him a treaty in the summer of 1921 which would have saved him the Hejaz had he renounced his [*pretensions to*] hegemony over all other Arabic areas: but he clung to his self-assumed title of "King of the Arabic Countries" ~~and we weren't having that.~~ So Ibn Saud of Nejd outed him and rules in Hejaz. Ibn Saud is not a system but a despot, ruling by virtue of a dogma. ~~So~~ [*Therefore*] I approve of him, [*as*] I [*would*] approve of anything in Arabia which ~~is~~ [*was*] individualistic, unorganised, unsystematic.

" 'Mr. Churchill ~~and I~~ took a moderate line in Palestine ~~and have~~ [*to*] obtain~~ed~~ peace while the Zionist experiment is tried. And in Transjordania we [*he*] kept our promises to the Arab Revolt and assisted the home-rulers to form a buffer-principality, under the [*nominal presidency*] ~~rule~~ of Feisal's brother Abdulla, between Palestine and the Desert.

" 'So as I say, I got all I wanted [*for other people*] ~~and more~~ —the Churchill solution exceeded my [*one-time*] hopes —and quitted the game. Whether the Arab national spirit is permanent and dour enough to make itself into a modern state in Irak I don't know. I think it may [*at least we were in honour bound to give it a sporting chance*]. Its success ~~will~~ [*would*] involve the people of Syria in a similar experiment. Arabia will always [*I hope*] stand out of the movements of the settled parts, ~~and~~ [*as will*] Palestine too, if the Zionists make good. Their problem is the problem of the third generation. Zionist success would enormously reinforce the material development of Arab Syria and Irak.

" 'I want you to make it quite clear in your book, if you use all this [*letter*], that from 1916 onwards and especially in Paris I worked against the idea of an Arab Confederation being formed politically before it had ~~been effected~~ [*become a reality*] commercially, economically and geographically [*by the slow pressure of many generations:*] ~~whether this con-federation were under Hussein in Mecca, Feisal in Damas-cus, or someone else (call him X) in Bagdad.~~: how I worked to give the Arabs a chance to set up their provincial govern-ments whether in Syria or in Irak: and how in my opinion Winston Churchill's settlement has honourably fulfilled our War ~~promises~~ [*obligations*] and my hopes.'

"There is little to add to this account beyond recalling that the French have had great trouble in Syria since Feisal left and their repressive methods have involved them in war with the Druses and a wanton bombardment of Damascus; and [*in heavy*] ~~the~~ expenses in running the province ~~cannot nearly be met by the revenues which they get from it.~~

"Of Lawrence during this political period there are many stories which one day will be collected, true and false together, in a full-length 'Life and Letters' which this book does not, of course, pretend to be. I can, however, vouch for the truth of two typical ones. Lawrence went to Jiddah in June 1921 and tried to make the treaty with Hussein to which he refers above. Hussein kept him ~~waiting~~ [*arguing*] for two months in the heat [*hoping to break down British opposition to his paramount position above other Arab princes*] and finally put him off altogether, suggesting that he should ~~carry on~~ [*continue the*] negotiations with his son Abdulla in Amman. Lawrence sent a cipher cable to Lord Curzon, the Foreign Minister: 'Can do nothing with Hussein. Are you fed up or shall I carry on with Abdulla?' Curzon, who was a stickler for the diplomatic phrasing of official despatches, asked his secretary, 'Pray, what does this term *fed up* signify?' The secretary, who had a sense of humour, replied, 'I believe, my lord, that it is equivalent to "disgruntled" '. 'Ah,' said Curzon, 'I suppose that it is a ~~cant~~ term in use among the middle ~~and lower~~ classes. ~~I had not met it before this.~~' When 'carry on' had also been explained Curzon gave consent to the Abdulla negotiations and Lawrence carried them on. Meanwhile the secretary, a friend, had told him in a private letter of the 'fed-up' episode. So Lawrence, having successfully concluded his negotiations with Abdulla, again cabled to Curzon in cipher. 'Have wangled things with Abdulla. Details follow by letter. Note, ~~I find that~~ the ~~valuable~~ [*necessary*] ~~word~~ [*verb*] "wangled" is absent from the diplomatic ~~dictionary of~~ ciphers~~, and~~ [*I*] ~~therefore~~ submit that a ~~separate~~ letter-group be allotted to it ~~from the emergency groups; thus avoiding building it up~~

[*to save spelling it each time*] letter by letter.' The word is now in the cipher book."

[The writing of the *Seven Pillars*]: "Lawrence does nothing by halves and not only set about making the book a history of the Arab Revolt which the Arabs themselves would never write, but one that he would not be ashamed of as literature. For this last ambition he secured the advice of ~~some~~ [*several*] of the best-known English writers and taught himself with their help to write professionally."

G.B.S. and E. M. Forster?

". . . there is such a thing as a book being too well written, too much a part of literature. Lawrence himself realises this and was once, indeed, on the point of throwing it into the Thames at Hammersmith. It should somehow, one feels, have been a little more casual, for the nervous strain of its ideal of fault-lessness is ~~almost~~ oppressive. Lawrence calls it 'literary prig-gishness', but that is unfair. His aim was, all the time, sim-plicity of style and statement, and this he has achieved in the most expert way. But he has, somewhere, confessed to a general mistrust of experts, and it may be that he should have carried it further, and dispensed with expert advice in literary matters too."

(If you ask the experts mentioned above, you'll learn that I did!)

"On the whole I prefer the earliest surviving version, the so-called Oxford text, to the final printed text."

I've just heard from Edward Garnett, whose competence as a critic I vehemently admire, strongly maintaining the opposite view. He says that my revision has done wonders, in turning a shapeless story into a shapely one. I hope his view is right. It would be hard luck to do four years work on a text, without bettering it: indeed I think it would be impossible, if the writer had any good in him.

"The historical accuracy of Lawrence's account has been jealously questioned by many [? *some*] reviewers of *Revolt in the Desert:* he has been accused of self-interested exaggeration."

I don't really think the reviews matter, and I should not refer to them, in your place. All the documents of the Arab Revolt are in the archives of the Foreign Office, and will soon be available to students, who will be able to cross-check my yarns. I expect them to find small errors, and to agree generally with the main current of my narrative.

"*Seven Pillars of Wisdom* will not be reprinted in Lawrence's lifetime. It is not a book that should be published for a popular audience. . . . Also popular publication would [*might, they say,*] involve Lawrence in a series of libel actions: he spares nobody in his desire to tell the whole story faithfully (least of all himself)."

I do not think it at all likely. I see little or nothing libellous in the book.

"Again, the censor would probably ban as obscene some of the more painfully accurate accounts of Turkish methods of warfare."

Nor do I think there is an obscene passage. However standards differ. Agreed there are plenty of horrors. See over-page.

[Over-page]:

The reason that the Seven Pillars is not published is because it is a full-length and unrestrained portrait of myself, and my tastes and ideas and actions. I could not have deliberately confessed to so much in public: and so could have not written the book had there been any chance of its coming out. Yet to tell the whole story was the only justification for writing anything at all.

You can also say that the prior knowledge that he is not going under any circumstances to benefit financially from his book affects an author's conduct profoundly: even an author so comparatively careless of money as myself.

As for its historical accuracy—as I've said, I cannot guarantee anything, except that I have tried not to be inaccurate throughout. I suspect heaps of minor errors, due to imperfect memory, confusion of events, haste of action. Sometimes I must have confused what I was told with what I saw.

There are also faulty places, which I know of: darns in the tale. Many things I was ashamed to tell of, because they were sentimental, or too good, or weak, or horrible, or just simply insane. We were mad, off and on: and I've suppressed these incidents or motives; even where they were of great importance, and have drawn together the edges of what went before and what came after, so as to hide the excision. Everybody who spent long at a war-front will understand what I mean.

I've read a lot of reviews, but in them all no one has challenged any particular incident as untrue: and I don't think they ever will: but I could not defend myself against charges of having told less than the truth, deliberately. Only, I think, I'd not enter the lists with any challengers. Let 'em say what they like.

A. T. Wilson, whose review I have just got, only accuses me of garbage mongering, and mutual admiration. No harm in that. Admitted, I did him great harm 6 years ago. He was in my way. If this comforts him now, he is welcome to say what he likes. I'm not answering.

"I have more than once caught him foxing, but nobody has ever caught him lying for self-advertisement. On the contrary, there are many true incidents of his life that he has concealed because their mention might seem boastful. And none of the British officers who were actually with him in Arabia have ever spoken a word against the accuracy of his account."

There were forty or fifty British out there. Lots of witnesses really.

"It has been ~~falsely~~ suggested that Lawrence's"

I have said so: and surely I know?

"part in the Eastern war was devoid of serious military significance."

Our fighting was a luxury we indulged in only to save the Arabs' self-respect. To get a true picture of whether we had a military value you should get hold of Bartholomew, a friend of Alan Dawnay, and ex-B.S.G.S. of Allenby. His is the only opinion that would weigh with me, but I don't think the point is important enough to print.

"In August 1922 Lawrence [*having finally renounced the use of that name*] enlisted in the Royal Air Force ~~under the name of Shaw~~. He did all the usual duties of a man in the lowest grade of the Force and steadfastly refused promotion. ~~The men at first were most suspicious of him, taking him for a spy from the Air Ministry, but soon grew to like and trust him.~~"

No: for six months I raised no suspicion at all. At Uxbridge they seemed to like me, though I was very sick and raw, and clumsy at the new life.

"Unfortunately an officer recognised him and sold the information for ~~fifty~~ [*thirty*] pounds to a daily paper, with the result that there was an unwelcome publicity-stunt made of it."

And then the suspicion that I was an A.M. spy arose. They little knew old Trenchard, if they thought he would use a spy.

"~~A question was about to~~ [*The Secretary of State for Air feared that questions might*] be asked in the House of Commons as to what he was doing there under an assumed name."

An assumed name is not a military offence: only false statement of age or previous service.

"~~The Air Ministry had no alternative but~~ [*so he judged it necessary*] to dismiss him; in February 1923. This was most disappointing to Lawrence [*who had got through the first hardship and bitterness of his recruit's training only to be thrown out.*]
"The following month he re-enlisted, ~~secretly~~ [*with War Office permission*] in the Royal Tank Corps [*having obtained a qualified*

assurance that if he served without incident for a while in the Army his return to the Air Force might be considered] ~~in the hope of eventually getting back to the Royal Air Force;~~ and [*he*] remained in it for [*more than*] two years, stationed near Dorchester. He found life ~~much~~ rougher but made many friends among the soldiers and was fortunate to be near Mr. and Mrs. Thomas Hardy, to whom I had the satisfaction of introducing him; much of his leisure time was spent at their house."

Tea every third Sunday was the usual!

"It happened often that journalists and celebrity hunters would break in on Mr. Hardy's quiet, and meeting there a little figure in ~~ill-fitting~~[1] khaki and a quiet almost filial regard for the old poet, would not give him a second glance."

Why? clumsy, ugly, humble: but it was generally neat, and fitted as well as could be expected.

"Whereas, as Mrs. Hardy has told me, 'they would have given their ears, almost, for a conversation with him had they known who he was.'

"Lawrence was never without a Brough-Superior racing motor-bicycle. Each year he ~~was given~~ [*used to wheedle*] a next year's model [*from the makers, by hook or crook, and ride it to death*] to test and report on ~~for the makers.~~ [*it*]. He nicknamed ~~them~~ [*his machines*] 'Boanerges' (sons of thunder) and they carried him well. He had five of them in four years and rode 100,000 miles on them, making only two insurance claims (for superficial damage to the machine after skids) and hurting nobody. The greatest pleasure of his recent life has been speed on the road. The bicycle would do a hundred miles an hour, but he is not, he says, a racing man. ~~Only once did~~ [*The first time*] he really let Boanerges [*the Third*] go, in the early dawn on a long stretch of road near Winchester,"

[1] "Ill-fitting" was Mrs. Hardy's word in a letter to me.

Oh no: I never took it for a ride on a dry road without letting it out, all out, at least once for every hundred miles I rode. Just to keep it and me from getting sluggish.

"he was curious to see the speed-dial make two complete revolutions. It did, and broke [*with a scream*], so he ~~does not know exactly how fast he went~~ [*flattered himself that he scored an unknown number of miles*] beyond the hundred ~~miles~~ an hour. [*But this was not his daily gait.*]"

Make this sound like a quotation from a letter.

"~~It was, usually,~~ [*It's usually*] my satisfaction to purr along gently ~~between~~ [*about*] 60 ~~and 70~~ m.p.h. ~~and~~ drink[*ing*] in the air and the general view. I lose detail ~~at~~ even [*at such*] moderate speeds but gain comprehension. When I ~~used to~~ [*open out a little more, as for instance a*] cross Salisbury Plain at 80 or so, I'~~d~~ feel the earth moulding herself under me. It ~~was~~ [*is*] me piling up this hill, hollowing this valley, stretching out this level place. Almost the earth ~~came~~ [*comes*] alive, heaving and tossing on each side like a sea. That's a thing that the slow coach will never feel. It is the reward of speed. I could write ~~for hours~~ [*you pages*] on the lustfulness of moving swiftly.'[1]

"He only once had a conflict with authority in the Tank Corps when he was brought before a Court of Inquiry on the charge of assaulting a Corporal. He was, however, released without a stain on his character and the Corporal was reduced."

I had several conflicts with authority: but this is not accurate as it stands. I'm told a man called Devers, who left the Tank Corps soon after I joined, has written a yarn about me in the July number of "The World Today".

[1]See L.H., p. 160, l. 16.

[In correction of a story that I had recorded, from memory, after hearing it from Eric Kennington it seems that two stories had been run together]:

At Uxbridge on our first C.O.'s hut inspection the Wing Commander was asking all us recruits personal questions. He saw a few not ordinary books in my locker, (where they were quite in order) and said, "Do you read that sort of thing?" "What were you in civil life?" "Nothing special", said I. "Working in an architect's office lately" (Herbert Baker's, of course). "Why did you join the Air Force?" "I think I must have had a mental breakdown, Sir." "What! What! Sergt. Major, take this man's name: gross impertinence." Next day I was "up", and was able to explain that he had misunderstood me. A decent old seaman: Wing Commander Breese.

At school in Uxbridge (the R.A.F. makes much of education) the master, a civilian, asked us to write a confidential first essay, for his eye alone, detailing our previous education, and saying what subject we were weak upon, and would like to study. He was obviously decent and sincere. So I told him I'd got scholarships and exhibitions, from the age of 13 onwards, which had helped pay my school and university bills, till I'd taken honours in history, and been elected to a research fellowship in political theory. That later events arising out of the war had constrained me to enlist, and that I found myself over-educated for my present part in life. The subject on which I was weakest being the polishing of greasy new boots! He got a lot of fun out of it, and was very kind to me, afterwards, giving me books to read in school hours, and a quiet place to sit in. Colonel Pillars, now at Halton Camp, in Bucks.

I've tried to think of some significant moment or moments in the Tank Corps to take the place of your Court of Inquiry story about the Corporal, but I can't remember anything worth telling. My R.T.C. "crimes" were mainly the work of an over-zealous Sergt. Major, who wanted to ride his company on the curb, and made a pride of collecting all our scalps, periodically. I gave him mine, quietly, to please the little pet. Afterwards, when I wanted to return to the R.A.F. a clean character-sheet became advisable: and I managed it for the skilful expenditure of 2/6: better not tell this story. Someone might look up the record and punish someone else!

The Corporal story is so garbled that you'd better not tell it. It was not my quarrel, and I did not lead against him; I was only one of 20 victims of his. You know I take most things lying down, when they concern myself alone.

"He ~~writes~~ [*wrote to me some while ago:*—] '~~If you think it worth while, in this book you are doing, will you make it clear that~~ I like the R.A.F. The being cared for, the rails of conduct, the impossibility of doing irregular things are easements. The companionship [*of "shop"*] the ~~interesting~~ [*enforced routine of simple*] labour, the occasional lectures are actively pleasant. While my health lasts I'll keep in it. I did not like the Army ~~so~~ much, but the R.A.F. is as different from the Army as the air is from the earth. In the Army the person is at a discount: the combined movement, the body of men, is the ideal. In the R.A.F. there are no combined movements: its drill is a joke except when some selected squad is specially trained for a tattoo or a ceremony.' "

Men in the Services aren't allowed to write for publication. You may publish the substance of this, but must change it, so as to be obviously a private letter, written to you, and by you published without my authority. Otherwise I see myself on pack-drill, which is not good for mind or body, out here. Make them extracts from more than one letter: give 'em verisimilitude. Forge anything you like in this sense. See back. Date them, if possible, to Xmas 1922.

[On the back of the page]:

"Why am I in the R.A.F., does old P ask you. Tell him because I like the R.A.F. etc. etc. . . . tattoo or ceremony.

"Our ideal is the skilled mechanic . . . machine. Our job is the conquest of the air, our element. That's a more than large enough effort to comprehend all our intelligence. We grudge every routine duty, such as are invented for soldiers to keep them out of mischief, and perform our parades deliberately ill, lest we lose our edges etc. . . . the more of them. Drill in the Air Force is punitive, in the eyes of men and officers alike. Whenever the public see . . . office hours."

If you can, bring out the homeliness of the R.A.F., the unaffected intercourse between us. It's like a lay monastery.

("I must here interrupt the account with a story. In the R.A.F. in 1925 Lawrence outdid himself in self-effacing efficiency. He found himself chosen as one of the squad to rehearse arms-drill for the Cenotaph ceremony on Armistice Day. He was most unwilling to take part in this for fear of being recognised. . . . 'Well, how did you get out of it, T.E.?' 'Oh, I waited for the final rehearsal and then dropped my rifle in the middle of the two-minutes' silence.' ")[1]

I deny this with oaths. I may be bad at rifle drill (I hate it so) but never have I dropped a rifle. I was rejected for the Cenotaph in 1922 because I was under 5'8" in height.

[Sergeant Pugh's account of Lawrence's re-engagement with the R.A.F.]:

" 'S. Joins the R.A.F. Second Time

" 'An amusing item was told of his second admission to the R.A.F. All recruits must pass an educational test before admission. S. had to do a paper of a visit to some place or other and accomplished this with such speed, tact and general show of a born author, that the Officer I/C asked him why he came to join up and yet could turn out his "stuff" with so much apparent ease. His reply was, "Chiefly a mental rest", which took the wind completely out of the officer's sails, and yet the mask on his face of mildness floated him clear of trouble.' "

This rejoining yarn really was rather funny. I went up to West Grayton, in R.T.C. uniform, to transfer. For educational test they

---

[1] Story from Eric Kennington, who may have misheard, but is not a person who invents. Possibly Lawrence said that he was warned for the Cenotaph guard, but would if necessary drop his rifle at the final rehearsal.

gave me an essay (on my favourite game or some such rot). I wrote the necessary few perfunctory sentences, just to show that I was able to read and write. The examining officer read it, looked at my name, looked puzzled, called me out: said 'Have you been in the R.A.F. before?' 'Yes Sir.' 'Some years back?' 'Yes Sir.' 'Under another name?' 'Yes Sir.' 'Did you then write an entrance essay on your native place?' I gave up, completely floored. The fellow had remembered it all those years, without any knowledge that I had any particular history behind me. It's the greatest literary compliment I've ever been paid.

[Sergeant Pugh again]:

" 'Out riding one summer evening, he came across a smash-up between a car (driven by an oldish man) and a pedestrian. When the unconscious pedestrian had been ~~safely disposed of~~ [*stowed in the back of the car, for carriage to hospital*] S. was asked to swing the car for the old boy. Nervousness and excitement caused ~~him~~ [*the driver*] to leave the ignition fully advanced and on S. swinging the starting handle flew back and broke S.'s right arm. Without so much as a sign to show what had taken place S. asked if he would mind retarding the offending lever, and swung the car with his left hand. After the car was at a safe distance S. got [*an A.A. scout*] ~~a man~~ to "kick over" his Brough, and with his right arm dangling and changing gear with his foot S. got his bus home and parked without a word to a soul of the pain he was suffering. Through some unknown reason the M.O. was away ~~for over an hour,~~ before his arm could be "done". That is a man—S., I mean.' "

It was not set till next morning as a matter of fact.

[Sergeant Pugh]:

" 'He will want to cancel this but let me tell you as his friend his broken arm was the 33rd broken bone he has had at various times, including 11 ribs.' "

(? I've lost count, myself)

" 'This last sentence must be known whether he approves or not. In his book *Seven Pillars of Wisdom* he mentions a fact about his capture by a Turkish officer and his treatment under his captor's hand. A bayonet had been forced after two attempts between his ribs,—those scars are on his body still and are noticeable at once when he is stripped.'

" '*Nights Out*

" 'Asked his idea of a good night out, he told me that to take a man [*pillion*] on his Brough to a decent town ~~and give him~~ [*for*] a good feed and general good time was O.K. to a limit. That limit was that his companion on those rides must [*preferably*] be ~~a man who had a criminal tendency~~ [*mildly a ruffian*].' "

I prefer my modification. The other phrase means too much.

" 'and his pleasure was derived in studying the man's peculiarities unseen to the man himself. "There are too many honest men in this world and a few more rogues would make the world a very interesting place." Never sly, he would weigh up a cute scoundrel and gently smile at the result of his observation.'

" '*Coal*

" 'A good incident took place when the strike was on; all coal issues were stopped and "B" Flight had [*only*] a lot of coal dust and slack.

" 'S.'s sheer cheek got to work, and calmly filling a huge bucket with dust he enquired the name of a Big officer who had stopped the issue. Walking point blank to his office, he [*found the officer had not stopped his own coal issue so he*] exchanged his load for some wonderful pieces of coal as big as himself. No one has found out who changed the dust yet. His comments were a broad grin and silence.'

" '*A Visit*

" ~~'He visited the Union Jack Club once just to try it.'~~ "

As a matter of fact in London I usually stopped there.[1]

" 'He came back and gave us his views. He said what with sleeping in a dormitory with a drunken sailor on one side and a "blind" marine on the other there was nothing to do but swear.' "

"A Visit

"He used to Brough down to Smoke (London) most Saturdays, to look after his book being printed, sleeping at the Union Jack Club. One night it was full, but they shoved him in somewhere. He came back and gave us his view etc. . . ."

"His future plans are simply to stay out his full time in the Royal Air Force, and afterwards to settle down quietly in [*some room in*] London, 'the only possible place to live in permanently', with a country cottage ~~in the West of England~~ [*somewhere*] for his occasional retreat [*and a pair of mechanical wheels to tie the two bedrooms together*]."

[Undated, and enclosed in the packet returning me my last batch of typescript]:

Dear R.G.

This I think is all. The writing gathers itself together towards the end of the book. The narrative of the blown up trains was first-rate —much better than my telling of it. And so was much of the final fighting. I sent off all that by yesterday's sea-post, and kept these last pages to think over. I didn't write that long letter for publication, so that I've had to alter a lot of it. I hope this will not trouble you. Winston was my very friendly chief, and has still his career to make. So we must give him credit for all he can carry. It would be wise to show those pages to Eddie Marsh.

The other post-war pages I've cut about also: but not so seriously. Your paragraph of my throwing my bread upon the waters, and

[1] See L.H., p. 187, third line from bottom.

it coming back at the next tide, much swollen, pleased me: and I thought Segt. Pugh's stuff great fun. I have changed a thing or two in it, for correctness sake, or to hide a name.

You will write a preface, of some sort, perhaps, saying where you got your stuff from. In this (if you do) hadn't you better say that you got my permission to use copyright material from my books? And that you wrote me specific questions; and sent me rough drafts of nearly all your material. But that owing to pressure of time your complete text could not be submitted to Shaw before publication, and that you apologise to him for such regrettable incidents as there may be put in or left out?

Privately I think there has been a deal too much attention paid to my little business. But I have already endured in silence so many well meant or ill meant inventions, and so much embroidery of my true story that my skin, originally thin, is now quite horny. So you may hope for forgiveness! Draw a line between my approval of your writing, if anyone had to write, and your own responsibility for your facts and opinions. Your book cannot possibly be regarded as mine, because it is not the least the sort of thing I would say or think about myself. I don't see why everybody should leap to the conclusion that I'm better than average, just because I happen to be odd or different. It's at least as probable that my oddness makes me below average.

And I think nothing of my literary product, either. The *Seven Pillars* is all full of weakness, and has few merits, outside the typography and page-design.

Don't worry about answering A. T. Wilson, or anything of the sort. I never write to the Press about myself. It's soonest over, that way.

I am remorseful at having *suggested* the cutting down of so many of your pages. Though I do you no harm in throwing you back upon your own writing. This book is not "good" in the sense that your former poetry and prose is good; because there is too much of me in it. The more you write the better it will be. I think you need a technical summary, of this sort:—

"This is not the place, and it probably is not the time, to weigh up Lawrence's military strategy and tactics during the Arab Revolt. Of the strategy he makes no secret whatever. It lies open in *Revolt* to anyone who uses a map. The *Seven Pillars* contains yet fuller details: and the first number of the *Army Quarterly* contained a long article by him upon irregular war—an article which summarised the results of his sick-bed theorising in Emir Abdulla's camp. The obvious comment upon his strategy is that it enabled the Arab Revolt, in the sphere of politics as of war, to assume a much larger share of influence and attention than its material importance justified. Lawrence would probably take this judgment as the highest praise, for we find him throughout insisting, with almost agonised study and iteration, upon extreme economy of means. He would be proud of having made much ado out of little or nothing.

"Tactically his conduct is less clear. A casual reading of his books might lead one to suppose that he fought his battles with bluff and crimson banners for main armament. In fact, they seem to have been as artificially thought out as his general principles: and his reasons for darkening counsel as to the means he used are connected with the political relations between the Syrian Government and the French in 1919 when he wrote his book. Both sides were preparing for armed struggle in Syria, and Lawrence apparently determined not to contribute anything to their conflict. His later redraftings of his book modified the form of his sentences, by smoothing or heightening the emphasis of his prose, without adding or subtracting anything material to its meaning or content.

"He had to select the materials to be used from his two active years severely, to compress the history of them into a single volume (his self-imposed limit for the work): and whenever possible it is the details of fighting which have been sacrificed. He apparently fought some fifty armoured-car actions, enough to evolve a whole system and scheme of battle for them. *Revolt in the Desert* only hints at this. Nor does it recite more than two or three of the nine occasions on which he was wounded: nor are the private engagements in which he tempered his bodyguard into a real fighting weapon recapitulated. We can only gather, by casual allusions, that he did not leave the tactics of the desert as he found them.

"He founded his strategy on an exhaustive study of the geography of his area: of the Turkish army; of the nature of the Beduins and the distribution of their tribe-masses. So he founded his desert tactics on the raiding parties of the Arabs. He shows us this self-education, repeated again and again till after the occupation of Akaba. Only by graduating in the Beduin school could he gain the competence and the prestige to modify its practice.

"Exactly what he did is nowhere explained. His English companions knew the difference between an Arab raid when he was present, and when he was not present: but they were not professional soldiers nor students of war, and he himself, except in the battle of Seil el Hesa before Tafileh, slurs over the spectacle of himself in command. Seil el Hesa demonstrates (what we knew) that his reliance was on automatics, not on rifles. Bayonets he rejected, with the memorandum (to G.H.Q.) that they were 'unintelligent masses of steel, generally fatal to the fool behind them.' Machine guns, except when armoured, were too heavy for the 'tempi' of his battles. Automatics (Lewis, or preferably Hotchkiss, since the Hotchkiss endured mud and sand) were his choice, and the files of 'Egyptforce' were full of his demands for them. Seil el Hesa is a pretty example (not, one gathers, by any means his first) of attack by infiltration. Lawrence seems before this to have cut his gun-crews to two men per gun. His bodyguard of forty-eight men had in one fight with a Turkish cavalry regiment twenty-one automatics.[1] He himself carried an 'air-Lewis' in a bucket on his camel saddle. He said once that he would supersede the rifle, if he could get control of an arms factory to make him Hotchkiss guns.

"His use of heavy machine guns, (Vickers) in the armoured cars developed, from the first tentative efforts after Akaba, till he could undertake combined operations of camelry, armoured cars, and aeroplanes. Likewise he was able to refine upon the regulation uses

[1]The historical parallel drawn between Belisarius, the Byzantine general (see pages 152, bot., and 185, l. 3, and L.H. p. 9, l. 20) and his admirer Lawrence is substantiated here. Not only did Belisarius admit on two occasions (at Carchemish and Sura) that he avoided pitched battles whenever he could attain military ends by indirect means—as Lawrence did—but his sharp-shooting bodyguard of horse-archers was the prototype of Lawrence's sharp-shooting bodyguard of camelry. During the Defence of Rome (A.D. 536) they gradually broke the *morale* of the Gothic lancers and foot-archers, who enormously outnumbered them, just as Lawrence did for the Turks: by the same hit-and-run tactics and superiority of armament. Lawrence mentions to L.H. (see L.H., pp. 24, l. 6, and 50, l. 7,) that as a schoolboy he read and even translated parts of the histories of Procopius (Belisarius's military secretary) which chiefly concern Belisarius's campaigns, and that he had learned from Belisarius (see L.H., p. 132, fourth line from bottom).

of high explosive. He was able to fire electrical mines along the telegraph wires, and to introduce petards into the fire-boxes of railway locomotives by 'salting' their wood-fuel piles with infernal contraptions. But he always saw his own ingenuities as things alien and incongruous in the Arab setting: and so we are left with only shadowy clues as to their importance and effectiveness in the more native scheme of things."

[Sergeant Pugh had given me the following note about Lawrence at Cranwell:

"Civil Police

"He was stopped by a 'copper' on point duty for furious driving in *Town* (Sleaford) and reported the matter to the Superintendent. He pointed out that the police were the servants of the public, paid by the public, and he did not think the 'copper' on point duty knew his job, that he was decidedly inefficient and a '*Swede*' (Airman's term for villager). The Super. and S. had a grand argument, but S.'s eloquence floored the Super, and left him wondering what the R.A.F. had enlisted."]

[Undated]

Dear R.G.

Two 11th hour news. Probably too late, but anyway unimportant:—

In Sergt. Pugh's stuff.[1]

---

[1] The following additional notes were given me by Sergeant Pugh, but I did not use them in my book. They may be of interest here:

"Tate Art Gallery

"On one occasion of leave he happened to walk into the above and stood by his portrait hanging in there. At the same time it was crowded with people, some admiring and some doing the other, which our man stood, looked, listened, smiled broadly and walked away. Such, as he said, is fame. On some later occasion he was invited to a private show of Art and his bust by Kennington stood on view. Admiral Beatty stood by and turning to Shaw said, 'What a horrible looking fellow'. Later he was introduced to Beatty! with *curtains* for the latter.

"Tax Collectors

"S. had not been long here before he had a letter from an Income Tax collector asking for the sum of £10 to be forwarded. S. thought for a few seconds, then he went to the Pay Office to have an allotment made out to the collector for the sum of 6d per week to be drawn at the post office and so pay off his amusing debt."

For "Stopped for furious driving in the town (Sleaford)"—this has never happened to me.

Read: "held up on three several occasions by the same constable on point duty in a traffic muddle:" . . . add: "This constable is now permanently excused traffic control." But the point of the story will be lost on most of your readers: they do not know what cavalier treatment fellows in uniform receive, usually, at the hands of jacks in office. The Cranwell people were astounded that I was not arrested for making a protest at the inefficiency of a police constable. Government is the enemy of the poor.

Please modify this paragraph yet further, in which he describes my taking out for a trip, to Nottingham or somewhere, a fellow from the camp: on condition that he was more or less of a ruffian. I took out most of B. Flight, one time and another: and they were all of them very decent fellows. Sergt. Pugh's note refers to a Corpl. in the Pay Section, whom I took out twice or thrice, as a reward for his looking after my credits, and backing them for me. Admitted he was a vulgar fellow: but I am interested in all sorts, and experienced enough to chance my arm amongst such. Don't let "B" Flight think I thought them rough or ruffianly. I liked them and admired them.

There was one more line in that confession book. Is it too bitter? For "my greatest wish" I wrote "To be forgotten by all my friends". I wish it often, and am yet ashamed of it. Old T.H. once said to me, "If we had been given the chance of being born, would not every one of us have refused?" I had to agree with him. All things are better not.

Mrs. Shaw is angry with me for telling you that she had letters and diaries of mine. Do not take any notice. I will smooth her. She quite rightly feels that the letters were private things: and the diaries she was asked to burn. So there will be nothing to come from that.

If you are gravelled for more stuff, there is one other thing I've remembered: in an early number of the *Arab Bulletin*, a secret magazine of Middle East politics, is an article of mine, called *20 or 30 or 40* (or some number of) *articles*. These are advices to British Officers attached on liaison duty with Sherifian forces, on how they should deport themselves.

You will find a copy of the *Arab Bulletin*, my property, in the Middle East room of the Colonial Office. They have a copy of the

Burton *Arabian Nights* and several other books of mine there—or had them. If you show them this letter they will let you take them away, probably. I just left them there, since they were being studied at the time I resigned, by Major Young, who is now in Gibraltar.

Failing the C.O., D.G.H. might let you copy the article from his bound volume of the *Arab Bulletin*. It is not uninteresting, and not worse written than my usual stuff.

Yours

T.E.Shaw.

Tear this off before the C.O. see it. They won't like the idea of your reprinting any part of the *Arab Bulletin*, which was very confidential ten years ago. Tell 'em you are going to store it for me. Actually Mrs. Shaw would probably accept it later. If you get it, let me know, and I'll write and ask her.

S.

D.G.H. is Dr. Hogarth. It was too late for me to take advantage of this letter. For the *Articles* see L.H., p. 185, l. 20.

17.VIII.27

Dear R.G.

I want to write to you about your poems and all sorts of things: and have not, because this life of me is always getting in the way. When it ends we will declare a moratorium of about six weeks, and then begin again with a clean sheet.

Of course you have "done me very well"—but I don't really care a hoot about that. The thing that was really important was for you to do yourself really well, and I don't feel that it's up to the level of your other prose. In the rushed circumstances it could not be: and you will doubtless pull it together in the revise. . . .

Your other quid[1] has just arrived. Don't worry yourself about these. It hasn't cost me anything like £2, and you have your responsibilities. The worst that can happen to me is to be broke till next Friday!

I hope your book will come out this Autumn and get itself over and follow *Revolt* into the Desert of last season's books. Then the way will be open for me to return, in 1930 or so. The best thing about

[1]Postage money.

yours is that it follows mine so closely. Surfeit 'em with me: and they will spue me out.[1]

Yours
T.E.S.

22.IX.27

No, of course that book will make no difference: but I shall be glad when it is out. I know, from my own experience, how much the work in hand fills all the horizon of the man who is writing it: and so much of the beginning and end of that draft you sent me was genuine R.G. work, that I suspect you are as deep in it as if the first motive of it was not get-penny. I hope it will get thousands, and that its effect on the public will be surfeit. Let them say "We have too much of this odd fellow": and very quickly they will open their judgements to hints of the A.T.W. sort. He disported himself too much like a blood-blinded bull of Bashan: but some subtler devil will soon arise who will sap round me artfully. That's why I begged you not to champion me again in the Press. Let 'em say. The more the better, they are doing everything I most wish done. Without my reputation I could live ever so well, like a pipe from which its huge bubble of soap-suds has fallen.

I'm a funny card really. I'd have been all right, apparently, if I'd never tried to do any of the things I have probably done well: or if I'd failed to do them. It's like having succeeded in all the details of a scheme, and then to have forgotten what was the master-scheme into which the bits were to fit.

I read your "Kipling": acute: but Laodicean. I'd have written both hot and cold, by turns: for he is a very wonderful fellow and a very mean fellow. There was not enough anger in your critique. Anger and generosity and warmth are all parts of the same feeling.

Tit for tat. Here's one of my later critical efforts: Oh yes, rotten of course: I'm not a writer by trade. But I know it, which is a mark of decency. (NOT SENT).[2]

If your life of me is very profitable—but how can it be? It enters a market depucellated by *Revolt*, and more than half inclined to sniff at my pretensions—but if—why then by all means do us good

---

[1] See L.H., p. 38, l. 7.
[2] "NOT SENT" is his own subsequent note.

with records. The R.A.F. of Drigh Road hang round this room on the sultry evenings like hornets round beer. It is too hot for beer, the real beer: and there are no diversions in camp.

I want you not to send the things unless you are rolling in wealth, and reprinting your past and present works every hour of the day: then you may send us from Alfred Imhof, of 110 New Oxford Street, a Polydor record of Hugo Wolf's Fussreise and Gesang Weyla's: and Haydn's Surprise Symphony (in Parlophone: not Columbia) and Brahms Sapphische Ode, sung by Gerhardt for Vocalion: and perhaps (if it's not too bandy)[1] Haydn's Emperor Quartette. That will drink up a month's dividends!

Best of luck.
T.E.S.

A press-extract has just recalled a grimmish joke to me. When I was working up from Akaba, once I took a mobile hospital up on a raid. All the stretcher-camels were loaded full with dynamite. The R.A.M.C. H.Q. in Palestine heard of this, and telegraphed to observe the Geneva conventions in future. So next time I left hospital and *doctor* behind. G.H.Q. wired again. I replied that transport could not be wasted on non-combatants. This made the Surgeon General hopping mad. To catch me he wired a peremptory request to know how I proposed, in the absence of my M.O., to dispose of my wounded. I sent back "Will shoot all cases too hurt to ride off". He shut up; and afterwards Allenby got rid of him.

1.X.27

'Ware photographs, old thing. They are more dangerous, to-day, than portraits: for by the great extension of the habit of cinema-going, people have learnt the camera-technique, and are able to recognise a man as easily by his photograph, as you or I would by his portrait. So I hope that if you decide to publish any photographs of me they will be of small scale and not characteristic. If necessary have the face changed a little by retouching.[2] People believe that the camera cannot lie, and so they will credit your false photograph.

I got your letter with the prints of me on my "bike," last Sunday. They shall be returned to Sergt. Pugh. Also I saw with pleasure that

[1] i.e., suggestion of a military band.
[2] No retouching was done.

you were cutting out the A.T.W. paragraph. Also the G.B.S. paragraph. It's hardly fair to bracket him with Lytton Strachey. The only
portrait which I've seen of his, lately, (deliberate portrait) was that
one of William Archer prefixed to three of Archer's plays: and it was
direct and wholesome. Strachey is never direct: and not, I think, in
himself wholesome. But I don't know him, and my memory of his
books tangles itself with my memory of Henry Lamb's marvellous
portrait of an outraged wet mackerel of a man, dropped like an
old cloak into a basket-chair. If the portrait meant anything it
meant that Lytton Strachey was no good.

That pen was too awful. So I go back to the tiny point with which
I learned to correct proofs. And at once I run into a further difficulty:
—that there is nothing more I've got to say. You are exhausted,
obviously, in mind and body, with the strain of writing all this stuff
about me against time. It astonishes me that you should have got
as far as you did. I'd have given up the effort. The bits you sent me
in the last few batches were good: and you must discount my criticisms of the narrative of the Arab War. I knew all that part so well
that your re-writing of me was no food to my curiosity. We all read
to find something new, and in pages and pages you put in nothing
that was new (to me, that is). G.B.S. wrote that all you could do of
the Arab War was to retell my story less well than I had done it.
The last phrase I can't agree to: for my telling was not good: but I
had hoped to find someone who would retell the story of the Arab
Revolt, from the available eye-witnesses, leaving the "I" of *Revolt
in the Desert* out of it: whereas you only turned first to third person.

There are plenty of people about to tell you the whole story:
Winterton put four articles in *Blackwood's*, years ago. Young put
something (which I never saw, except in extract) in the *Cornhill*.
Besides there are so many people who rode with me, each of whom
could say something: Joyce, most of all: Stirling, who has a bright
eye and a sense of colour, and liveliness: Wood, who rode with me
to the Yarmuk bridge: Alan Dawnay: Peake, who lives at Amman,
and has kept his memories of the war alive by continuing to campaign in its later area: Goslett, who lived at Akaba: his friend
Makins, an active R.A.F. pilot: etc. there are dozens of them:
besides people like Jaafer, Nuri Said, Zeid, and of course Feisal
himself. If Doran and Cape had financed you to go round and see

some of these, and collate their stories with the reports of the *Arab Bulletin* . . . then you'd have produced that most valuable thing, a cross check on my accuracy or inaccuracy. A history of the Arab Revolt would have been definitive. Whereas a "life" of me cannot be. I've not finished: and the last five years are a closed book, unless I write it.

Yet of course what the publishers want is a cheaper edition of *Revolt*, to tap the wider public without 30/– or 3 dollars to spare: and yet with enough of shape and new material about it to be worth reading on the part of those who liked *Revolt*. This, I fancy, you have provided, and I hope that it will sell hugely. I think it will, though of course much depends on the price, and the accident of what other spicy books come out this autumn.

Don't stress too much the part I have had in the production. It would be bad business, for it would cut at the root of your independence: and I can't assume responsibility for any of your judgements. I've tried to correct your text, where I thought it significantly wrong. Where it was merely one of these idle stories which every man collects about him as he journeys through life, as a ship collects barnacles— well, then I haven't often bothered. You know I am profoundly tired of this current impression of my greatness. You'd have only to see me now, on the fourteenth bed of the room (a corner bed is a benediction, and I was lucky in Room II to take the place of the old fourteenth man) to realise that actually the legend was all untrue. Isaacson and Weir and Sheen and Search are units just as integral and just as potential as myself. Nobody could live, as I do, inside myself for year after year, and preserve any illusion of unlikeness. During the Revolt I had a motive, within me, for activity, and therefore became capable of imposing my will on others. The very accident that normally I am empty of motive, helped make the rare motive, when it finally came, overpowering. Now that is all over, and the only sense in which I am now remarkable is that I am, compared with other men, an empty room. They like all manner of things, and want all manner of things. I often think that there is nothing in the world I care of, or for: and nothing of which I could say "I know" or "I do not know". If this is greatness and power, then greatness and power are very different to what they are commonly called.

There, enough of this. I'm glad you have got the job over: and I hope you will regard it as a pot-boiler, and get back, after you have overcome your exhaustion, to the life of ideas, in which you move more naturally. Let's hope that the pot will boil for two years with the sale of the book. That was, as you are aware, my motive in thinking of you as the person to write it. Had an ordinary commercial writer tackled it, he would not have had my help. I've wished all my life to have the power of creating something imaginative: sculpture, painting, Literature: and always I've found my gift of expression ludicrously inadequate to the conception I felt. Perhaps I should say that my conception never passed the state of feeling, into visualisation. It stayed woolly.

This brings me back to ——. You said he was in great trouble, and the remark has paralysed my writing arm, towards him. It can only be with his wife, I suppose. I hope that some later news from you will clear up the difficulty.

After your book is out we will forget it, and write one another decently, again. I have your very beautiful vellum edition, with the extra poems, and have seen a few inadequate reviews of it. But the time for me to write about that, and for you to read it, isn't yet.

Yours ever
T.E.S.

—— is a very good little fellow, who is simple and torments himself. He, too, is in trouble, and all his friends would like to help him, and cannot. Sometimes I think it is impossible for one live thing to touch another live thing. You can have physical contact, and mental contact, and spiritual contact. But these are only names for inadequacies and self-deceptions.

7.XII.27

Dear R.G.

The little books came (two of them, advance copies) and I have read them all: so henceforward there is no reason why we cannot write to one another, once a blue moon or so, and forget Cape and Doran. I hope you will meet Doubleday some time. His second name is Heinemann: so he bestrides the Atlantic.

The book again, the book. I call it very good. I'm trying to forget that it was about my past. I call it very good. The middle is a more fluent repeat of *Revolt in the Desert*, which is easy to read, and pleasant to read. You have taken the strain out of its pages. The public should thank you for that: and the death of *Revolt* gives your re-telling of its matter a very just raison d'être. So all's well in the middle.

The beginning is first-class. You draw a portrait of the mind and manner of a living person. I do not know if I am like that: you know my blindness towards my own shape: but I do know that your re-construction can stand up and walk on its own feet. People will call it absurdly flattering. That is no sin in my eyes. But it is astonishingly life-like. I can see your reading of me persisting finally. Only I do hope I won't be self-convinced, and act as you would have me act. It's a temptation.

The last part? The political part is less good. You have not realised the things we were all fighting for or against (why should you? as if they mattered to anyone but us) and so your political pages have not the grip of the personal or warlike pages. If the book had ended with me in the Colonial Office you would have been a loser: but, perhaps for your sake, I went into the R.A.F. and so put myself on a plane, and in a milieu, which were fitted to your pen. So the thing is rounded as a work of art. Really the balance of the book is beautiful.

I'm glad you sent that paragraph to Lord Stamfordham: it was worth your while. The King's paragraph is quite a good little addition to the text. You realise, of course, that the apparent discrepancy between our versions is really agreement. Good, after nine years! I forget the date of my communication to you of the substance from which you wrote that paragraph. Possibly it represents the sum of three or four relations, years apart?

I regret only the Curzon story. It is a little sorrowful, and puts me and Lord R. Cecil in a bad light. Sir Eyre Crowe (dead) late Under-Secretary of the F.O. used to tell it, in those words. My memory of the occasion is less clear cut: Curzon and myself were fundamentally antipathetic, and it was best that we differed at once, and sharply— or so I felt. But I've outlived the poor old man, and am sorry for his shade.

Sergt. Pugh carries off great honour for his pages. I hope they will not get him a court-martial. I don't suppose anything will come to me of it.

Your preface stresses my responsibility just enough and not a bit too much.

I'm glad you took my Azrak photograph. A difficult telephoto bit of work. Also the Wejh photograph, and the one of the house in Nakhl Mubarak. The photo of Feisal was by MacRury, a Major of A.H.Q. in Egypt. A good negative, which he gave me, and I lost with my MSS at Reading: so only that print survives. It's awfully good of F.

Fahad was one of my Ageyl bodyguard: not of the Beni Sakhr: Lowell Thomas' photo of Abdulla the Nahabi and Rahail, together, pleased me. On the whole a very good book. May it add a little wealth to your coffer! It will not harm me: and in 1930 expect me on your doorstep, very happy.

Sophy! We went sore with laughing: and all the camp came over to our room to listen. She had to be lent one night to the Officers' Mess. I did really enjoy the Surprise Symphony, and the Gerhardt songs: and I'll be glad when Sophy is dead. She plays all day, so it will not be long.

T.E.S.

"Sophy" is Miss Sophie Tucker. A red-hot-mammy record of hers was sent to Karachi to correct the Classical music.

I would not have reprinted the Curzon story here—see p. 108, l. 15—but that it was widely current in various forms long before I recorded it in *Lawrence and the Arabs*, and has been frequently quoted since from me. I feel called upon to give my authority for it in T.E.'s own words, and at the same time to quote Viscount Cecil's disclaimer of the part in it attributed to him: made to the Lady Cynthia Mosley, Lord Curzon's daughter, shortly after my book appeared.

"39, Grosvenor Square, W.1
"28th November 1927.

"Dear Lady Cynthia,

"Very many thanks for your letter of the 23rd. I have no recollection of any such incident as Mr. Graves describes. It is quite true there was a Committee of the Cabinet over which your father presided, called the Middle Eastern Committee, and it is also true that I remember on one occasion Colonel Lawrence attended that Committee. Beyond that my recollections are vague, but my impression is that your father gave one of his inimitable surveys of the whole position to which Colonel Lawrence listened with the most marked attention, and spoke to me afterwards in the highest appreciation of your father's attitude. It is true that there was, I believe, some difference of opinion on policy between your father and certain other members of the Committee of which I was one, but I feel quite certain that your father never burst into tears, and I am even more certain that I never have addressed him in the way described under any circumstances.

"You are quite at liberty to use this letter in any way you please.

"Yours very sincerely,

"[Signed] Cecil.

"The Lady Cynthia Mosley."

The following letter is typewritten:

Karachi, 24.12.27

Dear R.G.

Part of my present duty in camp is to play upon this machine, in execution of the Office correspondence. Do not judge my usual by this present. It is pitch dark, as I have only just opened the Shops (key-orderly . . . a job which has its compensations, in absenting me from first parade) and daylight now, in the winter-time, does not properly come till half-past seven. I fill up an empty while, therefore, in trying to type to you by instinct. It is hard to frame sentences, and spell words at once, on an unfamiliar bit of machinery.

Somebody sent me a letter you had written in reply to some rot of Philby's. Really you shouldn't do these things. Reviews do not matter in the least—or rather the rightness or wrongness of them doesn't. They are to help sell the thing, and one attack is worth three praises. Also authors do not notice groundlings, and you know why P. is peeved with me. Why tell the world? You have written what is the only book about myself in which I will lend help . . . and I hope it will sell like cakes and do its bit, properly. But between ourselves we must recognise it is a thing which is finished. The whole of it does not carry so much meaning, to my judgement, as the single poem about Alexander in your collection. Not to call *The Clipped Stater* your best poem—but it is related in subject to the long book. I put any poem by you above any prose effort you attempt . . . just because poetry is inevitably more tight in form, and because the reader can put into it as much of his own subtlety and desire as he pleases. Look for instance at how much more you get out of Shakespeare in the old spelling.

However, we will change subjects. Forget that you were the authority on me and refuse to keep the public up to date in my movements, bodily or mental. By the way I nearly got a move the other day. I suppose the C.O. had been studying *L. & the A's* and had got up from the book too impressed with the potentialities of my character. At least, he told his second in command that I was at the bottom of all this bolshevism in camp (the poor second had not known there was bolshevism in camp . . . but that's a detail) and sending for me, told me that I was in need of a change of air, and so would be posted up country. I was naturally upset at being sent away with a black mark, after behaving for the last year like a plaster saint. So when Salmond happened to turn up from Delhi next day, I asked him to lend me a hand. He did; and I am not going up country. All this is for your private eye only. Probably my saying so will enrage you. But it is hard to stop an activity, and the collection of yarns about me has been so fierce an activity of yours for the last four months, that you'll find yourself doing it in your sleep. The fellows here like your book much better than mine. I agree with them, on the point of order, but reluctantly; I would like to think mine the finer. Yet I agree that my writing is no cop. It is when people come to particularities of criticism that I begin to wish to say good of the bit attacked.

I am reading the book of criticism by L[aura] R[iding] and yourself. Cummings will be pleased at the place he takes in your thoughts; to see so much of himself in your mirror will help him write. I liked his prose, more, in the days when I read books. Indeed, I once tried hard to get his *Enormous Room* published in England. Cape wouldn't touch it; nor could Curtis Brown, who touted it round with a very cautious little note from me, place it anywhere. I call it one of the very best of the war-books—to which, by the way, *War-birds* now adds itself, amidst applause from the flying crowd. The last Cummings verse I saw was called *40 Poems*, and was held in a marvellous gold outer wrapper:—but the inside was more like Oxo than the normal flesh of poetry. It struck me that in his refusal of phrases with a past there lay as much irritation as power. Power does not get ruffled to such assertions, readily. Unless he had special cause, he should not let the worn condition of words hamper his re-use of them. In my own tiny case, I actually looked for the traditional words. They seem richer to my taught senses. I suppose he is naturally rebellious, and that his treatment in France inflamed him, and that he belongs to some clique which worships reaction more than action. A pity, for I think his gifts are too good to be wrapped up in shorthand. Modern historians have put history on the shelf (or rather handed her over to non-historians) by being so scientific that their writing is only for themselves. Hence I like a poet to put a little sugar with his strength. I cannot remember by heart any of Cummings' poetry, because of its tightness of texture.

At this point we turn the page over: one gets fun out of the machine at its stopping and beginning places. Where was I? At talking impertinently of Cummings. Enough of him. Isn't there better Sandburg than the example in your book? I must plead blindness to Robert Frost. He reminds me of Freeman; not to mention Hardy and Willis. Incidentally Hardy there is not *the* man; to him I want to take off all the hats the R.A.F. supply for airmen's use.

I have given away Sophie Tucker. She was worn to the bone, after about two hundred playings; and I find her just as intellectually suggestive when she comes down the wind to us from the next barrack-block ninety yards away. A splendid woman, doubtless, but she inclines me against matrimony. Imagine her greeting you at breakfast, day after day.

To-day is the 27th of December, and the camp is getting over the confusion of its Christmas. It has not been as wet as the Tank Corps, but a very fair second. I was on guard on the feast-day itself, for that is the cushiest day of the year to do a guard, and I'll confess that the ordeal of mounting and duty gives me creeps, ordinarily. This time it was a really good guard, and so I feel that the holiday has not been a dead loss. My Office job gives me the keys, too, and so a place to myself in off-duty hours. Think of it:—four days to myself.*

It will be June before Cape settles with you for the next instalment of your royalties. I hope they will be substantial, and should like to hear how many printings the demand pushes the book to. Short of getting profits myself (an unattainable heaven, in Arab affairs) I like to hear of the right people picking up something. Did you see that my monstrous book had reached £570 at auction in London? I rejoiced, for my subscribers' sakes. You know some of them were millionaires, like Philip Sassoon, and some were airmen of my own circle. The thirty guineas was a risk for the small men to put up, and I'm delighted their speculation has turned out profitable. Unfortunately some silly fellows are letting sentiment tell them not to part with the thing. As if a six hundred pound book could ever be anything but a nuisance.

I have been trying to keep up with Wyndham Lewis in his philosophy, and his *Enemy* and in his stories; and must confess that I cannot see where he wants everybody to go. Behind so many words there must be something to say . . . but he cannot convey it to me. If he wants to change the spirit of the age? but that is done by invention, not by criticism . . . give it up. I also have to give up the *Criterion*. They synthetise like a lot of blind cats on a church roof. What in God's name has Thomas Aquinas to do with philosophic doubt? Also they say they want to restore the intellect to its place in life and letters. Go to.

My judgement inclines my reading more and more to the easy men. I prefer Bennett and Wells and Galsworthy and Tomlinson and Kipling and Forster to Lewis and Joyce and Stein. Is that mental fatigue, or the ossification of age beginning?

T.E.S.

The "book of criticism by L.R. and yourself" was *A Survey of Modernist Poetry*.

*This is after three of them, here: they have been wasted in an effort to write a review of H. G. Wells' short stories: I can't write reviews, yet want to, badly! [Footnote by T.E.]

PART III

1928–1935

Drigh Road
26.1.28

I am uncharitably hoping that Lowell Thomas has been driven
off the shelves by your onset. It was a sad coincidence that led
Hutchinson to put his baby effort forward simultaneously. On the
other hand he has had a free run in the States.

Do not worry about Philby.[1] He is really a very good fellow: only
a natural opponent: and he suffers from an excess of personal feeling.
To him a person is bigger than a movement or idea or principle.
He is also very radical in home politics, and a man with a grievance.
Such a pity, for as I say, he is really a fine administrator, and a good
scholar. His writing is bad, and he is no politician: but I respect him
too much to wish to see him attacked.

No, your book contains nothing to make me hide my head any
deeper in the sand than it now, very uncomfortably, is. It is my own
books, and Lowell Thomas, which did all the possible harm. I
wonder a little how much more your book will sell, and what Cape's
plans are, in the direction of reprints. Probably he will eventually
put it in some one of his 3/6 series, I suppose. Let me know if you
know anything. I still cling to the hope of coming home in the spring
of 1930—which feels now like next door, with us already into 1928.

Yes, I got the *Survey*, and much enjoyed it: a clarifying book, and
not, I think, very hard to do. Also a legitimate book. Such explanations have to be done, time and again. I read less and less as the
months pass. There is a restlessness in my brain, which makes me
more inclined to talk to the other fellows or to play something on the
old musical box: also I now do a good deal of overtime in the office

[1]Mr. St. John Philby had published something in a Sunday paper belittling Lawrence.

147

. . . often more than an 8-hour day, which is held good, for India. This is a country in which the whites easily go slack.

I'd like a version of Mozart's Jupiter Symphony: there are two or three rival versions: send the least expensive, if there is a difference, for the import duty into India gives me a proper knock when a parcel of records arrive. However the post office knows our weakness, and never reports a parcel till Friday!

No, please don't send *Transition*.[1] If Joyce's new book is in English I shall read it gratefully. But I don't want to read any foreign stuff, just now. Too hard work.

Yours
T.E.S.

29.3.28

Dear R.G.

I should have written when the Alligator Crawl and its fellow arrived: but I seem to have run down, somehow: and can hardly move a pen or make a gesture in anyone's direction. The Crawl was too much for the room: they begged me to exchange it for something less furious, from the next room, which adores jazz. Certainly your records wake the camp up. Poor Sophy Tucker was lifting up her voice over in A.R.S. last night, just before ten, when I was getting ready to go to bed. A quiet night, it was, for the power station had broken down, and we were in the dark. The power station often breaks down.

We must be travelling different ways. You are getting exasperated, hating the dullness and stupidity of mankind, and especially of writing mankind. I'm losing my cutting edge, and therefore understand better, sympathise with, people like W—— and Bennett and the rest, who slide down the easy slope into fatuity. Only I'll try to slide down silently. A man whose buttons are coming off should not exhibit himself. So I won't write any more.

This is a défaitisme about this business: and I find that even marking-time (which I once thought the R.A.F. was) is too difficult for me. Now it is standing still, or sitting still, and letting its current carry me. While you are in the Air Force you have the illusion of belonging to so much: of being buttressed and supported and accom-

---

[1] I offered to send *Transition*, a magazine published in Paris, because of a book of James Joyce's, *Work in Progress*, appearing serially in it. It is still appearing serially in it (1938).

panied and paralleled by ever so many thousands of your likes.*
You are one man against the world. I've dodged (no, not dodged:
too active a word) all that loneliness, and am one cell in a honey-
comb. Just an empty thing for my employers to make use of.

That's perhaps why I want to be employed, now, always.

Now I'm going to crawl back to the room and be inactive for the
rest of this Thursday: Thursday is a troops' whole holiday in India.

T.E.S.

19.5.28

Dear R.G.

For most of this (Saturday) afternoon I've lain on my back, on a
bed as hard as turf, and listened to the Jupiter Symphony, which is
not perhaps the greatest bit of music, but assuredly one of the most
beautiful. We played it twice: once I got up and down doing the
needful: and the second time Smith (L.A.C. Smith, 755 RAF) went
through it, while I lay and lazed, luxuriating in it.

My gratitude to you for sending it flamed up again into action:
I got on to my feet, and staggered to ERS Office, to write you this
word: which will be my last from Karachi, for a while. On Wednesday takes effect my posting (by own arrangement) to Peshawar
(20 Squadron, RAF), to avoid a local situation which was fast
becoming disagreeable. Peshawar will be, at least, a new beginning.

On the way up to the Office my gratitude switched over from the
personal obligation of the Jupiter, to the general obligation, which
everybody owes you for that volume of collected poetry . . . [*Here he
lists his preferences.*] There isn't any of that wriggle in them as though
they'd been pried, unwillingly, from the spiral depths of some shell,
with a pin and great pain. I wonder how you do it? One's sober
judgement sees how hard worked they are, and how many words of
felicity have come as afterthoughts: but it's the first breath, still alive
in them, which makes them priceless. (One feels your poetry in the
hollow diaphragm, just under the cage of ribs.)

Alas, that word "priceless" has been deflowered, in English, and
also in French. However, time gives back their virginity to languages.
So let's let it stand. The ink will be three weeks old before you see it.
One could write the *Iliad* in 3 weeks.

*Literally likes. [Footnote by T.E.]

Incidentally Arnold Bennett warmed me, in an article on the young who write, by coming out handsomely on your side. There is something quite peculiarly of the craft about Bennett's criticism. It does not allow itself to get philosophical; or to speak of religions and ideals and principles; it takes a book as something which somebody has written (damn all readers, thinks A.B.: it's writing which is the job) and considers it as that. Whenever I get hold of a bit of Bennett's critical stuff I push it into my belly with delight, and rise up hungry; for he chops it into little bits, to fit newspaper columns, and is provokingly patchy: but he writes like a Lord, as though he didn't care who read him. No damned merit, no nonsense: yet such an admirable straight scent. Oh yes, really good. (Yet he wrote those awful 5-towns, or was it 7-towns, novels!)

This is rather a stupid letter. Virtue has gone out of me, not in the New Testament sense; but finally, I think.[1] The orange is squeezed dry. Nothing but the climate of England can revive this flesh: and even that will not do it, unless the Met. can maintain depressions over Iceland, in abundance, in sequence, for ever and ever.

Now I'm going back to have an Elgar Symphony. This old music box I lose, (no more records, please) by going up country: So I am making it meat and drink, for these last days, in the hopes of surfeit and a turned stomach.

Do you see S.S.? or is he also amongst the suits you have worn out? I'm afraid of S.S.: but I'm sure he is a great man. Regard me to him, if ever you meet, unexpectedly, on some neutral pavement.

T.E.S.

338171 A/C Shaw
R.A.F. Detachment
Miranshah Fort
Waziristan
India
30.6.28

I have dug myself right away now, in a tiny garrison (behind barbed wire, with searchlights in towers on the enceinte) among the hills, only ten miles from the Afghan Frontier. A quiet queer little place.

[1] See p. 71, twelfth line from bottom.

Alas, no gramophone. We are considering ways and means: but the ways are long and the means small. So no more records, I beg you.

I apologise to you, for the women who write to you about me. Choke 'em off, I beseech you.

Sorry the kids were ill: but you say they are better now.

Diphtheria isn't very pleasant, is it?

Humour? I doubt whether humour has changed much since B.C. 800: for of late I've been reading Homer. Juvenal might be a point on the other side: but was he ever thought funny?

Ralph Hodgson? Does he ever write any more, now-a-days?

Yours
T.E.S.

[Written on a typewriter]:

Miranshah
5.8.28

Dear R.G.

You are a queer mixture. You scold the world like a slutty Joan Keel-the-pot, in one line, and append a poem like *To the Galleys* a minute later. The galley-slave applies to yourself, you say. It applies also to half your generation, (and mine) and to S.S. and H. G. Wells, and Arnold Bennett and Barrie and God knows how many more. You are a psychologist in one eye, and jaundiced in the other. Thereby you have the advantage over so many of us, who are scathing upon the subject of humanity, whenever we are not talking forpublication. Goodwordthatforpublication.

Are there no just men in Sodom? Well, that depends on the point of view, I suppose. For them and for you . . . I am delighted that you are still writing poems. You have never turned backward to a mood after leaving it. Perhaps you were made without a reverse gear. As your studies of man happen generally to put me on the track of something I'd not thought of, but had been growing to unconsciously suspect—(O Muse, help me to get out of this sentence)—therefore your stuff is good for me.

Cape sent me the *Enormous Room*. I read it all again, after the years. And I feel sure that it is worth while. There is stuff in it which I have seen nowhere else. And a taste of reality. And it is not yet out of date. If a book can get over its first ten years, it must be really original,

I think. I suppose Cummings regards it as one of his deadliest sins, now: but I feel delighted that it's having another go at the public.

. . . . That Island. For my part, I have got the offer (the tentative offer) of a night-watchman job at the Bank of England, when my R.A.F. days are over. So nice and central, the Bank. So nice and centrifugal, your island. Really, of course we are looking for the same thing: some place to live in, in which ourselves won't be. Some hope.

G.B.S., whose wings are sprouting with every year he lives, has sent me off a gramophone. I expect it in a fortnight. Then will Miranshah be really fully furnished, for me. I have everything else I want. It is an odd feeling to be satisfied. I think that makes me content to like Bennett's books, and Wells' stories and John Buchan. Williamson, the *Tarka* merchant, has good stuff to come, I think. Also I like and look forward to more D.H.L., more E. M. Forster, more S.S. That makes seven or eight producing people who enlarge my wits. Not bad for a single age. There aren't seven yet-alive Elizabethans. . . .

Send me another poem whenever you remember Belisarius. To desire such obols is not to deny my satisfaction. I like sunlight, too. And the sun does not demand a diploma-in-justice from us all.

[In blue chalk on the reverse]:

Sorry for sending you the note on the back but this machine doesn't always work accurately. I do hope you'll go on with poetry. The things are building together so well.

                                                                    T.E.S.

The Enormous Room was E. E. Cummings' account of life in a war-time prison-camp in France, which Mr. Cape had finally decided to publish; I wrote a preface.

The Belisarius reference is the most interesting thing in the letter. Lawrence, looking round for a more historical parallel for his present case than the Alexander of my poem (to which he had made appreciative reference again in the letter before this) hit on Belisarius (A.D. 500(?)–565). The Dictionary of Classical Biography says of him: "As a general he was dis-

tinguished as well by his personal prowess and his unconquer-
able presence of mind as by the rapidity and comprehensiveness of his movements, and also as never having sustained
defeat without good reason, and as having effected the greatest conquests with the smallest resources. In a private capacity
he was temperate, chaste, and brave; but his characteristic
virtue, which appeared to Gibbon 'either below or above the
character of a man', was the patience with which he endured
his rivals' insults, and his loyalty to Justinian. . . . Lord Mahon
in his life of Belisarius, on the authority of an anonymous
writer of the eleventh, and of Tzetzes in the twelfth century,
has revived the story which he conceives to have been handed
down by tradition in Constantinople: that his eyes were put
out and that he passed the remainder of his life sitting in the
streets of Constantinople and begging in the words preserved
in the metrical romance of Tzetzes."

> Miranshah
> 27/8/28

Dear R.G.

I've sat down straight, and read your poems through. Your journey continues: one or two of these you *might* have written two years
ago: only one or two. More later.

You mustn't send me cash. I have rejected this lot. Please don't
be hurt. I am happy, and have all I want. If I'm sent more I only
play the Lord Bountiful, by giving or lending books, records, etc.
These are vanities. There is absolutely nothing I want for myself.
O Miller of Dee!

My leading this ramshackle but joyous life wouldn't be justified,
if I took things; it's the happy knowledge that I'm *not* doing things
which makes me so pleased with life.

More about the poems next week. No, *Anarchism is not Enough*[1] did
not come. Some scared Babu somewhere:—or drink-dulled English
official: or timid India-Office Jew.

> Yours
> T.E.Shaw.

[1]The title of a book of Laura Riding's.

The writing of this last letter is huge and vigorous, in contrast with the tiny disorganised writing of one or two of the letters from Karachi: the effect of the mountain air is apparent.

Lawrence now sent me the manuscript of his book, *The Mint*, a contemporary account of his recruit's training in the R.A.F. at Uxbridge in 1922. I had not known of its existence. He asked me for my opinion. In the main I liked it very much, better than *Seven Pillars*, because it had obviously been written straight off, not brooded over. (There was one particularly good chapter about Queen Alexandra's funeral-parade.) But it also contained a few noticeable examples of what he evidently thought was "style" and what I thought was bad taste in language—pseudo-poetic ornament. I instanced ". . . resides not in drill" and "pencillings of light". I said that I hoped he would not tease at *The Mint* as he had done at *Seven Pillars:* there was no mystery about good writing, given something to say—all there was to be done really was to write with ink on paper. People who pursued style in this fin-de-siècle sense ended up as Eminent Literary Men, like old Saintsbury, whom I had recently visited (accidentally) at Bath, where he lived in a hyena-den filled with old books, medicine bottles and second-rate statuary. I also corrected his spelling of the title of a Welsh song. And I defended arms-drill, which he ran down; saying that there was as much rhythmic satisfaction in watching (or performing) really good arms-drill as there was in ballet-dancing. I offered to get *The Mint* privately printed, at my expense, in ten copies not for sale. And I sent him Siegfried Sassoon's *Memoirs of a Foxhunting Man*.

He replied:

Miranshah
6 XI 28

Dear R.G.

This is two excellent letters you have given me about *The Mint*. The poor little thing interests me: because it's my only effort at really writing something about nothing. *Seven Pillars* was a historical necessity: I don't call it an option: but *The Mint* was a pure wantonness. I went to Uxbridge with the deliberate intention of writing something about service life: and I put down those notes evening after evening in the hut, with the blankets up to my chin, writing on the support of my drawn-up knees. They are the perfect exemplar of journalism, in its antique sense: and it interests me very much to find that you and Garnett and Forster (three very different people) all see something in them. It shows that the daily record needn't be as transient as, for example, the *Daily Mail*. A fellow can't read (even at Miranshah) a month-old *Daily Mail*.

About printing *The Mint*, as you suggested:—thanks very much, but no. "They" would hear of it, and say I'd written another book: and *The Mint* is 1922, and not a book. It's better left just as a manuscript diary. Diaries exist in thousands, and are thought no harm of.

Your second (and unpublishable!) gave me a lot of keenly improper laughter. It was a good effort: though it would have shocked Squad IV!

Your remarks on Form and Style tickled me, also the instances. "Resides not in drill". That, you say, is style. I like style, I fancy. The anticipation of antithesis, which is not fulfilled, is good. Old Asquith's speeches were intolerably boring because all the anticipations were bitterly fulfilled. You say, "All there is to be done is to write with ink on paper". Alas, that is the last and easy stage. It's the balancing your subject before you begin on it: the scheming proportion for it, the adding wings and feathers to carry all your prepared ideas, fitly: and the spacing the few ornamental ideas each of us have, so as to relieve the monotony of the plainer surfaces:— that's all got to be done before the easy ink-on-paper stage.

I know you didn't mean the remark to be taken so literally. You fall foul of my ornament, not because it is ornamental, but because it isn't: and you're sure right there. It comes in the wrong places, and it is clumsy. Yet the "pencillings of light" were just as clear, (are just as clear) to me as the sweat and swear-words. Only they are so much harder to put down. Anybody can catch the ugly to the life: but to make the smoothly beautiful at once beautiful and not sticky —aha, that's where the poet scores. Look at the *Memoirs of a Fox-hunting Man* to see how magically simple things, like birds, come to life again, on paper, specially for Sassoon, without any twisting of words, or strange words. A man's a great writer when he can use plain words, without baldness. See how bald Theodore Powys is, despite all his power and merit. It's because he's not big enough.

If a fellow isn't big enough he must do the other thing:—what you call style:—surface his work. It is a mode, too. The War-and-Peace plainness is better, perhaps: but one is fonder, often, of the rather-less-big work. It feels more homelike. That's the reward of secondary writers. They don't knock-out: but by their very smallness, or middle-size, they become good companions for ordinary people.

Lately I've been reading the *Odyssey* a great deal: and when I get tired of it I take up the *Aeneid:* and it is like stretching out in bed after a hard day, like stretching out in my bed is going to be, in half an hour, when I come off sentry: for it is half-past two in the morning, and I'm sitting on a box under the pilot-light beside the arms-rack, scribbling away. We have to guard the beastly rifles, in memory of 1919 when the Mahsuds used to try to steal them.

So I am quite unrepentant about "resides not", "resideth not" is Wardour Street; "does not reside in" is too loose. "There is no something-or-other in" is too bald: had I used the last my statement would have been seen through. "resides not" carried you on to expect more and you found a full-stop, and forgot the argument. So So.

Drill may be beautiful: but beauty is not perceptible when you are expecting a punishment every moment for not doing it well enough. Dancing is beautiful:—because it's the same sort of thing, without the sergeant-major in the "office". Drill in the R.A.F. is always punitive:—and is always practice-drill, never exercise-drill or performance-drill. Airmen haven't the time to learn combined rhythm. If they did learn it their (necessarily) individual work with screwdrivers and spanners would suffer. Rhythm takes months to acquire, and years to lose.

No, I will never be an eminent literary man. Yet theirs are not the only hyaena-dens. There is a hyaena coughing just outside the Fort now: and in many barracks you get very near the den stage. I think literary men are probably not really different from you and me.

Thanks for "Ar hyd y *Nos*": but I don't suppose I'll ever see the

MS. again: I gave it Garnett for keeps: and it probably won't ever be published.

Your last page, with its positive, comparative, superlative, defeats me wholly. You have a standard, and it enables you to be censorious. I only see what's better than my *performance* (quite different to a mental standard, that) and so I admire and enjoy Wells, and Bennett, and Forster, and Sir Thomas Browne, and Rossetti, and Morris and everybody who deliberately tries to better his every-day speech. Mind you: but an effort to better it. It's the trace of effort which warms my diaphragm:—beg pardon, cockles of my heart—whatever are cockles?

Ever so many thanks for the *Foxhunting Man*. It is a *book*.

T.E.S.

But in 1933 in a letter to L.H. he seems to have revised his attitude to style. (See L.H., p. 65, third line from bottom.)

Shortly after this, Lawrence was sent back to England. On his return he wrote:

338171 A/C Shaw
R.A.F. Cattewater
Plymouth.
20.3.29

Dear R.G.

Here we are. A good little camp, on a neck of rocks jutting into Plymouth Sound. The sea 30 yards from one window of the hut, and 70 yards the other way too. When it gets warm we will be enviably placed. About 100 airmen in camp. C.O. considerate. Camp all new, but apparently going to be easy. The main-plague is too much fire-piquet. I am working in the Orderly Room for a fortnight, and then going over to the Motor Boat Section, as deck hand. Boat-hook king, in action: polisher in peace-hours.

L.R. would describe this as life; I'm unregenerate, and regard even Humbert Wolfe's poems as better than silence. However, we will agree to laugh at both Art and Life!

The Bike is a heavenly machine. If only I could ride her for a week of sunlight. It has been very cold.

T.E.S.

[Typewritten]:

338171 A/c Shaw
R.A.F. Cattewater
Plymouth
5.5.29

Dear R.G.

Forgive the typing. It is a new machine, on which I am to be efficient tomorrow: this is Sunday, and I'm taking my rawness off on it, by typing a dozen private letters, before tackling any R.A.F. stuff. . . . Honestly, R.G., hasn't the scale of your judgement been out, lately? It is not my business, and I cherish my own freedom to do as I like too much to dream of interfering: but you have been so drastic in your condemnations of ordinary people, of late, that I've been afraid to stay near you. You see, I know by the best of all proof (contiguity with ordinary men in barracks) how ordinary I am; and because ordinariness is not wholly a flattering feeling, I have been led to look for my own likes in ordinary people: and from that I have grown to see the ordinariness in nearly everyone. But whereas that makes you rage and condemn, it makes me feel akin and friendly. I like your stuff, because so often you seem to me to say clearly something that all our generation is trying to say. There is no monopoly of feeling: lots of people are feeling like you: but only an occasional man can say it decently. It is a great thing to have the power of words: but it does not make one man different from another in kind, as something that L.R. said when we last met half-implied.

God Almighty, what a sermon when you are down with an abscess (that is rotten, but cures itself) and unhappy and do not want to ramble about inside the meaning of life. It is raining here, has been raining dismally since last night. I have done a Church parade, and the Hut is full of Wireless and gramophone music (by the way, I never thanked you for the new Sophy, which added a new horror to life for weeks. Sophy is always a battleground, like all things vitally vigorous. The Hut is divided into pro-Sophy and anti-Sophy, and squabbled as nearly as Huts can squabble) and I have come back into the Office to hammer out this stuff for you. I should be doing Camp Standing Orders, Order no. 15 (Fire Orders) but it is too cold for my fingers to type sensibly: also I've been thinking about you since yesterday when the letter came. There is a horrible little trawler outside, that keeps on edging nearer and nearer to the rocks on the South side of the Camp. I suppose it's the wind, dragging her anchor. They are getting steam on her, to save the expense of a tug. If she does not get her steam going in the next hour or two, the little beast will go ashore in front of the cookhouse, and then the duty boat (for one of whose crew I'm a stand-by this afternoon) will have to go out and do the life-saving stunt. It is humiliating to save someone's life at no risk to one's own. Also it is as cold as charity. Since I came back from India, I have been always cold. I wish England could be towed some thousand miles to the South.

I cannot get up to London, now. In this camp they give us leave for weekends only from after-duty Saturday till mid-night Sunday; and from Plymouth it is too far to get up in less than six hours' hard riding. So I cannot reach London till after dark on Saturday night, and have to set out on my return at noon or so on Sunday . . . to keep a bit of time in hand against a puncture or a crash. By train it is worse still. So I think I must make up my mind to let London go till I get a real holiday—Whitsun or annual leave. The annual I cannot have till after the Schneider Cup Race on the seventh of September. I am doing clerking and correspondence for our C.O. who is the big noise on that. So it will be months before we can meet, unless you want to get away from London, and from what you tell me you can hardly do that. . . .

Well, for a dismal airman who sat down to practice typing on a dismal day, to another fellow in dismal circumstances . . . Don't bother to answer this if you are hipped.

Yours
T.E.S.

Lawrence was very busy now trying to persuade himself that he was ordinary: towards the end he was almost convinced. But in the process he and I lost touch. He was not justified in saying that I condemned ordinary people. I had not condemned ordinary people for being ordinary. But I had said that people who could think and act for themselves should not, as he was doing, sentimentally and defeatistically sink themselves in common humanity, which was an unreal aggregate of ill-assorted qualities, natural and artificial, good and bad and indifferent. And I had been quarrelling with his new and, to me, repugnant view of poetry as a fancy craft which existed only by favour of the more substantial "human" ones —such as building or piloting aeroplanes, or writing popular novels. Many of the poets whom Lawrence admired I could not admire just because of the fancy-craft element in their work. An interesting case is W. H. Auden, of whom Lawrence (according to L.H.) spoke with "near-awe". Auden, who began as a fancy-craftsman, has since openly exploited the common-humanity view of poetry, evolving a synthetic style of writing which disguises the fundamental shakiness of his poetic individuality.

Lawrence wrote on the 16th of May:

My freedom is very circumscribed here, for to help the C.O. (a really decent fellow: one of the best I've met) I've agreed to take on some extra jobs: and these fill most of the time that should normally have been my own, like week-ends. It's not so much duty, as self-imposed stuff, even harder to get out of, as there can be no substitute.

In July I told him that I was soon going abroad to live. Spain was one of the places considered. He wrote in August:

The Mediterranean. I have just been seeing some drawing of old Saguntum: and feel sort of homesick for ruins and diggings and bright colours. Plymouth sea is good; and its houses and humans rotten.

That summer I wrote an autobiography, *Good-bye to All That*, and he read it in typescript and made a number of suggestions:

It is not a book with the sex-appeal of S.S.'s *Foxhunting Man*, but it should go all right. You are frankness itself and the perfect— Fusilier! Really, I mean by that that you never give offence except where it is due. The war is the best part (horrible idea: is the war always going to be the thing we do best?) S.S. comes out very well. I'm glad of that, for I like him; peculiarities and all. He's a fighting man, and generous. Your pictures of wounds and nerves are exactly as they should be: sane, decent, *right*.

In *Good-bye to All That* I mentioned Lawrence in several contexts. Only at one mention did he make any important correction. The passage referred to an incident in March or April 1920: An American oil financier had come in one day when I was visiting Lawrence and said: "I am here from the States, Colonel Lawrence, to ask you a single question. You are the only man who will answer it honestly. Do Middle Eastern conditions justify my putting any money in Mesopotamian oil?" Lawrence, without rising, simply answered: "No". Lawrence now made it "Hejaz oil". Whether it had been Hejaz oil that was asked about, or whether it had really been Mesopotamian oil (as I could have sworn it was) and Lawrence had warned the financier against investing his money in it because there might soon be another Arab revolt in the Middle East, but was now pretending that he had not, for fear that the story might be misunderstood—I do not know.[1] And he altered a 1925 letter of his I had quoted about Egypt, explaining:

I've toned my letter down, in the first sentences: and suggested slight cuts later. Is it moral to cut out parts of letters already written and sent? Or should they appear whole? I do not know: but if you can modify this one as I suggest, then it will be kinder to Egypt. One says more to a man's back than to his face.

This was during his Schneider Trophy work. On the 23rd of August from Cattewater:

Tomorrow I am to move to Calshot for 15 days. Busy up to my eyes.

[1] See L.H., p. 228, l. 4.

On the 3rd of September from Calshot:

So you're off soon. I'll hope to see you, if you are still in England when I am free—if I am ever free. We work from seven in the morning till eleven at night here. I hope it will end soon. This Calshot is the hell of a place for mails. We get nothing through.

On the 13th of September from Cattewater again:

Ouf! I'm glad that Schneider Cup is over. Too much like work.

I left England in October 1929 and except for a brief visit in September 1930, when he and I met for the last time, did not return there until forced to leave Spain by the civil war. After his Schneider work he resumed the translation of the *Odyssey* he had been working on in India.

> 338171 A/c Shaw
> R.A.F.
> Mount Batten
> Plymouth
> 30.XII.29

Dear R.G.

I have not been out of camp for five weeks. "Odyssey" all day and every day till further notice. I meant to finish it this coming year and am only half-way. I told you, didn't I, that I was doing the *Odyssey* into prose for an American? He pays well.

The Mediterranean sounds good, but I felt from your letter, which didn't bear an address, that there was a catch. I wouldn't like it myself. Agreed that sunlight and sea are good things: but there's a streak of vulgarity in me which passionately enjoys English gutters and mud and wet winds and fire-sides. Pure Dickens, all of that, yet it makes me want to live in England for ever. My Clouds Hill cottage should be cheap to live in; not as cheap as where you are, but cheap. Soon I hope to have an assured £3 a week, the invested proceeds of my Epping Forest Land, which the Chingford Council are buying off me. That might be enough for independence at Clouds Hill; and I'd prefer that to independence out of England, anywhere.

Also, I don't feel like you about people. Partly, it's living in a hut of twenty. They convince me every morning that I'm just ordinary. So I can't get your feeling that this person is significant, and that person not significant. I've got the toleration which comes from not caring very much about anything: whereas you people are always hot about something.

Poor little ——[1] He must be getting stiff-minded. You know you should be rather sorry for the little man. He's only a little poet, and nothing is worth being unless it is very good of its kind. —— can only look forward to thirty or forty more years of writing poems indistinguishable from his last ones. Look at John Freeman, and the others, who've died like that. . . .

Len Lye sent me a ticket for his film.[2] It reached me on a stormy Saturday. I was duty crew, and half-drowned after trying for hours to keep two moored boats afloat. (They both sank eventually): the show was next day, so I did not see it. If he had given me more notice, I could have managed it perhaps. I wish I had. I like Len Lye because he seems to have common clay tendencies. I have not yet ever seen a film that began to be the sort of thing I want to look at: and his promised to be unlike the standard film, and so I had hopes that perhaps it would hit people like me, who are rather tired of realities and pictures of realities[3] and bric-à-brac and clothes. . . . If I go on writing I'll start using Homeric epithets.

T.E.S.

Tell me, if there is anything I can do for you in England. It will not always be winter and Odyssey: and next summer I hope to splash a lot in the sea, here. An American millionaire has given our C.O. a racing motor-boat: and the Moth is here again: only, the Air Ministry forbids me to fly. Curse the Air Ministry.

When I saw Lawrence in England he explained to me that the motor-boat was one that the American millionaire had continual engine trouble with and offered to the C.O. (Sydney

---

[1]Someone whom he had met in my company at Oxford and who had recently attacked *Good-bye to All That* as ungentlemanly.

[2]*Tusalava.*

[3]But see p. 181, l. 15.

Smith) in case he could make anything of it. Lawrence cured it and used to go dashing about the harbour in it.

Lawrence had been "grounded" by the Air Ministry; or rather by Lord Thomson, the Air Minister, with whom Lawrence had once had a row in Paris during the Peace Conference. The sentence had originally been more severe, and Lawrence's fault had been a technical conversation in Italian with Air-Marshal Balbo, the Italian Air Minister who had come to England with the Italian Schneider Cup team. Lord Thomson affected to believe that the conversation had been treasonable. Lawrence told me that he had been summoned one day in September to the Air Ministry in London and informed that he was discharged. Pleas and arguments were useless. Lawrence walked despondently through Whitehall and happened by a lucky accident to meet a Public Personage who stopped and greeted him.

"Hullo, what are you doing now?"

"I've just been honourably discharged from the R.A.F."

"You're free, then?"

"I'm afraid so."

"I'm free too. So what about that trip across the Desert we talked about once?"

Lawrence made up his mind quickly.

"Right, any day you like."

Within a few hours the Foreign Office, terrified of international complications, was ringing up the Air Ministry, asking them to persuade Colonel Lawrence by all the arguments they could muster to remain in the Royal Air Force. Which was what Lawrence had foreseen.

Lord Trenchard, a few days later, told Lawrence on what terms he would be allowed to remain in the R.A.F. Lawrence had the greatest regard for Lord Trenchard, and that the message came through him softened the rigour of the sentence, which was that he should not fly, should not leave England, and should not visit or speak to any "great men"—which included most of Lord Thomson's political opponents.[1]

Two or three letters in 1930 are about my poems: but blankly appreciative rather than critical in the old way. We met in September that year, in London. As usual he looked ten years less than his age. The most striking change in him when we met was that his speaking intonation had changed: from Oxford University to garage-English. Probably the change had been a slow one, but by 1930 it was most marked. I do not mean that he spoke ungrammatically, but the accent was that pleasant compound of (perhaps) North London and Birmingham and Sheffield that one associates with men who drive lorries or have to do with mechanical bits and pieces. I commented on this, and he grinned, showing a row of gold teeth, which called for further comment. Common-clay vulgarity: no All Souls fellow could possibly have showed up with a mouthful of gold like that. He agreed, but said that gold was practical. I remember that he gradually returned in accent and humour to the old Lawrence. He began talking about himself as a writer and said that he had failed: he was far happier now on his Brough or in a speed-boat than with a pen in his hand. He also described the pleasures of "hedge-hopping" in a plane. We—Laura Riding was also present—discussed subjects for books; and L.R., with whom I had been doing some printing and publishing (The Seizin Press), suggested his writing a little book for us to print on the subject of Speed.

The idea appealed to him. He said that speed, and especially the conquest of the air, was the greatest achievement of civilisation, and that it was one of the very few subjects now left to write about. All right, he would try. A

[1]See L.H., p. 31, l. 19, *et seq.*

lighter topic was what to do with old safety-razor blades: I said that I would give him a "Rolls" and then the problem wouldn't arise. And we discussed a certain painter-author, whom Lawrence had commissioned in 1925 or '26 to do a portrait for *Seven Pillars* and paid in advance—but who had failed to deliver the goods. L.R. had happened to meet this person the day before, and he had asked her, if she saw Lawrence, to say that the matter had slipped his memory: he would write to Lawrence immediately if she gave him his address, which she did. He wrote to us on November 8th:

I am sorry about that book on Speed: but I cannot. The itch to write died in me many years ago, and I do not think it will revive. I hope not, for writing was a vexation and disappointment to me always, when I looked back on it. —— did not write. His conscience is still alive, I suppose. It must be giving him a time, too. Nothing less dignified than his antics over this new book of his can be imagined. He puffs it brazenly, poor worm. I am not going to read him any more.

I got your respective *Experts are Puzzled* and *But it Still Goes On.* They came together a day back and lie unread and rather disappointed, I think, on my office table. In the week-end both will be read: and next week they will be borrowed by enquiring airmen, bent on bettering themselves. I think not? What do you say?

The new razor is a success. It takes more leisure than the other sort, and works much better. So on the roundabouts it gains, and wins on points. Apparently it will last for ever. I have not yet exhausted its first edge.

I want to read Len Lye's *Letters:* will you lend or send them me some day when they are published?

The new Secretary of State will be all right for me, I think.

Yours
T.E.S.

The "new Secretary of State" was Lord Amulree, who succeeded Lord Thomson, recently burned to death in the *R-101* dirigible at Beauvais.

L.R. and I were writing a burlesque novel, *No Decency Left*, (later published pseudonymously by Messrs. Cape) and needed a somewhat fantastic autogiro for use by the Princely hero. We asked Lawrence to supply us with one. He answered us:

[Undated]

I have been trying to write to you for months, but couldn't. All manner of jobs have descended on me, for the Air Ministry (after we had been campaigning for two years) suddenly decided to have a try at new types of marine craft for the R.A.F.: and with poetic justice pitched on me to conduct the trials. So imagine me as mainly a mechanic and tester, oilskin-covered, urging speed-boats up and down Southampton water through the rain and wind at noisy rates. In your sunshiny warmth a pleasant picture; here it is wintry weather, and I am frozen and soaked, but interested. A job quite worth doing. Very difficult, engrossing and very exhausting.

It paralyses all my hope of finishing that beastly *Odyssey* to time, nor can I read anything. By evening my eyes are raw with salt-water and rheumy with wind and I go to bed. So I can only acknowledge receipt of your two books: and Len Lye's.[1] I have looked at them: skimmed them even, unworthily, and descended to *Tit-bits* and the *Happy Magazine* which seem to go with speed-testing and water-sports.

All that you have promised me has come: and many letters from you both. I am an ingrate: yet I cannot help. Only in sheer necessity can I put pen to paper, except to report engine performance, consumptions, and hull design modifications.

Fortunately your last night's letter (I am in lodgings at Hythe, near Southampton, and shall be here till some time in May) provided such a necessity. On the back are notes for a Jules Verne aircraft of about 1980 A.D. Too long for your need: rather technical perhaps. Only a rag, of course. Your letter did not give the date of your hero. If he is to be alive tomorrow, then perhaps his aircraft is a bit too advanced for him. If so, make the motors petrol-electric. Cut the blade protrusion to .5mm, double the landing speeds: reduce ceiling to 12,000 m.: make his speed what you think fit (I aim at sound:

[1] Three Seizin Press limited editions.

about 800 feet a second, say 960 k.p.m.). This machine would have to be oxygenated at full speed and height, of course. The designer should be a Spanish lady, I think; the aircraft trade being by 2000 A.D. entirely in the hands of modistes: or is your hero a strong silent man?

If the skit is too Verne-y, then cut out the technical terms till the paragraphs run: and delete the antennae like cat's whiskers and the rotor propulsion.

In great haste: just going down to try an entirely new *British* marine motor: something designed to challenge U.S.A. predominance.

Yours

T.E.S.

[*On the back*]:

"For the benefit of air-minded readers a short account may here be given of this admirable little machine, which had been specially designed to His Highness's requirements by Senora ——, the Madrid [modiste: *del*] to provide the ultimate degree of private comfort consistent with safety and speed.

"All structural members were drop-forgings of cellular colloidal infra-steel, rubber-faced. The monocoque hull was proofed against sound and temperatures by panels of translucent three-ply crodex, between whose films were managed the ducts and condenser areas of the evaporative-cooling system for the eleven Jenny-Ruras picric-electric motors in the under-body.

"Their power units were universally coupled by oil transmission and magnetic clutches alternatively to the lifting vanes (for hover or direct ascent) or to the propulsive rotor for horizontal travel. The vanes were geared into centrifugal governors which automatically varied their lifting angle according to load and air resistance.

"In the rotor, the blade-pitch was adjustable at will, for speed and air density. The blades were set (with a clearance at maximum protrusion of .05m.) in the internal drum of a rotor-turbine of (tractor) Townend type, revolving about the nose of the fuselage which was paired for lead-in and baffled for internal turbulence. The slipstream was deflected by scoops at the exit upwards against the bearing surfaces of the vanes, to increase lift in rare atmospheres or from salt water. A syphon-regulated ballast tank was fitted, to trim by the tail when taxying in rough water. The aircraft's landing springs were castored for ease of garaging and retractable for marine use. Landing speeds as low as 4 k.p.h. (downward) and 2 k.p.h. (forward) were attained. The maximum speed at 22,000 m. was — k.p.h.

"All controls were of course directional operated, at will, and gyroscopically stabilised. Baehlen beam-antennae (of four-cycle frequency) were energised by the rotor-brushes. These were set to indicate by sound-signal to the pilot the presence of any body of more than atmospheric density within 300 metres. At 200 metres they began to induce deflection in the controls, and absolutely refused nearer approach than 18 metres until the motors were throttled back to landing speed. Antaeus indicators recorded height and earth-direction continuously and nitro-generators supplemented the power-units at great elevations."

Nearly all of Lawrence's letters to me of 1931 and 1932 have since gone astray. Towards the end of 1932 he was sent a sample of some critical work that L.R., myself and some others were engaged in: he had always wanted to know what was "happening". His reaction as of low-brow to high-brows surprised me, and I was sorry that I had suggested to L.R. that we should send the stuff (she had been doubtful of his intellectual patience). I wrote to tell him that I felt that he was not playing the game, in assuming that plain-man tone with such forced ingenuousness: during all my years of association with him he had behaved as my intellectual equal. The change was sudden; and unfair, because sudden. Had all the past interest in my work been just another kind of game? He replied:

Plymouth
24.1.33

Come off it, R.G.! Your letter forgets my present [state]. It is so long since we met that you are excused knowing that I'm now a fitter, very keen and tolerably skilled on engines, but in no way abstract. I live all of every day with real people, and concern myself only in the concrete. The ancient self-seeking and self-devouring

T.E.L. of Oxford (and T.E.S. of the *Seven Pillars* and *Mint*) is dead. Not regretted either. My last ten years have been the best of my life. I think I shall look back on my 35–45 period as golden.

Enough of myself: but understand that I enjoy books and pictures and sights and sounds more than I ever did: and new books and new sounds, still. Taste with me has not yet stood still, nor retreated into its past. I am alive and capable with most of our daily emergencies.

Now regard yourself. Recall the hundreds of times we have met and talked. You cannot know how much I have seen in you, and learned of you—but please take it for written. R.G. has been a main current influencing my life, for nearly 15 years.

Wherefore it is, and always will be, that any line from you matters more than screeds from others. I know you—almost: and I do not know S.S. or any of my other past. I think Frederick Manning, and an Armenian, called Altounyan,[1] and E. M. Forster are the three I most care for, since Hogarth died.

Of course there are many people here, in the R.A.F., with whom one lives. And they are well enough: but it is the life of the mechanic: concrete, superficial, every-day: unlike that past excitement into which the war plunged me. I know the excitement in me is dead, and happier so: but the three or four big contacts remain as memories at least.

I said "as memories", for in my new life I am grown hard of hearing. It is disuse of the pineal ear! . . . I read the thing several times before answering: and now I have read it and your letter again, carefully: and I'm damned if I have the foggiest idea what it and you are driving at. Further, I'm prepared to swear that did the Air Ministry similarly word their instructions issued in A.M. W.O.'s, not a station in the R.A.F. would comprehend.

Be merciful, Lord, and explain it again, but very plainly, in text-book language. A text-book was the last thing I wrote. A "Handbook to $37\frac{1}{2}$ foot motor boats of the 200 class" . . . and I pride myself that every sentence in it is understandable, to a fitter.

Now then, preach——

Yours
T.E.S.

---

[1]Dr. Altounyan is Irish-Armenian, a physician from Aleppo, like his father whom Lawrence knew in his archaeological days before the war. For Frederick Manning see L.H., p. 40, sixth paragraph.

In *Lawrence and the Arabs* I had recorded that Lawrence never lied for his own glorification, but that I had often caught him foxing. This was a case of the sort, I thought. There was something in the writing he was sent that, he felt, called for some intellectual effort of self-examination: which he did not feel like making. I wrote very plainly about this and said that I thought that in "playing silly" and putting our, to us, seriously practical thought on an obscure abstract level he was handing over the contemporary field to those second-rate talents with whom his self-depreciative technique had led his intelligence to flirt. I mentioned some of the names and asked: were these his plain man's delegated spokesmen? I added that, if he really had quite suddenly lost his grasp of the meaning of any English but the sort used in R.A.F. standing orders and technical instructions to mechanics, it was hopeless to expect much from him, now. But when he left the R.A.F. he would probably recover his thinking powers: I greatly looked forward to that day. He replied:

> Plymouth
> 28.2.33

Well, there we are. I only wish I was playing silly: for it is not good to be unable to straighten out that stuff and that letter. It tried us too high. . . .

My *Odyssey* has sold 11,000 in New York at $3\frac{1}{2}$ dollars and is to reappear as a school edition, very cheap. Three of us share the royalty, so I have not bought a motor car: but I am putting a bath and boiler into my cottage, in anticipation of next settling day. I hope the dollar does not now crash.

I'm not very sure of my address for the moment. They are trying to shift me about again, and I'm like Charles II, rather too old. So I may retreat to my cottage and set up as a gent of leisure on £2 a month. It belongs to me, now, and is beautiful in my eyes.

> Yours
> T.E.S.

So now I felt as removed from Lawrence as he felt from me: I, clearly, was not going to turn mechanic-minded in order to keep our direction the same. Nor could I believe in the permanence of this common-clay mood for him. Some reaction would follow: Lawrence must in some way live as *himself*. But I hoped that, when the reaction came, he would not turn literary or artistic again. His "present state" seemed to me to be a repudiation of his mind; yet it was true, I now realised, that his interest in literature and art—in fact in everything not "practical"—had always been that of an outsider. He could, and did at times, write extremely well—when he confined himself to reporting the external aspect or mechanical workings of things. But he could not with any hope of success undertake work that required the exercise of fundamental values; because he did not believe in such values—he distrusted the mind. (See p. 74, third paragraph from bottom.)

A publisher wrote to me, as Lawrence's biographer, asking whether there was any chance of publishing *The Mint*, and whether I would approach Lawrence about it. (Lawrence apparently had allowed scores of people besides myself to read the book. Technically there had been no "publication". But Lawrence was always anxious to know of the effect he had on other people: he was like a child who hides behind a curtain and keeps showing little bits of himself to dramatize his sense of being in hiding.)

I forwarded the letter to Lawrence, who replied:

Clouds Hill
Moreton
Dorset
30.VII.33

Dear R.G.

Actually this comes from Southampton, whither I came from the Isle of Wight a week ago; and where I hope to live for at least two weeks. My life, since Plymouth, has been restless and errant.

That enquiry about the *Mint* amused me. I am still R.A.F., so no question of printing it can arise. Nor will it arise when I leave (discharge date is March 1935: and I hope not to anticipate it!) for I have vested the copyright in the Chief of Air Staff for the time being. Also I have lost the typescript! Or rather, it was in the hands of Sir Geoffrey Salmond, the late C.A.S., when he suddenly died: and nobody knows where he put it.

It is long since I wrote. The air at your end seemed to be sultry, and so I'd better go slow, I thought. Time will probably show that my failure to understand was natural and not meant. I have fallen in love with concrete things, and get impatient with the mind, because it wanders so.

Books lately? Yes: *The Book of Talbot*, by Mrs. Clifton. Quite unusual: *A Blasket Islander's Memoirs* of his boyhood. Goodish: *Log of the Sea*, by Felix Riesenberg. Very sound and honest. The new de la Mare Poems were a big step-up, for him, I thought. Also E. E. Cummings has done a vivid book about Moscow, called *Eimi*. That is not a bad shelf-full for seven months.

If you have found any winners, do send me names. Beef-filled grinning books, if possible.

My affairs? I have been foolish. The U.S.A. reprint of the *Odyssey* sold very fast, at first: and the dollar stood high. So I plunged into amending my cottage (now lived in by one Marshall, a bookseller-out-of-work) with damp-courses, bookshelves, a new floor, a bath and water-heating plant. Then the dollar fell, and the crisis stopped all American book-sales. So my $\frac{1}{3}$ of the translation's royalty will not meet the builder's bills.

Robin Buxton, who is still my banker, has come to the rescue with an overdraft: but now prophesy to me. . . . Will books revive in the States, or am I stuck for good? I deprecate an English reprint of the *Odyssey*—nor is there money, here, in new versions of the classics.

There, this letter is all about my side lines, and has not dwelt on that boat-building for which the R.A.F. employ me. They go well, the boats. And your affairs? I trust your country is still warm and quiet. We no longer envy you the sunlight. This is the finest English summer of my experience.

Yours

T.E.S.

I sent Lawrence the galley proofs of my novel, *I, Claudius*, asking him to note any inaccuracies he came across. He wrote me three letters about it, from which I shall quote only the more relevant passages.

Clouds Hill
Moreton
Dorset
12.XI.33

Dear R.G.

I hope your life goes well, with enough in hand. In about a year I leave the R.A.F. and try to live there. It will feel strange to be my own master, again.

I have now to write to you about Claudius, after going through the proof from Arthur Barker and marking it and returning it to him. A conference at Air Ministry took me to London on Thursday, and so I took the chance of handing the galleys back to him personally. I am very rarely in London now. Always boat-building.

Practically I was useless for the Claudius job. Even in my schooldays I was no classic, and to-day I am twenty-five years rusty. You have made your scenes your own, and there is little parade of research: the tone is deliberately modern, and I like that. Two trifles jarred on me for some reason, your use of "French" and "France", which seemed a pity when everybody knew of "Gaul" and "Gallic": and your calling the German spears, in the story of Arminius, always "assegais". "Assegai" is bastard Bantu, I think. It was a very broad-bladed paddle-like stabbing spear. The early German spears were throwing-spears, I think, with leaf-shaped blades: not very like assegais. I'd have said javelins for them: and *not* javelins for the pilum of the legionaries. The pilum was a weapon on its own. Bothered whether I know what to call it. And were the vine-shoots of the Roman N.C.O.'s really the rods that kill? I envisaged them as light cane-like minor punishments.

About the book—and there I am in a difficulty. In every direction you take the way of crime, so that your chronicle becomes more scandalous than the most hostile Roman story. There may be chapter and verse—the amount of study you must have done for the book is appalling—but there is hardly average on your side.

In so much human nature there would have been some good specimens, surely?

It gripped me, against my will. I couldn't help reading at it, long after bed-time, with the bed-room of my lodging here in Southampton growing deadly cold—and an early call in the morning facing me. I give you very high marks for the sustained effort. And yet—and yet—*quo vadis, Domine?*

You have gone a long way from your beginnings, now: and I have a feeling that you ought to come home, at least for a while, and meet people who don't care enormously about poetry—and who aren't as foreign to you as the Spanish. You are losing your englishry—and not taking on another habit.

Yours
T.E.S.

All this long letter about nothing but the book.

He was wrong about "assegai", a French word of Arabic origin which has been in English use from three centuries; and I had geographical reasons for not using "Gaul" and "Gallic", which I put into a prefatory note. The vine-rods frequently killed.

13, Birmingham St.
Southampton
17.XII.33

Yes, your prefatory note to Claudius helps it much: it saves us from having to find out your intentions as we go: and that forestalls criticism.

I still feel that the "assegai", whatever its pedigree, is now too localised a word for classical use. Words die, as words are born. For instance "pictures" now mean cinema performances: and one couldn't describe Claudius as "broadcasting" news through Rome. "Blooming" died because the cockneys fell in love with it. Kipling murdered his infant "far-flung". Morris overlaid "wan". Perhaps you will bring back "assegai" to broader use.

As Claudius recedes from my memory, it leaves on me more and more the impression of unrelieved crime and horror. As you rightly say, there are normal characters in it: but in relation to normal life these are as rare as criminals.

This mild sense of having been shocked is likely to be personal to me, I think: for in daily life crime leaves me cold. I skip all the immeasurable columns of the papers which deal with yesterday's murder. I have never finished a detective yarn—nor for years begun one. I know that many people read them: more, even, seem to write them. It is perhaps a need of the age which has passed me by. There are so many thousand cares of the generations of yesterday and to-day which seem to have missed me. If you do come home you will find me haunting Dorset like an aurochs. Remote enough, I hope, to be interesting to you.

This is Sunday night, and I am just back from my cottage (all put to my liking now, as my home. In March 1935 the R.A.F. push me off, and Clouds Hill then receives me) ready for a last week of boat-testing before Christmas. The new ones are certainly the best boats we have had.

But tomorrow I have an interlude that would amuse you—S.S. is being married in the morning, at Christchurch near here, and I have promised to go over and see the deed done. If any of my generation has earned harbour after storm, it is S.S. and I am hoping for him.

Good wishes for poor Claudius. He deserved a harbour, too, but got Messalina instead, I fancy. *Quelle vie.* Jew Süss was nothing to it.

Yours
T.E.S.

13, Birmingham St.
Southampton
4.V.34

Dear R.G.

Barker sent me a very early copy of *Claudius* and I have taken the chance to read it through much more easily and fluently than was possible in his huge galley-bundle.

You know, it's a grim tale. You will say that so was the epoch: yet if Blunden had written it, it would have been a bucolic lyric! I think we must be subjective animals.

I hope Claudius pays. It seems to me too grim: but then as you discovered, I do not read crime books, and I skip the court news in the papers. So I'm a bad judge. . . .

Boats, boats, boats: that is what I do. They grow slowly better. Today's, for instance, was a very good boat. If only everyone would drive them with understanding.

Yours
T.E.S.

I did not keep the galley proofs of *I, Claudius* with Lawrence's comments, but still have his comments on the page proofs of *Claudius the God*, the sequel. Here are three typical ones:

"Philo said: 'Herod Agrippa came from Edom: wearing a purple cloak—Basra purple—and stepping like a king.' "

Bozrah (in Transjordan) is the O.T. original. Basra in the Persian Gulf, has no purple. Bosrah presumably used Tyrian *murex* yarn.

"Though Bardanes held Ctesiphon, the city on the opposite bank of the Tigris, he did not command the river itself, and the strong Seleucian fleet could introduce supplies into the city, bought from friendly Arabian tribes on the western shore of the Persian Gulf."

How? By rowing? I wonder if this is really true. The river current near Ctesiphon runs 6 m.p.h. at times.

"My brother Germanicus used to say that the only way to win the respect of Germans was to treat them with brutality. The German must always be struck to the dust and struck down again as he rises, and struck again as he lies groaning."

May be true, but is a little too plainly post-War to carry credence, or be very palatable.

T.E.S.

He initialled this comment to show how strongly he felt about it. As a matter of fact, it really was Germanicus's view, as recorded by Tacitus (who thought very well of the Germans, and also admired Germanicus), and that of Germanicus's father Drusus. It was no fault of mine if people read the passage as "post-War". It was also post-War for Germanicus; the remark having been made only a few years after the ambush and massacre of Varus's army by German friendlies. Lawrence always, so far as I know, spoke in kindly terms about Germany; often with admiration.

Ozone Hotel
Bridlington
Yorks.
13.1.35

Dear R.G.

I cannot remember when I wrote to you last, for often I think of doing it and my mind gets confused. *I, Claudius*, which I shrank from when I read it, you described as a crime-book, and I was confirmed in my dislike of crime. But *Claudius the God* is utterly different—the sun has risen. I put much of my pleasure in it to your sympathetic picture of Herod. In the other volume there was nobody (not even battered Cassius Chaerea) whom one could like. Herod is charming: and even Claudius wins a battle. I am so glad the gamble came off, for a historical novel is a desperate gamble, I think . . . unless, perhaps, it is translated from German!

Other books that I have liked lately? Two that Cape published, one called *Winged Victory*, by Yeates, which is a handbook to air fighting on a Sopwith Camel (so you can see why I like it) and the other *Desert and Forest*, by Nesbitt. That was travels in Abyssinia, and I found it curiously restful. The party seemed to have left themselves behind before they started; so they saw the country and people objectively: and there was a curiously old-fashioned dignity about the prose. It felt like a classic of some while ago.

Also I have read and liked *It Was the Nightingale*, some autobiography by Ford Madox Ford. Wry, witty, humorous stuff, done with all the ease of carpet-slippers, and with great skill, in all the major requirements; but with a clumsy handling of many sentences, and with the word "that" excessively prominent.

That is not a great bag of reading for a year; but I am feeling all the while now that my R.A.F. time is almost over (March, it ends) and I'm like a miser trying to make much of the little left. Till it ends, I shall not value anything else. I am very sad that it ends.

My plans, afterwards, are a blank. I go to Clouds Hill and try to hold out there on the 25/– a week which will be my saved balance. I had set aside £2 a week, for reserve: but the rate of interest dipped and dipped. It looks like going to 20/–, soon! Instead of trying to make more, I am going to try to need less. People offer me jobs, but I've never had much leisure yet, and want to try it. If I like it, I shall try to keep it. My address will be Clouds Hill, Moreton, Dorset.

Selfishly I go on wishing you would come back to England. Not for keeps, I mean, but for a visit.

I think the public now expect you to write a life of Nero. I would like you to spend some imagination, instead, in early Galilee: those Greek-Syrians have been overlooked.

Yours
T.E.S.

I asked Lawrence to let me help him with his cottage troubles and reminded him of the time when I had let him help me. (But Lawrence was better at giving than at receiving[1] —in London in 1921–22 he had starved rather than apply to his friends for help.) At the same time I asked him jokingly what was I to do about a request that had just come from a London daily newspaper, asking me to write a memorial notice of him to file away in their "morgue". The editor had written: "We have no reason to suppose that Colonel Lawrence is in failing health, but the present biographical details are many years out of date." I asked whether he would like to take on the job himself and, like the Aztecs, leave nothing to chance. Once, when I had officially died of wounds during the War, my biographical details had duly appeared in the same newspaper, supplied by my father: I did not much like his view of my life. I wrote, too, that I was pleased that he

[1] See p. 14, l. 17.

was soon finishing with the R.A.F. When it was over, many things might come to life again.

He replied:

Ozone Hotel
Bridlington
4.II.35

Dear R.G.

I have been—by lack of thought—guilty of a great fault in taste, and I am so sorry about it. Please believe it was neither conscious nor subconscious. When I told you that I might be short of money at Clouds Hill I had completely forgotten—as for years I have forgotten it—how, long ago, I was able to help you when you were in difficulties. I was stupidly thinking aloud. Long ago I found out what income I needed for retirement and set it aside, invested. The rest—what I had and what I made—I spent on friends and books and pictures and motor-bikes and joys of sorts. Five years ago I found I needed more, to spend on improving my cottage; so I did that *Odyssey* translation, and put in bath and heater of my own choosing and designing, always secure in the knowledge that the income was safe and intact . . . and then down goes the rate of interest and the income shrinks. It is enough to make a saint swear, for had I foreseen it, I would have reserved more. Now when I wanted to be at ease (I have a deep sense that my life, in the real sense, my Life, is over) I have to make about £700 more.

It is very good of you to offer to share the job with me . . . but needless. I can easily make that. Easier still could I make ten times that; it's the stopping short that is skilful. I blame not circumstances but my own bad calculating. I pride myself on being knowing and did not foresee the Treasury-induced spell of cheap money. Another eight or nine years and the rates will bound up. Meanwhile my peace must be mixed with effort. Damn. Claudius, I think, has put you safe now for a while. Your next book will be bought on the merits of your last, always supposing it is not poetry! That is a comfortable state . . . but less comfortable than mine, for I am safe now, and only need another slight effort to be comfortable for all time. You may not ever look to cease to work, wholly. If you hear that I have done something else, you will be able to put the motive to it. I shall be rounding off my capital. You will be a reserve only if ever I get meshed (like you at Boar's Hill) and unable to help myself; which will be bad management, with my notoriety to help me.

New page, new subject. I saw Alexander Korda last month. I had not taken seriously the rumours that he meant to make a film of me, but they were persistent, so at last I asked for a meeting and explained that I was inflexibly opposed to the whole notion. He was most decent and understanding and has agreed to put it off till I die or welcome it. Is it age coming on, or what? But I loathe the notion of being celluloided. My rare visits to cinemas always deepen in me a sense of their superficial falsity . . . vulgarity, I would have said, only I like the vulgarity that means common man, and the badness of films seems to me like an edited and below-the-belt speciousness. Yet the news-theatres, as they call them (little cinemas here and there that present fact, photographed and current fact only), delight me. The camera seems wholly in place as journalism: but when it tries to re-create it boobs and sets my teeth on edge. So there won't be a film of me. Korda is like an oil-company which has drilled often and found two or three gushers, and has prudently invested some of its proceeds in buying options over more sites. Some he may develop and others not. Oil is a transient business.

Money explained, films considered. Let us now pass to the epitaph.

Yes, Hogarth did the morgue-men a first sketch of me in 1920, and they are right to overhaul their stocks. Rather you than Liddell Hart, who seems to have no critical sense in my regard. I won't touch it myself, but if you do, don't give too much importance to what I did in Arabia during the war. I feel that the Middle Eastern settlement put through by Winston Churchill and Young and me in 1921 (which stands in every particular . . . if only the other Peace Treaties did!) should weigh more than fighting. And I feel too that this settlement should weigh less than my life since 1922, for the conquest of the last element, the air, seems to me the only major task of our generation; and I have convinced myself that progress to-day is made not by the single genius, but by the common effort. To me it is the multitude of rough transport drivers filling all the roads of England every night, who make this the mechanical age. And it is the airmen, the mechanics, who are overcoming the air, not the Mollisons and Orlebars. The genius raids, but the common people occupy and possess. Wherefore I stayed in the ranks and served to the best of my ability, much influencing my fellow airmen towards a pride in themselves and their inarticulate duty. I tried to make them see—with some success.

That for eight years, and now for the last four I have been so curiously fortunate as to share in a little revolution we have made in boat design. People have thought we were at finality there, for since 1850 ships have merely got bigger. When I went into R.A.F. boats in 1929, every type was an Admiralty design. All were round-bottomed, derived from the first hollow tree, with only a fin, called a keel, to delay their rolling about and over. They progressed by pushing their own bulk of water aside. Now (1935) not one type of R.A.F. boat in production is naval. . . . We have found, chosen, selected or derived our own sorts: they have (power for power) three times the speed of their predecessors, less weight, less cost, more room, more safety, more seaworthiness. As their speed increases, they rise out of the water and run over its face. They cannot roll, nor pitch, having no pendulum nor period, but a subtly modelled planing bottom and sharp edges.

Now I do not claim to have made these boats. They have grown out of the joint experience, skill and imaginations of many men. But I can (secretly) feel that they owe to me their opportunity and their acceptance. The pundits met them with a fierce hostility: all the R.A.F. sailors, and all the Navy, said that they would break, sink, wear out, be unmanageable. To-day we are advising the War Office in refitting the coast defences entirely with boats of our model, and the Admiralty has specified them for the modernised battleships: while the German, Chinese, Spanish and Portuguese Governments have adopted them! In inventing them we have had to make new engines, new auxiliaries, use new timbers, new metals, new materials. It has been five years of intense and co-ordinated progress. Nothing now hinders the application of our design to big ships—except the conservatism of man, of course. Patience. It cannot be stopped now.

All this boasting is not to glorify myself, but to explain; and here enters my last subject for this letter, your strictures upon the changes I have made in myself since the time we felt so much together at Oxford. You're quite right about the change. I was then trying to write; to be perhaps an artist (for the *Seven Pillars* had pretentions towards design, and was written with great pains as prose) or to be at least cerebral. My head was aiming to create intangible things. That's not well put: all creation is tangible. What I was trying to do, I suppose, was to carry a superstructure of ideas upon or above anything I made.

Well, I failed in that. By measuring myself against such people as yourself and Augustus John, I could feel that I was not made out of the same stuff. Artists excite and attract me; seduce me. Almost I could be an artist, but there is a core that puts on the brake. If I knew what it was I would tell you, or become one of you. Only I can't.

So I changed direction, right, and went into the R.A.F. after straightening out that Eastern tangle with Winston, a duty that fell to me, I having been partly the cause of the tangle. How well the Middle East has done: it, more than any part of the world, has gained from that war.

However, as I said, I went into the R.A.F. to serve a mechanical purpose, not as leader but as a cog of the machine. The key-word, I think, is machine. I have been mechanical since, and a good mechanic, for my self-training to become an artist has greatly widened my field of view. I leave it to others to say whether I chose well or not: one of the benefits of being part of the machine is that one learns that one doesn't matter!

One thing more. You remember my writing to you when I first went into the R.A.F. that it was the nearest modern equivalent of going into a monastery in the Middle Ages. That was right in more than one sense. Being a mechanic cuts one off from all real communication with women. There are no women in the machines, in any machine. No woman, I believe, can understand a mechanic's happiness in serving his bits and pieces.

All this reads like a paragraph of D.H.L., my step-namesake. I do not think for a moment that I have got it right, but I hope from it your sense of character will show you the difference between your view of me and mine. Laura saw me too late, after I had changed direction. She is, was, absolutely right to avoid communication with me. There are no faults on either side, but common sense, the recognition of a difficulty too arduous to be worth the effort of surmounting, when there are so many other more rewarding activities within reach. Don't worry or regret or desire me to change the face of nature. We are lucky to have proportion and toleration to pad our bones.

Yours
T.E.S.

What a whale of a letter. Five minutes' talk would have been so much more fun!

When, two days after his death, this letter appeared, with my consent, in a London evening newspaper, some editing of it was found necessary. L.H.'s name was, naturally, omitted. He now good-humouredly authorizes its inclusion.

I cannot think that Lawrence literally meant that L.H. had "no critical sense" of him. He had not long before told a mutual friend how much he appreciated L.H.'s biography and wished that none others had been published (which meant that he wished I had not published mine). How is one to reconcile this apparent contradiction? It will help, I think, to recall Aesop's fable of the Satyr who saw a man first blowing on his porridge to cool it, and then on his fingers to warm them; and decided that he could not trust a man who blew hot and cold alternately. We should not decide that Lawrence could not be trusted, but rather that his blowing hot and cold with different people was always relative to some different aspect of himself. L.H., he knew, had come to see him as a historical character, the most recent of a long line of Great Captains, with Alexander and Belisarius as his predecessors. Lawrence was conscious that his part in the Arab Revolt had earned him the historical niche that L.H. had carved for him, and was pleased to accept it at the hands of a military historian whom he respected. But the purely historical portrait was, after all, not enough: when Lawrence faced the idea of his own obituary the romantic temptation to be recorded as something more than another "Great Captain"[1] overcame

[1] See L.H., p. 138, eighth line from bottom.

him. He wanted to be given validity, on a poetic, non-historical plane: as the Alexander of the *Clipped Stater* and the Belisarius of Marmontel are not the Alexander of Plutarch and the Belisarius of Procopius. This turning to me for his epitaph meant, I think, that he had not really been whole-hearted in dropping the threads of those "intangible things" which his letter mentions. And yet not only did he not pick them up: he glorified in letting them lie. L.H.'s portrait of him must be the one that stands; any poetically glamorous one that I might have attempted, from old affection and confidence, would have been both historically and poetically untrue. And did Lawrence really mean that his Life was over? He was made (in a phrase that he had once applied to me) without a reverse gear. He had finished with digging up the past, making new military history, trying to be an "artist", being a plain man. Now came (see L.H., p. 222, bot.) the temptation to dramatize himself politically, using all the psychological resources that his experience in the ranks had given him—to become a more legendary Hitler, a shrewder and more powerful Mussolini.[1] He knew that this was against his principles of freedom, yet he played with the temptation as an exciting alternative to the do-nothing Sunday (see L.H., p. 229, l. 9) that he had promised himself in his Clouds Hill cottage. Lawrence, I think, wanted me to write an elegy that would give some coherence to his diversities. But he had—even to the end—fought coherence. I could not, and cannot, do for him what he had set his face against doing for himself.

L.H. wrote to ask me whether the suppressed name was his own. He had a psychological reason for asking, he said. I guessed the reason, and we compared notes.

The passage about Augustus John and myself I also suppressed at the time: I print it here, however, because it is an

[1]See L.H., p. 211, tenth line from bottom.

integral part of the story. I had never encouraged Lawrence to think of me as a resounding literary name; and while I knew Lawrence incapable of placing me in my proper category, it was nevertheless a shock to find myself linked in his mind with the painter for whom of all contemporary painters I have perhaps the least sympathy. It had been easier when I was younger to treat humorously his desire to make a big gun of me—and of all his other potential selves. Now I was ashamed of the picture: Lawrence measuring himself against the contemporary giants, and I one of these poor giants. The sad thing was that he should have reckoned himself a failure by such standards. He was unable to be healthy in his attitude to writers and painters; he regarded writing and painting, in fact, as interesting disorders. So in 1922 he had in a sense been asserting his essential integrity by seeking the kind of animal health that life in the ranks provided.[1] But to the other kind of health, which would have demanded more fundamental simplicity and discipline, he never dedicated himself—because it suited his philosophy to doubt its existence.

The queerest thing he did, towards the end, was to become a member of the Irish Academy of Letters—he who was "no writer". He might just as appropriately, I thought on hearing of it, have joined the United Service Club. Yet this late assertion of his Irishness was significant. Although he was at pains to tell first me and then L.H. that the men of his family had been careful not to marry Irishwomen, Irish he undoubtedly was: of those Plantation settlers who became (as Geraldus Cambrensis once noted of the English who went over with Strongbow) more Irish than the Irish. He had all the marks of the Irishman: the rhetoric of freedom, the rhetoric of chastity,

---

[1] For an interesting parallel between Lawrence and the French poet Rimbaud, supported by a letter from Lawrence to Laura Riding, see *Epilogue*, Vol. 1, page 65. (Seizin Press and Constable.)

the rhetoric of honour, the power to excite sudden deep affections, loyalty to the long-buried past, high aims qualified by too mocking a sense of humour, serenity clouded by petulance and broken by occasional black despairs, playboy charm and theatricality, imagination that over-runs itself and tires, extreme generosity, serpent cunning, lion courage, diabolic intuition, and the curse of self-doubt which becomes enmity to self and sometimes renouncement of all that is most loved and esteemed.

T. E. Lawrence
TO HIS BIOGRAPHER
LIDDELL HART

Information about himself, in the form of letters, notes, answers to questions and conversations.

PUBLISHER'S NOTE

On pages 77–124, 147–62 and 174–85 references to matter in the typescript of Captain Liddell Hart's book, "T. E. Lawrence: in Arabia and After", together with references in the corresponding pages of the published book on which this matter may be found, are given in this way: "T. 3, B. 16 (5)", which means that the matter commented upon was on p. 3 of the typescript and may be found on p. 16 of the Cape edition of the book and on p. 5 of the Dodd, Mead edition. (The book was published in England by Jonathan Cape, Ltd.; in the United States by Dodd, Mead & Co., under the title, "Colonel Lawrence, the Man Behind the Legend".) T. E. Lawrence's comments and changes, set in a smaller type, follow the matter quoted from the typescript. In general, all Lawrence's letters and his answers to Captain Liddell Hart's questions, etc., are set in the smaller type. Throughout this section the footnotes are by Captain Liddell Hart, except where they are specifically attributed to T. E. Lawrence. The letters R.G. before page references indicate the companion work by Robert Graves.

FOREWORD

In the preface to *T. E. Lawrence: in Arabia and After* I have related how that book, intended as a history of the Arab Revolt, necessarily evolved into a biography. It was published a year before T.E.'s discharge from the Air Force, and fourteen months before his death. During its preparation he gave me the most generous help in the way of suggesting sources, answering questions, and commenting profusely on the successive drafts, as well as by providing much light on himself in letters and conversations. But, at his wish, I refrained in my preface from disclosing the full extent of his help, lest the acknowledgment which I wished to make might be a cause of embarrassment to him in his relations with authority. Now that such restraint is no longer required, it is a duty to history to place his own evidence on record so that it may be available to those who are interested. There was much of it which I could not use in my original book. And, for the rest, a man's own words are often more illuminating, especially in regard to his trend of thought, than a summary of the evidence by another. In this case the evidence that T.E. gave Robert Graves on the same events from a different angle provides an invaluable cross-bearing towards determining his true position.

In collating the material it has been my aim to incorporate everything that may be useful to history and to the historical understanding of T.E.'s thoughts, feelings, and actions. I have had to make a small number of excisions in T.E.'s remarks, some for legal reasons, some to meet the wishes of the Lawrence Trustees. The places where they occur are indicated by omission marks. But little that is of historical value has been left out.

My thanks are due to the Lawrence Trustees for permission to include material in which they hold the copyright, and for making this, together with Robert Graves's companion volume, an exception to their rule against the use of copyright material. In deference to their wishes, no popular edition of these books will appear until six months after the publication of the official *Letters*, which are to be edited by Mr. David Garnett.

My thanks are also due to Messrs. Jonathan Cape, Ltd., and Dodd, Mead—the publishers in Great Britain and the United States respectively of my *T. E. Lawrence: in Arabia and After*,[1] from the original draft of which I here reproduce passages that T.E. corrected or annotated. Likewise to Messrs. G. Bell, the English publishers of my book on *The Decisive Wars of History*, and to Little, Brown & Company, its American publishers, and to Messrs. Faber & Faber, Ltd., and Yale University Press, English and American publishers respectively of *The Ghost of Napoleon*.

L. H.

[1]The title of the American edition is *Colonel Lawrence, the Man Behind the Legend*.

T. E. LAWRENCE TO HIS BIOGRAPHER, LIDDELL HART

In 1927 the work of preparing the new 14th edition of the Encyclopaedia Britannica was undertaken. When making up the list of articles in my province, as Military Editor, I thought it was desirable to have one on "Guerrilla Warfare"—and T.E. was obviously the man to do it, if he would agree. This I hardly expected; yet his article, "The Evolution of a Revolt", in the first number of the *Army Quarterly* (Oct. 1920) had discussed the subject in the very way I wanted it to be treated. So in writing to him I suggested that if he could not manage a fresh article the original might serve.

> 338171 AC 2 Shaw
> Room 2 ERS
> RAF Depot
> Drigh Road
> Karachi
> 25.X.27

Yes, I remember giving Gen. Dawnay that article, years ago, and your letter to me about it. But since then you've gone on being interested in combined movements, and I've been doing none but individual movements. The problem of the ranks in the R.A.F. is to produce the mechanic of individual intelligence!

Your book on war[1] interested me, the other day: though you did not take the lid off, enough, to reform things: nor screw it down

---

[1] I cannot recall which book this was: probably *Paris, or the Future of War* (in the Today and Tomorrow series); possibly *The Remaking of Modern Armies*.

tightly enough to produce a philosophy: at least so it seemed to me: but probably your book is only an interim production while you make up your mind which way you will go. I suspect there is not much value in the philosopher of war—it isn't a subject from which the emotional element can properly be divorced—so I hope you'll be a reformer. There is much room. I was three years in the Royal Tank Corps.

However, back to Irregular War—— As you clearly expected, from your letter, it isn't possible for me to write you a special article. These things are so long ago, now, and I have dropped all concern with them, deliberately.

As for reprinting the Army Quarterly article: as you please. So far as I can recollect, Guy Dawnay asked me for something for his new venture. I had my account of the Arab Revolt by me, and boiled down two chapters of it (excising some sections, I fancy) into a review article. I can't remember if I recast any part of it. Possibly.

You might well be able to re-hash up something more satisfactory, to your experience, if you got hold of a copy of that book of mine (it has the queer name of the "Seven Pillars of Wisdom", and both Guy and Alan Dawnay have copies—or had them, and would lend them you. Also Gen. Bartholomew at the W.O.: or D. G. Hogarth at Oxford: you are sure to know some of these personally) and boiled the original two chapters together into a brew of your own. I haven't a copy of it, myself, nor of the Quarterly article: but I think that a puzzlement about the general principles of war came about page 100, when I was ill in Abdulla's camp: and that some notes on tactics came later, about page 350, after Akaba had been captured. But probably the whole book is strewn over with remarks —more or less rude—about war, regular or irregular.

1. If you boiled the stuff out yourself, or employed some devil to boil it for you, it would avoid your having to mention me in the article. Please regard all the material of any technical military interest in the Seven Pillars as at your disposal for the purpose of hashing-up an article.

2. If however you prefer to quote blocks of it, textually, in inverted commas, then I'll have to ask you to put a note in somewhere, saying where it came from: the Seven Pillars was registered as by

T. E. Shaw. I gave up the (assumed) name of Lawrence some five years ago. . . . You are at liberty to quote from the Seven Pillars any paragraphs dealing with general theories of war, or application of these theories, or any tactical disquisitions. If the quotations are going to be unreasonably long, then the Encyc. Brit. must pay me some fee for their use. The Seven Pillars isn't publickly-published, and I do not want people to assume a habit of quoting from it freely.

3. If you prefer the old Army Quarterly article, then reprint as much of it as you please, naming the source. If you attach my Lawrence name to it, then you must put it in inverted commas, for legal reasons.

What a lengthy and clumsy letter! I apologise. The alternatives 1 and 2 will probably give you a better article than 3 . . . though I have rather forgotten what the differences were. All that sort of thing is a long way away.

If your Encyc. pays its contributors, and you adopt alternative 3, then I'd be very glad of your persuading them that even second-hand stuff was worth something. Service life in India is much dearer than it was in England, and I have some more years of it to do. Smallest contributions thankfully received!

Acting on his suggestion, I compiled an article from his reflections (it appears in the 14th edition above the initials T.E.L.), obtained as good a fee as I could for it, and sent him the fee.

> 338171 A/C Shaw
> R.A.F.
> Miranshah Fort
> Waziristan
> 17.X.28

It is very good of you to have played editor to such purpose with those pages on irregular war. The cheque delights me. I fancy Guy Dawnay only paid £10 for the original article.

To provoke the soldiers to battle on my own ground I kept on limiting what I said to irregular warfare. Unhappily they would not be drawn. I intended what I wrote to have the larger specious application which you have discovered. For "irregular war" you could write "war of movement" in nearly every place, and find the argument fitted as well or ill as it did.

The logical system of Clausewitz is too complete. It leads astray his disciples—those of them, at least, who would rather fight with their arms than with their legs. There is, in studying the practice of all decent generals, a striking likeness between the principles on which they acted: and often a comic divergence between the principles they framed with their mouths. A surfeit of the "hit" school brings on an attack of the "run" method: and then the pendulum swings back. You, at present, are trying (with very little help from those whose business it is to think upon their profession) to put the balance straight after the orgy of the late war. When you succeed (about 1945) your sheep will pass your bounds of discretion, and have to be chivied back by some later strategist. Back and forward we go.

I am very grateful to you for your kindness.

In 1928 my book, *Reputations*—a study of ten of the chief military figures of the War in the light of ten years after—was published, and I sent T.E. a copy.

> 338171 A/C Shaw
> R.A.F. Cattewater
> Plymouth
> 19.3.29

"Reputations" came to Miranshah just as I left the quiet little place. I pushed it into my kit bag, flew to the coast, and read it at great leisure in the Rajputana on the way home. The Joffre pleased me hugely. It ends with the most complete and pointed and neat judgement of a general that I've ever read.

The Allenby was very just. He was so large-hearted and clean-judging a chief that all we varied devils worked hard for him, without having leisure to see what a rotten gang we were (or the other fellows were). For actual tactics he depended for success on his staff: Guy Dawnay, first: Bartholomew lastly. I suppose you had to do the Americans, to fill some contract. They didn't get under the skin, like the Frenchmen and the Englishmen. The book would have been a better book if it was all like its best bits. Parts of it feel as if done to order: but then some of your people were not interesting to me. I'd like to know all about Weygand: and Hentsch, and Conrad von Hotzendorf. Sorry about Falkenhayn. I had thought him pretty good. I suppose old Ludendorff was really a good general. [*Note by L. H.* Here T. E. made a remark caustically reflecting on Ludendorff as a peace-intellect, and bracketed him in this respect with Foch.]

I'd like to see your new philosophic work on war.[1] I fancy you do that 100 times better than journalism. In journalism you are not encouraged to use words in their real meaning: you have to write for the hurriedly reading eye: whereas in a thinking book you tend to choose your phrases for what they meant before everybody else started chucking them about.

Unfortunately Plymouth is so far from London that I shall have few chances of seeing people. We get only "short" weekends from this camp. My hopes are inclining towards a chance of annual leave, for perhaps a fortnight, in London in the early autumn . . . only you will probably choose that moment to fly off to U.S.A. or somewhere. We ought to meet, somehow, you know: and talk about something. Not war! I'm too rusty there!

[1] In writing to T.E. I had mentioned that I was writing a book on "The Strategy of Indirect Approach"—it was eventually published under the title *The Decisive Wars of History*. Its theme was, in brief, that a direct approach to one's mental object, or physical objective, tends to stiffen resistance and thus lead to a negative result as well as a waste of strength; and that the dislocation of opposition, psychologically and physically, should precede the attempt to overcome it. In view of his interest I sent him the proofs for criticism. He sent them back with several pages of notes.

T.E.'S NOTES ON PROOF OF
"THE DECISIVE WARS OF HISTORY"

338171 A/C Shaw
RAF Cattewater
Plymouth
31.3.29

Excuse pencil. It is easier in barracks: and I'm writing by the stove, because it is cold at night, here by the sea.

I've read your book during these holidays, which I've had to spend in camp, on Fire Picquet. It's uncommonly good: so lively and interesting, and wide. You establish your thesis: but I fear that you could equally have established the contrary thesis, had the last war been a manoeuvre war, and not a battle war.[1] These pendulums swing back and forward. If they rested still that would be absolute truth: but actually when a pendulum stands still it's that the clock has stopped, not that it has achieved absolute time!

I fear that I am too long out of the game. My life now deals so wholly in non-military things that I couldn't get into the swing of your thinking, so as to help you with real comments. Once I think I could have: for the practice of war which followed on my book study seemed to clarify my sight, and I thought I could see war whole. Illusion, no doubt: but for the moment I felt I *knew*.

These notes, on a few sheets, and here and there in the margins of your proofs, aren't really anything, except babble. But please believe

[1] The remark was characteristic of T.E.—an expression both of his sense of futility and of his sense of humour: to emphasise that we were merely the creatures of circumstance. But I have grounds here for questioning his view. For in my youthful pre-war studies I had a strong natural tendency towards the manoeuvre thesis, and only yielded this as I found that the weight of authoritative opinion was on the other side—in my immaturity I was always ready to assume that authority was right until facts proved the contrary. Experience in the war, and reflection upon it, progressively released me from the straitjacket of the battle-dogma.

6

that I've liked your book immensely. It is quite first-rate: and I fancy that you will find the soldier, rather reluctantly, admitting it. If you had worn your learning rather more ponderously, they'd have admitted it at once—but failed, ever after, to read the book. Whereas now, I fancy, they will read it. I hope they'll buy it, too!

It was very good of you to lend me the sheets. I'd not have missed it for a lot.

Let me know if you do decide to run down into the West for a holiday. I'm mobile, on Saturdays and Sundays, and even on Wednesdays, after noon: and could run out and meet you for lunch or tea: to my profit—because, as I said before, I'm out of date, militarily, now.

T.E. appended several sheets of notes referring to various pages of the galley proof. His notes are set in a smaller type following passages quoted from the proofs of *The Decisive Wars of History:*

(P. 6.) This dealt with Xerxes' invasion of Greece, and contained the comment:
"When the menace developed, in 481, this time on a grand scale, its very magnitude not only consolidated the Greek factions and states against it, but compelled Xerxes to make a direct approach to his goal. For the army was too big to be transported by sea and hence was compelled to take an overland route. And it was too big to supply itself, and so the fleet had to be used for this purpose. The army was tied to the coast and the navy tied to the army—each tied by the leg. Thus the Greeks were able to be sure as to the line along which to expect the enemy's approach, and the Persians were unable to depart from it."

The size of the Persian army imposed "direct" approach. Very few people will use skill if brute force will do the trick. The worst thing for a good general is to have superior numbers. Only an Allenby can resist that temptation.

(P. 10.) This began an analysis of the campaigns of Epaminondas—

"who may perhaps be termed the most original genius in military history. He not only broke flagrantly with tactical methods established by the experience of centuries, but in tactics, strategy and grand strategy alike laid the foundations on which subsequent masters have built. Even his structural designs have survived or been revived. For in tactics the 'oblique order' which Frederick made famous was but a slight elaboration of the method of Epaminondas."

I agree as to the greatness of Epaminondas: but I do not like the "most original genius in military history". An original genius: of whom we do not know enough to classify him precisely.

(P. 15.) This concluded an analysis of the campaigns of Alexander which contained the comment:

"His logistical strategy is direct and devoid of subtlety. The cause would appear to be, first, that in the youthful Alexander, bred to kingship and triumph, there was more of the Homeric hero than in the other great captains of history; and, still more perhaps, that he had such justifiable confidence in the superiority of his instrument and his own battle-handling of it that he felt no need to dislocate preparatorily his adversaries' strategic balance. His lessons for posterity lie at the two poles —war-policy and tactics."

Alexander was part knight-errant, and part experimenter with life. He is so above rules that ordinary people daren't follow him. [See R. G., p. 33, l. 4.[1]]

(P. 18.) This dealt with Hannibal's invasion of Etruria and how he surprised the Romans by taking a route through the marshes instead of one of the normal roads. It contained the comment:

[1]The letters R.G. before any page reference indicate the companion volume by Robert Graves.

"Normal soldiers always prefer the known to the unknown; Hannibal was an abnormal general, and hence, like other great captains, chose to face the most hazardous *conditions* rather than the certainty of meeting the enemy in a position of their own choosing."

A good point about the general not fearing *natural* hazards. You will find the best examples of this in the history of Montrose. Read John Buchan's book about him, if you have not yet seen it.

(P. 23.) Here, the examples from ancient warfare closed with the campaigns of Caesar, while making the comment: "During the period of 'the Decline and Fall', during the centuries when Europe was shedding its old single-coloured skin for a new skin of many colours, there is profit to be got from a study of the military leadership. Sometimes much profit, as in the case of Belisarius and later generals of the Byzantine empire. But, on the whole, decisiveness is too difficult of definition, turning-points too obscure, purposeful strategy too uncertain, and records too unsafe, to provide a basis for scientific deductions."

I'm sorry you didn't go into Belisarius.[1] One of the most queer cases of an old-fashioned "regular" army defeating less regular forces. It would have been worth more than the Caesar pages, for C. wasn't (I think) a very good general.

(P. 31.) This dealt with the Hundred Years' War and how, after the victories of Edward III and the Black Prince, du Guesclin turned the scales against the English. "The strategy by which he carried out this policy was to avoid battle with the main English army while constantly hampering the movement and contracting the territory of his opponents. Far removed from a passive evasion of battle, his strategy exploited mobility and surprise to a degree that few

[1]See R.G., p. 130, footnote.

generals have matched, cutting off convoys, cutting up detachments and capturing isolated garrisons. Always taking the line of least expectation, his surprise attacks on such garrisons, often by night, were helped both by his new and rapid storm methods and by his psychologically calculated choice of objectives where the garrisons were discontented or the population ripe for treachery. So also he fanned every flame of local unrest as an immediate distraction of the enemy's attention and an ultimate subtraction from his territory."

du Guesclin was helped by his operating in friendly country. The English were by now foreigners in France: and their garrisons were so many isolated rocks in a French sea: also the lack of an English main body meant that the garrisons had no hope of relief.

(P. 39.) This concluded an examination of Cromwell's campaigns with a discussion of the final one in which he overcame the Royalist army, posted at the gateway to the Highlands, by enticing it into England, where he shepherded it into his net at Worcester:

"When, late in June, 1651, Cromwell was fit enough to resume operations, he was faced with a difficult problem. And his solution for subtlety and masterly calculation compares favourably with any strategic combination in the history of war. Although now, for the first time, the superiority was on his side, he was faced by a canny adversary established in a region of marsh and moorland, which afforded every natural advantage to the weaker side in barring the approach to Stirling. Unless Cromwell could overthrow the resistance within a brief span he would be doomed to spend another trying winter in Scotland, with inevitable suffering to his troops and the likelihood of increasing difficulties at home. And to dislodge the enemy would not suffice, for a partial success would only disperse the enemy into the Highlands, where they would remain a thorn in his side. Let us watch the unfolding of Cromwell's plan. First he menaces Leslie in front, storming Callender House, near Falkirk. Then he passes, in stages, his whole army across the Firth of Forth and marches on Perth, thereby not only turning Leslie's defensive barrier across the direct approach to Stirling, but gaining possession of the key to Leslie's supply area. By this manoeuvre he had, however, uncovered the route to England. Here lies the supreme artistry of Cromwell's plan. He was on the open rear of an enemy now threatened with hunger and desertion—and he left one bolt-hole open. As one of them said, 'We must either starve, disband, or go with a handful of men into England. This last seems to be the least ill, yet it seems very desperate.' "

I doubt whether the "bolt-hole" was intentional. Charles too nearly won, anyway, for it to be a good intention. It's the sort of mistake a solid man, like Cromwell, easiest makes: and as it ended well, his friends will gloss it over. If he did mean it, then it was his brainiest effort.

There is no conclusive proof in Cromwell's own words that his conception was as subtle as I have suggested. While his letter to Lenthall (the President of the Council of State) provides a clear hint of such a conception, it may be argued that this letter was not written until Cromwell had news that the Royalist army was marching southward. But there is strong indirect evidence of how his thought ran. We know that a march into England had been long expected; that at the end of June, before opening his own campaign, Cromwell had arranged with Harrison, then on the Border, to send parties into the passes in readiness to delay the Royalists if they attempted to march that way; that three weeks later, just before Cromwell moved across the Forth on his turning manoeuvre, Harrison came north to receive Cromwell's orders and was given further reinforcements; that a week after, when he heard on approaching Perth that the Royal army was heading for the Border, he reversed his own direction with a celerity that would hardly have been possible unless the move had been foreseen and prepared. Moreover, the letter he sent to London on July 26th was so couched that it gave sufficient warning of a possible southward bolt by the army, to make the Government hasten preparations without alarming them over the boldness of his own. And the course of events subsequently, until the net was closed round the invaders at Worcester, moved with a precision that bears the stamp of design. The balance of evidence seems to weigh heavily against T.E.'s doubts, while there is little to support his view that Charles was anywhere near success.

T.E. then interpolated the remark:

I was sorry to find no discussion of Saxe, one of my highlights in war.

The omission was due to the fact that Saxe's campaigns had less significance than his subsequent reflections, and less bearing on my theme. I had devoted a whole chapter to Saxe's ideas on warfare in a previous book, *Great Captains Unveiled*.

(P. 43.) This was the first page of a long analysis of Marlborough's campaigns, and contained an incidental reference to Catinat as Eugene's opponent in Italy.

Marlborough had an astonishing opinion of Catinat. I always meant to isolate his (C's) actions some day and study them. I wish you would. Your Marlborough chapter is very good.

(P. 49.) This dealt with the significance of the campaign that led to the capture of Quebec, contrasting the costly failure of the original direct approach with the astonishing success that crowned—

"his final hazardous landing on the French rear above

Quebec . . . an illuminating example of the truth that a decision is produced even more by the mental and moral dislocation of one command than by the physical dislocation of its forces."

Wolfe was very lucky. He did nothing worth success.

(P. 50.) This was an analysis of Frederick's campaigns, pointing out that his advantages—e.g., absolute power, a superior instrument, and a central location—were much greater than is often recognised and examining the causes why his fortunes declined as his roll of victories grew.

The succeeding chapter was on Napoleon.

You are very acute and interesting on Frederick the Great. I am with you all the time. A second-rate mind, who threw away enormous assets.

The Napoleon study, by bringing out the rapid decadence of his military talent (almost from the end of the Italian war he ran down hill) is most valuable. You should also have stressed the hare-brained ignorance of his Egypt and Russia expeditions: only a false conception of geography could have led him to attempt such follies. What we call the "Intelligence" Services were at fault in letting him dream of Constantinople and India and Moscow.

The chapter on the Napoleonic Wars included a section on the Peninsular War which emphasised the predominant part played by the Spanish guerrillas. The analysis ended with the comment:

"This happy conclusion could hardly have come but for the moral and physical support of Wellington's presence in the peninsula, and his activities, by distracting the attention of the French in part to him, repeatedly facilitated the spread of the guerrilla war. Yet it is a question, and an interesting speculation, whether his victories in 1812 by stirring the French to cut their loss and contract their zone did not improve their prospects and make his own advance harder in

1813. For the wider and the longer they were dispersed throughout Spain, the more sure and more complete would be their ultimate collapse. The Peninsular War was an outstanding historical example, achieved by instinctive common-sense even more than by intention, of the type of strategy which a century later Lawrence evolved into a reasoned theory, and applied in practice if without so definite a fulfil-ment."

I've long wanted to see greater justice done to the Peninsular War truth—that the English forces were there only to sustain the Spaniards in their rebellion: and that the more irregular the Spanish forces, the greater their effect. Weakness made the Spanish unconsciously adopt the tactics my weakness made me consciously adopt. If Wellington had had the mental nimbleness to develop his Spaniards into a deliberate guerilla scheme he'd have done quicker, and cheaper and better. Instead he was always trying to organise them into formations: which only spoilt them! In the same way they were always at me to drill the Arabs: I used to reply that if we wanted drilled men we'd borrow English troops: who weren't qualified, by nature, to be irregular.

It always puzzled me that Wellington made no real use of sea-power, to harry the French lines of communication by means of local risings in Catalonia and elsewhere. If he'd kept the French main forces on the border of Portugal, and then cut them, back in the Pyrenees, he'd have wiped out the lot.

(P. 78.) This was the beginning of a large section devoted to the American Civil War. After showing how the decision was produced in the West, I remarked that the disproportionate attention given to the campaign in Virginia by British military students might be traced partly "to the spell cast by Henderson's epic, *Stonewall Jackson*—perhaps more epic than history."

Your analysis of the American Civil War interested me very greatly. I've not studied it: but am prepared to believe all evil of the

Henderson book. It struck me as just about the pre-war standard! It's not really epic, you know!

The suggested difference between autocratic and democratic warfare is very fruity.

(P. 87.) At the end of the long survey of past wars, from the Persian invasion of Greece to the Russo-Japanese conflict, the book devoted a chapter to "conclusions" and another to "construction" before making an analysis of the war of 1914–18.

The putting your conclusion here is very wise of you. It rounds off the thesis, and leaves your readers to try to *apply* it to the Great War.

Again you stress the unimportance of *undefended* natural obstacles. This is most valuable.

(P. 91.) Here the chapter on "Construction" began by discussing Clausewitz's definition of strategy, suggested that— "if the government has decided upon a 'Fabian' war policy, the general who, even within his strategic sphere, seeks to overthrow the enemy's military power may do more harm than good to the government's war policy. . . . We can now crystallise our thought into a shorter, simpler, and perhaps more exact definition of strategy as—'the distribution and transmission of military means to fulfil the ends of policy.'

"As tactics is an application of strategy on a lower plane, so strategy is an application on a lower plane of 'grand strategy'. If practically synonymous with the policy which governs the conduct of war, as distinct from the permanent policy which formulates its object, the term 'grand strategy' serves to bring out the sense of 'policy in execution.' For the role of grand strategy is to co-ordinate and direct all the resources of a nation towards the attainment of the political

object of the war—the goal defined by national policy. . . .
Furthermore, while the horizon of strategy is bounded by the
war, grand strategy looks beyond the war to the subsequent
peace."

Your discussion of the definition of strategy is worth doing. We
know (dimly) what it is: but when we try to see it exactly it fades.
Your limitation of it on p. 93 is V.G.

(P. 100.) This dealt with the French and German plans in
1914.

You get right down to the naked truth, about the two plans: and
draw blood from the French, whose staff work deserves all it gets
from you!

(P. 104.) This concluded an analysis of the Battle of the
Marne by remarking:
"Finally we see that the actual decision, the move which
compelled the Germans to retreat, if no more, was due to an
'indirect approach' so unintentional as to form an act of
pure comedy. This was the 'disappearance' of the British
expeditionary force and its happily belated reappearance
opposite the strained and weakened joint of the German right
wing. French critics have reproached it for this slowness, not
realising that here was a superb if somewhat different testimony to the fable of the hare and the tortoise. Had it returned sooner the joint would hardly have been so weakened."

The humour of the Marne is well-placed, and timely: but I've felt
humour often in reading the book: just like a smudge across the page,
and gone before one knew it: yet a great relief, each time it did
appear.

(P. 113.) This referred to the change in the German
Supreme Command in 1916 when Falkenhayn was replaced
by Hindenburg, with Ludendorff as his right hand; it com-

mented on "the firm's" loss in leaving Hoffmann, formerly Ludendorff's right hand, in the East.

I wonder how much Hoffmann stood for. I saw how first Guy Dawnay and then Bartholomew were essential to Allenby's success: and wonder.

(P. 118.) This began a discussion of the Gallipoli campaign by commenting on the abandonment of the "traditional amphibious strategy of Britain" and the neglect to exploit the military advantage of sea-power.
"In October 1914 Lord Fisher had urged a plan for a landing on the German coast. In January 1915 Lord Kitchener advocated another, for severing Turkey's main line of eastward communication by a landing in the Gulf of Alexandretta. The post-war comments of Hindenburg and Enver have shown how this would have paralysed Turkey, but it could hardly have exercised a wider influence or been an indirect approach to the Central Alliance as a whole."

I am unrepentant about the Alexandretta scheme which was, from beginning to end, my invention, put forward necessarily through my chiefs (I was a 2nd Lieut. of 3 months seniority!). Actually K. accepted it, and ordered it, for the Australian and N.Z. forces: and then was met by a French ultimatum. A landing at Alexandretta in Feb. 1915 would have handed over Syria and Mespot. to their native (Arab) troops then all in their home stations, and complete, and automatically established local governments there: and then attracted to Ayas (it was Ayas, not Alexandretta) the whole bulk of the *real* Turkish armies:* and that would have been the moment for the Dardanelles naval effort.

(P. 120.) "The Middle East expeditions hardly come within the scope of this survey. Strategically they were both too remote to have any hope of exercising a decisive effect, and considered as diversions they both absorbed far larger forces

*to fritter itself against the Arabs, not against us. [Note by T.E.L.]

of the British than they detained of the enemy. In the sphere
of policy a case can be made out."

I hope you will some day write a study of the Mesopotamia campaign. It's a British disgrace, end to end.

(P. 122.) This followed a discussion of the Palestine campaign by remarking that—
"in the desert to the east and south a curious campaign was
not only helping to weaken the fighting strength of Turkey
but shedding some new light on strategy and, in particular,
on the indirect approach. This campaign was the Arab
Revolt, with Lawrence as its guiding brain. If it falls into the
category of guerrilla warfare, which is by its very nature
indirect, its strategy had such a scientifically calculated basis
that we should not miss its reflection on normal warfare. . . .
". . . With all its unconventionality this strategy merely
carried to its logical conclusion that of following the line of
least resistance. As its author has said: 'The Arab Army never
tried to maintain or improve an advantage, but to move off
and strike again somewhere else. It used the smallest force
in the quickest time at the farthest place. To continue the
action till the enemy had changed his dispositions to resist it,
would have been to break the fundamental rule of denying
him targets'. What was this but the strategy evolved in 1918
on the Western front? Fundamentally the same, but carried
to a further degree. Its application to the problem of normal
warfare is conditioned by the factors of time, space and force.
While a quickened and active form of blockade, it is inher-
ently slower to take effect than a strategy of decision. Hence,
if national conditions make a quick decision imperative the
latter appears preferable. But unless the end is sought by
an indirect approach, it is likely to prove slower, more
costly, and more dangerous than the 'Lawrence' strategy.

Lack of room and density of force are also handicaps, if rarely insuperable. A reasoned verdict is that in normal warfare the choice would fall on the form of indirect approach which aims at a quick decision, by 'trapping' the opponent, if there is a good prospect of its success. Otherwise, or after it has failed, the choice should fall on that form of the indirect approach which aims at an eventual decision by sapping the opponent's strength and will. Anything is preferable to the direct approach."

I agree that we attained (in 1917) the strategy of 1918: and we also, independently, invented for ourselves the filtration tactics by machine-gun parties. War is all much of a muchness.

(P. 124.) This discussed Allenby's plan for the final offensive and pointed out that—
"To get a grip on Deraa would sever the communications of all three armies and the best line of retreat of the IV.
"Deraa was too far to be reached from the British front in a time short enough to exert a prompt influence on the issue. Happily, the Arabs were available to emerge like phantoms from the desert and pounce upon and cut all three of its railway 'spokes'. But neither the nature of the Arab tactics nor the nature of the country nor Deraa lent itself to the formation of a strategic barrage across the Turkish rear. As Allenby sought a quick and complete decision he must seek a closer site for such a barrage . . ."

Deraa was admittedly not the place for a strategic barrage: but at Sheikh Saad (20 miles N. of Deraa) I put in the sort of barrage which I could afford, and held it for 2 days.

I think you do me rather too much justice, compared to the scale of your book. Only my show is such a neat example. A perfect netsuké of a campaign.

(P. 126.) "One other south-eastern theatre requires incidental note—Salonika. The despatch of Allied troops thither arose out of a belated and ineffectual attempt to send succour to the Serbs in the autumn of 1915. Three years later it was the spring of an offensive which had vital consequences. But while the retention of a foothold in the Balkans was necessary during the interval for reasons of policy, and of potential strategy, the wisdom and necessity of locking up so many troops, ultimately half a million, in what the Germans ironically called their 'largest internment camp', are open to doubt."

I laughed over your Salonika paragraph.

(P. 126.) The chapter on "The Strategy of 1918" opened here with the comment:
"Any study of the military course of the final year is dependent upon and inseparable from an understanding of the naval situation preceding it. For, in default of an early military decision, the naval blockade had tended more and more to govern the military situation.

"Indeed, if the historian of the future has to select one day as decisive for the outcome of the World War he will probably choose Aug. 2, 1914—before the war, for England, had yet begun—when Mr. Winston Churchill, at 1.25 a.m., sent the order to mobilise the British Navy. That Navy was to win no Trafalgar, but it was to do more than any other factor towards winning the war for the Allies. For the Navy was the instrument of the blockade, and as the fog of war disperses in the clearer light of these post-war years that blockade is seen to assume larger and larger proportions, to be more and more clearly the decisive agency in the struggle. . . .

"Helplessness induces hopelessness, and history attests that loss of hope and not loss of lives is what decides the issue of war."

I am so glad you do the sea-power of the war justice. That is a great honour to your judgment and range. Few soldiers ever see it at all.

(P. 130.) This dealt with the great German offensive of March 1918. The passage to which T.E. referred in particular was, apparently:

"The break-through proved quick, the exploitation rapid. Yet the plan failed. Where did the fault lie? The general criticism subsequent to the event and to the war was that the tactical bias had led Ludendorff to change direction and dissipate his strength, to concentrate on tactical success at the expense of the strategical goal. It seemed, and was said, that the principle was false. But a closer examination of the German documents, since available, and of Ludendorff's own orders and instructions, throws a different light on the question. It would seem, indeed, that the real fault lay in Ludendorff's failure to carry out in practice the new principle he had adopted in theory; that he either did not grasp or shrank from the full implication of this new strategic theory. For, in fact, he dissipated too large a part of his reserves in trying to redeem tactical failure, and hesitated too long over the decision to exploit his tactical successes."

Your study of the last great German push deserves a book to itself. I think it is the real stuff, and you've got hold of the clues to failure. Tactically, of course, our victory was spelt TANKS.

. . .

Early in May I arranged to take a holiday and let T.E. know that I was driving down to Cornwall.

338171 A/C Shaw
R.A.F. Cattewater
Plymouth
7.5.29

Thanks for your letter. I've put in for a week-end which will set me free about 12.45 on Saturday May 11: till nine o'clock at night on Sunday. On Tuesday we have an A.O.C. visiting us (spitting and polishing hard, everybody, now!) but I hope to get the pass nevertheless: and my pocket will be delighted to pass as your guest! It is good of you to suggest it.

Car or bike? Well, that is partly for you to say. If I bring the bike you can run out to wherever you wanted to go: and I can find my own way home. If you take me out, you will have to take me back to some point within bus or train distance of Plymouth, so that I can be in camp before dark. The bike is best, in fine weather: but if it rains you'd have me cleaner in your car!

If bike, then there is no need to bring you down the 3½ miles of by-road to Cattewater. I can meet you (say at 1 o'clock) anywhere within five miles of Plymouth on the road. If car, then you will have to pick me up. Possibilities are

(i) Cattewater, at our Guard Room. If you come in from London then turn left (hairpin) on meeting the first tram-line: cross LAIRA Bridge: take first on right some 400 yards across bridge, turn left under a railway arch: and then God help you. The rest is a maze of bad by-road, for 1½ miles.

(ii) Plymouth. There is a ferry which takes us over to Plymouth, and I could meet you opposite the General Post Office, or at the hotel you had had lunch in, from 2 o'clock onwards. I think you would find this easier than coming to Cattewater, unless you are in a great hurry to get away.

Complicated things, operation orders, as you will agree, where troops of more than one arm have to be conjoined.

We called for T.E. at Cattewater, drove in to Plymouth for lunch, and drove on to Newquay, where I had been many times in boyhood but had not seen since the War. We spent the night at the Atlantic Hotel, where our reception took an amusing turn owing to T.E. being in aircraftman's uniform. While I was telling the porter what luggage to take off the car my wife went upstairs to see the rooms. She made a choice and was then asked, "You'll want a room for your chauffeur?" She, momentarily puzzled, said, "We haven't got one—my husband's driving the car." "But what about the man in uniform?" "Oh, that's a friend." The temperature palpably dropped, and when we went down to dinner we were put at an out-of-the-way table, half hidden behind a pillar from the respectable guests. T.E. signed the hotel register as "T. E. Ross". Next morning we drove out to Bedruthan Steps, back to the Headland at Newquay for lunch, then on to Perranporth and St. Agnes, had tea at Truro, then drove down the river, and back in time to put him on a train for Plymouth that evening.

We crowded an immense amount of talk into that short week-end, and some of the things he told me were of such interest and so fresh to me—I have since learnt that some of the things he told me had not been mentioned even to close friends of his youth—that I jotted them down.

Born at Tremadoc. . . . Paid for own schooling by scholarships. Took history at Oxford, but studied war since about 16 years of age, because filled with idea of freeing a people and had chosen Arabs as only suitable ones left. Began studies in Risorgimento and the Condottieri. Translated extracts from Procopius and other authors. Interests archaeology, military history, etc., and took 1st in history on war questions —originality in treating.

Enlisted in artillery about 1906—before going to Oxford— . . . and did 8 months before being bought out. Contrast with present, especially drink and roughness.

Enlisted after war in R.A.F., was thrown out in 1922 by Sam Hoare on discovery, then to Tank Corps, and back to R.A.F. by Buchan's influence with Baldwin against Hoare's will. Trenchard good friend.

Debarred from France, Turkey, etc. In India, never went out of camp at Karachi, Peshawar, or Miranshah (1 flight station) except when flying over hills in aeroplane. Indian government spiteful. But never sick and never too hot.

On return saw Trenchard, who asked him where he would like to go and suggested Scotland as out of way. But too cold, and so chose Cattewater. Immense admiration for Trenchard. Geoffrey Salmond's capacity for detail. Trenchard's no eyewash in inspections—clean copy-books! March-past—"There will not be any today"—after a C.O. had spent weeks in preparation.

Flew 2000 hours in war with 7 write-off crashes. Broken collar-bone, wrist, and several ribs. Has rib sticking into lung —so one lung useless and bleeds if heavy exercise.

Often took over controls while in air but only once landed and then took off under-carriage. . . . Now wants to fly again in commander's Moth. Doing Schneider Cup arrangements. Going Scilly Isles by motor-boat to arrange base.

Brough, motor manufacturer, whom he has helped in design, gives him each new model (part-worn) whenever one comes out. Has done 94 m.p.h. on road on present one. Averaged 54 m.p.h. Durham-Cranwell—highest average, but usually reckons on 40 m.p.h. average. Slows to 35–40 at crossroads and careful in traffic and corners. Love of speed.

Has cottage near Wool, now let to Sgt for several years, 15 acres in Epping Forest and use of attic in Barton St. Westminster—favourite part of London.

Reason why does not live at All Souls—because £200 a year too little, and need to maintain decent appearance and hospitality. Ideal is to have £300 a year, for single man. "Enough for place in town and in country". How to get, because won't use name "Lawrence" for "family reasons".

Does a lot of foreign translations, "better than writing". Has written two other books.

Service in R.A.F. expires in 1935 and doubts whether can last until then, because feeling old and life hard. Trenchard insisted on right to discharge him at any time and so, as sop, gave him right to leave without any claim of Government upon him.

Discussed MacPhail's essay on him in *Three Persons*—L. spoke of MacPhail's capacity for misunderstanding the point, e.g., the Arabs were essentially humane; the only time they were not it was at T.E.'s orders in avenging Turkish brutality.

.   .   .

T.E. expressed his admiration, fundamentally, for Lenin as the one man who had conceived, applied, and recast a theory. Of Mussolini he was dubious, emphasising that he had failed to create a successor.

T.E. said he never played any game—disliked them partly on competitive ground. So much did he dislike competition that although he had cultivated a garden at his air station, when others followed suit and the C.O. in consequence was led to offer a prize, T.E. gave up tending his own to avoid competing.

.   .   .

Told of his encounter with Thurtle and Maxton when he called at House of Commons on his return from India.

.   .   .

Jessie happened to indulge in one of her rhapsodies about policemen—T.E. said she would have a less idyllic view of them if she belonged to the poorer classes and saw them from that angle.[1]

We talked of writing as we stood on the rocks at the end of the headland; he remarked that he never had difficulty in finding words to describe what he saw—they surged up. I said that I often found it difficult to find the exactly right words I wanted; like a bath with a narrow outlet, there was more floating in my mind than I could get out easily. He said that descriptiveness came easy to him; also analysis, but he lacked the power of synthesis, which I had.[2]

[1]See R.G., p. 132, l. 10.
[2]*Ibid.*, p. 64, l. 2.

In writing him a few days later from St. Ives, I expressed a wish that he would let his friends help him in some way that would not infringe his scruples.

> 338171 A/C Shaw
> RAF. Cattewater
> Plymouth
> 17.V.29

I, too, enjoyed those two days immensely. I haven't talked war for years: and civilised persons are not common even in the R.A.F. So it was altogether excellent. I only fear that we chattered too constantly and bored Mrs. Liddell-Hart. She hasn't had the vexation of serving under Bols or Archie Murray, or the pleasure of Trenchard: and so couldn't properly follow our short-hand remarks. Please apologise for me, if she feels she had an overdose of tactics!

On the cash question, I'm afraid things aren't so simple as that. Life can be divided into two categories: leisure, which is *hors concours:* and work. Leisure, to my mind, is to have £300 a year, assured, with nothing to do for it except to go on breathing. Failing that, one falls back on work, and I find the R.A.F., as I now live, the best work possible. I could get more pay for other work, but will not change. Leisure is a different thing, and if I could afford it, I would enjoy it straight away. Only no one alive will assure one of £300 a year for nothing at all. Why should they?

My R.A.F. life seems reasonably sure until 1935: and if my father's family felt inclined, my dream of £300 assured might come off between now and then. If not there might be an accidental drop of money from some kindly Heaven: or the Epping Forest Commissioners might cough up £7000: or some venerable unknown admirer might leave me a fortune: or one of my legs might drop off, with old age, and a compassionate Government put me on the civil list. With so many possibilities a fellow needn't despair so far as to start working for himself! I haven't ever done that yet, thank God!

Does this sound flippant? I hope not. Being a lone hand I haven't anyone to care for, and feel quite confident that I'll never reproach myself for improvidence: and meanwhile I get quite a lot of vividness out of every-day living. Which is more than nine people out of ten can say. I value it more than the comfort they have chosen.

My "notes" on RAF reform-trifles will be sent to Trays Hill[1]; not to spoil your holiday. The weather has been noble the last two days. I hope St. Ives is good, & the car performing suitably. Au revoir.

I was so much struck by the wealth of knowledge shown in his notes on my study of the Indirect Approach in history and subsequent amplification of them in our talks, and also by his evident revival of interest in military questions, that I suggested he might write a preface.

> 338171 A/C Shaw
> R.A.F. Cattewater
> Plymouth
> 6.VI.29

I began this letter as you see the date above: then Incursions and Invasions drove me (i) to Portsmouth (ii) to London (iii) to Sussex: so now your second letter has crossed my intention.

I sat on your preface suggestion (it was a great compliment you paid me) for quite a while: putting down on a sheet of paper headings of what I might say if I wrote such an introduction: and it dawned on me as I worked at it that I had so little to say that it was not worth saying. To express agreement would help nobody: and compliments would be out of place. The introduction should be useful and stimulating. I don't believe in anything strongly enough to say it with conviction.

So on Thursday I sat down to thank you, and say no. I'm afraid you'll think me rather a useless person to do a job. I cut myself too completely out of the action world, and haven't a leg left in the business.

As I try to write this my silly head keeps on nodding forward asleep on to the paper, and then the pen scrabbles wildly. Please forgive the mess. Dead tired.

The notes are half-ready. I'll send them as soon as possible. Very good of you to help with them.

[1]In our talk he had mentioned various small things, irritating or humiliating, which by their effect on those who were serving in the ranks of the Air Force tended to react detrimentally on recruiting the type of young man that was needed. I had suggested that if he would jot down some of these points I would bring them to notice privately.

"Tray's Hill" was the name of my house.

Corfe
14.VII.29

I'm here, temporarily settling some problems concerning my Dorsetshire cottage. Going back this afternoon. I hope this letter will arrive in time. Your wire was sent on to me.

1. Directly, the C.A.S. might abolish, by a word, bayonets and walking-out canes. Bayonets because they are costly (16/-each), take long to maintain (about 1 hr. per month, except where a buffing-wheel is available) ugly, and useless. I'd call them dangerous, for there was an idiot Squadron Leader who used to practice open-order attack, in France: waving a sword himself. A fool like that might easily throw away a squadron. Aircraft are a long-distance weapon, and bayonets are out of place in them.

2. The walking-out cane I can leave to common sense. You saw mine: and saw that it's a silly bodkin of a thing, no use as stick or weapon, and no ornament. It was designed, I believe, to keep troops' hands out of their pockets: but R.A.F. tunics and breeches have inaccessible pockets, in which no man can keep his hands. Whereas hands and stick both go into our overcoat pockets.

The C.A.S. (Trenchard) has already done two or three of the reforms I urged on him, and repeated to you. So the job is lightened.

3. Kit Inspection is another bore. It's supposed to be held monthly, and troops have to show all their kit. This is ridiculous. Our working dress is inspected daily, our walking-out dress weekly, in the normal course of duty. All that is required (besides these two suits, in case of active service which is the justification of kit inspection) is spare socks, spare shirts, pants. Instead of laying everything, which confuses the eye of the Inspecting Officer, and involves everything being very tightly folded, to be got on the bed, troops should (once a quarter) leave out on their beds their spare underclothing, and go off to work. And the inspection should be done by the Flight Officer and his N.C.O., at leisure. It shouldn't be a parade, or a beauty-show: but an inspection to make sure that our normally-invisible kit was serviceable and complete. There is no need for us standing by. That makes us hot and ashamed, and the decent officers feel like nosy-Parkers, and avoid looking at us.

4. The last thing is a very small point. In the navy, an officer or

N.C.O. entering the men's mess takes his hat off, whether on duty or not. The airmen would like this to become the general rule in the R.A.F. It is in some stations, where the C.O. is ex-navy.

There were many other things I'd like to talk about: marriage-establishment rosters, overseas-rosters, posting of airmen in England to the stations most convenient to them (a Scotchman in Plymouth: home fare—£5: an Englishman in Leuchars: ditto). Pillion-riding on motor cycles (airmen are the only people in England forbidden it: not soldiers, not sailors. It's rather an insult to what we fondly hope is the most dangerous service). The week-end pass (I'd make after duty Saturday till Reveille Monday free for all men not warned for duty. Every station keeps a duty crew). I'd make an Air Ministry regulation about plain clothes. At present one C.O. allows them, and another restricts them. Chaos and irritation. It is a very valued privilege, I'm sorry to say. Church parade. This is the most annoying parade of the week. Couldn't it be made voluntary? I think I could get the consent of the two archbishops to that, if the Air Ministry is shy of the C. of E.

29.VII.29

Alas: I serve everyone that way, now, in letters. You see I am in arrears with my Form VI and my Logs and Indents: and it feels wrong, somehow, to touch private paper while my R.A.F. paper is overdue: so between one way and another nothing gets done. Each day a new wave of R.A.F. stuff (not by any means all paper: many actual activities) rolls over: and we begin again sorting over yesterday's debris after it clears.

It was very good of you to have tried, tactfully, to soothe Lord Thomson's troubled mind.[1] I wonder what has stung him? He offered me the R.A.F. History[2]: yes. I was then in the Tank Corps, and had been for two years asking for permission to return to the R.A.F. The History was an appalling job, which had killed Ralegh, and frightened Hogarth away. You know how little I esteem myself as a writer. Nevertheless I agreed to do it, if they would let me back into the

[1]Lord Thomson was then Secretary of State for Air; he had come into office in June. Lunching with him soon after, I had found him prejudiced against T.E.'s presence in the Air Force. Knowing that I was a friend of his, Thomson had told me of some things over which, he considered, T.E. had caused offence.

[2]See R.G., p. 28, thirteenth line from bottom.

R.A.F. at the end of the two years it would take: even I would do it free of charge, to this end. Only they wouldn't. I'm glad, now, because I got back without the labour of the History.

Game I don't know, but they all say that he's a very nice fellow. I believe he is leaving the R.A.F. at once. He's not likely to have told Lord T. anything good or bad, on my account.

The Crusades were geographically very important to me: as an invader across the same patch of country. They have no general interest, and you would not gain anything (on the head of "principles of war") from their study. Only they do tell one how to conquer Syria from the East. So does Mohammed.

As for coming out of here, even for a night—it seems impossible. My last 2 week-ends have been cancelled, by work turning up. After September 7th, perhaps, I tell myself and everyone else. Only it will not be true, I suppose. I'd rather do R.A.F. stuff than private work, that's the truth of it: and so I gladly let everything slide when they press me. No Odyssey since Easter—and I've a contract to finish that next summer! Ever so sorry.

That autumn, soon after the Schneider Trophy race, the storm burst. This international seaplane race, with its assurance of new record speeds, excited public attention to a remarkable degree and drew to the Portsmouth area a vast crowd of spectators. It was inevitable in such circumstances that it would provide an opportunity for those who resented T.E.'s normally inconspicuous presence in the Air Force. For he was closely concerned with the arrangements for the race, as clerk to his commanding officer, Sydney Smith, who was a member of all the three committees which shared the responsibility. Thereby T.E. came into undesired prominence.

I had been away from London since July on my usual tour of the Army training, but came back in late September for a few days before taking a holiday. The evening after my return T.E. dropped in to see me and told me that he was under sentence of expulsion from the Air Force—by the original arrangement, his contract of service could be terminated at any time by either party. He had come up to London to make a personal protest against the decision, and I gathered from him that certain friends were interceding on his behalf. Next day I did what I could to help, and was lunching with one of the authorities concerned when he was called to the telephone by a call from a governmental quarter that was aimed, I gathered, in the same direction. A day or two later I heard from T.E. that he had been reprieved—I cannot remember whether I learnt of this by telephone, letter, or visit. But I did not hear full details until a month later when he came in to see me after I had returned from my holiday. This time I found time to make notes of some of the points he mentioned, and had a particular reason for doing so.

TALK WITH T. E. SHAW

He blew in just before 7 p.m. and despite objection about uniform stayed to dinner, and late.

T.E. came to-night with puttees inside out—his method of changing and hiding mud after motor ride—as he never wears overalls lest they spoil pleasure of riding—free and light.

T.E. had interview with Trenchard (not on Thursday Sept. 27, as arranged, but) on Monday Sept. 30. . . . T. told him he was reprieved on condition that henceforth he did an ordinary A.C's job solely; never went out of the country, even to Ireland; never visited or spoke to any "great men"— e.g., Winston, Austen, Birkenhead, Sassoon, Lady Astor (i.e., all politicals). G.B.S. not banned—and when he told G.B.S. the latter rather annoyed at not being counted.

T.E. feels that R.A.F. is foolish not to get more than daily 3/-d. worth out of him. Had, however, only done ordinary A.C's job until Schneider Cup. Real cause of trouble was that he was seen talking to Balbo at Schneider meeting. Because R.A.F. put a working party on to their own slipway to clean it and left Italian one slippery with green scum. And T.E. got Italian slipway cleaned at Balbo's request.

. . . .

Talking of his enemies, T.E. said, "Enemies never do one any real harm; that is only done by friends".

T.E. met Philip Sassoon recently and told him, "I mustn't speak to you".

—— intervened by suggesting to Air Ministry, etc., that if T.E. were to be thrown out of R.A.F. he might go to Arabia. Frightened them.

.   .   .

T.E. says people never recognise him in uniform (!) but often in mufti. Cannot walk through London without 6 or 7 stopping him. Doorkeeper at W.O. still remembers him.

He wanders about London streets by night. . . .

He had been to Motor Show with G.B.S. to-day—G.B.S. chose it because half crown entrance to-day. G.B.S. a dashing driver, in 6-year-old Vauxhall that he has put in ditch several times—can only steer one way. Now hesitating between Lanchester and Bentley. . . .

.   .   .

G.B.S. once said to T.E., "Why have I never thought of your idea [of no review copies] to advertise my plays?"

.   .   .

T.E. hates Paris and Frenchwomen. Likes American women. French countrywomen most capable, but hard and grasping.

He has made no progress with translating Odyssey yet. Must get down to it, as needs money.

.   .   .

He is being painted again by Augustus John—had three sittings already down at Fordingbridge 10–4. Made to sit *absolutely still*—which he finds no trouble. Is being given oil sketch for his trouble. (His face in sketch looks as if pounded and discoloured, and the tunic is like no tunic ever seen.) John always had something original to say on everything—

never repeats others' opinion. He thinks John only painter of to-day with greatness.

Has fondness for picture galleries, but no talent himself— because no technique. That's why he turned to writing, as only art which required no technique.[1] No trouble to find words to describe things—wished he could have gone on Far East cruise with Cave-Browne-Cave.

.   .   .

He has only had 2 skids in last 5 years. Once at Cranwell, bringing back sausages for supper and struck ice patch at 45 m.p.h. in dark—he went to one grass border and even-tually found bike on other. Second time going up Highgate Hill (just before going to India), skidded on tramlines and sheered all side off the bike.

T.E. agreeable to me writing book as Cape ask, but doubts whether sufficient material, unless Alan Dawnay will help.

He laughingly said he often thinks when he writes a letter, "This will come in my 'Life and Letters' " and so tears up and sends a telegram instead—not much use to print tele-grams!

He hates letters and yet certain fascination in opening them. Takes an occasional wet day at Cattewater to answer twenty or so, but lets majority answer themselves.

He remarked that it didn't matter how much garbled stuff was written about him—wilder the better—but danger when written by friends, because truth hurts.

Alan Dawnay, different to his brother though outwardly a Guardsman.[2] . . . Always immaculate, even in desert he had polished boots. . . . D. acted as G. 1 and actually was senior officer of force.

[1] See R.G., p. 183, l. 7.
[2] *Ibid.*, p. 51, l. 4.

Vickery left early because he thought service in Arabian show was professional suicide—wanted decorations. Vulgar, and lowered white prestige; but clever and could even read and write Arab.

.   .   .

T.E. cannot speak Arabic now; had vocabulary of about 5,000 words (?) but could only speak ungrammatically.[1]

. . . He would like to see Allenby again but doesn't like to call unless bidden. Allenby very much the great chief.

.   .   .

T.E. admires Maurice Hankey, who knows so many secrets yet never portentous, and can be always interesting without giving anything away.

.   .   .

T.E. argued that ordinary English peasant's vocabulary is far more than 500 words.

His A.Q. article of 1920 was thought to be above heads, and beyond vocabulary, of ordinary soldier-reader!

He suggested that I couldn't write a book of more than 20 pages on his method of war.

A few days before this talk I had been approached by Jonathan Cape to write a book that would—

"supplement and round off the picture presented first by Lawrence himself in *Revolt in the Desert*, and next by Robert Graves. What has so far been left undone is an estimate not only of Lawrence and his work, but of the relation of this work to the immense affairs of which it was an important part, and in which Lawrence was one of the leading figures; its relation, too, to the course which events have subsequently taken."

[1]See R.G., p. 57, l. 19.

The special argument for me undertaking it, as conveyed by David Higham, was that—

"Such a book is quite certain to be written sooner or later. Whoever writes it, it is bound to have a considerable circulation, and that will mean, quite probably, that a bad book— one quite probably which doesn't tell the truth—will be read by many, and whatever steps might be taken to refute it, a good deal of misrepresentation would survive into history: and one feels that history, not only general but military history, ought not to be so ill-served. Cape are definitely of this opinion and it is one of the strongest reasons why they, who published the two earlier authentic books, want to be the publishers of this later one when it is written: for this reason, also, they will want such a book to be written by you with your standing as a military historian—and indeed as a more general historian also now—and with your special knowledge of the subject."

This argument overcame my original hesitation, and I agreed to consult T.E. about the proposal—as I intimated that I would only consider it if he were willing. I had an immediate opportunity to do so, as he came to see me on October 25th. He proved quite agreeable to me undertaking it, and seemed to like the idea of achieving a proper historical account of events, although he expressed a doubt whether I could find sufficient material unless I could obtain assistance from other sources, Alan Dawnay especially.

After further thought on the question next day, I wrote to T.E. to enquire how far he would be able to help, and to give him a fresh chance of turning down the idea of such a book if he felt any objection to it. His reply showed, as so often, a characteristic reaction, if only a partial one, from the ready response of a few days earlier. The letter follows:

[Posted London]
28.X.29

I'm here for an hour, and found your note. The weather has turned against motor cycles, at last.

Cape is foolish, to go on exploiting my vein. The public will vomit when it feels the surfeit come. However.

You know the tenderness of the R.A.F. towards me, and must realise that I dare not associate myself with anyone who brings out books or articles upon me. They imagine, apparently, that I pay for all "appearances" in the Press.

Of course I'd do what I could, privately, to help you to avoid errors: but your difficulty will be that your sole source is my Seven Pillars. That was not intended as a military manual. It leaves out vital parts (vital as tactics: not as narrative) and slurs lots of things. The S.P. is a private publication: copyright. You can't quote it: and if I keep it private (at financial loss to myself), so I must prevent other people publishing a paraphrase or re-hash of it. "Revolt in the Desert" doesn't matter. S.P. does.

If Alan Dawnay has enough materials to let you get the other sides of the story, then it might well be the subject of a military thesis of some value. If not—And I haven't the time, or the inclination, or the heart, to dig very much into my own memories of those times for anyone's sake.

Sorry not to be explicit: but it's as explicit as I feel. I don't care a bit, either way.

(No less characteristically, when I began serious work on the book three years later—after browsing in the subject meantime as opportunity offered—T.E. gave me far more help, and took a far greater interest in the book, than I had ever dreamed that he would. Even then, however, he would continue to have intermittent reactions—thus, after approving, and suggesting numerous personal additions to, the first and second drafts he had a sudden qualm on the score that it was too personal; he came to see me, began by suggesting radical modifications, went through it again pencil in hand, and ended up by deleting only one insignificant passage besides a few minor changes of phrase.)

8.1.30

You win. I forgot Christmas and New Year. Surely I should have written to say that I hoped they would go well. Those two periods are the most critical of the modern year.

I passed them quietly, in an almost empty camp, doing my weekly spell as "duty crew". Nobody wanted us. So I sat in a luke-warm office and slaved at Homer. Soon, ever so soon, I shall have finished half of his or her poem, the Odyssey, and pouch £100 on account. Hallelujah.

Apart from which I have no news, and have done nothing. For two months my only outings have been in search of haircuts, to please our very humorous S.M. I hope the new house grows on you, and that Sherman is nearing his production-moment.[1]

338171 A/C Shaw
R.A.F. Mount Batten
Plymouth
5.3.30

I spend every spare hour I have now doing Homer; and shall do yet for months. It is a waste of time, but profitable in the money sense: and reading the Greek so carefully is good mental exercise.

This preamble neatly explains why I have taken three weeks to read "Sherman": for you will have understood that I would not answer it till I had read it.

The striking thing about it is the power of writing. From you one expects military knowledge, and a sense of reality, so far as campaigns are concerned—and gets them: but this Sherman is really fine biography, wherever the dust of battle settles a little bit and shows the man. I think it is an extraordinarily good book: and after reading it again next month I shall know it.

[1]This was a study of the American Civil War woven round the man whom I had come to regard as the most interesting and significant soldier of that period. I had actually finished the book in the summer, but although I had discussed it with T.E. I had forborne to bother him with it in the proof stage. Although published in America in the autumn it did not appear in England until February, when I sent him a copy.

That may strike you as a bit perfunctory: but it is partly your fault. You have written it so clearly that most of the reviewers will forget you and think only of Sherman, as he is so very lucently shown in your pages. The reality of the man, and his uncommon genius, and the strange conditions amidst which he fought::::: altogether I put this very high among military books. You have never done anything with more scale and sense of country, and with a more living personality to pull it all together. I give it absolutely full marks.

Your honesty in suppressing footnotes and authorities is beyond praise. Indeed they are slovenly things.

No, I had never heard of Forrest before I read your book. He must be somebody, for your prose always breaks over him like a rock in the sea whenever you come to mention him.

Saxe gives you better stuff, though, does he not? Saxe is so human in his writings.

Marlborough is a great study, too. I think he was a rare fighter and strange fellow.

"Her Privates We" is by Frederic Manning, son of a Colonial Office official (overseas): an exquisite, and an exquisite writer. I wonder how he really got on in the ranks. Too fine a mind, I think, for real contact: but he has drawn a wonderful picture of the other ranks as I know them.

I hope Greece shines upon you, as it has always done to me. A magic country, except in Piraeus and Corinth and Missolonghi. Prepare Mrs. Liddell Hart for landscape of extraordinary purity of line. Greek hills are conscious works of art, I think. She will enjoy their shapes and colours.

About this time there was a debate in the House of Commons in which a number of military and naval peers hotly denounced the inhumanity of "air control" on the frontiers of the Empire. As their connection with the older services raised a doubt whether their view was impartial, and their motives purely humanitarian, I was moved to explore this question for myself. As one step I tried to find out what truth there was in the assertion that air control was "stirring up feelings of bitter hate and resentment", and whether the natives regarded it as worse than the intrusion of a land force. I consulted a number of people who were acquainted with the native point of view, writing to T.E. among others.

The letter of his which follows is the answer to this. It also refers to another book of mine. After finishing *Sherman* the previous summer I had completed a history of the war of 1914–18 which was the product of studies spread out over several years. It was published under the title of *The Real War*.

Plymouth
26.VI.30

Alas, I got the Real War weeks ago. From before that date till now I have not opened a book to read it. The weather? Malaise? A great deal to do? Odyssey? I do not know: there are so many causes.

I was at the Shaws' last week end, and they asked if I was reading it, saying it was particularly good in its characters of generals. I expect it is. O for a wet week, to drive me back upon books again! Only in summer time, by fits and starts, books seem impossible things.

Arab reactions to air bombing? I think they feel our own intense irritation and vain rage at an attack to which there can be no response. There is something cold, chilling, impersonally fateful about air bombing. It is not punishment, but a misfortune from heaven striking the community.

The R.A.F. recognises this, and bombs only after 24 hours notice given. So the damage falls only on immovables.

It is of course infinitely more merciful than police or military action, as hardly anyone is ever killed—and the killed are as likely to be negligible women and children, as the really important men. Only this is too oriental a mood for us to feel very clearly. An Arab would rather offer up his wife than himself, to expiate a civil offence!

[Postmark Plymouth]
11/XII/30

I'm working at the Odyssey like a tiger, in great hope of finishing it next spring: it takes all my nights and half-days, and I have promised myself to have no holiday till it is over. Barring business interruptions it should be over in April: and then for a lazy summer, with full pocket and no liabilities! The cloud on the horizon is that threatening Schneider Cup—but perhaps it will fizzle.

The Real War is out-and-out the best war-history yet. It is packed with stuff and yet readable. Only I have not read it through. It sits on my table, and I pick out of it, like a plum a month, some side-show in which I feel interest and swallow it. The French campaign is rather too large. I cannot read more than its episodes. I admire the technical skill in which you have kept your main personalities as tie-rods to hold the periods together. The characters make it lively, and unlike a book of reference—which yet it is, under another aspect.

Till Spring, then. I hope you and Mrs. L-H will find some good place to spend some winter-days in, chasing sunshine or warmth. This England is depressing, now.

Mount Batten
13 April [1931]

I'm a poor correspondent, I fear. Many times I have been on the edge of writing to say that your war-history has become one of my constant reference books, for the main war; and that its chapters on the side-shows are so crisply black-and-white as to make exciting stories of them. Only you know all this, and I'd ten thousand times rather tell it you by mouth.

Now arrive these two letters, and by a chance they find me at Mount Batten. My two-year war with Air Ministry over the type of motor boats suited to attend seaplanes is bearing results now, and experimental boats are being offered by contractors. I've become a marine expert, and test the things for them, acquiring incidentally and by degrees quite a knowledge of the S.W. coast of England! A minor consequence is extensive absence from home, and a major (secondary and indirect) consequence is the paralysis of my Odyssey translation. It is stuck at Book XXI, and I begin to despair of finishing it. Motor-boat-testing is an all-time job, and leaves one too exhausted to write.

I hope you have a good holiday. Myself, I am craving only for a little home-life, at the moment. You must arrange to include Plymouth some day in your orbit of duties, and come speed-boating with me. It is fun, for a time.

The P.E.N. suggestion is rather astonishing. A million times "no" and thank them very much. I thought they always guested writers—and they can hardly call me that on the strength of a war memoir written twelve years ago and only privately printed—or are writers and celebrities all running short and the second rank now due for turns? It is a queer invitation: but such things do happen. I must tell you some day of offers I twice got for honorary degrees at Scotch universities. My second reason, above, is operative in Scotland. You did, I fancy, "guess my reaction" successfully: only don't be too brusque with Ould. I do not know him, but he may be decent.

The Foch book cannot, I fear, be greatly interesting. He was rather a drab creature, surely, with more teeth than brains. It was irony that made him the successful general of the last phase.

After finishing my history of the war, I had started on what was in the nature of a biographical supplement to it—a study of the actual workings of the high command as seen through the eyes, and expressed through the mouth, of Marshal Foch. This occupied me so fully that I had little time to think of seeing friends, and contact lapsed. But in July I was to visit the artillery practice on the Okehampton ranges, and wrote to let T.E. know.

15.VII.31

I'm glad Foch is finished: and that you are out of Germany in this tremulous moment. It is a time to be at home, apparently. I wonder what will happen.

Today's Wednesday: we are rather troubled by the Prince of Wales being in Plymouth. Tomorrow you move to Okehampton, which is near. On Friday I move to London, to do some trustee business, and I am due back here on Sunday midnight. So that prevents our meeting, I fear, for I cannot get either Friday daytime or Monday daytime off, at short notice—or indeed anyhow, for long week-ends are tabu in the training period.

I am sorry, for I have had too much work this year and feel stale: —a bad feeling, for I have that Odyssey to finish by September and no heart for it!

Telegram from Plymouth, 17/7/31:

Railway journey arriving Plymouth 8 p.m. Sunday.

T.E., however, came back to Plymouth earlier than expected, and we spent the evening together. This time I find that I again made some notes of our talk—but only a few odd ones.

TALK WITH T.E.

PLYMOUTH, 18 JULY 1931

Met him at the railway station early in evening—off train from London. A woman had also come to meet him in car, unasked, so he had to put her off first. Then we went to the Grand as before.

Talked of how he had left the Colonial Office in 1921—had promised Winston Churchill, lightheartedly, he would come back if the Middle East blew up; not otherwise.

How he had written 30,000 words in 22 hours when working on *Seven Pillars*—had worked 12-hour stretches usually, without food.

Talked of my book on Foch—and of how he never had much opinion of him from the time when, in his youthful reading, he discovered Foch had taken a whole big section of his book, the *Principes de Guerre*, from a German writer.

Of Henry Williamson, whose work he admires.

Of his own love of music.

Of how he had been commissioned by an American, Bruce Rogers, to do a prose translation of the Odyssey—for £800. He had received half. Wanted in a year—he had said it depended on circumstances—perhaps by 1929.

Of how he spent his leave in his two-roomed cottage near Wool.

Of his idea of speedboats for the R.A.F., and how he had

got it taken up by the Air Ministry (crew of 2; 30 m.p.h.; glassed in; 17 ordered, at about £1800 each). Of a trip to Penzance in very rough sea.

I asked if he had flown again recently. He said he felt absolved, since Thomson and Trenchard had gone, from his promise not to fly, but had been debarred for 15 months, and now felt uneasy in the air.

Plymouth
4/XI/31

This is the penalty of my going away—typewritten letters to everybody. It means that there are so many letters on my table waiting reply that I have to tackle them in my office (R.A.F.) time. Rattling away on a typewriter sounds like work to them, so I can do it hour after hours; whereas to stop the noise and write would be obviously scrounging.

I got your first letter just the day I went away; & as usual I went away all standing, leaving my table just as it was. Then when I got back there was your second in its place among its contemporaries. The Post Corporal and I have evolved a marvellous system of arrangement, by which I get mail in its historical order, however long my delay. I had marked it for reply, by not throwing it into the fire basket—I do all my filing in the office stove—when up turned No. 3, yesterday.

So I have departed from strict justice, and am knocking this off to you before its fellows.

My travels are not yet over. I go away again on Friday week, for about ten days, and am to test another motor-boat engine after that, before Christmas. So it looks as though I should be booked fairly until the year ends.

One thing the outdoor work does allow—plenty of evening. After work we must write up our logs, and eat, and the rest of the night is ours, till bed-time, and bed-time is ours, too. No private bugles blow for us.

Foch: you astonish me with the news of it. I had an idea it was for the spring. Yes, I would very much like to see it; only you have given me so many books. Why not lend it? Then if it is as I hoped, I'll have

to buy it, after returning you yours. I have ten days here, as a mathe-
matician would deduce from two paragraphs up.

Do you like Foch now? When you spoke of it, you were anxious not
to attack or demolish, and puzzled how to make him appear anyhow
big.

I hope this financial season has not hit you hard. They started out
by cutting a quarter of my pay away, but after a naval demonstration
let me off with 10%. Good for the Navy, we thought, for we profited
by them, and kept our reputation for loyalty, too. Even the 10%
makes a difference, I find.

However some storm losses are inevitable.

> Myrtle Cottage
> Hythe
> Southampton
> 25.IV.32

Indeed I am a sinner: yet not so bad as you judge, for I wrote at
length about your Foch. That was last year, in my last visit to Plymouth, between two spells in the boat-yard here. The R.A.F. needed
to re-equip itself with new motor-boats, and chose me to test and tune
the new boats, and to watch over their building.

Foch is too far behind me, now, for that letter to be re-written.
The gist of it was that you left me with a better opinion of Foch, the
man, than I had had. You demolish him thoroughly as a soldier:
as a politician he needed no other evidence than his own to discredit
him. But as a human being he came out well and honourably in what
you wrote.

I met the old boy only in 1919, when he was only a frantic pair
of moustaches. So I was glad to see the better side.

Surely I sent you the letter? Did it miscarry, to a wrong address—
you are as nomadic as myself, and I never know where to imagine
you—or did you get it and forget it? At least I remember writing it.
Not a real critique: but enough to bring out my feelings. You touched
on Colin, I think, too: but my memory is too full of chines, transoms
and engine torques, which have driven all books out of it. Sherman,
being more in perspective, made a rounder and firmer biography.

My Scotch visit was a 3-week affair only, to deliver one of the new boats to its station.

Mrs. L-H? This is her postscript. I hope she finds Geneva a little less dull than I remember it. Isn't there a Conference there, on Armaments? I faintly remember my friend Dawnay going from his cottage in the Forest here either to Geneva or Lausanne. Happy Swiss: they get all the conferences!

(P.S.) Do you "Telegraph" yet? Is it happy on its new lines, and prosperous?

I should be here till late in June, I think.

> Myrtle Cottage
> Hythe
> Southampton
> 30.VIII.32

This new book of yours,[1] which reached me yesterday after it and I had wandered in two diverging orbits for half a century—is amazing. I have only read 116 pages, and only read those for the first time, in my ranging way which when it finds a book worth study gallops over the ground for a bird's eye view, and returns at leisure for study: but if there is nothing whatever in the last 2/3, still it will remain a memorable book. Your reasonableness is so utterly sweet that your deadliness is half-concealed. I have not before seen anyone mould and occupy history and geography so much to clarify his own ends.

The last chapter that I have read is your study of the metaphysics of military terminology—and it delights me wholly. So clear, so simple, and so gay. You have mastered the art of expression in your searching after the power to convert souls. It is fine as writing, and would be fine writing, if it were only a description of how to brew hops.

I wonder what the rest of the book is, but shall not know for ever so long, as I go off again tomorrow. The wandering Jew, poor mug, did his best: but his lack of mechanisation makes his career look stagnant

---

[1] "This new book" was *The British Way in Warfare*. The chapter to which he specially refers was one on "Strategy Re-framed". In the preface to the book I had specially warned readers that "there is one chapter, V, which means effort in the reading. It is, for example, unsuited to quick digestion just before bed—unless perhaps it is used intentionally as a potion to induce sleep".

beside mine. I didn't want you to keep wondering what or where I was (and where are you?) until fate settles me for a week here again. I keep it as an address, and here books and letters pile up in waiting; so many books and so many letters that I only open a fraction of each pile. . . .

I may overestimate the goodness and value of your book because it hits my tender spot. In the Seven Pillars I wrote a chapter on theory, which was an expression, in terms of Arabia, of very much of what you argue about the aim of war. Of course yours is war proper, and mine was a tussle in a turnip field: but the lesser sometimes mirrors the large.

I send this to the Daily Telegraph, in the hope that you are still on its pay-roll. These are difficult days, and you will not sell more than 5000 copies of this book, I fear. It will be widely read abroad.

We are lucky in England to have anyone who can put the case so clearly. If only our mandarins could read.

(P.S.) My regards to Mrs. L-H. I hope she and you have been able to enjoy some of this year's good weather. It has been a wonderful summer. I have web feet now, and live on the water, in motor boats.

Although I had taken opportunities from time to time to gather sidelights on the history of the Arab Revolt, it was not until April 1932 that I took the first serious steps towards the book that had been long in prospect: obtaining permission to consult certain sources of information. Even then, my annual tour of the army training interrupted the process of exploration, but by April 1933 I had sufficient data to begin the actual writing of the book. However, I had not gone far with the draft before I found the need to consult T.E. on various points—and wrote to him accordingly. The book might be described as the result of three years' browsing, a year of intermittent digging, three months of writing, four months of revising and adding.

QUERIES—I

(Answered in writing)

1. When did you begin to read books on the theory of war as distinct from history?

In my sixteenth year, when at school at Oxford—about 1903 (?).

2. What books did you begin with?

The usual school-boy stuff—Creasy, Henderson, Mahan, Napier, Coxe: then technical treatises on castle-building and destruction: Procopius, Demetrius Poliorcetes and others which I have forgotten. I also read nearly every manual of chivalry. Remember that my "period" was the Middle Ages, always.

3. When did you come to Clausewitz?

Not till 1906 or 1907, I think: and from Clausewitz, being dissatisfied, I worked back to Napoleon.

4. When about in the sequence did you reach (a) Saxe and (b) Guibert?

I read some French study of Napoleon's Italian campaign, and then browsed in his despatches, a series of about 25 vols. These interested me in his text-books, and so they got me to Bourcet (?), Guibert, and Saxe, in that order. Then I read other "manuals of arms" of the 18th century.

5. Was it ever a habit of yours to study battlefields, and if so when and what?

Yes, I made a series of maps of them, and visited Rocroi, Crecy, Agincourt, Malplaquet, Sedan and two other Franco-German War places whose names I forget. But my interests were mainly mediaeval, and in pursuit of them I went to every 12th century castle in France, England and Wales, and went elaborately into siege-manoeuvres, via Viollet-le-Duc! I also tried to get an idea of the bigger movements, and saw Valmy and its neighbourhood, and tried to refight the whole of Marlborough's wars.

6. When did you first see Greece?

Not till after I had finished with Oxford, I think perhaps 1910 or 1911. Three or four visits between then and 1914.

7. On what side were you at School?

They wanted me to stand for a Maths. scholarship: so I did rather too much of that till nearly 18—when I suddenly changed to history, and after six months of that tried for a history scholarship at St. John's College—but failed. Next shot, at Jesus, I got an exhibition for history. The City of Oxford School is a day school and had no formal "sides". (N.B. I don't think any of my "education" mattered. I knew French as a boy, and could read and write before I was 4. The rest of what I learned came from the books I used to obtain for myself. School was usually an irrelevant and time-wasting nuisance, which I hated and contemned.)

8. I remember your telling me that before you went up to Oxford you enlisted in the Artillery and did some eight months. (a) When exactly was this? (b) Where did you serve? (c) How did you get on under discipline at that time?

This is hush-hush. I should not have told you. I ran away from home . . . and served for six months. No trouble with discipline, I having always been easy; but the other fellows fought all Friday and Saturday nights and frightened me with their roughness. I'd rather keep this out of print, please: the whole episode. It is negligible, militarily, like my subsequent O.T.C. training.

9. How did it happen that you were a member of Magdalen after Jesus?

I took History Finals from Jesus and got a first. That was 3 years. I had thoughts of a 4th year, and a B.Litt. on mediaeval pottery. Magdalen, by influence of Hogarth, offered me a senior demyship for 4 years, to study this, or middle-east archaeology. So I became a member of Senior Common Room there, 1911–1914 and then the war intervened to suspend the job before the 4th year ended. So I was still a member of Magdalen in 1919.

10. Is there anyone you can suggest now living who knew you in your Oxford days?

I don't know anyone who read with me: nor have I kept touch with my Jesus College people. My tutor, Reginald Lane Poole is still in Oxford, but very old.

11. Is it true that roof-climbing was a sport of yours?

Not formally. I used to go up all the towers and roofs, to get new angles of photography for architectural reasons. You know I did a great deal of mediaeval study.

12. Did you ever print or have you any copy of your thesis? If not can you tell me anything about it, particularly any new idea or suggestions that it contained?

No, I refused to print it, and have not even seen the (unique) copy since the war. It was only a preliminary study, and not good enough to publish. Its general conclusion was that the Crusaders brought more military architectural science to Syria than they took away. Their "borrowing" from Byzantine was meagre.

13. Was it in 1909 or 1910 that you spent the Long Vacation in Syria?

I don't know, I'm afraid. It was the year before I took Finals but exactly when that was I have forgotten. It may be in the University Calendar. (*Note by L.H.* It was 1909.)

14. What was your route out and back from the time you landed?

Help! I went to Sidon, from Beyrouth; thence to Lake Huleh and Trans-Jordan: back via Nazareth to Athlit and Acre and Beyrout. Then to Tripoli, and up and down the hills to the Antioch latitude. Then to Aleppo and across to Urfa and Harran: then back via Aleppo; but I was also at Damascus, and I forget how I got there.

I saw 60 castles, and took 4 months, my route being like a spider's web over Syria.

15. Did you have any companion at any time during it?

No.

16. How did you live during it?

I was walking, and so entitled to hospitality in villages. Generally went to the Sheikh's house, if there was no Khan or inn.

17. Can you refresh my memory as to the murder attempt and the bouts of fever?

No, I have no very clear recollection. I had had malaria long before (exploring Aigues Mortes and Camargue, probably) and it only came back on me in Syria. The murder effort failed because it was a Webley pistol, and I pulled out the trigger-guard (so collapsing the pistol) before the Turkman got it from me.[1]

18. Any further incidents?

Millions, I expect; but it was 25 years ago, and it would take me days to get back into that train of thought. I was mainly interested in photography and planning the castles. Pirie-Gordon (now "Times", I think) had preceded me to Syria a year or two before, and gave me many hints.

19. Were you able to converse in Arabic at this time?

I had had lessons in conversational Arabic from a Rev. N. Odeh, a Syrian Protestant clergyman living at Oxford as an Arabic teacher. So I had the rudiments at any rate. All I needed were road directions, and food and sleep and money terms.

20. Can you suggest anyone who could throw light on the Carchemish period? And can you tell me of any incidents outside those with the Germans?

Hogarth is dead. . . . I do not think the German affairs were as large as Woolley says. I wonder if Mrs. Hogarth has many letters from him, of that date? . . . We dug hard for 6 months and I used to travel

[1]See R.G., p. 61, l. 21.

for the rest of the year. We were there for 4 years and it was the best life I ever lived. The British Museum might show you our reports. I did the photographs, sculpture, pottery, and copying of inscriptions, besides generally helping Woolley.[1]

21. I have a recollection of your telling me a story about Gertrude Bell, but it eludes me at the moment. Can you recall it?

I think this must have been Hogarth's story, about Gertrude's visit to our camp, and the villagers' decision that she came to marry me! Not a very amusing story, and already in print, somewhere.[2]

22. When you did your trip to Egypt to Flinders Petrie was it true, that story of his saying, "They don't play cricket here"? And if so, what kit were you wearing?

Hogarth sent me to Petrie, to get digging experience, after my first term at Carchemish, in the winter: At Carchemish I always wore shorts: so at Petrie's camp I turned out for work in blazer and shorts, which he seemed to think was better for cricket. He meant football, I expect. Shorts were not "worn" pre-war, in Egypt.[3]

23. When exactly was your trip to Sinai, and when did you realise it was mainly for a military purpose?[4]

Winter, 1913–1914. Woolley and I were in Aleppo, resting after Carchemish, and were telegraphed to from London to go down. When we got to Gaza Captain Newcombe told us the whole history of it. We wrote a Palestine Exploration Fund annual volume, the Wilderness of Zin, upon it. Published about 1915.

24. Is the story of your lone visit to Aqaba correct?

Woolley and I divided forces after doing N. Sinai: he went N. and I S. to Aqaba. Thence I went to Maan and Damascus. I had three or four Arabs in my party, I think; no English.[5]

---

[1]The diary of T. E. Lawrence during his travels in 1911 has been printed by his friend, Viscount Carlow.

[2]See R.G., p. 67, tenth line from bottom.   [3]*Ibid.*, p. 63, l. 19.   [4]*Ibid.*, p. 69, l. 16.

[5]This account is given in R.G.'s *Lawrence and the Arabs*, p. 39 (pp. 25–6 of the American edition, *Lawrence and the Arabian Adventure*).

25. Was there anything on the island besides ruins—i.e. of a military nature?

Jebel Faraun was all ruined and even the cisterns were broken. I was looking for constructions of the 13th century—Renaud of Chatillon or Saladin.

26. When did you first meet Kitchener? What sort of impression did he make on you, and what happened?

First met in 1913, and then again in 1914. He was . . . wooden, and normally dull . . . but every now and then he would appear to have second-sight, and be quite dogmatic about something utterly problematical—and was then as often right as wrong. A very limited imagination . . . and sure of himself: not honest according to ordinary men's codes. He inspired very little personal devotion.[1]

27. What racial strains come to you from (a) your father's, (b) your mother's side?

Father Anglo-Irish, with 1/4 Dutch. Mother Anglo-Scotch with a dash of Scandinavian.

28. When the war broke out, when and where was it you tried unsuccessfully to enlist?

I did not try to enlist. For the first few months of the war I was working on our Sinai book, and then went to the War Office to do the Sinai map, in the absence of the surveyors, who had all gone on Active Service. In the W.O. my chief was Colonel Hedley (now Sir —and retired) and he put me into uniform without medical examination or formality. So I had no trouble. I have always been very fit physically.[2]

29. Didn't you make any immediate attempt to get out to Egypt?

No: but in December when Turkey came in, Colonel Hedley and Newcombe decided I would be more useful in Egypt, where the making of maps of Turkey would now be transferred.

[1]See p. 163, l. 17.
[2]See R. G., p. 49, fourteenth line from bottom.

PREFATORY NOTE TO QUERIES—II

Field Marshal Earl Kitchener had been British Agent and Consul-General in Egypt since 1911. When the war broke out in 1914 he was on leave in England and was then made Secretary of State for War.

Hussein was the Sherif of Mecca. The Emirs Ali, Abdulla, Feisal and Zeid were his sons. Unwilling subjects of the Turkish Empire, Hussein and his sons longed to recover their freedom and dreamed of a great Arab confederacy which should revive the glories of the Abbasside Empire.

Sir Henry McMahon succeeded Lord Kitchener in Egypt, being appointed with the title of High Commissioner when a British Protectorate over Egypt was declared.

Mr. (later Sir) Ronald Storrs was Oriental Secretary to the British Agency.

Brig.-General Gilbert Clayton combined the office of Sudan Agent with that of head of both the Military Intelligence and the Political Intelligence in Egypt.

Dr. D. G. Hogarth, the great archaeologist who had been Lawrence's patron, was appointed Director of the Arab Bureau in Cairo in 1916.

General Sir Reginald Wingate was Sirdar of the Egyptian Army and Governor General of the Sudan. (In 1917 he succeeded Sir Henry McMahon as High Commissioner in Egypt.) The control of operations in the Hejaz was placed under him, and he sent Lt. Col. C. E. Wilson, Governor of the Red Sea Province of the Sudan, across to Jidda as his representative.

General Sir John Maxwell was in command of the British Forces in Egypt. He was succeeded early in 1916 by General Sir Archibald Murray.

Captain (later Colonel) S. F. Newcombe, Royal Engineers, had been accompanied by Lawrence and Woolley in a pre-war survey of the country beyond the eastern frontier of Egypt. He was later a leading member of the British Military Intelligence and became the senior officer of the British Military Mission which was sent to the Hejaz late in 1916.

Mr. Philip Graves, who had been the correspondent of *The Times* in Constantinople before the war, was taken into the British Military Intelligence in Cairo and entrusted with the compilation of the enemy's "Order of Battle" (i.e., the day-to-day disposition of the Turkish forces).

Colonel (later Sir Coote) Hedley was head of the Geographical Section of the General Staff, in London.

Sir Mark Sykes, a well-known traveller and politician who had conducted special missions, was deputed by the Foreign Office to negotiate an agreement with the French on the future division of the Middle East.

M. Georges Picot was the French representative in these negotiations.

Colonel Edouard Brémond was head of the French Military Mission which was sent to the Hejaz in 1916. He returned to France at the end of 1917. In 1931 he published an account of the campaign, as seen through French glasses at long range, under the title of *Le Hedjaz dans la Guerre Mondiale*.

Sir Arthur Nicolson (later Lord Carnock) was Permanent Under-Secretary for Foreign Affairs from 1910 to 1916.

Enver Pasha was one of the leaders of the Young Turk revolution. In 1914 he was the Turkish War Minister.

Fakhri Pasha was placed in command of the Turkish forces at Medina shortly after the outbreak of the Arab Revolt. He remained there until the end of the war.

When T.E. merely referred me to other sources or gave an uncertain answer, the questions have been omitted.

Queries—II

(Answers given verbally and jotted down)

1. Did Kitchener know of Arab ambitions before Abdulla visited him in Feb. 1914?

K. knew vaguely beforehand. There were, I think, two conversations, but K. was too canny to commit himself although doubtless giving Abdulla impression of a concrete assurance. K. was clever in that way—he could utilise the Arab ambitions later, or not, according to circumstances.

2. What was Hussein's aim then—autonomy within the Turkish Empire or more?

The aim was independent of the World War which only provided an opportunity. Abdulla had a scheme, earlier, of seizing all pilgrims and thus involving the Great Powers. Ja'far might throw more light on the point.

3. Who took Kitchener's message to Abdulla in Sept. 1914? Had Abdulla sent one earlier?

Storrs had an agent called Ruhi, who used to go down to the Hejaz, and "looked like a mandrake". He was probably the bearer. There were two messages. R. E. M. Russell might throw further light.

4. Was there any real move in negotiations between Nov. 1914 and July 1915? Did we ask for Revolt to begin after our landing at Gallipoli?

(a) Wingate was doing a lot indirectly, if not with Hussein.   (b) No.

[*Note by L. H.* McMahon says he had been looking for an opportunity to disintegrate the Turkish forces. Negotiations really started by Hussein's message to McMahon saying it had come to the "parting of the ways".]

5. On what grounds did Hussein refuse to proclaim *Jihad?*
[*Note by L.H.* "Jihad" is the Holy War—of all Moslems against Christians.]

Turks were not very keen. It was a matter for the Khalif rather than for the Sherif.

6. Was Hussein's letter of July inspired by any person or development?

Yes, it was prompted by our blockade.

[*Note by L.H.* I questioned Newcombe on this point and he told me that Storrs actually wrote the letter, in high Arabic at the Residency. The British could not find the copy subsequently. On telling this to Lawrence, he said that it was not correct. "The letter was written by some Assyrian poet on Abdulla's staff. Came as a bombshell to Storrs. Storrs not really interested in politics."]

7. Did it refer to the Khalifate?

Hussein never asked us for Khalifate—didn't think it our business and only referred to it when *we* offered it—that fact, that we offered it, was the reason why it was kept secret. It was *not* McMahon who wrote the "Khalifate" letter. Wingate's adviser raised the matter.

8. How far was McMahon's reply influenced by the Foreign Office?

It was written by McMahon and Storrs in consultation with Clayton and referred to the Foreign Office.

[*Note by L.H.* McMahon's telegram to the F.O. insists on the importance of keeping faith.]

9. Was there a meeting on the Red Sea Reef with British officers, and if so, when?

Hogarth met the Arab leaders. (Hogarth wrote an article on the Arab movement. Mrs. Hogarth has it—write to her, mentioning at Lawrence's suggestion.)

10. Re our proposed landing at Alexandretta[1]—was the Arabs' idea to make peace after securing freedom?

Yes; we should have connived at this.

[Newcombe says that he was going as Intelligence Officer. We were banking on the Armenians to help.]

11. Was Intelligence about Arabia in 1915 gathered more by military or by McMahon's secret service?

Wingate's Intelligence was not passed on to the Military Intelligence—but presumably to McMahon. Clayton handed over M.I. to Newcombe as regards the enemy side, keeping the internal and political.

12. Did Sykes conduct negotiations with Hussein? (Cf. Arthur's Life of Kitchener, III, 154.) Who appointed Sykes? Where did he go?

Sykes did not himself see Hussein until May, 1917. Sykes came out to Egypt, saw McMahon and Wingate, then on to Mesopotamia, and then to Simla—where he gave offence to the Viceroy by dining in khaki. The mission was made on Sykes' own initiative, not Kitchener's. He fixed it up with Sir A. Nicolson.

13. Did McMahon warn the Foreign Office about the danger of an Agreement and the importance of keeping it?

Yes.

14. When did McMahon know of Sykes-Picot treaty?

Not until Sykes told him—Sykes saying casually, "Haven't you heard of my Treaty?" Others nearly threw up.

15. Is there a map showing Sykes-Picot zones exactly? And what was Russia's share?

Uncertain of where to find.

[1]See pp. 17, l. 18, and 88, l. 12.

16. Were areas A and B contingent on the Arabs freeing themselves?

No: separate declaration later.

17. Was our blockade of W. Coast of Arabia exercised against the Hejaz during 1915?

Uncertain.

[*Note by L.H.* Newcombe says the blockade was starving the Hejaz. We said we should tighten it more if they did not join us.]

18. Did howitzers arrive from Egypt at same time as mountain artillery from Sudan?

Howitzers arrived after.

19. Falls (*Official History*) says Fakhri carried off surviving women and children. Lawrence (*Seven Pillars*) says massacred all. Which is correct?

Fakhri carried off surviving women and children from Medina itself. He had massacred them in one suburb.

20. Was any promise given before the Revolt to cut Hejaz Railway?

No; one of Hussein's sons asked [C. E.] Wilson that this might be done. But Hussein refused offer of both explosive and experts.

21. Did Newcombe go out to Egypt with you in December 1914, or was he already there?

I went out with Newcombe on a French Messageries Maritimes liner from Marseilles—Dec. 8 (?).

22. How did you come to receive instructions for Mespot. Mission?[1]

I had put the Grand Duke Nicholas in touch with certain disaffected Arab officers in Erzerum. Did it through the War Office and

[1]See R. G., p. 82, l. 12.

our Military Attaché in Russia. So the War Office thought I could do the same thing over Mespot., and accordingly wired out to Clayton.

23. When did you become a captain?

I was Staff Captain. I lost it on going to Mespot., so Hedley arranged a local captaincy.

24. Were the General Staff going to get rid of you too?

While we were together on Maxwell's staff Holdich was my greatest ally. When appointed to Murray's staff his attitude changed.

[*Note by L.H.* Newcombe says that he used to hear from Holdich, now dead, who was very bitter about T.E.—jealousy and resentment of what was regarded as T.E.'s cheek. The Murray crowd were trying to down Clayton as well as Lawrence.]

[Philip Graves and T.E. got out Handbook of Turkish Army; may have been a dozen editions; I supervised the printing of them. T.E. and Graves spent most of their time among the Turkish prisoners and came to know more about the Turkish Army than the Turks themselves.]

25. What led Wilson to change his view about sending troops?

Probably owing to better information about Turks. I said *it wouldn't do* to send troops.

26. Had Wingate been opposed to despatch of a Brigade as said by Wavell, page 55?[1]

Wingate wobbled. . . . If a brigade had been sent it would have been under him and he would have been G.O.C.

27. Did you conceive idea of taking a hand in the Revolt immediately after, or before, your visit to Feisal?

[1] *The Palestine Campaigns*, by Colonel A. P. Wavell.

Thought I was a God-sent Intelligence Officer. But had not imagined myself in the other capacity—the difference between O. and I. had been drummed into me so strongly by Holdich.[1]

28. Were any officers besides Garland at Yanbo when you landed in December?

Garland was a sick man, an ex-Sergeant . . . apt to stand on his dignity at the wrong moment. Not the type for the job. Garland was alone.

29. What was the strength of Arab Army, regular and irregular, at Rabegh and Yanbo in December?

About 2–300. Troops at Rabegh sometimes included a negro battalion and sometimes not. At Yanbo, about 80 mule-mounted infantry and 150 infantry. Didn't really increase until Wejh—about 700, at Aqaba about 3000.

30. Did Bremond discourage a move to Wejh? (Cf. his proposals to Wingate at Khartoum Dec. 14.)

Brémond mentioned in conference at Khartoum about localising.

31. Were you or Feisal responsible for suggestion about Abdulla?

It arose thus: In discussing the project T.E. said that on second thoughts he doubted if Abdullah could maintain himself at Khir . . . Feisal said, "You mean Wadi Ais". Until then T.E. had never heard of Wadi Ais but on learning about it he at once saw possibilities and the fact that it would make a move possible. So jumped at it.

32. Falls says the march began on the 18th. This does not seem to fit the dates.

Probably means from Umlej.

33. How did two days' delay occur in the march?

Because the Arabs jollified over the news of Abdullah's victory.

34. Did Vickery handle the Wejh attack?

T.E. explained how this was launched. "Navy were spoiling for a fight".

[1]"O. and I." is short for "Operations and Intelligence."

35. Who is "S.A." of the dedication to S.P.W.?

One is a person and one is a place. [Vague][1]

36. What was the "personal motive" in epilogue?

(Talk notes, 27.5.33. See p. 68, l. 14.)

37. Did you know that an eclipse was due on July 4th, 1917?[2]

Yes.

38. How many miles had you ridden in the two months before reaching Aqaba?

About 1700 miles.

39. How do you reconcile your action in abstaining from attack on Maan with your argument to Brémond?

Wanted access to Maan plateau, not Maan itself. Could advance on railway as long as we were holding Wadi Ithm.

40. Why were there no previous arrangements for supplies to be ready at Aqaba?

Had arranged with Boyle to put in when possible. The ship had actually been there and departed about an hour before I reached Aqaba.

Tullibardine's Brigade was still ear-marked for Aqaba when I captured this place.

.   .   .

119 Clarence Road
East Cowes
Isle of Wight
Friday, 19.V.33

I stayed only a few nights in Felixstowe. Then went to Hythe: then here for two nights. Then to Nottingham and Manchester and returned this afternoon to find your letter waiting.

[1]See p. 143, l. 3.

[2]This had reference to the attack on the Turkish post at Kethira, when the local Arab sheikh demurred to it on the score that there would be a full moon, whereat Lawrence overbore this excuse by "promising that tonight for a while there should be no moon".

I'm sorry: I had not realised that you wanted to come to Felixstowe to see me: but I shall not be there for a long while now. My jobs lie in Hythe and in Cowes, and I move between them.

There is rumour of my coming to London next week or the week following for an afternoon conference. That would probably afford you time for us to meet. Cowes is not very good: it means a voyage by ship as well as a trip by train. Or do you fly down? I expect to be here for 3 weeks, at least.

119 Clarence Road
East Cowes
I. of W.
23.V.33

I will try to come to Hindhead on Sat. night, if that will suit you. I could get there in the afternoon and stay till late, and then go on towards London, probably: but that depends on your other engagements.

I have not heard anything from the Air Ministry about the London Committee meeting, so it looks unlikely before Whitsun: but I can get away for Sat. night, almost certainly, if you can tell me where to come, and when you are most likely to be free.

Don't worry about your prose style, or mine. It's not how you say it, but what you say. I only write well when excited.

(P.S.) Reply early, as the Island has slow posts!

TALKS WITH T. E. LAWRENCE
27 MAY 1933

(*From Diary*)

Went to Hindhead in afternoon . . . to Adrian's school sports. T. E. Shaw (Lawrence) arrived just after tea on his Brough bike. Came down to school and was v. good about coming to prize-giving and submitting to admiring chat. Good exercise for his sense of humour.

After leaving I asked him if he would like to see Lloyd George again. He took to the idea—said despite differences he admired L.G. immensely—L.G. had "towered above everyone else at Peace Conference"; Clemenceau and Wilson narrow mediocrities compared. Also thing that struck him above all about L.G. was his desire to do what was right, not merely playing for national advantage like everyone else. (This would surprise most of the people who talk about L.G. —the last thing they concede him.)

I rang up L.G. and he said he would be delighted to see Shaw, so I took him down in the car with Adrian. Intending to stay a few minutes, I could hardly drag him away after an hour. They talked hammer and tongs, both at their best. I was content to be little more than an audience.

Then back to school to drop Adrian, and then to the Moorlands. After dinner T.E. and I talked till 1 a.m., first about Arab Revolt and then about philosophy of life.

T.E. and I had breakfast together. . . . Then walked about

garden and talked all morning until T.E. left about 12.30 on his way to Dorset cottage en route back to Cowes. Wouldn't stay to lunch, as prefers to ride on empty stomach!

Intends to settle down, after his service ends in 1935, at his cottage as "hermit"—not complete, will go up to London to concerts, theatres occasionally, see people, and do translations to pay for his luxuries. Prefers translations, can be done to order and to time-table. Enjoys doing nothing and doesn't think he needs action to drown his sense of futility of everything.

.   .   .

Has lost his Barton St. attic because Sir H. Baker has had to move. So he uses Union Jack Club chiefly.

Cottage at Bovington (where road N. from Bovington crosses ridge. Looks towards Dorchester), 2 rooms. No water, but own spring. 5 acres—only grows rhododendrons, trailing. No drainage. Gets his meals at Bovington when he wants them—advantage is several cheap soldiers' cafés. Otherwise finds cheese, etc., under 2 or 3 glass covers. One meal a day and any hour will do. No bed—sleeps in any chair that he is sitting in, and as he is—saves so much time dressing and undressing. But chairs are all long enough to lie full length.

Walls of cottage (200 years old) were standing when he bought it. Scrounged slates from builders all over Dorset, and slated roof himself (9000 were needed).

Father's family came from Leicestershire, cousins of Walter Raleigh, at that time. Settled in County Meath, estates round castle. . . . Never intermarried with Irish, always with English or Scot, especially with Yorkshire. Father had no interest in land but in field-sports—one of finest snipe and pheasant shots. Also a yachtsman. Golf later. Never read a book till late in life. . . .

Talking of early 18th century warfare, he said Catinat was the best of all the French, better than Villars. Real brains.

Written 3 books:

1) One before the war that he burnt—also called *Seven Pillars*.

2) *Seven Pillars.* 1922, original, and then with verbiage reduced in 1926. Wrote *S.P.* in sections in 22–24 hour sittings, averaging 1000–1500 words an hour. Between each section knocked off for week or so. Trimmed afterwards. Wells called it a great human document but not a work of art. T.E. remarks: the opposite—not a human document like Xenophon's *Anabasis* but an artificial straining after art. A "depressing" book. No message.

The "personal" motive mentioned first in the concluding bit was the "S.A." of the opening poem. But S.A. "croaked" in 1918. T.E. says he could never write fiction, because trained himself to *see* everything in full detail, to neglect of other senses.

3) *The Mint*, an account of life in the R.A.F., written in 1922, 1923 and 1925. First and main part about life at Uxbridge Depot, showing moral effect of Bonham-Carter. Later chapters about Cranwell to show happier contrast—if artistically spoils.[1]

"Out-Joyces Joyce" in giving exact language, etc., of the men. Unpublishable? But finer writing than *Seven Pillars*. Two typescript copies—lent one to Geoffrey Salmond. Manuscript copy to Edward Garnett.

Spoke of a phrase in this book on life in the R.A.F.—"The only thing military in the R.A.F. is the intelligence of some of the senior officers."

The root fault of the Army, and of the services in general, was "lack of *independent* courage". Feel uncomfortable unless

[1] See R.G., p. 155, l. 12.

in a herd. Guardsmen the most hopeless—they "seem to choose N.C.O.'s for their straight-backed heads". Had I noticed them? R.A.F. men were developing better—because their job is so individual and technical.

On Lone Trip through Syria. June 1917.

There is an official report to Clayton upon this episode. Rode so much that kept no notes, except a few words. Carried nothing from Feisal. Travelling with Syrian revolutionaries.

Ras Baalbek.

Blew up bridge, 4-lbs. (?) block. Poked in the bridge holes. Took an old sheikh he had known before the war.

1. Rode with him to Burga (E. of Jebel Druse).
2. Then to favourite spring half way across mountain range between Palmyra and Damascus.
3. Then near Ras Baalbek (great monument).
4. Then back to Nebk.
5. Skirted edge of Damascus. Ali Riza (Turk Base Cmdt.) came out to see him. Had sent message from Nebuk. T.E. told him what we were doing; asked him to keep Damascus quiet—told him he (T.E.) was going to Aqaba (in order to spike Nesib's wild plans and avert a premature rising).

No posters, as alleged. (Reward offered only vague.)

Just before got back to rejoin Nasir again, suspicious of Sheikh of Beni Sakhr. . . .

Sleeping in tent, and the Sheikh's brother crept in and whispered, "They've sent to Turks to say you are here". T.E. crept out through back of tent and mounted. . . .

At Peace Conference.

Lawrence wore Arab dress when with Feisal; British uniform when regarded himself as member of British delegation. Once delivered a speech in English, French & Arabic by turns.

Lloyd George towered above everyone else—Clemenceau, etc., mere mediocrities. Far the greatest man there. He really strove for what was right, not merely what was expedient. Impressed T.E., too, when he asked where Teschen was. Only man who would ask such questions, instead of pretending he knew—and so remaining ignorant.

T.E. said that Hussein was very like . . . —intensely narrow and oblique mind, seeing through a slit. But very honest fundamentally. He regarded everyone else as crooks.

TALK WITH T. E. LAWRENCE
28 May 1933

Wanted to go off before lunch—rides (motor-bike) best on empty stomach. Food after work. Yet admitted it had effect on his *mind*. Lack of food, and still more lack of sleep (especially when he reached Damascus in 1918) made him light-headed.

Weighed once in Cairo—only 6 stone 10 lbs.

Constantly ill during his life, but abnormal endurance.

After thrashing, able to ride all right. Same when suffering from boils on ride from Wejh. Believes his impression of thrashing is accurate.

Has now a new Brough, weighing $\frac{1}{4}$ ton, developing 57 h.p. and doing maximum of 97 m.p.h. If not quite so fast it is worth sacrifice because much quieter and easier in towns.

Lawrence this time carried a small black attaché case—quite luxurious—used to carry merely a toothbrush in his pocket. Had patent black oilskin motorcycling overalls—copied specially from his working overalls.

Told me of Coastal Area order—"Multi-engined aircraft are not to be rolled or looped"—because of trouble with the Sidestrand type. Sent to his flying-boat station. (Flying boats couldn't possibly do either!) So T.E. inspired reply that same instructions, not to *roll*, should be given for 50-foot *pinnaces*.

.   .   .

In 1913 T.E. went up 4–5 miles of Wadi Ithm—enough to realise it was impregnable. Could have turned it by going 10 m. S. of Aqaba, via Rum, and then down the Ithm. (No one, however, knew at the time.)

Cars were a lot used. Could only keep touch by cars or air. No wireless. Front longer than Western Front.

.   .   .

Hejaz show cost about £ 11 million. Only 2 Englishmen killed (except in Buxton's raid).

(Jotted down as T.E. talked):

Pre-War.

Knew Hogarth long before he went to Syria. Attracted his notice by the way he arranged the mediaeval pottery cabinets in the Ashmolean, which had been neglected. Hogarth arranged demyship at Magdalen which gave T.E. £100 a year. While digging at Carchemish he got 15/- a day, and rest of year while travelling he lived on his demyship.

His (youthful) sympathy was not with Crusaders but with those Crusaders who settled there and learnt civilised ways, only to be cried out against by rougher new arrivals.

For about a year he had studied approaches to Syria from desert side, and this study from Saladin's point of view helped his own, although Saladin did not operate at same places (and the railway was a fresh addition). T.E.'s problem and Saladin's were not far apart. Saladin's conquest of Syria was an accident, born of lopping off the edges.

General.

William of Tyre appealed greatly to Lawrence—a real historian, not a mere chronicler.

Talked of Caesar's Gallic War. I said it reminded me of Falkenhayn's concealment of truth. T.E. said the account of the bridging the Rhine was obviously an interpolated report from

"Caesar's C.R.E." Pity he had no Naval Transport Officer
to write a similar account of crossing the Channel that would
have covered up the failure of Caesar's invasion of Britain
like the other had covered up failure on Rhine.[1]

In R.A.F., practice of hot baths in waterproof suits—better
than rum to warm after being chilled.

Post-War.

After the war, Flinders Petrie offered T.E. field-work. But
T.E.'s desire to take up archeology again was useless in view
of the fact that he was not allowed in any of the "digging"
countries, except under political surveillance.

T.E. had the intention of enlisting in the R.A.F. from last
year of war. Put it off for 3 years while settling Arab affair.
Told Geoffrey Salmond; so in 1919, when he told G.S. of his
desire to join R.A.F., G.S. suggested he should be his assistant
in Egypt. To this T.E. said—"I mean to *enlist*".

T.E.'s view—that the air is the only first-class thing that our
generation has got to do. So everyone should either take to
the air themselves or help it forward. Now it is virtually
accomplished.[2]

I tackled T.E. about the change in him and the better balance in him since I first knew him, and asked was this a reason
also for enlisting. T.E. admitted it was, and that he was
"nearly dotty" when he enlisted. The strain of writing *Seven
Pillars* had been too much, *excited* him too much. Now he was
"more human" and "genius had gone out of him".

War.

Hubert Young (in his book *The Independent Arab*) was wrong
about Lawrence being adverse to Arab Regulars. T.E. had
been responsible for them, in getting them equipment, etc.
T.E.'s "child". But Young was also wrong about thinking

[1]See p. 9, tenth line from bottom.
[2]See R. G., p. 181, seventh line from bottom.

that Regulars did anything. Battle was always decided before they arrived—they merely occupied.

One thing we did not want to do was to *maintain* a force in the North. T.E. made his trips always in the harvest when food easy, and so no transport needed.

He brought Buxton's force (200) across Jordan to give idea that Allenby was coming across again (his first two attempts were stupid, unpurposeful strategy). The Camel Corps had gone before, so it naturally encouraged delusion. Arabs had no idea there were so many Englishmen in the world. T.E.'s one idea of real value was to strew area with bully-beef tins.

1932–33.

T.E. was happy at Mount Batten until new C.O. . . . . came. The sort of man who wins gold-medal essays. A paper man. More important to organise than to fly. So atmosphere in station changed and T.E. threatened to leave service.

Geoffrey Salmond talked of various special jobs, e.g., Auxiliary Air Force (T.E. remarked would have been splendid publicity, but Air Ministry afraid of publicity, unlike Admiralty). Also spoke of Malta. Finally settled on speedboats. On his own there. Geoffrey Salmond promised, and John fulfilled, £3000 for experiments on speedboats with Napier Lion 500 h.p. engines, with which T.E. is confident of raising present 30 knots to 50 knots. (Had previously raised it from 15 knots.) Would have 300-mile radius. T.E. declared to me, and L.G., that the new boats would make it impossible to conduct any submarine campaign against our coasts. Even from France.

M.L. class used in war did only 18 knots, and P-boats, which were technically defective, did about 30.

N.B. T.E. also said (to L.G.) that our air force completely superior to French, whose latest fast machines are 50 m.p.h. slower than the Furies. Ours would drive them out of the air.

In sending back the first batch of the typescript, he accompanied it with the following letter:

26.vi.33

Dear L.H.,

You talk of a summing up to come. Will you (if you agree with my feeling) in it strike a blow for hard work and thinking? I was not an instinctive soldier, automatic with intuitions and happy ideas. When I took a decision, or adopted an alternative it was after studying every relevant—and many an irrelevant—factor. Geography, tribal structure, religion, social customs, language, appetites, standards—all were at my finger-ends. The enemy I knew almost like my own side. I risked myself among them a hundred times, to *learn*.

The same with tactics. If I used a weapon well, it was because I could handle it. Rifles were easy. I put myself under instruction for Lewis, Vickers, and Hotchkiss (Vickers in my O.T.C. days, and rifles, and pistols). If you look at my article in the Pickaxe you will see how much I learned about explosives, from my R.E. teachers, and how far I developed their methods. To use aircraft I learned to fly. To use armoured cars I learned to drive and fight them. I became a gunner at need, and could doctor and judge a camel.

The same with strategy. I have written only a few pages on the art of war—but in these I levy contribution from my predecessors of five languages. You are one of the few living Englishmen who can see the allusions and quotations, the conscious analogies, in all I say and do, militarily.

Do make it clear that generalship, at least in my case, came of understanding, of hard study and brain-work and concentration. Had it come easy to me I should not have done it so well.

If your book could persuade some of our new soldiers to read and mark and learn things outside drill manuals and tactical diagrams, it would do a good work. I feel a fundamental, crippling, incuriousness about our officers. Too much body and too little head. The perfect general would know everything in heaven and earth.

So please, if you see me that way and agree with me, do use me as a text to preach for more study of books and history, a greater seriousness in military art. With 2,000 years of examples behind us we have no excuse, when fighting, for not fighting well.

I like your little book—wherever it does not repeat a told tale. It starts at Chap. II by the way, and goes on to page 335.[1] That's what you've sent me.

Yours,
T.E.S.

T.E.'s note attached to first page of the typescript of the first eighteen chapters of L.H.'s book:

The book puzzles me. I found it interesting, for the pictures it drew, quite apart from the soldiering. It seems to me that L-H. is a writer, and would be even if he was not dealing with the military subjects on which he is an authority. Exactly why he is a writer puzzles me, for he does not show love for the shapes of sentences, and some of his phrases are worn with use. I think it may be for the interest he takes in his human beings. Clausewitz had no humanity, and so his War became a monstrous inanimate science: it lost its art. Saxe was flesh and blood, and so his creation of war came to breathing life.

---

[1] Chapter I was originally numbered II, as I had the idea of composing an opening chapter on the general background; I later decided, however, to incorporate this further on in the book.

SOME OF THE COMMENTS AND CORRECTIONS MADE BY T. E. SHAW ON L.H.'S TYPESCRIPT DRAFT OF THE BOOK EVENTUALLY ENTITLED "T. E. LAWRENCE: IN ARABIA AND AFTER"

Comments at top of first page:

Sorry: margin all speckled with suggestions. But you asked for it. I told you you need not show it me!   T.E.S.

Page in typescript, 1; page in book, 13 (3):

"The County of Carnarvon in North Wales points like an arm into the Irish Sea. At the armpit lies the village of Tremadoc, close beneath the foothills of Snowdon. This resemblance, which catches the map-gazing eye, offers a convenient method of indication. It is also an apt symbol for the career of one who was born at Tremadoc on August 15th 1888. History hardly offers a clearer case of a man born for a mission, of a life moving along a path pointed out by fate—even though twists in its course may have hid the *ultimate direction*."

T.E. underlined the words here italicized and made the marginal comment:

"But even now I'm not dead!"

He put the remark, "*suggest cancelling this*", against the remainder of the original page 1 and the whole of page 2 and attached a considerably longer substitution written by himself. It ran as follows, except for two small changes of wording

77

which he himself made subsequently (the revised version is given here):

Your p. 1.

The second paragraph. There are (as I hinted at Hindhead) things not quite desirable in this. Without wanting to censor I suggest alternatives—written with the allusiveness that hints at knowledge refusing to betray itself except between the lines.

"He was of mixed race. His father's family were Elizabethan settlers from England, favoured in gaining land in County Meath by Walter Raleigh, a connection. During three hundred years of Irish domicile they never married into Ireland, but chose their wives from intruders such as themselves, from England, from Holland even. His mother was Island Scotch in feeling and education, but her parentage was part English, part Scandinavian. The sympathy of his home was Irish, all the stronger for being exiled. Wales of the Atlantic coast had no share in him, after his first year.

"The friends of his manhood called him 'T.E.', for convenience and to show him that they recognised how his adopted surnames— Lawrence, Ross, Shaw, whatever they were—did not belong. The father's self-appointed exile reduced his means to a craftsman's income, which the landowning pride of caste forbade him to increase by labour. As five sons came, one after the other, the family's very necessaries of life were straitened. They existed only by the father's denying himself every amenity, and by the mother's serving her household like a drudge.

"Observers noted a difference in social attitude between the courtly but abrupt and large father, and the laborious mother. The father shot, fished, rode, sailed with the certainty of birthright experience. He never touched a book or wrote a cheque. The mother kept to herself, and kept her children jealously from meeting or knowing their neighbours. She was a calvinist and ascetic, though a wonderful housewife, a woman of character and keen intelligence, with iron decision and charming, when she wished.

"T.E.'s father's family seemed unconscious of his sons, even when after his death recognition of their achievement might have done honour to the name. The five brothers, accordingly, were brought up to be self-sufficient, and were sufficient till the war struck away

two and left in their sequence gaps in age that were over wide for
sympathy to cross. Then their loneliness seemed to rankle, sometimes.
To friends who wondered aloud how he could endure the company
of the barrack-room and its bareness T.E. might retort, almost
fiercely, that he had gone back to his boyhood class and was at home.
'The fellows' were his: but this declaration of birthright seemed to
strain the truth."

(Not perhaps as much as you feel. I can be on terms with scholars,
or writing people, or painters or politicians; but equally I am happy
with bus conductors, fitters or plain workmen: anybody with a trade
or calling. And all such classes are at home with me, though I fancy
none of them would call me "one of them". Probably my upbringing
and adventures—and way of thinking—have bereft me of class. Only
the leisured classes make me acutely uncomfortable. I cannot play or
pass time. Lots of people go about saying that they alone understand
me. They do not see how little they see, each of them separately.
My name is Legion!)

"His first eight years were wandering—Scotland, the Isle of Man,
Brittany, the Channel Islands, Hampshire. Eventually the family's
migrations brought them to Oxford, for reasons of education. T.E.
arrived there with a child's lip-knowledge of French, and a fund of
book-learning. He had learnt his letters through hearing his eldest
brother taught them and in his fourth year was reading newspapers
and books. Latin at six, through private tuition, and then at eight
began his attendance at the City of Oxford School, a day-school
small in numbers and low in fees. The fees he made lower for himself
from the age of twelve upwards, by winning scholarships in a series
that covered his tuition till he had taken his degree at the University.

"'School,' he said later, 'was an irrelevant and time-wasting
nuisance, which I hated and contemned'. Formal lessons were small
beer against his private reading, which had already ranged relatively
far and wide in the three languages he understood. The discovery
of grammars for English, French and Latin was an unpleasant
interruption to the enjoyment of their books; just as the long school
hours and the plague of homework cut into the pursuit of archaeology
that was already the child's passion. He hunted fragments of Roman

or mediacval pottery on every site or in any chance excavation and went . . ."

PUBLISHER'S NOTE

[*In the pages that follow, references to matter in the typescript of* T. E. Lawrence: in Arabia and After, *together with references to the corresponding pages in the published book on which this matter may be found, are given in this way: "T. 3, B. 16 (5)", which means that the matter commented upon was on p. 3 of the typescript and may be found on p. 16 of the English edition of the book and on p. 5 of the American edition. (The title of the American edition is* Colonel Lawrence, the Man Behind the Legend.) *T. E. Lawrence's comments and changes, set in a smaller type, follow the matter quoted from the typescript.*]

T. 3, B. 16 (5):
"The theme of the Crusades caught his imagination, if his sympathies were attracted rather by the opponents of the Crusaders who seemed less conventional."

I doubt this. Bohemond was not conventional, nor Raymond: and there is only one "human document" (Usamah) on the Arab side. The Franks have it!

T. 3, B. 16 (5):
"But the idea of a Crusade, the idea underlying it, revolved in his mind, giving rise to a dream Crusade, which implied a leader with whom in a sense he identified himself yet remained as himself a sympathetic observer. Naturally, it would be a Crusade in the modern form—the freeing of a race from bondage. Where, however, was he to find a race in need of release and at the same time of *sufficient* appeal to him? The Arabs seemed the only suitable one left, and they fitted in with the trend of his interests."

T.E. changed the word italicized here into "*historical*".

T. 14, B. 17 (6):

"He was still a schoolboy when . . . he ran off and enlisted in the Artillery. He served some six months before he was brought out."

T.E. put this in brackets and wrote, in substitution:

In his teens he took a sudden turn for military experience at the urge of some private difficulty, and served for a while in the ranks. He has remarked—

T. 5, B. 17 (6):
"severity of discipline."

T.E. put brackets round these words and made the note:

No, there was little imposed discipline; less than now. It was the "brutality of conduct and manners".

T. 5, B. 18 (7):
"He *took no* part in the ordinary College life."

T.E. put brackets round the words here italicized and made the note:

? refused to take.

T. 5, B. 18 (7):
"and the other undergraduates would hardly have realised his existence if his imperceptibility had not been pressed so far as ultimately to provoke *curiosity*"

T.E. underlined the word here italicized and made the note:

! There was friction over my refusal to take interest in sport, as a matter of fact.

T. 5, B. 19 (7):
"In his studies Lawrence was equally 'free'. He had decided to read for the History School, but he paid little attention to the prescribed books, and perfunctory attendance at the prescribed lectures. His reading widened with every oppor-

tunity, pursuing many interesting if academically irrelevant avenues, from medieval poetry to modern strategy . . . It was always the unexpected, the undiscovered, or the inaccessible sources that he sought."

T.E. added:

Originals and sidelights, not compilations.

T. 5, B. 19 (8):
"To this *Lawrence* replied"

T.E. underlined the word here italicized and made the note:

? T.E. throughout whenever the comment is personal.

T. 7, B. 19 (8):
"When he mooted his idea of spending the 'Long Vac' in Syria Hogarth warned him that the summer was a bad season for such a journey, and that in any case it would mean considerable outlay on the necessary retinue and camp-equipment. To this T.E. replied that he was going to walk, and going alone. The fact of walking would entitle him to hospitality in the villages he passed through."

It would also have led to my immediate arrest by the suspicious Turkish Government—but Lord Curzon obtained for me, from the Turkish Cabinet, an open letter to its governors in Syria, to afford me every assistance! This was a piquant passport for a tramp to carry.

T. 7, B. 20 (8):
"back by Nazareth / to Acre"

T.E. made a stroke as indicated and inserted:

and over Carmel.

T. 7, B. 20 (8):
"his route like a spider's web over / Syria."

T.E. made a stroke as indicated and inserted:

mountain.

T. 7, B. 20 (8):

"to Urfa" /

  T.E. made a stroke as indicated and inserted:

and Harran.

T. 8, B. 20 (9):

"He had no craving for *either* drink or meat"

  T.E. put a circle round the word here italicized and inserted:

European or conventional or normal or accustomed.

T. 8, B. 22 (10):

"It was Hogarth who now induced Magdalen College to give him a four years' senior demyship, or travelling endowment, and took him on the British Museum expedition to Jerablus on the Upper Euphrates, the presumed site of ancient Carchemish of the Hittites. On this first trip Lawrence . . . proved his value best by his knack of keeping the native labour-gangs in a good humour."

  I wonder. I know I did all the pottery, and produced, before the season ended, a complete stratification of types and rims from surface to 30 feet down. Also I did the photography.

T. 9, B. 22 (10):

"When the November rains came and interrupted the work, Hogarth sent T.E. to Egypt in order that he might learn something of *the latest* scientific methods of digging under Sir Flinders Petrie" . . .

  T.E. crossed out the words here italicized and wrote in the margin:

  Not quite!

T. 10, B. 23 (10):

"excavation in Egypt soon palled . . . it had become a *too highly* organised branch of research for his taste."

T.E. put brackets round the words here italicized and wrote, in substitution:

too minutely.

T. 10, B. 23 (11):
"He returned to Carchemish again the following year with Hogarth, and subsequently assisted Woolley there right up to the coming of war in 1914. The work offered plenty of variety, for his province embraced the photographs, sculpture, pottery and the copying of inscriptions. Twenty years later he remarked: 'It was the best life I ever lived'."

T.E. added:

—better even than the R.A.F. which was the refuge of his maturity.

T. 10, B. 23 (11):
"Even in the off-seasons, during the long winter floods and the heat of the summer, he only went home occasionally for short spells, and spent the rest of the time travelling round the Middle and Near East, or staying at the diggings alone. During the digging season he received fifteen shillings a day; during the rest of the year, while travelling, he lived on his demyship of a hundred pounds a year, supplemented by casual earnings of queerly varied kinds. Once, for example, he took on a checker's job in coaling ships at Port Said."

At the end of this paragraph T.E. added:

In five years he came to know Syria, like a book, much of North Mesopotamia, Asia Minor, Egypt and Greece. He was always going up and down, wherever going was cheap.

T. 10, B. 23–4 (11):
"his profound understanding of native ways . . . essentially different from the acquired knowledge of the outside observer."

Particularly, my poverty let me learn the masses, from whom the wealthy traveller was cut off by his money and attendants.

T. 11, B. 24 (11–12):

"It was by this complete abandonment not only of the conventions but of the *comforts* of civilized life, by what other Europeans would have considered an abasement, that T.E. became a naturalized Arab instead of merely a European visitor to the Arab lands."

T.E. bracketed the word here italicized and wrote:

? resources.

T. 11, B. 24 (12):

"It was while at Carchemish that he adopted the habit of wearing Arab dress on his / wanderings"

T.E. altered "Arab" into "*native*", crossed out "his", made a stroke as indicated and inserted:

occasional and specific.

T. 11, B. 24 (12):

"Short and slight, fair and clean-shaven, he was apparently the last man to carry off such a guise successfully . . ."

It was easy in N. Syria, where the racial admixture has produced many fair natives and many with only a broken knowledge of Arabic. I could never pass as an Arab—but easily as some other native speaking Arabic.

T. 11–12, B. 25 (12):

·"But to imagine him as always brooding would be essentially false. He was no hermit."

I travelled always with someone from our Carchemish digging gang, and we thoroughly enjoyed ourselves, taking a few camels on hire-carrying, sailing down the Syrian coast, bathing, harvesting, and sight-seeing in the towns. Certainly no hermitry!

T. 12, B. 25 (12):

"those who meet Lawrence see a facet of his personality that largely depends on their own cast of thought. And so is very different . . . It has led some of his friends to christen his the 'human chameleon'."

At an O.T.C. field-day I was once told to disguise myself as a battalion in close order: and have done, ever since!

T. 12, B. 27 (14):

"He made frequent trips on it [the Euphrates] defying its dangerous currents, in a canoe . . ."

T.E. inserted:

"Water work had come to him naturally, from his childhood in his father's sailing yachts . . ."

T. 16, B. 31 (17):

"That winter, after his return to Syria, a more serious mission awaited him. Woolley and he were at Aleppo, resting after a hard spell at Carchemish, when a telegram came from London telling him that they were wanted to take part in an expedition to Sinai. They went south accordingly and were met at Beersheba by Captain Newcombe, a Sapper officer, who was to be their companion. They learnt that their part in the expedition was to be an archaeological camouflage for a military survey, by Newcombe and his assistants, of the country beyond the frontier of Egypt . . . The survey was made *at the instigation* of Lord Kitchener, then Consul-General in Egypt." . . .

T.E. substituted "*at the initiative*" for the words here italicized and in the margin wrote:

K. paid the bills!

T. 18, B. 34 (19–20):

"This expedition, with its veiled military purpose, gave a reinforcement to thoughts which were already stirring in

Lawrence's mind since his sojourn at Carchemish.* He had watched the construction of the Baghdad railway with his own eyes, and thus had the keener perception of its potential menace to the outposts of British."†

T.E. wrote the insertions:

*His basic intention in exploring Syria was always to write a strategic study of the Crusades: but incidentally he saw many other things. From Carchemish he had watched . . .

†The Armenian revolutionaries had come to him for help and advice, and he had dipped far into their councils. The opposition party of the Kurdish reactionaries against the Young Turks had encouraged him to ride in their ranks and seek opportunity in the Balkan crisis. From the Arabs among whom he moved he had heard . . .

Chapter II (originally numbered III)

T. 32, B. 38 (24):

"As Napoleon wrote in 1808—'Who is to have Constantinople? That is always the crux of the problem'.* It proved to be so for another century."

*Nor have we any reason to think it settled yet!

T. 35, B. 40 (25):

On the rise of German influence at Constantinople in the years before the war:

"The / British Ambassador during these critical years *was a man whose personality* lacked both the necessary prestige and strength/."

T.E. made a stroke before "British", inserted the word "*successive*", changed "Ambassador" into the plural, deleted the words here italicized, inserted "*of personality*" at the end, and wrote the note:

The Ambassadors were Lowther (an utter dud) and Louis Mallet who was pretty good and gave fair warning of the trend of feeling. I blame much of our ineffectiveness upon Fitzmaurice, the Dragoman, an eagle-mind and personality of iron vigour. Fitzmaurice had lived half a lifetime in Turkey and was the Embassy's official go-between and native authority. He knew everything and was feared from end to end of Turkey. Unfortunately he was a rabid R.C. . . . The Young Turk movement was 50% crypto-Jew and 95% Free-mason. So he regarded it as the devil and threw the whole influence of England over to the unfashionable Sultan and his effete palace clique. Fitzm. . . . prestige . . . was enormous and our Ambassadors and the F.O. staff went down before him like ninepins. Thanks to him, we rebuffed every friendly advance the Young Turks made.

T. 41, B. 47 (31):
"On the entry of Turkey into the war, Kitchener mooted the idea of a landing near Alexandretta, but was advised that a large force would be required. So, dropping the project,* he came to the conclusion that the passive defence of the Suez Canal was the only possible way of protecting Egypt."

*The project was issued to Maxwell in Egypt in Feb. 1915 by K. as a tentative order, and not finally dropped till Ian Hamilton decided on Helles.

T. 44, B. 50 (33):
"Already, in October [1915], when the evacuation of Gallip-oli was in the air, he [Kitchener] had urgently demanded from Maxwell a report on the Turkish communications in Asia Minor and Syria."

Don't I know it. Gave me a lot of unnecessary work.

Chapter III (originally numbered IV)

T. 49-50, B. 55 (37):
Regarding the Ayas Bay project of Oct. 1915:
"He [Kitchener] agreed that Maxwell's estimate of 100,000 troops would suffice not merely to cut the Turkish communications but to hold a position that would keep them severed indefinitely with security to itself."

This reply was due to action of myself upon Guy Dawnay!

T. 51, B. 57 (39):

"*A curious stretch of imagination* . . . had led the British command to magnify beyond all reason the size of the Turkish forces which might be assembled for the invasion of Egypt."

T.E. underlined the words here italicized and made the note:

Not at all: it was misrepresentation by our chief of intelligence in Egypt, against the protests of Philip Graves, Jennings Bramley, and myself—the three active intelligence staff officers.

Chapter IV (originally numbered V)

T. 60, B. 66 (45):

"The British in answering . . . Hussein . . . remarked that the discussion of boundaries was premature, and *cloaked* the question of the Khalifate in discreet silence."

T.E. substituted the word "*dropped*" for the word here italicized, and made the note:

We had raised it; not Hussein!

Chapter V (originally numbered VI)

T. 71, B. 84 (60):

"Meantime, in ignorance of these dramatic events, Hogarth and other members of the Arab Bureau had come across the Red Sea to meet the Sherif's representative. Expecting to discuss the future revolt, they found it in being. When they landed . . . on the 8th . . ."

No: Hogarth's visit was in full knowledge. I think you have the date wrong.

(N.B. The date, taken from the Official History, was wrong. Hogarth landed on the 6th. But, as the revolt only broke out the day before, Hogarth, obviously, could not have left Egypt in full knowledge, as distinct from expectation, of it.)

T. 74, B. 87 (62):

On the Arab:

"A Cavalcade was more in his line than a Crusade."

Good!

T. 81, B. 93 (67):

"When the war came, in August, 1914, Lawrence had been back at Oxford, working on his part of a record of the Sinai trip which he had made with Woolley. Undisturbed by the general upset of life in England Lawrence continued work on this book, which was published in 1915 by the Palestine Exploration Fund under the title of *The Wilderness of Zin*. It is interesting to observe that Lawrence's literary style in this book, although lucid and well-expressed, is plain and almost curt, in contrast to the spaciousness and splendour of his post-war prose, which followed the tradition of Doughty's *Arabia Deserta*."

A dangerous remark. Woolley wrote nearly the whole of it, and edited my small share!

T. 82, B. 94 (67):

On Lawrence's first steps when the war came in 1914:

I think you are adrift here. Turkey was not in the war, but was sore about the Sinai survey, which it felt had been a military game. K. (the only begetter of the survey) insisted on the Palestine Exploration Fund's bringing out its record of our archeological researching, p.d.q. as whitewash. Woolley and I had instructions to get it done instanter.

Nor is the next paragraph correct. Woolley and I wrote to Newcombe, when the book was finished, and asked his advice about a war job. They were difficult to get. Newcombe told Cox, of the Intelligence, about us, and got our names on the waiting list. Woolley lost heart, waiting, and wangled a Commission in the Artillery. I asked Hogarth (prominent in the R.G.S.) if he could expedite me something—and he asked Hincks, who got Hedley to take me. The interview with Hedley was by Hogarth's appointment. Of course Hedley was drawing the Sinai map, and knew about me. He had only one assistant left, Capt. (Walter) Nugent, who was within a week of departing to France. Nugent hurriedly instructed me in my G.S.G.S. duties: we were M.O.4: O and I being one!: and Hedley and I were left alone in the office.[1]

T. 83, B. 96 (69):
"In December, after Turkey had entered the war, it was decided to strengthen the Intelligence service in Cairo. Newcombe . . . was to go out to Egypt . . . to take with him several officers, among them George Lloyd, / Leonard Woolley, and Lawrence."

T.E. made a stroke as indicated and inserted *"Aubrey Herbert"* . . .

At the bottom of the page he added the note:

Newcombe and I went then. The rest independently.

T. 83, B. 96 (70):
"Here Lawrence soon made his mark, and his knowledge was utilised not only in preparing maps but in compiling the enemy's 'Order of Battle' . . ."

You must mention Philip Graves (now on the Times) whose work the first number of the Ordre de Bataille was. Ask him about it. Philip was our Turkish Army authority.

T. 83, B. 98 (71):
". . . from the examination of prisoners."

I always knew their districts, and asked about my friends in them. Then they told me everything!

T. 87, B. 102 (74):
In the spring of 1916 Lawrence was sent on a secret mission to Mesopotamia, to accompany Aubrey Herbert on an em-

[1] See pp. 55, l. 23, 192, l. 16, and R.G., 49, l. 30.

bassy to Khalil Pasha, who commanded the Turkish forces then besieging Townshend in Kut. The hope, which proved vain, was that Khalil Pasha might allow Townshend's force to go free in return for a money payment—the first offer was a million pounds, and it was then doubled. While in Mesopotamia Lawrence took the opportunity of examining the conditions of the British forces there and wrote a pungent report on their defects. I quoted Colonel Stirling's description of the sensation his criticisms caused among the General Staff in Egypt when they read his report.

"Sir Archibald Murray, who knew of his visit to Mesopotamia, asked to see the report. 'There was consternation that night in the General Staff, for we were convinced that, if he were to read it, apoplexy would be the result and we should lose our C-in-C. Hurriedly, therefore, we sat down and bowdlerized the report until we considered it fit to be put before his professional eye! Lawrence, however, was abundantly right in most of his criticisms—particularly on the medical question— as was proved by the tragic muddle which occurred when the wounded first started coming down.' "

I was not distressed at their editing it, for Webb Gillman, a War Office investigating general, had been my only fellow-passenger on the ship from Basra to Egypt, and had discussed every page of my original with me, before starting to write down his own submissions.

T. 87a, B. 103 (75):
Later in 1915 Lawrence was "absorbed into Murray's swollen staff organisation where his chief, Holdich, was a man who could not tolerate Lawrence's 'cheek' or his superior knowledge."

It went further than this. My estimates of enemy strengths always were issued to the nearest hundred: he suppressed them and put forward his own, which seemed to me to be only in the farthest ten thousands. Holdich was excellent in O. and fatal in I.

Chapter VI (originally numbered VII)

T. 99, B. 114–15 (85):

"Lawrence [on return from his first visit to the Hejaz] . . .
was opposed to the idea of sending British units into the
Hejaz, having formed the opinion that such a landing would
turn the tribes against the Sherif. In both these views, however, he found himself in a minority."

"I found myself in a minority". Qualify this. Clayton in Cairo
asked me for a note on the "troops to Rabegh" question, which I had
traversed already in my report to Wingate. I wrote for Clayton a
short and very pungent note, opposing the dispatch of a brigade, root
and branch, also pointing out the existence, 15 miles inland of
Rabegh, of great water sources.[1]

Murray and his staff turned round and said I was a broth of a boy.
They telegraphed my note in extenso to Robertson, who sent me a
message of thankfulness. Wingate bleated a bit at my irregular conduct, but Clayton took the responsibility of having asked for my
views.

Chapter VII (originally numbered VIII)

T. 111, B. 123 (93):

Regarding Brémond's attitude in pressing for the despatch of
troops to the Hejaz:

"He [Lawrence] suspected the French of having political
motives for their eagerness, and did not hesitate to say so
(in his report)."

Not in my first note: later, after Brémond came to me in Yanbo or
Wejh and made certain suggestions.

T. 113, B. 125 (95):

(Quotation from *Revolt in the Desert*):

"As our revolt succeeded, onlookers have praised its leader-

---

[1] This would enable the Turks to move direct on Mecca, short-circuiting any British
force at Rabegh.

ship: but behind the scenes lay all the vices of amateur control, experimental councils, divisions, whimsicality."

Yes: for amateurs lack the tradition and without prejudice will try
everything—once. Had a tried soldier like Dawnay been with us, we
should have been spared much repetition of experimental work,
already disproved elsewhere.

T. 123, B. 134 (102):
In January 1917 Feisal's army, hard-pressed by the Turks
in the Hejaz, turned the tables on them by a strategic flank
march up the Red Sea coast to Wejh, from which it could
threaten the railway from Damascus, the Turks' line of
communications:
"His own [Vickery's] informal way was affronted by Lawrence's, and especially by what seemed airy talk of the Arab
army *being* at the gates of Damascus within a year."

T.E. underlined the word here italicized and made the note:

Not "being"—"tapping" was my phrase. I meant raiding.

T. 123, B. 134 (102):
"Vickery insisted on wearing a British helmet under his Arab
headcloth, which offended Lawrence's sense of fitness . . ."

I'm afraid I laughed. Our old Arab guide, when he saw Vickery
riding in front of him, cried out, "Mashallah, the head of an ox"—
astonished at the spread of the headcloth: and that collapsed me.

T. 123, B. 134 (102):
"Vickery disappeared from the scene too early to share in
the ultimate triumph . . ."

He said of Arabia, "Service here is professional suicide."

T. 123, B. 134 (102):
Regarding the Arab forces which advanced on Wejh:

The 200 "regulars" (m.i. and gunners and machine-gunners and
a company of infantry) were all of them my godchildren over whom
I had worked for weeks.

T. 129, B. 140 (113):
  T.E. made the note at the end of the chapter:

I would like more frequent comparisons, in your text, of the comparative numbers of Turks opposing Murray and opposing us. The figures were rather consoling to me, usually. I counted as ours, all from Maan downwards to Medina and Asir—not Yemen, of course.

Chapter VIII (originally numbered IX)

T. 139, B. 157 (121):
On the invasion of Palestine, January 1917:
"To meet the advance of three British infantry divisions, and two mounted divisions, the Turks had only one weak division and the remains of a second."

They had, according to what I remember, within 500 of the strength that was opposing us!

T. 140, B. 158 (122):
"Early in March a telegram from Djemal Pasha was intercepted *on the Hejaz railway*. Only part of it could be deciphered. That part, however, seemed to suggest that the evacuation of Medina was being arranged, and that the Turkish forces were to retire north in mass."

T.E. put brackets round and underlined the words here italicized, substituted "*by wireless in Cairo*", and made the note:

I got it fuller than this, verbally, from McRury who was sent down by special ship to tell me. It suggested an order of march, with luggage and H.Q. on an accompanying train. Fakhri, old fanatical Moslem refused to obey—said he couldn't!

Chapter IX (originally numbered X)

T. 149, B. 164 (127):
"Only in the East, especially the Middle East, was mobility given opportunity, and the opportunity taken. But there, more significantly, arose a new and extreme theory of mobil-

ity, which was applied with dramatic success and had a far-reaching effect in irregular warfare. But it has, also, a message for regular warfare, of still greater potential range. . . . That theory evolved/from the reveries of Lawrence as he lay on his sickbed in Abdulla's camp."

T.E. made a stroke as indicated and suggested the insertion:

? into expression.

T. 150, B. 165 (128):

On Lawrence's pre-war studies in military history:

"This had inspired Lawrence with a desire to study the textbooks that Napoleon himself had studied/".

T.E. made the note, as an addition:

and I was fortunate in having access to the advice of Oman and Reginald Lane Poole, who had read every book, and remembered the best ones. R.L.P. was my most unpontifical official tutor at Oxford!

T. 151, B. 166 (129):

"Plunged suddenly into action at Yanbo, Lawrence's immersion had been too complete hitherto for him to rise to the surface and get his head above water. Now, however, enforced inactivity served him as a life-buoy."

True as it stands: but the implied criticism is a bit 'ard. Upon entering Hejaz first of all I had put forward a reasoned appreciation. Upon my second arrival I had been faced with the need to act instantly—and had acted by (I) starting to equip Feisal with Arab technical units. and (II) moving him to Wejh. Both instincts were sound, if dumb.

Chapter X (originally numbered XI)

T. 166, B. 180 (141):

"This gave Lawrence the opportunity of laying his first mine."

The Martini-lock to fire it was a device used by the Boers in S. Africa against us! I got it from either Garland or Newcombe.

T. 168, B. 182 (142):
On Lawrence's expedition to capture Aqaba:
"What he had in mind was far more than an alternative offensive . . ."

Perhaps you should point out that the venture was a private one. I had no orders to do it, and took nothing British with me. Feisal provided money, camels, stores, and explosives. That explains why I had no help from the Navy.

(Yet the Official History remarks that it "became desirable to extend the operations of the Arabs further north and to open a new base at Aqaba. The mission was *entrusted* to Captain Lawrence" . . [!])

T. 169, B. 183 (143):
"Lawrence was convinced that the longest way round would prove the shortest way there—his mind was ever on the mountain wall that towered behind Aqaba and could be so easily used by the Turks to block any advance from a landing."

One of my first jobs for Holdich had been to make out a tactical scheme for the occupation of Akaba by amphibian expedition—and I had confessed that such a landing party could nohow cover itself. The proposed operation was indefensible. I said this in Jan. 1915, in my paper upon an Akaba landing.

T. 173, B. 186 (146):
On his first stage; the ride to the Sirhan:
"They pushed on relentlessly, driven by the thought of the waterholes of which Sharraf had told them . . ."

Sharraf's waterholes were W. of the railway, near Dizad.

Chapter XI (originally numbered XII)

T. 190, B. 200 (157):
On finding the Turks encamped at Abu el Lissal:
"This ill-stroke of fortune was a lesson to Lawrence in the accidents of war that may wreck the best-laid plan unless

it has variants. And here no variant was possible.* But a sense of time and an instinct for surprise may change the balance of fortune. And here both were shown."

T.E. put an asterisk as indicated and made the note:

*My alternative plan—for I hardly expected to crush the battalion at Aba el Lissan—was to hold them on the defensive, and force them to fight their communications open again to Ma'an. This would take all their reserve and transport. While so occupied they would not be able to look towards Akaba: but half our force would have gone down via Batra towards Rumm, and fallen upon Guweira, and then marched down the (Wadi) Ithm to Akaba, which we would have taken while the (Turkish) force at Lissan was being contained. It was inferior to what we did, as the destruction of the Ma'an garrison at Lissan gave us leisure, at Akaba, to organise it as a base and for defence.

Chapter XII (originally numbered XIII)

T. 199, B. 209 (165):

On Lawrence's dispositions, after the capture of Aqaba, to hold this key-point:

"It was arranged to cover all the possible approaches to Aqaba, not by a series of interdependent posts, but by four independent ones, sited in places as nearly impregnable by nature as possible and each menacing the enemy's rear if he tried to advance by the others, so that while not one could be easily taken, none could be neglected."

You need to be a high-speed geographer to site posts of this kind successfully in a hurry. My map studies with Hedley and the survey of Egypt (Director, Sir Ernest Dowson) were of great value to my plans, always.

T. 199, B. 209 (165):

"a fourth [post] at Delagha up the Wadi Araba through . . ."

Not quite. Delagha lay E. of the hills. In 1915 the Turks had bettered the road from it to Wadi Gharandil, in the Araba, on their way from Maan to Sinai. Now I was not sure of the Sinai and Beer-sheba Arabs, who had been much Turkised (later we sent Sherif Abdulla el Feir and converted them: it was they who took the Turkish fleet in the Dead Sea): so I put posts at Delagha and Gharandil, to prevent Maan and Beersheba joining hands against Guweira & Akaba.

T. 205, B. 214 (169):
Quotation from *Revolt in the Desert* telling how, by Allenby, he was "given stores and arms and a fund of two hundred thousand sovereigns . . ."

The £200,000 had become £500,000 before Damascus fell—and I had only £10,000 balance then, to return.

T. 205, B. 214 (169):
"Before going to Yanbo he had tried to evade the responsibility of being adviser. Now he sought the far greater responsibility of being leader . . . when Clayton objected that even irregular war did not reverse regular methods so far that the most junior officer should take command, Lawrence willingly fell in with the practicable alternative that Joyce should be sent as commanding officer at Aqaba . . . For with Joyce . . . he would be assured . . . of a free hand. . . ."

I did not ask for command: but that *my* policy and tactics should be adopted by those of us who were working in the Arab area. In other words, I wanted the northern plan to be adopted as the official one.

T. 205, B. 215 (169):
"Lawrence was more than willing to accept . . . that Joyce should be sent as commanding officer at Aqaba. For with Joyce . . . he would be assured not only of a free hand but of solid backing. Joyce would make a strong shaft for Lawrence's spearhead, and all the stronger because Joyce had

the capacity for that necessary organisation which Lawrence *preferred to escape*."

T.E. underlined the words here italicized and made the note:

If you had been in my place, and knew that your guidance & impulse were essential not merely to Feisal, but to all the individual tribal leaders; and that this was a 24-hours a day job—wouldn't you have wanted someone else to do the stores, ammunition, telegraphy, & routine work? "Anxious to escape" is quite true, but only part of the truth. Necessary to escape, or to delegate, perhaps: not preferred to escape. I had no choice.

Also remember that long experience had shown me that I had to be the spear-point in any big drive I needed. The others had courage and good-will: but they lacked ingenuity. I knew my ground, my material, my allies. If I met fifty checks, I could yet see a fifty-first way to my object. The others used to confess themselves baffled, sometimes. Now, if I had to be the spear-point, dared I weary myself over ship-loads of flour and rice?

The same with the Arab Regulars. The formation and equipment of Jaafar's force was full-time work for several people. Because I delegated this, am I to be called indifferent? I controlled it all generally (refusing them e.g. bayonets, because I wanted to keep them long-range, & heavy guns, because I wanted them light-footed, & horses, because I wanted to carry them through the desert, & Vickers guns, because $\left.\begin{array}{l}\text{Hotchkiss}\\\text{Lewis}\end{array}\right\}$ were lighter) and Jaafar always came to me when he was stuck: and I used them, tactically & strategically. The man who has to do everything himself will never be big. Akaba operations throughout 1918 were big: 400-mile front, 5000 regulars, unlimited irregulars, armoured cars, aircraft—a perfect war in miniature.

T. 206, B. 216 (170):
"Lawrence realised, *whether he liked it or not*, the Arab peoples in the north could only be freed through the aid of the British Army . . ."

T.E. underlined the words here italicized and made the note:

I liked it well enough! Allenby was a trump. With Murray it would have been different!

T. 206, B. 216 (170):

". . . British and Arabs were long-range collaborators rather than direct associates. Such was Lawrence's idea, and in Allenby he found a ready response to it."

We agreed to keep the Dead Sea & Jordan between us—except when he gave me notice he was going to Amman, and I gave him notice I was recruiting in Sinai.

T. 207, B. 217 (171):

"Lawrence's *own dream of a united Arabia* had shrivelled in contact with Arab realities . . ."

T.E. underlined the words here italicized and made the marginal note:

Not even in boyhood, I think.

At the bottom of the page he wrote:

Surely not! I never, to my knowledge, suggested it. You may be quoting something I have forgotten: but the physical difficulties alone make it a plan too wild for me. Remember I have always been a realist and opportunist in tactics: and Arab unity is a madman's notion—for this century or next, probably. English-speaking unity is a fair parallel. I am sure I never dreamed of uniting even Hejaz and Syria. My conception was of a number of small states.

T. 207, B. 217 (171):

"Feisal should be the fuse, as a personification and projection of the past glories of the Ommayad and Ayubid dynasties. He should come among them as a new *Saladin*."

T.E. underlined the word italicized and made the note:

Not very happy. Saladin was a Kurdish nobody. Feisal thought himself better than that!

Chapter XIII (originally numbered XIV)

T. 213, B. 221 (175):
"On the debit side was the detachment of the Billi from the Sherifian cause. Early in May their Sheikh had joined the Turks at El Ala . . . and although he evaded their invitation to attack Feisal, he induced his brother to leave Feisal's army . . ."

This may be true, but I doubt much of it. We mined a train that was bringing down Suleiman Pasha Rifada, the head of the Billi, from Damascus to Medain Saleh, & killed the poor old man. He had never joined Feisal, or left the Turks.

I don't think the brother left Feisal for the Turks: so far as I remember, he only went to his tents.

T. 217, B. 225 (178):
"Without doubt Lawrence, who has no care for his own money, was prodigal of public money in his efforts to forward the cause."

It was money or my life—or other fellows' lives.

T. 218, B. 226 (179):
"By the beginning of September they [the Turks] had concentrated 6000 men at Maan . . ."

All from the NORTH. None from Medina.

(He thereby emphasized that the menace of the Arabs' northward advance had drawn to meet it further troops who might otherwise have been used against the British.)

T. 219, B. 227 (180):
". . . Air co-operation . . . An advanced landing-ground was reconnoitred at Quntilla . . ."

It took me two days hard work to choose and mark this landing ground, & take up their stores. I didn't tackle the line till afterwards. Too busy!

T. 225, B. 234 (185):
After the successful raid on the railway near Hallat Ammar:
"Lawrence himself rode out on a fresh venture / . . ."
T.E. made a stroke as indicated and inserted:
This time to train disciples in the art of demolition.

T. 226, B. 235 (186):
"During the next four months seventeen engines were destroyed, and scores of trucks."

Traffic was disorganised up to Aleppo, for we posted notices in Damascus, warning "our friends" not to travel by the northern railways, as our threat was about to be extended thither. The Turks had rail-guards up to Aleppo, soon!

Chapter XIV (originally numbered XV)

T. 231, B. 239 (191):
On the British plans for the Gaza-Beersheba attack of October 1917:
(Quotation from *Revolt in the Desert*): "We knew, better than Allenby, the enemy hollowness . . ."
Naturally, for we lived behind the Turkish front!

T. 237, B. 245 (195):
On the Hebron diversion in aid of Allenby's offensive, an effort "due largely to the initiative and self-sacrifice of another member of the British Mission to the Arabs . . . Newcombe . . ."

Newcombe, I think, showed imagination, courage, as well as self-sacrifice in this show. He was brave for six hours too long, but that was inevitable: he had no spies out to tell him when the Turks were coming in force. I am glad your study does him some tardy justice.

It had been suggested that we come up between the Dead Sea and Beersheba and press Hebron or Jerusalem from the S. and E: but

I feared that to brigade Arabs and English together would be a free fight—and so discouraged the idea. It was not so much the English I feared as their Australian and Indian auxiliaries.

Newcombe was too enterprising, too keen, too active . . . for my base commandant. What I needed was a man glad to stay still behind me. Newcombe is a man to like and respect.

T. 243, B. 251 (200):
On the raid which Lawrence himself made against the Tell el Shehab bridge:
"But now, one feels, he had for some months so strained himself . . . that his power of practical guidance was affected. Here, and not merely in the adverse conditions of the problem, one may find the explanation of what followed."

We were only a cat's whisker off success, you know—and it was the boldest thing we ever tried.

Chapter XV (originally numbered XVI)

T. 259, B. 267 (213):
"Nasir's direction of advance [on Jurf ed Derawish] offered him the *chance* of seizing a ridge which overlooked the station."
T.E. underlined the word italicized here and made the note:

Not chance. We had been there a few days before, and chosen the gun-position for him!

T. 266, B. 275 (219):
On the decisive movement in the Battle of Tafila:
"While they waited a fresh reinforcement arrived, about a hundred men from the neighbouring village of El 'Eime, or Aima. 'Their arrival decided us to abandon the precepts of Marshal Foch, and to attack from at any rate three sides at once; so we sent the Aima men, with three automatic guns to envelop the enemy's right or western flank' [quoted from *Revolt in the Desert*]. As they happened to arrive on the scene

from this direction, it is possible that geography had as much part as strategy in deciding the form of their attack."

T.E. answered this surmise by the note:

Zeid was calling them to him. I sent them back to their own side.

T. 267, B. 276 (220):
"the Turks fled in confusion . . . abandoning two howitzers and sixteen machine-guns . . ."

T.E. crossed out "sixteen", substituted "*all their*", and made the note:

We captured the whole 27. I have a jolly photo of them on parade next day!

(N.B. The figure "sixteen" was taken from the British Official History. I was subsequently able to check T.E.'s figure by obtaining the photograph.)

T. 268, B. 277 (220):
"Heavy snowfalls and a wind of razor-edge extinguished the Arabs' flickering impulse to follow up their success, and even Lawrence was constrained to recognize that the effort placed too high a tax on human capacity. The clumsy helplessness of camels in mud would also be a tactical danger.
But although his *body was chained* to Tafileh, his mind was projected towards his Dead Sea objective. . . . He bethought himself of Abdulla el Feir, camped down in the sunny, snow-free plain . . . so *a message was got* through to him . . ."

T.E. underlined the words here italicized and made the note:

Not in my memory. I went down to Abdulla el Feir in the Ghor and moved him.

T. 270, B. 279 (222):
"Movement forward was now practicable and Lawrence made a reconnaissance to the Dead Sea with that idea. But

when, on returning, he urged it on Zeid, he met difficulties, due still more to Zeid's entourage. The chief excuse was / that Zeid had spent all the money intended to subsidise the advance . . ."

T.E. made a stroke as indicated and inserted:

a pretence.

T. 271, B. 280 (222–23):
"After a ride of nearly eighty miles he reached Beersheba . . . Then he went on to Allenby's headquarters and luckily met Hogarth on the station platform. Here was a man to whom he could relieve himself. He blamed himself for Zeid's moral failure. He declared that he was sick of responsibility . . . Thus, for his own part, he wanted to go back and become a cog in the military machine, with things comfortably arranged for him. The harness of obedience was better than the self-applied spur of command."[1]

I was a very sick man, again, you know: almost at breaking point.

Chapter XVI (originally numbered XVII)

T. 273, B. 281 (224):
Opening sentence: "Immediately after the capture of Jerusalem, Allenby . . ."

Would you like to put in a paragraph saying what pleasure the capture gave to the Allies? Its moral value, which far exceeded any tactical success in France?

T. 274, B. 282 (225):
On Allenby's plans for 1918 and promised reinforcements: "Thus he [Allenby] would have ten infantry and four mounted divisions . . ."

Perhaps you might say what he had facing him! And what were facing us, the Amman troops being now contained by the Arabs.

[1]See R.G., p. 97, bottom.

T. 276, B. 284 (227):
"the Turkish strength was actually weaker in the spring, when Allenby might have attacked, than in the autumn when he wrought their collapse."

No: his rapidity of advance depended on his being able to feed his beasts—and men—on the newly gathered harvest. Spring N.B.G.

(N.B. The "might have" referred to Allenby's intention, not to its practicability, so T.E.'s comment did not affect the point of the sentence.)

T. 278, B. 285 (227):
"in the field (i.e. the open) the Arabs would easily defeat the Turks."

Remember that we had armoured cars, which once got into a Turkish battalion, and wholly dispersed it.

T. 278, B. 285 (228):
On the plan for a British advance across the Jordan:
"Allenby's Chief of Staff, Bols, wanted the Arabs in the north to help in the British advance, but Lawrence argued that it would be better to wait until the raid on Amman was over* and Es Salt permanently occupied . . ."

T.E. put an asterisk as indicated and made the note:

*I did not think close co-operation a possible achievement. Like mixing oil and water!

T. 280, B. 288 (229):
"The British had done little damage to the railway during *their stay*" (at Amman).

T.E. altered the words italicized here to: "*the five days it had lain in their hands*". He added the note:

I called it unpardonable carelessness. They went to Amman, not to take the beastly village, but to smash the railway. Miles of the line, from Amman southwards, were in their hands—and they hardly broke a rail!

T. 281, B. 288 (230):

"Lawrence . . . left Abu el Lissal on April 3rd with a convoy of two thousand baggage camels, carrying ammunition and food."

The size of this shows on what a scale we had prepared to act in the Madeba area. It was equipment for 10,000 irregulars for a month.

T. 282, B. 289 (230–31):

"Desert news seems for once to have travelled with curious slowness. For according to Lawrence's account it was fully a fortnight after the British had reached Amman that the Beni Sakhr, in their camp less than forty miles distant, heard of it and began moving towards Themed. Then, however, . . . Lawrence . . . 'grew seriously disturbed in the conflict of rumour, and sent Adhub . . . to Salt with a letter for Chetwode or Shea, asking for a note on the real situation'. This precautionary search for information seems to have been rather belated."

I think your timing is wrong, too. The British retreat from Amman was on April 1, I fancy: and they left Salt on April 3 or 4, and were in Jericho on April 6 (rearguard timings). I sent Adhub across on April 7, to Salt—three days, not a fortnight, after. You will remember the retreat from Amman was planned: so I was not worried about that, and was leaving local opinion time to settle. The Turkish garrisons of Ziza & its two neighbouring stations had taken refuge with the Beni Sakhr! We had to put them back on guard!

(N.B. The British actually retired from Amman early on March 31st, and quitted Salt in the night of April 1st/2nd. They had reached Salt on the 25th and Amman early on the 27th—so even if Adhub was sent on April 7th (I had made the time two or three days later) this was eleven days after the British "had reached" their objective. In these circumstances I saw no reason for modifying the implied criticism of his slowness to obtain information on this occasion.)

T. 283, B. 290 (232):

On the loss of Lawrence's two devoted followers:

"One of those who had died from the cold was Daud. His bosom friend, Farraj, did not survive him long, nor had he the wish to linger when shot through the body in a scuffle . . ."

This seems to me not very important, and it holds up the story.

(N.B. The story was so briefly told, while of distinct interest as a sidelight. T.E.'s objection seemed rather slight.)[1]

T. 286, B. 293 (234):

On the attack launched against Maan, April 1918, in Lawrence's absence:

"Auda's Abu Tayi, however, had not lived up to their Abu el Lissal reputation, doing little to help Nuri's attack. Even *Lawrence was constrained to recognise this*, and when Auda came in . . ."

T.E. underlined the words here italicized and made the note:

I should have said: "Even allowing for the difficulty of working regulars and irregulars together, the Abu Tayi had been disappointing, and when Auda . . ." Had I been there, the Abu Tayi would have been sent miles further off, & done something!

T. 288, B. 294 (235):

(Dawnay's camp): " 'The cars were parked geometrically here; armoured cars there; *sentries* and pickets were out, with machine-guns ready . . .' "

T.E. underlined the word here italicized and made the note:

The sentries were marching up & down. I had to post them in hiding and tell them to listen & keep still. They were giving us away across the quiet of the night.

[1]See R.G., p. 99, l. 9.

T. 290, B. 296 (237):
On the looting at "South Post": "Egyptians and Bedouin came / to blows over the food . . ."

T.E. made a stroke as indicated and inserted "*almost*" and, at the foot of the page, made the note:

This was really why I had come down. The antipathy of the Egyptians & the Bedouin was intense, and the Egyptian effort to save some of the loot from private plundering nearly started a fight. I had a very near call, but just managed to keep the Arabs in hand. Otherwise all the regulars would have been killed.[1]

T. 295, B. 301 (240):
On the failure of Allenby's second attempt to advance into Trans-Jordan and occupy Es Salt:
". . . the situation of the cavalry, who had exhausted their rations, certainly became awkward, if not so dangerous as they believed. That afternoon Allenby came down to see Chauvel and, confronted with 'a somewhat exaggerated report', decided to cut his loss and order the abandonment of the whole enterprise."

I was meanwhile sent for and asked to be ready to fly over to Salt, land, and lead the cut-off cavalry via Mabeba, Kerak, Tafileh, back to safety. It would have been possible, as there was lots of water and some food. The Turks would have been properly flummoxed! The staff thought the Salt force were probably cut off from the Jordan by forces too strong to pierce.

T. 296, B. 302 (241):
"From Lawrence's point of view the failure had one advantage in that it made the British staff more patient with Feisal's difficulties."

It much strengthened my personal position. They saw that moving irregulars was an art, like moving troops, & agreed to let me know if anything of the sort was ever required. . . .

[1] See R.G., p. 100, footnote 1.

T. 297, B. 303 (242):
Allenby's forces had been depleted by the necessity of sending
reinforcements to France. Until they could be reconstituted
there was danger of the Turks concentrating against the
Arabs:
"The Air Force promised, and rendered, still more definite
help to Feisal by repeated bombing raids on the railway which
disorganised traffic."

Not strong enough. They were invaluable now.

T. 300, B. 306 (244):
Young had been deputising for Lawrence in co-ordinating
the Bedouin operations, but his efforts towards extending the
railway attacks northward seemed to have little effect; he
was put off by excuses that seemed mere evasions.
"Yet with characteristic Arab *inconsistency*, no sooner had he
disappeared than Nasir moved north to the Wadi Hesa,
... and broke the railway ... effectively over a fourteen mile
stretch ..."

T.E. underlined the word here italicized and made the note:

Not quite fair. Timing in war depends on the enemy as much as
on yourself. Young refused to make allowances. The Hesa operation
was being steadily prepared all the while he fumed, & it was carried
out as soon as possible. He allowed no law for the political preparation, and no elasticity to compensate for the liveliness of the Maan
garrison....

T. 300, B. 306 (244–45):
"First he [Nasir] destroyed Hesa station and next day
Faraifra station, without having men killed. Between his
forays he fell back to a hidden valley, rich in pasture and
within quick support from Tafileh. These were the 'intangible
ghost' tactics of Lawrence's desire."

T.E. put a circle round "a" in "a hidden valley" and substituted "*his*". He made the note:

You rather underestimate the size of this operation, & its importance. I was afraid of the Arab regular army being attacked by a much re-inforced Maan. Breaks in the line by Jerdun were no help against this, Jerdun being too near Maan. So we projected this big break north of Tafileh, so close to Amman that it would occupy its garrison, & make Maan seem of secondary importance.

I wanted Young to try his prentice hand at it, so gave him the idea and my notions of what to use for the job. He upset everybody by being too cast-iron, and wore himself out. Maximum of friction. So I was not sorry when he went sick, except that I had then to take over the push myself.

Nasir took the Turks completely by surprise—& Peake & Hornby, with the labour assistance of their stalwart Egyptians (not fighting men: line-breakers) made an awful mess of the Turkish stations & line. We turned over great lengths of it, bending rails & sleepers, & even blew in cuttings, besides wells, water towers, pumps, points— all the railway. Nasir stayed up there, in Wadi Hesa which was full of air-proof caves, and as often as the Turks tried to mend a bit, he broke it again. We were in secure possession of Tafileh & Kerak, meanwhile, and the Turks had the proper wind-up. They thought we were coming on to Jericho[1]: and I went there, just to excite them!

As for the effect of the bombing, the war showed me that a combination of armoured cars and aircraft could rule the desert: but that they must be under non-army control, and without infantry support. You rightly trace the origin of the RAF control in Irak, Aden & Palestine to this experience. As soon as I was able to have my own way in the Middle East I approached Trenchard on the point, converted Winston easily, persuaded the Cabinet swiftly into approving (against the wiles of Henry Wilson)—and it has worked very well. The system is *not* capable of universal application.

Note by L.H. When I asked T.E. if I could quote this as a footnote, he agreed, but made a few revisions of wording in the

[1]*Note by L.H.* This northward ride into the Turkish zone is one that he did not mention in the *Seven Pillars*.

sentence before the last. One of these revisions is included in the sentence as printed here.

T. 313–14, B. 307–08 (245):
"On returning south Lawrence was able to assure Feisal that ample breathing space was assured until the Arabs, with the augmented mobility that the coming increase of camels promised, could renew their offensive at longer range and on a wider scale. In preparation for this he proposed that all the Arab Regulars now in the Hejaz with Ali and Abdulla should be transferred to Aqaba . . .

"Feisal accepted the plan and gave Lawrence letters to carry to Hussein. Knowing Hussein's jealousy of his son, Lawrence decided first to obtain leverage upon him from the British authorities. He went to Cairo and expounded his ideas to Dawnay, who saw their value . . . They next went up to Allenby's headquarters, on June 19th, where the unexpected awaited them.

"Lawrence found a remarkable lightening in the atmosphere. The reorganisation of the army was so far advanced, and also the vision of its chiefs, that Allenby was planning not merely to carry out the postponed spring offensive but to execute it on far bolder lines, with Damascus and Aleppo as the geographical goals. The offensive would be launched in September, and the Arabs were wanted, as arranged, to cover Allenby's flank and distract the Turks' attention by striking at Deraa."

My plan for containing Maan, holding the Moab plateau, and simultaneously raising the Hauran was actually to capture Damascus, & so destroy the Turkish Palestine army between my hammer & Allenby's anvil. He had assured me that he was immobilised, done for, by the drafts withdrawn for France. The new Indian material was not good, and could not be quickly embodied—etc. etc. etc.
This was now 1918, and stalemate across its harvest would have

marked the ebb of Feisal's movement. His fellows were living on their nerves (rebellion is harder than war) and their nerves were wearing thin. Also the big war was not looking too well.

So I made up my mind to take the offensive, encouraged to it by hints from the War Council, who also felt that it was Damascus in 1918, or never. Allenby agreed, unofficially, while not promising to pass the Palestine boundary: but I felt that did I get on to near Aleppo he would come along, too.

When Bartholomew took over, & the new troops' absorption was expedited, the plan of course changed. Allenby would do the big offensive, & my job again became a permeating one. So I didn't need the troops from Hejaz, and was rather glad to leave them alone.

Chapter XVII (originally numbered XVIII)

T. 316, B. 310 (248):
"Lawrence's experience of British staff calculations had made him healthily critical of them . . ."

So that I took the precaution to go into their offices and assure myself of the exact methods on which they were working.

T. 303, B. 310 (248):
"The chief of the General Staff was on leave, as well as the chief of the 'Q' staff, and . . . in their absence Bartholomew and Evans, their now unfettered right hands, were working out the material factors of the problem . . . The fighting troops of the army were now to be given comparative freedom of movement by the use of an elastic cord that could not only be stretched but quickly attached to fresh points."

There was also the definite intention of living on the country except for troops' rations during movement. Bartholomew and Evans did wonderful work in this redistribution of transport—only Bols & W. Campbell will not like being told that they were sent on leave!

T. 304–05, B. 311 (249):
"Well might Bartholomew express anxiety over the uncomfortably narrow margin between complete success and failure.

If the Turks got wind of the intention, and were wise enough
to retire in time, 'the British Army would then be left like a
fish flapping on dry land, with its railways, its heavy artillery,
its dumps, its stores, its camps all misplaced.' "

This is my remark, not Bartholomew's, by the way. Though he
felt it, of course!

T. 318–19, B. 313 (250):

On returning to Cairo, Lawrence and Dawnay received reports that the Turks were contemplating a fresh stroke against
Abu at Lissal. This threatened an interruption of the Arab
move to Deraa. To forestall the Turks they devised a preliminary distraction and for it obtained the loan of two com-
panies of the Imperial Camel Corps under Major R. V.
Buxton:

"The plan was not well received when it reached Aqaba.
Joyce and Young had been hard at work organising, under
manifold difficulties, the transport of the Arab Regular Army
for the coming move to Deraa . . . Dawnay's *telegram* was a
disturbing shock."

T.E. underlined the word here italicized and wrote "*letter,
I expect*". At the bottom of the page he made the note:

No: part of the trouble was that we did not use W/T for "operation" messages. Allenby every morning for breakfast had the log of
Turkish signals over the preceding 24 hours: we read their every
message—and I presumed they read all of ours. To keep our moves
secret we used air-mail or word of mouth. To keep the Turks' public,
one of my cares was to distribute wirecutters over their rear, and cut
their telegraph at least daily.

T. 320, B. 313–14 (251):

"Seeing the wider strategic aspects of the problem, Lawrence
was equally critical of Young's scheme, when it reached
Cairo. Knowing 'the muddy impassable roads' of the Hauran
in winter, he saw the practical weakness of a scheme which

placed a force there so late in the season. More pertinent still was the fact that it did not fit the particular case. For Allenby was going to attack about the end of September. Any sort of force at the right time was better than the most perfectly equipped force that arrived too late."

Three men & a boy with pistols—on the right day, Bartholomew used to din into me.

T. 320–21, B. 314–15 (251–52):
On the divergence of views between Lawrence and Young over the scheme for the Deraa raid:
"There was an entertaining passage at arms between them. Taking Young's schedule for the Deraa raid, Lawrence crossed out the provision for forage beyond the dump at Bair, saying that pasture was splendid this year in the Azrak-Deraa area. This removed the heaviest item. He cut down the allowance for food, saying that the men could live on the country. Young sarcastically remarked that the ten days' return journey would be a long fast. Lawrence retorted that he had no intention of returning to Aqaba. So it went on, Lawrence meeting 'regular' objections by repeating his irregular maxim that the Arabs lived by their raggedness and beat the Turk by their uncertainty."

Before making my Deraa scheme I had taken the trouble to look at the country—and before settling to go there in August and Sept. I had studied the pasture & water. So (pace Young) I knew
(I) where the pasture was rich enough for 2000 camels, and therefore the routes we would have to take to
(II) where the flood-pools lay (there is no natural water between Azrak and Mezerib—only rain pools). These pools are filled by floods coming down whichever valley runs in the spring—and they entirely conditioned our halting places. Had Umtaiye not filled we should not have gone that way—of course.
As for retreat—had we met disaster there was all Wadi Sirhan open to us, and Akaba afterwards, at our leisure. Sirhan was (in

Sept.) full of sheep and dates and flour. Also we had 2000 camels, each affording a meat meal for 200 men.

I knew my Arab soldiery, in and out, and they were much more self-sufficing and easier to feed than Englishmen. Young was treating them like an army: I wanted to treat them like the uniformed peasantry they were.

T. 329, B. 324–25 (259–60):

On the raid against Amman by Buxton's Camel Corps force, which Lawrence accompanied:

"From villagers they heard that several parties of Turkish mule-mounted infantry were quartered in the villages near the bridge, guarding the tax-gatherers. This force was not sufficient to prevent success, but it might make success expensive. In view of the ban on casualties, Lawrence regretfully decided to abandon the attempt, to the still greater disappointment of the Camel Corps.

" 'To gain what I could, I sent Saleh and the other chiefs down to spruce their people with tall rumours of our numbers, and our coming as the reconnaissance of Feisal's army, to carry Amman by assault in the new moon. This was the story the Turks feared to learn: the operation they imagined: the stroke they dreaded. They pushed cavalry cautiously into Muaggar, and found confirmation of the wild tales of the villagers, for the hill-top was littered with empty meat-tins, and the valley slopes cut up by the deep tracks of enormous cars. Very many tracks there were! This alarm checked them, and, at a bloodless price for us, kept them hovering a week. The destruction of the bridge would have gained us a fortnight.' " (Quoted from *Revolt in the Desert*.)

Gains counted against the concentration of forces for an attack on Jaafar's force before Maan. I wanted J. not to be actively engaged with an offensive enemy when we marched off his mounted men towards Deraa.

T. 331, B. 327 (262):

"On Lawrence's own methods of internal diplomacy Stirling sheds an amusing sidelight—'It was an education to listen to Lawrence at one of the Arab Councils. When in debate some sheikh became a little difficult, Lawrence, from his amazing knowledge of the past life and inner history of every leading Arab, would let drop a hint or reference to some small disreputable/incident in the sheikh's past'."

T.E. put a stroke as indicated and made the note:

Or reputable. I could flatter as well as flutter!

T. 319, B. 328 (263):

For the Deraa move "the fighting forces comprised 450 Arab Regular Camelry with twenty Hotchkiss guns, two armoured cars/, and Pisani's French mountain battery/."

T.E. made strokes as indicated and inserted "*and five tenders*" and "*and two aircraft*", and made the note:

I think the machine gunners have not been counted in the 450: Nuri Said had nearly 600 men. The camelry were really M.I. who fought on foot. For mounted men they had my bodyguard & Nasir's, & the Rualla horsemen.

T. 320, B. 329 (264):

" '. . . I could feel the taut power of Arab excitement behind me. The climax of the preaching of years had come, and a *united country* was straining towards its historic capital'."

T.E. underlined the words here italicized and made the note:

By united country I was not thinking of Hejaz—that was over & done with. By a momentary miracle we had truced all the feuds for this month, so that from Akaba up to Damascus all was clear going. As for the N. tribes being problematical—they were certain, though only success could say how many of them would show up. Some—enough—were certain.

It really did warrant a mood of exultation. I still think it was a jolly good effort: and nobody's but my own, for a change!

Chapter XVIII (originally numbered XIX)

T. 323, B. 330 (265):
"Upon them [the Arabs] much depended if the Turkish dispositions were to be paralysed before Allenby's stroke descended."

T.E. added:

,and while it developed.

T. 323, B. 331 (266):
"Lawrence shrewdly calculated that by the mere fact of establishing the Arab force at *Azrak* 'the first part of our plan, the feint, was accomplished'. 'We had sent our "horsemen of St. George", gold sovereigns, by the thousand to the Beni Sakhr, purchasing all the barley in their threshing floors: begging them not to mention it . . .' "

T.E. underlined the word here italicized and wrote, to emphasise his point: "*Azrak is dead opposite Amman*", and made the note:

You dismiss my distractions shortly. Actually they had been very careful and elaborate.

(1) I had visited the Madeba area myself, just beforehand, and there chosen and marked two large landing grounds for aircraft, hired Arabs to camp by them on watch, and left smoke signals and landing signs, with instructions for use. Of course I chose people sitting carefully on the fence for my confidences.

(2) I had had a census taken of all available sheep, & had four local agents making provisional contracts for them, "delivered to camp". I paid commission, but bought none outright.

(3) I had sent three or four buyers to the threshing floors, & *bought for hard cash* all the piles of feed barley for horses that they could spare. Terms that they should hold it for me, till warned at what camp, within a day's march, to deliver it.

(4) We were in touch with Arab Staff Officers of the [Turkish] 4th Army. I had warned these of a thunderbolt shortly to fall on them at Amman, from E. & W. and conjured them to so dispose their troops as to be ineffective on the day, both ways.

(5) I had put all my influence behind Hornby's push, personally attaching to him all the B. Sakhr sheikhs, and telling them that he would roll up Moab from the S. while I cut it off from the N. & E. I had also given him Dhiab of Tafileh, an old wind-bag, and two of the Majalli sheikhs of Kerak, who notably had a foot in each camp. Hornby had been given guns, money, troops, explosives, part of my bodyguard—even Sherif Zeid. It was quite a big affair.

T. 323, B. 332 (266):
"The idea of alternatives had also inspired a project of attack on Madeba by Hornby with the Zebn tribesmen. A feint in the event of Lawrence's success at Deraa, in the case of failure it could be converted into 'the old second string to our bow', through the Deraa force moving south to reinforce it. . . . The Turks had now upset this move by their new move against Tafileh . . ."

Not fully upset it—for as soon as our Deraa expedition struck, the Tafileh Turkish force would be withdrawn N. at the gallop. Our attack on Hauran was Hornby's opportunity. Had he taken it, the Maan garrison would not have got so far as Ziza.

T. 324–25, B. 333 (268):
(*The Deraa plan*): "As a conception adjusted by consummate calculation to the uncertainties of foreseen reality, this plan is a masterpiece . . ."

I think it was the best I could do: and so it should have been, after the pains & work I had put in on it.

T. 325, B. 334 (268):
"The main body marched forth from Azrak, heading for Umtaiye."

About 1200 strong, I think.

T. 325, B. 334 (268):

"Round the Regular core was now woven a gathering force of/Bedouin, Auda with some of his Abu Tayi, and the sheikhs of the Zebn and Serahin. Nuri Shaalan, cutting his ties with the Turks, had brought 300 Ruwalla horsemen;"

T.E. made a stroke as indicated, inserted "*picked*", and made the note:

These were the cream of the desert. Some really good stuff.

T. 326, B. 335 (269):

"If Deraa was to be cut off from the north and west as arranged, it must, for the security of the operation, be previously cut off from the south."

T.E. added:

Also he wanted Amman to be the nervous place, for the next two days.

T. 327, B. 336 (270):

"That particular demolition gave Lawrence great joy of craftsmanship." (The railway bridge near Jabir.)

You must remember that we invented our own methods of demolition. After the war I wrote an article for the Pickaxe (the Sappers' Journal) detailing them.

T. 329, B. 338 (271):

After capturing Muzeirib:

"Lawrence and Young had cut the telegraph, thus severing the main communication between the Turkish armies and their home-base"

T.E. added:

before proceeding to dynamite the rails and points & wreck the station and its rolling stock.

At the foot of the page, T.E. made the note:

There was also a tremendous pressure put on me to take Deraa itself: but I felt that if we did we should lose it so soon as to compromise ourselves. We had now to mark time for a few days, watching Allenby.

T. 330, B. 339 (272):

The idea of an attack on the bridge at Tell el Shehab in the Yarmuk Gorge was given up when news came that a train-load of German reserves had arrived there:

"Lawrence now began to *feel the irk of his forbearance* and sent off two small parties to cut the line at deserted spots on the far side of the bridge."

T.E. underlined the words here italicized and made the note:

Not really. I did not want the new enemy arrivals to go either to Deraa or back to Afuleh, soon: so I gave 'em something to think about. Mind you, we had to cross their line first thing tomorrow, ourselves, between Tell el Shehab and Deraa.

T. 331, B. 339 (272):

At the top of this page, T.E. made the note:

As we crossed the Deraa-Palestine line we destroyed the station of Muzerib that we had damaged yesterday.

T. 332, B. 340 (273):

"Lawrence's . . . three-sided cut at the focal point of the enemy's communications . . . had the mental effect of per-suading Liman von Sanders to send part of his scanty reserves towards Deraa. More significantly still he sent German troops, the precious cement that held up his jerrybuilt armies."

You see, my effort had to be precisely proportioned: too small to impose immediate retreat upon Liman v.S.; too near Allenby's date for Liman to alter his front-line dispositions, which were ideal—in Allenby's eyes!

T. 332, B. 340–41 (274):

On the ruses practised by the British before their offensive:

"*Dust columns had gone eastward by day*, while troop columns marched westward by night. Under cover of *manifold deceptions* Allenby had achieved an overwhelming superiority in the coastal sector."

T.E. underlined the words here italicized and made the note:

Wouldn't you say that these were frauds? I should mention a few.

T. 334, B. 342 (275):
On the inroad of Allenby's cavalry:
"They . . . seized not only El Afule but/ Nazareth, where the enemy's General Headquarters lay, still *ignorant of the disaster that had overtaken their troops.*"

T.E. made a stroke as indicated, inserted: "*temporarily occupied*", underlined the phrase here italicized and added:

because aircraft & agents had cut every telegraph.

T. 334, B. 343 (275):
"Only the Fourth Army, east of the Jordan, remained."

After "Fourth Army", T.E. made the note:

which yet had been much the strongest of the three

T. 335, B. 343 (276):
"The Fourth Army's chance of making good its retreat depended on whether it could brush aside the Arabs and reach Damascus before Allenby's Cavalry made a fresh bound/ to the aid of the Arabs in barring the way."

T.E. made a stroke as indicated, wrote in the margin: "*of—miles to Khan Denun*" and made the note:

The British were not quick enough to get after the 4th Army. The magnitude of the coast success staggered Chaytor, who let the Jordan units slip away unhindered.

The Beisan cavalry eventually moved towards Deraa, but a mishandled scrap at Semakh delayed them & shook them, & they exercised too much caution in advancing through the Aylus hills. So all the IVth Army was a day out of Deraa before they arrived.

The Galilee (Nazareth) cavalry came forward steadily and fast, along the Kuneitra road, and reached Khan Denun, where we joined them, just after we had finished off the rearguard of the IV Army. They missed its advance parties, too—as we did!

T. 335, B. 343 (276):
On the situation of the Arab forces at Umtaiye:

"For some days the Arabs would be in a precarious position as the wedge between the Deraa socket and the recoiling mass."

No. I didn't dare try to push between Amman & Deraa. The terrain did not suit. We hung on their flanks, & the RAF bombed them, into Deraa: but between Deraa & Damascus I intercepted them.

T. 335, B. 343–44 (276):
"An inferior force composed exclusively of regulars, without a guerilla screen, could not safely hold it: yet to that we should shortly be reduced, if our *air* helplessness continued patent."

T.E. underlined the word here italicized and made the note:

You will probably explain this air helplessness. I had started with 1 Bristol Fighter & 1 BE. 12: and had lost both machines in air fights —no pilots, fortunately.

QUERIES—III

(Answered verbally and answers scribbled down)

1. Hedley says you came to see him early in August and told him you had been rejected as of poor physique.

This is incorrect. I was not rejected, but the height standard had been raised—beyond my stature.[1]

2. Did you go to the War Office at Hogarth's suggestion or on your own?

At Hogarth's suggestion. He arranged with someone in the War Office.[2]

3. Were you imprisoned at Urfa for 3 weeks—sometime before the war?

For T.E.'s answer see note of 1/8/33 (p. 141).

4. Did you, and when, have an argument with Brémond at Aqaba?

Yes, after the capture of Wejh.

5. Brémond says you went "en automobile" to Abdullah, arriving March 13th.

Quite wrong about my method of travel. Brémond was nowhere near.[3]

6. Did you meet Raho and have a conversation with Abdullah on March 20th?

Yes.

[1] See p. 55, l. 20.
[2] See p. 90, bottom of page.
[3] *Note by L.H.* This had reference to Lawrence's gruelling journey to the Wadi Ais.

7. What books did you carry with you in Arabia?

Nothing in the early part. Later, at Azraq, I had Aristophanes' "Eirene", Morte d'Arthur, and the Oxford Book of Verse.

8. Surely your reference on p. 97 (of *Revolt in the Desert*) to "*counter*-offensive" at Aqaba is a slip.

Agreed that it was.

9. Was the railway reached on the 11th or 10th day of ride from Wejh (to the Sirhan, in May)?

Can't say, unless you can check it up.

10. Did Auda go to Jauf?

No. Nuri was up North.

11. Can you tell me the facts about the Baalbek ride?

(See notes of conversation, 27 May 1933, p. 69.)

12. Did you go with Nesib and Zeki part of the way (on the Baalbek ride)?

No.

13. Did you then learn of the Sykes-Picot treaty from Nuri, and when?

During the later ride.

14. Why did you go to Aqaba pre-war? Was your motive merely to see Jebel Faraun?

Yes.

QUERIES—24 JULY 1933

(Answers scribbled down as given, verbally)

1. Did Allenby suggest a diversion in October 1917 when you flew to see him?

I refused first suggestion, viz. to go where Newcombe went (in Hebron area) on political grounds—because the Arabs would have taken Jerusalem, with all its complications. Also would have crossed the space that I was careful to keep between British and Arabs. Incidentally, Allenby's attack was a month too late for real success. Lateness was due to his fear of a heat-wave, which was exaggerated.

2. Was your doubt of the British the real cause of postponing Deraa, if you expected Allenby to sweep forward to Haifa?

Yes: meant to wait at Azrak in case the British had such a sweeping success. Never expected halt to come when it did—whole of the British transport broke down. That breakdown was the reason why Bartholomew took it over himself—was largely due to jealousy between divisions.

3. How do you explain the slight effect of losing 20 (?) men in train escapade November 1917?

Didn't lose so many, only a few, and even so the Zebn tribe never did anything afterwards.

4. Was Allenby's idea of operating against Amman and Hejaz Railway due to you or not?

I said to Allenby: "Why not help us to join you at Jericho?"— to lever away Maan obstacle.

5. Was Ja'far present at October 27th show at Petra?

Don't think so; all due to Maulud.

6. Query about story of T.E. proposing himself for Naval D.S.O.[1]

At dinner, to Allenby. Also recommended himself for D.F.C.—for not shooting down two (Australian) Bristol Fighters. T.E. had given signal of friend by forming a ring.[2]

7. Why did you only hear news of British retreat from Amman between Oct. 6th and 11th?

Can't explain. (Three Turkish stations south of Amman surrendered to Arabs from Themed; held for 5 days.)

[1]See R.G., p. 97, l. 9.
[2]*Ibid.*, p. 101, fourteenth line from bottom.

8. Did you intend to blow up Yarmuk bridges at this time as Young says?

No; only in case of big movement. My objective here was Madeba.

9. Who advised Bols about Arabs over second Trans-Jordan?

Walter Nugent probably, or "Bosphorus Bill" (Woods), or Deedes: even perhaps Clayton—he seemed to have a guilty conscience about it. G.H.Q. thought they were scoring off me—as return for my gibes over not blowing up bridges near Amman.

10. Was there a real threat of [a Turkish] advance to Abu-el-Lissal?

No.

11. Why were armoured cars sent back to Azraq?

No more petrol: and could not have gone back to Jebel Druse because of ground.

12. Did you see the dispersion of the Turks' "cavalry" on 25th Sept?

Yes: drove them back on railway line westwards to prevent them going to Umtaiye because this direction would have been dangerous.

13. Is it true that there were heavy casualties inflicted in suppressing the Damascus rising on Oct. 2—Stirling says "heaps" of dead?

Only 5, apart from a certain number of Druses outside.

14. Did you have a row with Allenby at Damascus?

Definitely no. Had the greatest difficulty in persuading Allenby to let him go—wanted him to go on to Aleppo—"nice as pie".

15. Did Feisal really tell Jemal in August 1918 about the British attack going up the coast?

F. didn't know it was.

QUERIES—29 JULY 1933

(Answers scribbled down as given, verbally)

1. How did crash at Rome occur?

Had given up all hope of Paris Conference, so wanted to collect his papers from Egypt—they were not in a state anybody else could have brought them. Groves offered me a passage in a flight of Handley-Pages going out to the East. Went in advance machine. Was two or three days in hospital, then rang up Francis Rodd who arranged for him to be moved to the Embassy (Sir Rennell Rodd then Ambassador). Was here 3 or 4 days. Then flew on with the Squadron. The whole journey took 2 or 3 months. Many crashes. "Blazing the trail".[1]

2. Was the *S.P.W.* original, or only the second, written in 24-hour bursts?

Both. Wrote introduction on way down the Rhone Valley.[2] Had only sketched out before he went to Cairo. Moved to Arab Delegation headquarters in Paris and wrote there. Was complete in Paris—Went to Meinertzhagen to read—Romeo and Juliet act, letting down by string from balcony.

3. What made him decide to publish *S.P.W.?*

Gertrude Bell was the cause of his publishing the *S.P.W.* Asked him—"Wouldn't you consider publishing it for your friends?" Agreed—but found "friends" an elastic word. It cost £90 a copy to produce, although sold at 30 gns. Did it gradually, by enlarging (on illustrations, etc.) as subscriptions came in. Asked Robin Buxton —"Are you willing to cover (overdraft) by a public edition?"

Executed trust—with Buxton, Hogarth, and Eliot (lawyer); any profit over to go to (R.A.F.) charities. Earmarked for education of children of officers. A jape! The charity has taken £14,000 net, after paying income tax. Had first paid off debt of £7,000. Total royalties £24,000.

[1]For Francis Rodd, see R.G., p. 51, l. 6.
[2]See R.G., p. 55, eleventh line from bottom.

4. What was pre-war *S.P.W.* about?

"Descriptive with a moral". Cannot remember whether Medina was one of the cities. He had arranged to visit it, but had not gone when war came.[1]

5. Was title based on Book of Proverbs, or something more?

More fully elucidated in Jewish Rabbinical embroideries (medi-aeval Jewish) beginning with "M".[2]

6. Post-war chronology?

Member of F.O. delegation for Eastern Affairs, under Louis Malet. Went to Paris about January 1919. There till April (?)—then by air to Cairo. Returned to Paris in July (?). Demobilised in July, while there. Returned to London in Sept. (?). In November elected to research fellowship at All Souls' on past, present and future of Middle East. About a year later,[3] went into residence for 9 months, until asked to join Colonial Office. 1½ years with Winston before went into R.A.F.

7. Did you see Hussein before June 1921?

No. (Add: when driven out by Ibn Sa'ud, Hussein carried off Government Reserve Funds and his private property.)

8. Re decorations discussion with George V.

About December 1918. Before he went to see Feisal at Marseilles. Had told the Military Secretary that he would not take any decora-

---

[1]See R.G., p. 49, l. 23.

[2]*Note by L.H.* I am indebted for the following information to the Warden of Wadham College and Professor T. W. Mearon of Mansfield College, Oxford:

The Midrash gives two explanations of *She hath hewn out her seven pillars:* first, that she (Wisdom) was hewn out of seven firmaments and given to mankind; second, that the Seven Pillars are the seven lands. "If man (or Adam) is righteous and keeps the Law he will inherit seven lands; and if not, he will be dispersed into seven lands." This second explanation may have been known to Lawrence. Other explanations of the Seven Pillars are: the seven books of the Law; the seven days of Creation (Rashi); the seven years of Gog (Ezekiel, XXXIX, 9).

The Midrash explains *Wisdom hath builded her house* as follows: "First, this is the Law which hath built all the worlds. Second, what is this except that the Holy One hath said, 'If a man is righteous and learns Lore and Wisdom, it is reckoned before the Holy One as if he had created the heavens and as if he had established the whole world.'"

[3]Four or five months only.

tions, but the latter failed to warn the King. Thus T.E. had to explain again . . . (T.E. had told Allenby first of all when Allenby said that he had put T.E. in for a "K", and Allenby had wired T.E. home.) King took the explanation quite well. . . . (King recently sent T.E. a message by a third party saying that he was inclined to think that T.E. was the one really happy man in his Dominions.) In giving his reasons for refusing decorations T.E. said nothing about possibility that he might find himself fighting the British. . . . Stamfordham letter printed in Graves was incorrect on point about fighting the British. S. admitted it afterwards.[1]

9. When and how did Abdulla receive Trans-Jordan?

Abdulla went up to Amman with idea of reprisal for his brother's expulsion from Damascus by the French. Trouble threatened. T.E. suggested solution to Churchill: "I know Abdulla: you won't have a shot fired". T.E. fetched Abdulla to Jerusalem, avoiding taking him through city, and Churchill's personal decision was taken in half an hour's talk at Mount of Olives—it was exact contrary to the decision reached at Cairo Conference.

10. Re Foch—what is truth about T.E.'s retort?

Not as in Graves. Nothing like it. Foch said jokingly, "When I have the pacification of Syria, I'll send Weygand". T. E. retorted, "We'll be all right—so long as you don't come yourself".[2]

11. Re flying experience.

Sixth crash was in Handley-Page, seventh was in 1921 in Palestine.

12. Re T.E.'s personal weapons.

They were:
1) Lee-Enfield (originally belonging to 1st Essex) captured at Dardanelles and presented by Enver with gold engraved inscription to Feisal. T.E. collared it off Feisal. It is now in Windsor Castle armoury. T.E. offered it first to the Essex Regiment, but they never troubled to reply. Then the King asked for it, and T.E. gave it. Knotches cut in it when hit anyone.

[1] See R.G., pp. 106–07.
[2] See *Lawrence and the Arabs*, end of Chapter 29.

2) Dagger.

3) Pistol—stolen.

4) Carried an air Lewis gun, stripped. All the more reliable members of his bodyguard carried the same. Thus if 30 of them were with him, there were about 15 Lewis or Hotchkiss guns—heavy fire power.[1]

Early in the year I had given the Lees-Knowles Lectures at Trinity, Cambridge, and had taken as my subject "The Movement of Military Thought from the Eighteenth to the Twentieth Century, and Its Influence on European History". I arranged to publish them, with an additional chapter, in book form under the title, *The Ghost of Napoleon*. When I got the proofs I sent them to T.E. He and Spenser Wilkinson were the two men whom I knew to have explored the French military writings of the 18th century. He returned the proofs with the following letter and a number of annotations:

Whitmonday, '33

I have read this twice, once to get its idea, and once with a pencil in hand. It has been a queer experience—like going back, in memory, to school—for by myself (though with far less knowledge, and hesitatingly) I had trodden all this road before the war. It is a very good little book: modest, witty and convincing. You realise, of course, that you are swinging the pendulum, and that by 1960 it will have swung too far!

So far as I can see strategy is eternal, and the same and true: but tactics are the ever-changing languages through which it speaks. A general can learn as much from Belisarius as from Haig—but not a soldier. Soldiers have to know their means.

I can't write an introduction: none is necessary. Your sub-title should be "A tract for the times."

[1]See R.G., p. 130, l. 19.

SOME OF T.E.'S PENCIL NOTES UPON
PROOF OF L.H.'S "THE GHOST OF NAPOLEON"

(Pp. 16–17.) "The greatest military pioneer of the seventeenth century was Gustavus Adolphus, and he lives in history as the creator of the first 'modern army'. But if we examine his tactical formations, which more than any art were the secret of his success, we can trace his adaptation of the Roman legion and its manoeuvrable maniples. We know, too, on his own evidence how much he prized the teaching of Xenophon, than whom no man has had more influence on the history of the world; if influence on the minds of the makers of history be the gauge. The Cyropaedia was for Gustavus his military bible as it had been for the greatest captains of the ancient world, and as it would be for some who followed."

I am so glad to see this word of praise for Xenophon. The Cyropaedia is a good book. . . .

(Pp. 34–5.) On the *Reveries* of Marshal Saxe (pub. in 1757): "Saxe advocates that natural barriers should be fortified instead of towns. . . . For him, fortification was only a means to advantageous battle, a sponge to absorb the enemy's forces with small diversion of his own."

Torres Vedras and my Wadi Musa.[1]

[1] See *Seven Pillars*, pp. 341 and 391.

(P. 38.) "Napoleon was indebted to his forerunners for the new ideas that are linked with his name . . . he took but did not create.

"Saxe, in contrast, produced more than the military system could assimilate. A twentieth century mind was needed to appreciate the full significance of his proposals."

This reads as though it had waited for you—quite true, but you don't mean it! I suggest "The experience of the twentieth century was needed before the full sig. of his proposals appeared."

(P. 53.) "Calculated dispersion is often the only way to effective concentration. For obvious concentration simplifies the task of an opponent in concentrating to stop you."

?—by making it obviously safe for him to concentrate in turn.

(P. 55.) "The infiltration method introduced by the Germans towards the end of the World War . . ."

How about my m/g attack at the battle of Seil el Hesa? That was a real filter attack! T.E.S.[1]

(P. 56.) "Bourcet's cardinal principle—one of his most valuable contributions to the theory of war—was that 'a plan ought to have several branches'. 'One should study the possible courses in the light of the obstacles that have to be overcome, of the inconveniences or advantages that will result from the success of each branch, and, after taking account of the more likely objections, decide on the part which can lead to the greatest advantages, while employing diversions and all else that one can do to mislead the enemy and make him imagine that the main effort is coming at some other part. And in case all these diversions, counter-marches or other ruses fail of their purpose—to hide the real aim—one

[1]See R.G., p. 130, l. 18.

must be ready to profit by a second or third branch of the plan without giving one's enemy time to consider it'."

Or my picture of attack as a hand held out—with five fingers at the end of it, all possibles! T.E.S.

(P. 73.) Comment on Guibert's *Essai général de tactique* of 1772:
"He ascribed the prevailing tactical immobility to the 'custom of the pike' and the belief that 'the force of infantry consisted in the density of its order'."

The S-M's command "Shoulder 'hipe'" for bayonets, to-day, is a relic, I believe, of Cromwellian pike-drill. T.E.S.

(P. 102.) "General Bonaparte applied a theory which created an empire for him. The Emperor Napoleon developed a practice which wrecked his empire. And, a century later, evolved by Clausewitz into a system, it brought down three other empires in collapse."

Good! T.E.S.

(P. 114.) "His [Jomini's] teaching shows no sign that he had recognised the vital significance of Bourcet's argument that every plan ought to have branches, so that if one line is blocked by the enemy, another may be instantly developed to serve the same purpose. No theory of war could be adequate which overlooked that principle.

"For war is a two-Party affair. Thus, to be practical, any theory must take account of the opposing side's power to upset your plan."

GOOD!

(P. 120.) "Although Clausewitz . . . came to be taken by the world as the interpreter of Napoleon, he really expressed ideas that originated in his own mind. He was the prophet, not of Napoleon, but of himself."

HEAR, HEAR!

(P. 172.) "In exploring the records of the last war, I have frequently come on suggestions to the effect—'We might gloss over this' . . ."

I should damn the consequences, and put a footnote, "The official history of our campaigns in France and the East is guilty, here and there, of suppression that amounts to misrepresentation."

(P. 177.) "The tale of the tank—which could have been available before the war, for plans of such a machine had been contemptuously pigeon-holed—is but a segment of the mosaic of marble-mindedness. Its glassy opaqueness is as depressing to contemplate as the deadly uniformity of its pattern."

Good! T.E.S.

(P. 181–2.) Comment on the absence of military research and the inadequate study of military history that prevails in armies:
"Too many [of the books], compiled from secondary sources in an uncritical spirit, offer a worse than second-hand acquaintance with the facts. And selection of the books for study is often made with so little discrimination that the student unknowingly is led to feed upon fiction rather than upon historical fact. At the best, as we have seen, the study of military history in an army, even in Staff Colleges, corresponds to the level of undergraduate work in other branches of history. The repeated errors of the military profession in the past can be traced to this superficial treatment of the only alternative to pure theorising on make-believe and on fragmentary personal experience."

I'd put a footnote that the book known as "Hamley" is worse than useless.

(P. 185—the conclusion of the book): "Those who have studied war the most cannot avoid becoming acutely conscious that the exploration of war as a scientific subject has scarcely begun."
T.E. doubly underlined.
"Loyalty to truth coincides with true loyalty to the army in compelling a new honesty in examining and facing the facts of history. And a new humility."
V.G.

> 119 Clarence Road
> East Cowes
> Isle of Wight
> 15.VII.33

Mrs. Shaw was closing-house and going to Malvern: we did not know when you would get back, and so she sent me the Arab Bulletin volumes to hold for you. They are now being posted. Will you send them to her (at Ayot St. Lawrence, Welwyn, Herts) when eventually finished with? I think you will find a mass of news in them. Three volumes, one per year of the trouble! Full of military rumours and facts.

In thinking of your draft book, afterwards, I am sure that the value is in the technical part, and that the less biography in it the better. The life (except where it has a military bend) intrudes. Cape has already published one "life" of me and Hutchinson another[1]: both are available at 2/-a time. Only by being interested in work, rather than personality, can your addition justify itself. So I would advise your shrinking up the first part, even more than it is.

By the way Colonel Joyce (P.C.) was in London last week. He would interest you. Newcombe might know his address.

Mrs. Hogarth, who has his sketch of the Arab political history, has written to me from Northumberland (Greystead, Tarset, Northumberland), to say that her address will be 39a St. Giles, Oxford, which she

[1]See R.G., p. 147, l. 2.

has taken as a temporary house. She might lend the sketch to you, if you explained the circumstances.

(P.S.) Ekeby[1] must have been interesting. Sweden has some uncommon writers.

The theme of my lectures of the movement of military thought was so closely related to the course of his military studies and thought that it seemed fitting to dedicate the book to him. I mentioned the idea to him when we spent an evening together at Lyndhurst and, finding that it pleased him, sent him several alternative forms of dedication that had come into my mind, asking which he preferred. The first was:

"To 'T.E.'—who trod this road before 1914"

Alternatively, I had suggested the addition:

"—and thereby knew what was hidden from other commanders".

or:

"—and thereby knew where he was going better than any other leader of 1914–1918."

In pencil, T.E. tentatively added another alternative:

"—and so learned variety."

Another suggestion of mine was:

"To 'T.E.'—the last Great Captain".

He underlined "last", and wrote:

"Alas, no!"

> 13 Birmingham St.
> Southampton
> 30.VII.33

Excuse pencil. I write on a bed: laziness, not infirmity.

Here are the dedications back again. Sweetest are the victories of understatement: so I deprecate all but 1. If you praise me, or con-

---

[1] I had been staying at Rottneros, the house which, under the name of "Ekeby", is the central scene of the Gösta Berling saga.

trast me with British generals you weaken your case, by dogmatising
on what is debateable

As I see it, the interesting point is that these "primitives" were my
text-books, *after* Clausewitz; my merit is to have become dissatisfied
with that logician, and to have studied earlier practice and precept;
not professionally, but to please my mind.

(1) pleases me by its succinct modesty. Not that I trod all your
path, or understood it: but in so far as I did, I learned something.

Two days later I was at Hythe again on my way back from
Devonshire: on this occasion I made fairly full notes about
things he told me. Also a diary note:

"He showed us Scott-Paine's new American challenger—
has done over 100 m.p.h. with present 950 h.p. Lion engine
and is now fitting 1400 h.p. from 1929 Schneider Cup machine. Hull was impressively fast in design.

"T.E. also showed us over the 30 m.p.h. speedboats he
introduced for R.A.F.—amazing how every need of accessi-
bility is thought out. Took Adrian out for trip in speed-
dinghy. We saw Scott-Paine make one trial, but could not
wait for the second, as he asked.

"Then drove to Elderfield Hotel, Otterbourne, where we
spent night. T.E. left just before midnight."

TALK WITH T.E.
OTTERBOURNE, 1 AUGUST 1933

On the way to Otterbourne I chased him hard, and the way he shot through traffic led me to chide him about the risks he ran. He defended his riding, on the score that safety lay in his immense power of acceleration, whereat I argued that there were circumstances when it wouldn't serve—where someone suddenly swerved, etc.; that he didn't allow enough margin for fools. The argument ran on, till he suddenly said, in a pensive way—"It'll end in tragedy one day."

T.E. had been telling me how the King sent him a message saying he believed he was the one happy and contented man in his dominions. I told T.E. that was rather my impression, and asked T.E. frankly, "Are you really happy?" T.E. reflectively replied—"At times. No one who thinks can be really happy." Went on to say that he had learnt long ago that happiness lies within, not in externals, but also had learnt later that those who did not think could be happy, the kind he lived among now. Yet he was happy in spasms, great satisfaction in some job, especially in mechanical, well done.[1]

As a boy T.E. always thought he was going to do great things, both "active and reflective"—"I hadn't learnt you can't do both"—and determined to achieve both. All his work was done "against bogey".
Pre-War.

Told me of his trip, about 1912, when he was first a Turkish

[1] See R.G., p. 183, thirteenth line from bottom.

140

prisoner. Had heard about a place in the Valley of Upper Euphrates—report by workman of a statue of a woman seated on backs of two lions. Might have been Hittite. He went in native dress, with 2 workmen. Was pinched, with one of them, as possible deserters near Birijik (too far north for Arabs to have gone). Imprisoned all night. Kicked downstairs into lousy dungeon. Bruised all up one side. Other man had sprain. Bribed their way out in morning. (Spoke of Urfa, with magnificent Byzantine castle, and the best bazaars.)

Early War.

When war broke out Woolley and he were working on their book *The Wilderness of Zin.* When book was finished, Woolley joined the artillery. T.E. spoke to Hogarth, said he was too small to be taken. Hogarth suggested the Geographical Section at the War Office. (? Sept. late) There T.E. took Walter Nugent's place; was shown in to the job by him. Only Hedley and T.E. were left. Worked as a civilian for a time. T.E. had to show Belgian maps (printed for Expeditionary Force) to Rawlinson. R. had a fit when he saw T.E. in mufti: "I want to talk to an officer." Hedley said to him, "We must get you a commission". He went to Army & Navy Stores and got into uniform before his commission was actually through.[1]

Erzerum Incident.

He put Russian General in touch with Arab on Staff. (Deal gently with this because people still in Turkey.) Say something like this: "half-hearted defence of Erzerum possibly to be explained by Secret Service reasons."[2]

1918 Campaign.

Dawnay's April show finished the Turks' use of the Hejaz railway below Ma'an.

T.E. heard the news about the English giving up Amman

---

[1] See pp. 90, bottom of page, and 192, l. 15.
[2] See R.G., p. 82, l. 18.

on arrival in the Atatir. On hearing it he said, "It's quite all right. The English are going to keep Es Salt. Wait till they have consolidated."

Feisal never told him about his negotiations in the summer of 1918—Feisal was definitely "selling us".[1] He thought the British were cracking. The British had offered status quo to Young Turks (Talaat) if they would move the Germans. (Aubrey Herbert to Talaat in Switzerland. Herbert did not know our commitments.) Feisal heard of this within a week. Promptly took up with Jemal. (T.E. heard through "agents" in camp. T.E. stopped it when getting dangerous; pretended to take it as a piece of political tactics, and suggested to Feisal to develop. Feisal could not carry on when the English knew.)

T.E. stopped unpromising shows usually by one of two methods:

a) by going to Feisal and saying, "We won't pay for this show";

b) by causing a personal upset among the Arab leaders, which effectually put an end to a doubtful project. Left to themselves, the Arabs "would have chopped the tree all round".

T.E. went on to talk of strategy in general, in the light of what he had learnt from the Arab campaign. Dwelt on two points:

1. "Pass around obstacles, but don't branch the main stream".

2. Importance of distractions, but leave "an air space between them and the main stream—to prevent ruffling".

Pisani's guns were very important at the three cuttings of the line—Tell Arar, Muzeirib, Nisib. (The Arabs could not get mountain guns from the British or Italians.) But Pisani's guns did not count at Tafas, except to cause the Turkish

[1] See p. 189, l. 3.

swerve, or during the night show—which was a much bigger affair.

Talked of his dedicatory poem in *Seven Pillars* to "S.A." Asked him was there any real person or only symbolical. He said partly geographical. S. and A. were two different things, "S" a village in Syria, or property in it, and "A" personal.

Post-War.

When T.E. saw L.G. early in 1921, he stressed the mess Curzon had made of Middle East. Must take it away from him if L.G. wanted to straighten out the mess. L.G. was against sacking Curzon, but transfer the responsibility to Colonial Office. T.E. said the man was the important thing. . . .

Hence offer to W. S. Churchill. They thought of making him offer of Colonial Office and Air Ministry together.

W.S.C. asked T.E.'s advice. T.E. said, "You must take risks, make a native king in Iraq, and hand over defence to R.A.F. instead of Army".

.   .   .

T.E. joined Colonial Office in 1921 on Churchill's promise that he could do entirely what he liked, could quit any time, but meantime have free hand.

As salary said £1,000. W.S.C. said, "Most modest thing had ever been asked. We'll make it £1,600." Allowed him to have Young and Meinertzhagen as assistants.[1]

Everything staged before they went out for Cairo Conference. T.E. had settled not only questions the Conference would consider, but decisions they would reach. "Talk of leaving things to man on spot—we left nothing". Had them printed and wanted to distribute (!), but W.S.C. objected.[2]

[1]See R.G., p. 54, eighth line from bottom.
[2]*Ibid.*, p. 110, l. 10.

Before going out T.E. arranged things with Feisal (?) at Winterton's place in Sussex. Then Winston and Feisal met at lunch and W.S.C. (primed by T.E.) explained decisions to Feisal.

Out at Cairo, W.S.C. was masterly in handling Percy Cox and others. Cox said he had promised Baghdad Arabs that election of a king should be free as elections of M.P.'s in England. W.S.C. said they shall, pointed out to Cox that elections in no sense free—party organisations settle candidates and electors have simply choice of A or B.

Cairo conference completely satisfied T.E., gave Arabs more than he had ever hoped, British giving up claim to Basra. Only surrender to French over Syria could not be remedied.

Curzon not at all like popular picture. Very sensitive, fearful of his own dignity. . . .[1]

W.S.C. behaved splendidly to T.E.—who did not want any of the credit. Never any friction between them, and only one breeze when T.E. said Lenin was the greatest man, when W.S.C. was fondling Napoleon's bust.[2]

T.E. stayed 12 months. Then asked to go. W.S.C. wouldn't let him, but T.E. drew no more money and stayed on though nominally resigned. Then at last insisted, saying, "There will be no more trouble for 7 years". Others laughed—but who was right? We saved £16 million the first year.

Cairo Conference was T.E.'s outlet from public affairs; could then go, feeling satisfied that justice was done and our honour rehabilitated.

[1] See R.G., p. 108, l. 15.
[2] See pp. 209, l. 2, and 211, eighth line from bottom.

NOTES ON THE WRITING
OF "SEVEN PILLARS OF WISDOM"

(Given verbally by T.E. on 1 August 1933)

1st writing, his method was: Sketched out expedition to bridge again—from memory. Then took diaries and notes, and wrote on other side—took days. A composite process. Then "planing off into one smooth run".

2nd writing: Done from memory of 1st writing.

Details about loss of 1st: On train journey from London to Oxford. Went into refreshment room at Reading, and put bag under the table. Left it. Phoned up from Oxford an hour later, but no sign of the missing bag—it was a bank messenger's bag, the "thing they carry gold in".

T.E. joyously said to Hogarth—"I've lost the damned thing". (Alan Dawnay and Hogarth had read it.) Hogarth was angry—"You must write it again."[1]

(It was manuscript—on loose-leaf ledger; blank sheets, not ruled. Only wrote one side of page. None of it was ever typed.)

T.E. wonders—Did fancy (*involuntarily*) play with it?

It was written in Barton Street (only thing written by him at All Souls' was his introduction to new edition of Doughty's *Arabia Deserta*).

3rd rewriting was done when he was at the Colonial Office. Very slow. 1921–22.

Set up in type at Oxford in 1922.

[1]See R.G., p. 47, l. 13.

(Note jotted down by T.E.):

S.P.

1. M.S. written in Paris. Read by Meiner, Dawnay, Hogarth. Lost at Reading.
2. M.S. written at Barton Street. Not circulated.
3. M.S. Revise of 2. Printed verbatim at Oxford 1922. 8 copies of which 5 survive.[1]

    The published S.P. is 7/8 of the Oxford printing of (3), very much revised textually.

(Did not add any facts, but cut out a lot. Altered stylistically.)[2]

---

[1]All 5 copies belong to T.E.: 1 in cottage, 1 with Alan Dawnay, 1 with E. Kennington, 1 with Mrs. Bernard Shaw, 1 with E. M. Forster. He would burn them, but MS. is in Bodleian. In that MS. are the few surviving pages of (2) which he burnt at Chingford with paraffin and blow-lamp. Printing of (3) was done at Oxford Times Press. In "hay-making" order. Badly printed—2 columns to a page—cheaper than typewriting. Total cost about £80.

[2]See R. G., p. 116, bottom.

T.E.'S COMMENTS AND CORRECTIONS
ON TYPESCRIPT OF "T. E. LAWRENCE:
IN ARABIA AND AFTER"

In returning the second section of typescript of L.H.'s book, *T. E. Lawrence: in Arabia and After*, i.e. the last two pages of Chapter XVIII, Chapter XIX, XX, XXI (originally numbered XIX–XXII), pp. 337–91 (American ed. pp. 276–329):

13 Birmingham St.
Southampton
10.VIII.33

Dear L-H.

Major Barbara, for sure: but I have no Shaw by me now and cannot remember the quotation.

Comments on this section in margin. Very little to say. It overdoes my detail organisation in Damascus: I got the other fellows to take a subject each and put it on its feet. Those were 3 days of rush—with pits of silence intervening, and into them one fell unconscious. My mind is full of single snapshots of those days—not ever to be written down. I was a very unhappy atom, in a rough sea.

Yours,
T.E.S.

T. 338, B. 345 (278):

"Soon after dawn, the expected aeroplane from Palestine arrived and brought them the first news, astounding and exhilarating/, of Allenby's victory"

T.E. made a stroke as indicated, inserted "*in its completeness*" and made the note:

We were expecting a victory: not as big!

T. 356, B. 349 (282):

"On the 24th a British aeroplane came over to give them news
of further successes in Palestine and a warning that the
Fourth Army was now in retreat towards them. That same
day the Arab force moved back to Umtaiye, where a vitally
important council of war was held on the following morning.
In fulfilment of his new purpose Lawrence proposed 'that we
march north, past Tell Arar, and over the railway at dawn
to-morrow, into Sheikh Saad village'. Ten miles north of
Muzeirib on the Pilgrims' Road, and on the flank of the
Damascus railway, 'it lay in familiar country with abundant
water, perfect observation, and a secure retreat *west* or *north*,
or even south-west if we were directly attacked . . .'"

T.E. underlined the words here italicized and made the
note:

i.e. in the enemy direction. This was one of the points which
alarmed Young, who did not see that Galilee Lake covered the very
broken districts into which we should retreat. We could have stood
a fortnight's siege in them.

T. 343, B. 351 (283):

"The interruption had not only delayed the Arab move but
threatened it with a more serious and lasting interruption—
from a British source. For in camp that night Young urged
that the Arabs had now done enough, and would be justified
as well as wise in retiring . . ."

Young said the delay had prejudiced our chance of crossing the
line unopposed.

T. 343, B. 351 (283):

"The suggestion was most unwelcome to Lawrence. Morally,
because it seemed to sacrifice the Arabs' honour to their
safety, by leaving Allenby's troops to bear the final burden.

Militarily, because it threatened to forfeit the best chance of a quick decision."

T.E. added:

and politically, for it threw away the chance to consolidate the terrain for which the Arabs had been fighting two years. Remember the Cairo promise, "The Arabs shall keep what they take".

T. 344, B. 351 (283):
"Sheikh Saad would be a lever on the rear of Deraa, loosening all resistance this side of Damascus, and at present only the Arabs were close enough to exert such vital pressure on the Turks' retreat."

Which is tactics, I think; "grand tactics", perhaps.

T. 344, B. 351 (283):
"While Lawrence based himself on the higher issues, Young persisted in emphasising the immediate tactical risks."

Surely, if there is one military maxim of universal value, it is to press hard on a rout.

T. 344, B. 352 (284):
"He [Young] fell back on the line that he was a regular soldier and the senior one present. This familiar *refuge of mediocrity* was not suited to the unorthodox conditions of 'command' in the Arab zone". . .

T.E. put brackets round the words here italicized, wrote, "'*tag*' or '*refuge of authority*'—*Young is not mediocre*", and made the note:

Command in Arabia was like sovereignty in the British Empire—a power in commission, and very difficult to find!

T. 344, B. 352 (284):
"One may justly appreciate Young's view that Lawrence . . . was inclined to demand of the rather immobile Arab regulars what was for their own part an undue risk. But one can see

that Lawrence was using two-party scales—and weighing the
Turks' low morale against the Arab regulars' low mobility."

Nor would the momentum of our Damascus rush have been
checked much, by the loss of the regulars. Casualties do not matter,
in a successful pursuit.

T. 345, B. 353 (284):
"Absence of opposition encouraged Lawrence to enlarge the
plan / . . . . While the main body pursued its way to Sheikh
Saad /, Auda turned aside for El Ghazale station . . ."

T.E. made strokes as indicated, inserted:

and permitted me to detach forces to enlarge it. We concentrated for
the railway crossing

and, after "Sheikh Saad":

without having fired a shot.

T. 345, B. 353 (285):
"The Turks, receiving fantastic / reports of the Arab forces'
strength, had ordered the immediate evacuation of Deraa."

T.E. made a stroke as indicated, inserted "*night*" and made
the note:

and burned the six aeroplanes left there: their last hope of "seeing"
where they stood.

T. 346, B. 354 (285):
"Events multiplied hourly on the Arabs' front. Another British aeroplane came over to warn them that two large enemy
columns were approaching from the south. One of six thousand men was marching from Deraa and another of two
thousand from Muzeirib. It meant that the main mass of the
retreating Turks was now at hand. And there was as yet no
sign of the British cavalry who should have come to the Arabs'
assistance. Barrow's 4th Cavalry Division, which had been
on the Jordan around Beisan since the 20th, had / begun its
eastward march / early on the 26th."

T.E. made strokes as indicated and inserted: "*not*" and "*till*".

T. 347, B. 355 (286):
"The column moving north from Deraa was, obviously, too large a mouthful, especially as it was beyond convenient reach of Sheikh Saad."

Nor could I have gone for it, with the 2,000 across my track!

T. 347, B. 355 (286):
(On Turkish "butchery" in Tafas.)

Here I skip the familiar tale! Wouldn't you like to shorten it?

T. 349, B. 357 (288):
"The situation at Deraa had still to be secured."

I did not know what had happened to Barrow: and some such security as an occupied Deraa, or a junction with him, was essential as a prelude to advance on Damascus.

T. 349, B. 357 (288):
"The blood lust of the afternoon was not easily quietened, and under its intoxication the Arabs were remembering their own blood-feuds and tribal jealousies."

and were wanting to kill the prisoners, which Young and Winterton forbade.

T. 349, B. 357 (288):
"Nasir and Nuri/set off thither (to Deraa) with their men, and Lawrence / also . . ."

T.E. made strokes as indicated, inserted "*had*" and "*followed*" and made the note:

Both Nuris, this time, I think!

T. 349, B. 357 (288):
(Quoted from *Revolt in the Desert*):
"'I gave liberty to my camel—the grand, rebellious Baha—and she stretched herself out against the field, racing my

wearied followers for mile upon mile with piston strides like an engine, so that I entered Deraa quite alone in the full dawn'."

This was a crazy ride, through a country of murder and night-terror.

T. 350, B. 358 (288):
"Lawrence went out to meet them [Barrow's leading troops] and told them that Deraa was in the Arabs' hands."

This was a difficult situation to carry off. I took one man with me, only: I shaved & dressed in clean clothes & behaved with histrionic nonchalance, being treated first as enemy, then as native, then as spy, before I found Barrow.

T. 351, B. 359 (289):
"His repulsion may have been increased by his recent wit-ness at Tafas of the bestial license to which severely disciplined troops were prone when their curbed instincts were allowed an outlet. . . . It did not suffice to say that these were Turks— he could not help remembering the British troops at Badajoz."

   T.E. made the note:

and a reaction against our own reprisal

and (against the last words):

or the Aussies in Cairo—though it might not be tactful to say so!

T. 352, B. 360 (290):
"If Lawrence had shared the fellowship of the trenches, in a happy battalion, he might have qualified his judgment and even found extenuating circumstances. For in the approach to the fighting line authority became curbed to the benefit of individuality, which in many cases not merely survived but even grew stronger under the pressure of the experience. The front was the Moloch that consumed bodies, but souls were often tempered in its fire—the Moloch that hungered for them lay in the rear areas. One should remember that

Lawrence had only experienced the two extremes of soldiering, the cesspool of Cairo staff offices and the solitariness of
guerrilla war in the desert."

   T.E. marked this paragraph and wrote:

   Good!

T. 352, B. 360 (291):
"In weighing his reflections one must take account of his
state at this time, when an over-tried body dragged on a de-
pressed mind . . ."

   I think that strictly speaking my will was dragging on both body
& mind!

T. 352, B. 360 (291):
"Acutely conscious of the double nature of the part he had
played . . ."

and was yet to play.

T. 352, B. 360 (291):
"His dark mood in these days of triumph made an indelible
impression on his companions and, because of their affection,
grieved them."

   Did you ever see McBey's portrait of me (in the Imperial War
Museum) painted in Damascus a day after we got in? It is shockingly
strange to me.

T. 352, B. 361 (291):
"His reflection, moreover, helps to explain why he himself
later chose to serve in the Air Force."

   Perhaps you should assist the public here! They will not understand.

T. 353, B. (omitted):
"After his consultation with Nuri Said and Lawrence, Barrow
had sent the bulk of his division to Muzeirib, as the watering
facilities at Deraa were scarcely more adequate than at Er

Remta. If he had moved to well-watered Muzeirib in the first place he might not only have saved delay but also the chance of cutting off the Fourth Army."

I think he was too late in any case—and his orders said Deraa.

T. 354, B. 363 (293):
(Quoted from *Revolt in the Desert*):
" 'It irked Stirling and myself to see the caution of Barrow's advance . . . It marked the difference between our certain movements and the tentative processes of normal war'."

It also showed a total ignorance of the proper use of the air arm. We were flown over all day.

T. 357, B. 367 (296):
"Lawrence . . . stopped beside a little stream to wash and shave. He was interrupted by a patrol of Bengal Lancers who rushed up to take him prisoner."

In the desert I shaved daily. My burnt red face, clean shaven & startling with my blue eyes against white headcloth & robes, became notorious in the desert. Tribesmen or peasants who had never set eyes on me before would instantly know me, by the report. So my Arab disguise was actually an advertisement. It gave me away instantly, as myself, to all the desert: and to be instantly known was safety, in 99 cases out of the 100.

The hundredth case was always the eventuality to be feared. If I saw it coming, I would get into a soldier's cap, shirt & shorts, & get away with it, or draw my headcloth over my face, like a visor, and brazen it out.

No easterner could ever have taken me for an Arab, for a moment. Only the Bengal Lancers, & similar innocent foreign soldiery, here and at Deraa, & in Egypt, & in Allenby's H.Q. They started the notion of my skill in disguise—which was nil!

T. 357, B. 367 (296–97):
The arrival at Damascus:
"There were many Turkish soldiers who watched the entry

as apathetically as they waited for capture—over thirteen thousand were found in the barracks and hospitals."

Pellagra, the disease of despair, was killing them by battalions.

T. 358, B. 368 (297):
"He then went back to the town hall to deal with the Algerian usurpers. They had not returned, and when he sent a summons for their presence he received a curt reply that they were sleeping. He then told a relative of theirs that he would fetch British troops to search for them."

T.E. wrote in brackets:

(It was tactics only, not meant.)

T. 359, B. 369 (298):
(Quoted from *Revolt in the Desert*):
" 'Rebels, especially successful rebels, were of necessity bad subjects and worse governors'."

I think it is a quote from "Il Principe" of Machiavelli.

T. 360, B. 370 (298):
"An Australian detachment which had taken the surrender of the Turkish troops in barracks, sent guards to the *various public buildings* and *consulates*."

T.E. underlined the words here italicized and made the note:

I don't think so. Not the town hall, or post office or Railway Station: nor the Spanish Consulate, which represented 14 nationalities. I saw them only at the big barracks—but I was too busy to explore the town, so you may be right.

T. 361, B. 371 (300):
"At the first streak of light he [Lawrence] moved armed parties to the upper suburbs and carried out a drive that swept the rioters towards the centre."

Nuri Said did it, actually.

T. 362, B. 372 (301):
"His depression was the deeper because of a factor that had nothing to do with politics. In the haunting poem that prefaces the *Seven Pillars of Wisdom*, and again in the brief epilogue, he has confessed a personal motive that, like a magnet, had drawn him along the road to Damascus. Death had outpaced him on the road, and brought the dissolution of his dream."

Before we got to Damascus. Some time before.[1]

T. 363, B. 373 (301):
"On the following day he took his departure for Cairo. With peculiarly deep truth one may say that he shook the dust of Damascus off his feet."

That is one of the clearest memories I have, the silky coolness of the Damascus dust, as it lapped over my sandals and powdered my feet. Those white deep paths, under the trees or shaded by the house walls, were heavenly quiet and soft.

T. 381, B. 374 (302):
"In the crucial weeks while Allenby's stroke was being prepared, and during its delivery, nearly half of the Turkish forces south of Damascus were distracted by the Arab forces; pinned east of the Jordan by the subtle feints and nerve-paralysing pinpricks that Lawrence conceived and directed."

or needle-jabs? Pins stimulate me, usually.

At the end of this chapter T.E. made the note:

An eloquent and excellent—if very friendly summing up! T.E.S.

Chapter XX (originally numbered XXI)

T. 373, B. 386 (313):
"Feisal came on a British cruiser [to Marseilles], and was met by Lawrence *who donned his Arab dress*."

[1]See p. 169, l. 16.

T.E. put brackets round the words here italicized and wrote in the margin:

in British uniform.

After "Arab dress" T.E. made the note:

1) Arab kit—when worn in Europe
    a. to an evening at Mrs. Lindsay's—for fun
    b. with Feisal to B. Palace, as interpreter
    c. to be painted by Augustus John
2) Arab headcloth, with khaki uniform & British badges
    (a) to be photographed with Feisal in Paris
    (b) To the Council of Ten, to interpret for Feisal.

T. 373:
"He handed back to Brémond the Croix de Guerre that the French had earlier conferred upon him."
T.E. wrote in the margin:

not because of the rebuff, but to follow up my return of British decorations.

T. 373, B. 387 (313):
"After showing Feisal round England Lawrence returned *with him* to Paris in January for the Peace Conference"
T.E. underlined the words here italicized and wrote in the margin:

Not with Feisal—but independently as member of the British delegation.

T. 374, B. 387 (314):
"*Feisal was admitted to the Conference* only as the representative of his father, who was recognised merely as King of the Hejaz."
T.E. wrote in the margin:

All he asked for!

T. 387, B. 402 (327):

"A hundred [of the *Seven Pillars*] were printed for subscribers and nearly half as many more . . . for presentation . . ."

Rather more than a hundred for subscribers, besides the copies for those who took part in the Revolt.

T. 389, B. 404 (328):

"To the regret of his friends . . . T.E. *would not touch a penny of the profit. Unknown to most of them*, he executed a trust by which all profit, after the debt was redeemed, should go to a certain charity."

T.E. put brackets round the words here italicized, and made the note:

I gave copyright of "R in D" 6 months before pub. to trustees who had accepted my overdraft. Pub. of "R in D" is breach of copyright of S.P. which belongs to T.E.S.

"His reason for rejecting all personal profit / sprung from his fastidious sense of honour."

T.E. made a stroke as indicated and inserted:

and honours

T. 390, B. 405 (329):

"Significantly, the *Seven Pillars of Wisdom* bears no author's name on the title-page."

T.E. wrote in the margin "*typog.*" (and explained verbally that the name was left out for typographical reasons—because the title-page looked more effective without).

·   ·   ·

On August 11th, I sent him some further questions:

i) If there is any truth in the attached cutting?

This was from a London evening newspaper and said that at one stage during his 1921 negotiations with King Hussein the latter—

"declared, 'In these circumstances, Colonel Lawrence, there is only one thing for an honourable man to do'. At the same time he called for his sword. Colonel Lawrence bowed and said, with profound respect, 'In that case, Your Majesty, I shall carry on these negotiations with your successor'."

ii) Exactly when you left the Colonial Office?

iii) When enlisted in R.A.F.?

iv) What did you do in the interval?

v) How was your entry into the Royal Tank Corps arranged? (You have told me, but I'm hazy.)

vi) What was your work there?

vii) Did you go straight to Karachi from there, and when?

viii) Can you explain the appeal that speed on a motor-cycle has for you? [*Note by L. H.* Although he had often discussed various aspects of this appeal, I wanted to see if he could throw a fuller light on it.]

Bridlington.
Monday, 14.VIII.33

Here till Thursday, I think: and then via Southampton to Lympne & Manston, in Kent for three days, and thereafter in Southampton, where some boats will have come to ripeness, for test. Only address, Southampton, 13 Birmingham St.

Queries

1. Cutting: no truth. Suicide practically unknown amongst orthodox Moslems. King Hussein used to threaten to abdicate. I wished he would, but was never funny about it. The old man was a tragic figure, in his way: brave, obstinate, hopelessly out-of-date: exasperating.

2. Ceased salaried appointment to C.O. about Feb. 1922. Resigned honorary appointment about June 1922: no notion of exact date, but letters were published in press of the day, giving reasons.

3. August 1922.

4. Nothing at all, except tramp London.

5. By Sir P. Chetwode and others in the War Office.

6. Transferred from R.T.C. to R.A.F. for remainder of engagement: was sent to Uxbridge for one day to drawn airman's kit: then posted to Cranwell. My term of service was 7 active & 5 reserve, from March 1923. While in India, I extended, to serve my 5 reserve years in the active.

7. Aircraft-hand (general purpose unskilled man) in B.Flight, of the Cadet College. Each flight had half a dozen training machines for the cadets to learn flying: and three or four instructors, and a dozen or fifteen airmen (one third fitters, one third riggers, one third aircraft-hands) to look after the machines. We did anything there was to do.

7. [sic] Was posted overseas to India direct from Cranwell. Sailed in Dec. 1926 and upon arrival at Karachi was sent to R.A.F. Depot at Drigh Road there.

8. To explain the lure of speed you would have to explain human nature; but it is easier understood than explained. All men in all ages have beggared themselves for fast horses or camels or ships or cars or bikes or aeroplanes: all men have strained themselves dry to run or walk or swim faster. Speed is the second oldest animal craving in our nature, and our generation is fortunate in being able to indulge it more cheaply and generally than our ancestors. Every natural man cultivates the speed that appeals to him. I have a motorbike income.

On August 20 he came to spend the day with us at Farnham, and here went through the last chapter, "Fulfilment", and the Epilogue of *T. E. Lawrence: in Arabia and After*.

Chapter XXII (originally numbered XXIII)

T. 414, B. 406 (330):
"The most general idea . . . is that Lawrence condemned himself to servitude in the ranks as a kind of penance for his failure to secure the Arabs what he had promised them."

I did not enlist till I had (through Winston) straightened out the mess.

T. 416–17, B. 408 (332):
"As the year 1920 drew to its close, events were vindicating Lawrence's repeated warning of the dangers of playing fast and loose with national aspirations in the Middle East. A too inelastic adherence to our old Imperial policy and a too supple interpretation of our assurances had involved us in widespread trouble ... At a *chance* meeting with Lloyd George, Lawrence discussed the mess and Curzon's responsibility for it, suggesting that the only way to straighten it out was to relieve Curzon of responsibility."

T.E. underlined the word here italicized, wrote "?" (and explained verbally that he had definitely sought the meeting).

T. 417–18, B. 409 (332):
"Winston Churchill, then the occupant of a post-war War Office, was offered the Colonial Office with an extension of its responsibilities. ... And Lawrence was made Political Adviser. He accepted the post on the understanding that the wartime pledges he had made to the Arabs on Britain's behalf would now be honoured as far as lay within Britain's power. He also asked and was promised a *free hand*."

T.E. underlined the words here italicized and wrote in the margin: "*access to the S. of S.*" (and explained verbally).

T. 398, B. 410 (333):
"In March, Churchill / and Lawrence went out to Cairo."

T.E. made a stroke as indicated and inserted the name of "*Young*" also.

T. 403, B. 415 (338):
On positions that Lawrence might take:
"There is, however, that of counsellor without responsibility, and this, I think, he has a reviving readiness to fill ..."

T.E. substituted "*directing action*", then crossed it out and wrote in the margin: *"deciding policy"*. Still unsatisfied, he wrote a series of alternatives on the back:

determining the course of events through others' mouths
     King without the crown
Authority   "   trappings[1]
Counsellor to an executive.

T. 405, B. 417 (339):
Re *The Mint:*
"a book which T.E. considers his *finest piece of work* . . ."[2]
    T.E. underlined the words here italicized and substituted *"best writing"*.

T. 414, B. 427 (347):
How the name "Cattewater" was changed to Mount Batten: "one suspects that the change was inspired by T.E."
    No: I wangled it for S. Smith, who suggested it.

(N.B. Other additions and modifications in this chapter were made during verbal discussion with T.E.)

TALK WITH T.E., BUSH HOTEL, FARNHAM, 20 AUGUST 1933

Motor-Cycle:
    Christened one of the first "Boanerges", because so thunderous. Now calls them George's. Present one is George VII. Next year's model expected to do 150 m.p.h. Wonders whether Brough will trust him with it.
    Enjoys motoring so much that would not charge Air Ministry with the 1d. a mile strictly due to him for journeys on duty.
    Used to do about 400–600 miles a week when at Cranwell. If missed a week, his delight was immense on getting in the saddle again.

---

[1] *Note by L.H.* T.E. crossed out his own word "trappings" and substituted the word "reputation".
[2] See R.G., p. 154, bottom.

Smoking:

Has tried once or twice. But no particular liking.

Anecdote:

When reported at Felixstowe recently was asked to give name of next of kin. He replied, "Put down the Daily Mail—and mind you ask for a special rate."

Friends:

"One doesn't make real friends after twenty-five. The shell hardens".

"The Mint":

Now in Sir J. Salmond's possession.

Sex:

T.E. emphasised his "sexlessness", and the fact that his senses were quite different to those of most people.

Gin:

"The most beautiful limpidity of anything on earth".

"Kitchener had second sight, sometimes, and was a great man, if clay-footed".[1]

Self-explanation.

Pleasure or pain—a matter of judgment. But hunts *sensation*, in true meaning. Always keen on new sensation. Doesn't repeat if unpleasant to his judgment, e.g. pain would be "high diving". Not ascetic, but a hedonist. The more elemental you can keep sensations the better you feel them. He replaces all normal pleasures by something internal.

(Letter from L.H. to T.E. Shaw):

Bush Hotel
Farnham, Surrey
2.9.33

Dear T.E.,

May I inflict these further queries on you? So far in my revision I have been improving the pill more than the jam.

[1]See p. 55, l. 8.

On Monday we go to Salisbury. Saw L.G. again the other day and he expressed hope of seeing you again any time.

(Reply):

Wed. morning

Very Rushed about

Not good replies, I fear: some I cannot help you in: others no one could answer. Some I hate the idea of answering. Don't worry about sugaring the pill. The sugar melts: the pill is the thing.

QUERIES—I

1. What were the reasons that prompted you to leave Damascus as soon as Allenby arrived?

I had finished—what better reason? The Arab Revolt and the Turkish War were also finished. What was in my mind, as I went towards London, was to begin again—as a junior officer—in France, learning the new way of war. The East was sucked dry. Never outstay a climax.

2. Have you any objection to my quoting your caustic impression of Kitchener?

How caustic? K. had second sight, sometimes, and was a great man, if clay-footed. What did I say of him that calls forth this?

3. Is it true that Feisal sent to the Turks some of the tobacco you captured at Jurf Ed Derawish (Jan. 1917). If so, where and how did he send it into their lines?

By camel, to Tebuk, I fancy.

4. Is it true that you asked for the rank of full colonel in order to travel home on the train from Taranto? Was it temporary or active?

Sleeping berths were given only to full colonels and upward. I travelled with Chetwode, with the local (Allenby-conferred) rank of colonel: and so was comfortable. I like comfort! Troop trains took 8 days—and the Wagon-Lits Express only 3.

5. Is it true (and when about) that you once made a major stand up and return the salutes of some privates he had been cursing? If so, details please.

There was a squabble of this sort at Taranto: I think Robert Graves mentioned it. I understand that the major did not mean what I thought, in his action.[1]

6. Any other experiences of this sort? Was there one in Oxford Street?

No: I was never in Oxford in uniform, I think.[2]

[*Note by L.H.* In view of the account he gave R.G., it would seem that his misunderstanding was feigned, to suppress an incident.]

7. Did you ever work at coaling ships in Port Said before the war?

Yes: about 1909, for a few days. Checker.

8. How far were you in danger of being handed over to the Turks at Ziza?

We were fellow-guests of the Arabs, & very sympathetic towards one another. I should have been quite safe with them. We put them back in their station with apologies for having troubled them.

[*Note by L.H.* My question referred to his private visit in June 1917 to Sheikh Fawaz, from whose tents he fled in the night— see *Seven Pillars*, p. 531, and his supplementary information in our talk, 27 May 1933. He read my question, however, as referring to the time when he camped with the Beni Sakhr early in April 1918. His answer supplements his note on p. 282 of my draft (see p. 108) about the accompanying presence of the Turks—a fact which is not disclosed in the *Seven Pillars*. The Turks had fled from their posts at the news of the British

---

[1] See R.G., p. 93, tenth line from bottom.
[2] *Ibid.*, p. 94, tenth line from bottom.

advance into Trans-Jordan which had already, unknown to them, changed into a retreat. There is more than a spice of humour in the idea that Lawrence's men and the enemy whom they were expecting to "relieve" should be waiting in company—and should be still waiting when the cause had disappeared, owing to the British retirement.]

9. Have you ever piloted aeroplanes yourself? In particular, did you have the use of a Moth in 1929?

Never formally. The 1929 Moth was a dual bus, and its owner did first pilot always.[1]

10. When did your last "removal" from speedboat work occur?

About October last year, I think: or was it September? I am bad at dates.

11. Can you remember the chronology of
   a) Your telling Allenby of your hammer-and-anvil Damascus plan in summer of 1918?
   b) Your ride up to Jericho to play on the Turks' fears aroused by Nasir's Wadi Hesa rail-move?

(a) Unless the Seven Pillars dates the talk? It was when he gave up the idea of an attack himself. I did not know if I could hold the city afterwards: but told him it was better to have won and lost than never to have tried at all. The war was going against us, everywhere.

(b) I wrote a long account of this, in the "Oxford" Seven Pillars, and cut it all out as incidental. I forget its date.

[*Note by L.H.* From the indirect hint of a diary reference this would appear to have taken place early in June. But see p. 112, footnote.]

[1]See R.G., p. 163, fourth line from bottom.

12. I think you said to me re Hogarth, as you said to Graves,—"I owe to him every good job I've had except my enlistment in the Air Force". Can you confirm?

Yes, all this is true. Trenchard let me in to the R.A.F. Till then D.G.H. had been a god-father to me: and he remained the best friend I ever had. A great man.

QUERIES FOR T.E.

3 SEPTEMBER 1933

1. Would it be possible to publish the photo of the 27 machine-guns captured at Tafileh?

I think it was burnt in Lionel Curtis' house fire this spring. Will find out!

2. What reason did Brémond give you, if you were in British uniform, for removing you from Feisal's company in France, Nov. 1918?

That Feisal was guest of the French Government, whose duty (and pleasure) it was to do the entertaining. So a foreign hanger-on was out of place. He was quite nice and (I thought) right about it. He gave me no idea that his instructions were as you report.

3. *Seven Pillars* account of your Hallat Ammar raid in Sept. 1917 says *Salem* fired the mine (at 200 yds. distance). Your report in Arab Bulletin says *you* fired it (at 100 yds., for observation). Which is correct?

Salem was in a hollow, out of sight of the train. I was on the bank in front of him, about 100 yards from each. When I lifted my arm he pushed down his. Technically he fired the mine. Morally I did. A fine point! If anyone cared!

4. You told me that on the last lap to Damascus, when you caught up Barrow, you had changed to a camel. How did you get hold of one?

We caught up my bodyguard, who were accompanying Barrow's H.Q., and I took one of my camels to ride the two miles or so on to see him, and find out why he had halted (for water, it was).

5. You made a note on my page about the Tell el Shehab bridge attempt in Sept. 1918—"There was also a tremendous pressure put upon me to take Deraa itself". Whom from?

From the Sheikhs of Deraa, who had come in to us for the job, at Mezerib, during the evening. Deraa was in a panic, and almost evacuated.

6. On the page that refers to your depression at Damascus and its relation to the poem in *S.P.W.* you have put a cryptic note that does not refer apparently to any phrase of mine— "*before* we got to Damascus. Some time before." What does this refer to, and mean?

The unhappy "event" happened long before we got to Damascus. I only took D. (so far as that motive was concerned) for historical reasons.[1]

7. For what reason did you wear Arab kit when you accompanied Feisal to Buck. House?

I was attending Feisal as his interpreter—and had not been invited by King George to come.

8. Who rebuked you for doing this, and what did he say? What did you reply?

I think the point of dress arose before I went, between myself and Robert Synge, our attaché: and I pointed out the advantage of two liveries, to a man with two masters.[2]

[1] See p. 156, l. 8.
[2] See R.G., p. 107, ninth line from bottom.

9. When you went to the H. of C. on your return from India did you ask for Thurtle or Maxton? What was your remark to Maxton about his hair?

Thurtle. He dragged in M. But I'd rather you didn't repeat the yarn. I dislike seeing my gossip in print! Reaction against Castlerosse.

10. In your report on the Yarmuk bridge attempt, you do not mention the dropped rifle.

I suppressed quite a lot of that night! And still do, I think.[1]

11. An extract from your first report (p. 35 Arab. Bull.) about Tafileh seems to suggest that you had sent Abdullah-el-Faiz to stop supplies to Mezraa on Dead Sea *before* the battle of Tafileh. Can you clear up this point?

We had sent Abdulla el Fai*r* to the S. end of the Dead Sea about a fortnight before: with orders to stop the traffic. He eventually did!

12. Was Hincks the Secretary of R.G.S.?

Was, and still is, I think, Secretary or Librarian. Hogarth was one of the heads of the R.G.S., and knew him. I don't think I ever saw him.

> 13 Birmingham St.
> Southampton
> 18.IX.33

Tomorrow Sir P. Sassoon visits the yard. Wed. one of my bosses stays here all day, I think. Thursday is Scott-Paine's return from U.S.A., and he is received with a pageant of speed-boats.

So I can't tell. I'd like to see you, to talk about the book. Cape sent me the script yesterday, according to an old promise, and I want to talk it *all* over with you. He is repentant about the "story" part of it.

I'll wire tomorrow if I can get away on Wed. If not where are you over the week end?

[1]*Note by L.H.* T.E. later (31 October 1933) gave me a longer account, illustrating it with a diagram.

T.E. came over to Amesbury, where I was staying for the final exercise of the year's training. The Avon Hotel was full of generals, and it perhaps saved awkwardness, if at the sacrifice of amusement, that he did not wear uniform—his usual motoring kit. As it was, he had a somewhat incongruous air; hatless and coatless, in a cheap pull-over and grey flannel "bags", he would have been less perceptible in a bank-holiday crowd than in this decorous gathering. Among them there was one old acquaintance who on entering, later, was quick to notice him—General Bartholomew. Their talk was a savoury to a rather heavy meal. For T.E. had come armed with my draft to "talk it *all* over". Although he had been through it in successive sections, passing the third (and last) when he came to see me at Farnham, he had suddenly developed misgivings over the general effect. There was too much of himself in it, he complained. I retorted that his remonstrance was rather late, in two senses—for the real time to rectify this was sixteen years before. I had found, by examining the evidence and the witnesses, that his predominant part in the Arab Revolt was historical fact, and it was inevitable that it had to be treated proportionately. We had a bantering argument on the question of duty to history. Apparently unconvinced, he settled down, pencil in hand, to go through the whole typescript. I expected to see the pencil descend in slashing cuts. But taking it thus, point by point, he found cause only to alter a few odd phrases. He was almost at the end when, as if repentant of his own repentance, he pounced upon and struck out a passage referring to his cottage. This, he had not only passed when at Farnham, but had actually, I found, begun to amplify when reading the typescript just before his present visit.

How can one explain the difference between his expressed intention and ultimate action? By sheer kindheartedness?—he had it in abundance. By a reluctance to damage what another had created? By an inward admission of the justice of my complaint about his oscillation? Or because the opening historical argument had made an impression? By nature or education, he had a sense of duty to history that struggled with his sense of futility and instinct to loose all ties. There is significance in the remark in his letter of November 6, 1928[1] to Robert Graves—"*Seven Pillars* was a historical necessity: I don't call it an option". There is a further sidelight in his remark on Christmas Eve, 1927, that, while agreeing with any depreciation of his writing as a whole, "it is when people come to particularities of criticism that I begin to wish to say good of the bit attacked". I found this tendency strongly marked during our various discussions of my draft. While expressing indifference to what was said about him, he several times protested that my criticism of his action on specific occasions was too hard—and took pains to furnish the evidence I required before modifying them.

He was willing, and frequently eager, to see himself written down, as a whole, yet was often prompt to defend himself on any particular point—an attitude which arose, I believe, from an historian-like urge to see that each fragment was measured exactly. When the critic, however, came to weigh the fragments collectively, and was compelled to state the correct sum, T.E. was impelled to reject it. I noticed signs of such a reaction following the completion of my book; at the time, having attended the weighing of the points, he did not dispute the sum: as the months passed, and the impression waned, his instinctive doubts grew. That inconsistency may be traced to his self-confessed weakness in synthesis. Or to his instinct to avoid being pinned down—which is to be seen in what he said about Robert Graves' "astonishingly 'life-like' "

[1]See R.G., p. 155, l. 1.

portrait of him—"I do hope I won't be self-convinced, and act as you would have me act".[1] It would fetter his freedom to alter as he liked. There is a further explanation suggested in R.G.'s summing-up (see R.G., p. 184, bot.). But apart from the fact that the mountain of negation only brought forth a mouse-like deletion, there were other symptoms in this Amesbury labour which suggested that T.E.'s historian side had momentarily gained the ascendancy. He made a number of small yet significant alterations, for more exactness, in some of the biographical points; he also suggested that I might incorporate the "27 articles" on the art of handling Arabs which he drafted in 1917. Accordingly I composed a fresh chapter from these and sent it a week later for him to see.

[1]See R.G., p. 139, l. 9.

EXTRACTS FROM REVISED DRAFT OF
"T. E. LAWRENCE: IN ARABIA AND AFTER"

Chapter I ("The Crusader")

T. 1, B. 13 (3):

"The County of Carnarvon in North Wales points like an arm into the Irish Sea. At the armpit lies the village of/Tremadoc ... This resemblance ... is also an apt symbol for the career of one who was born at Tremadoc on August 15th, 1888."

T.E. altered "village" into the plural, made a stroke as indicated and inserted "*Portmadoc*" before Tremadoc; below, he crossed out "at Tremadoc" and substituted "*here*".

Chapter X (originally numbered XI)

T. 181, B. 193 (152):

On his mood when undertaking the "mystery" ride through Syria in June 1917:

"'To hell with them all' *was his inward comment* . . ."

I inserted this in the revised draft after he had expressed in these words his mood at the time. He now put a cross against the words here italicized, and, to meet his doubt, I altered them to "seems to have been his inward comment."

T. 181–82, B. 194 (152):

"Here, in brief, is the outline of this amazing ride. He took with him an old sheikh whom he had known before the war and rode first due north to Burga, which lies in the desert east of the Jebel Druse. Then he turned north-west and rode to a spring which lies between Tadmor, ancient Palmyra, and Damascus. Still continuing in this direction he reached the Aleppo-Damascus railway near Ras Baalbek. Here he blew up a small bridge—as reported in an enemy signal which was intercepted by our forces at the time. Then he bore south, travelling under the auspices of the Syrian revolutionaries; and he visited many of their leaders who promised to rise when the moment was ripe. He also took care to dissuade them from a premature move and to warn them against Nesib's allurements."

T.E. had passed this without remark, beyond the points already corrected when he first went through the draft. Now, however, he said that it was not exact and gave me, verbally, a number of corrections which I embodied in the following revised paragraph:

"Here is the partial outline of this amazing ride. He was unaccompanied by any of his party, escorted instead by successive local guides, among them an old sheikh whom he had known before the war. He passed by Burga, which lies in the desert east of the Jebel Druse, and subsequently turned north-west to a spring which lies between Tadmor, ancient Palmyra, and Damascus. Eventually he reached the Aleppo-Damascus railway near Ras Baalbek. Here he blew up a small bridge—as reported in an enemy signal which was intercepted by our forces at the time. Then he bore south, travelling under the auspices of the Syrian revolutionaries; he visited many of their leaders and discussed with them plans for a rising when the moment was ripe—he took care to dissuade them from a premature move."

T. 196, B. 206 (162):
"While the post was being looted, Lawrence raced on to Aqaba, only four miles further, and splashed into the cooling

sea. *If 'Thalassa, Thalassa' was not on his lips, it was in his thoughts."*

T.E. had made no comment on this in the first draft, but now he put brackets round the sentence here italicized and said that, in fact, his thoughts were entirely *"on his feet"*—his one idea was to plunge into the water and cool his burning feet.

Chapter XXI (originally numbered Chapter XXII)

T. 383, B. 398 (323):
"The advance machine in which he was travelling crashed at Rome, killing both pilots. Lawrence, more *lucky* than them in having a seat behind the engines, escaped with three ribs and a collar-bone broken."

T.E. underlined the word here italicized and put a "?" He objected to the word, saying that it was due to prudence— he *"had firmly declined invitations to sit in front with the pilots".*

T. 389, B. 404 (328):
"His reason for rejecting all personal profit and honours sprang from his fastidious sense of *honour."*

T.E. underlined the word here italicized and put a "?" in the margin. He said that it was due also to an acute sense of policy—to refuse personal advantage immensely strengthened him in achieving his impersonal aim. He also preferred the word *"honesty"* to "honour".

T. 389, B. 404 (328):
"I remember him once saying, half humorously, that having 'posed as a sea-green incorruptible' he must be consistent in maintaining it. But it was not a pose. Those who knew T.E.'s passion for baths, his one form of self-indulgence, and are also aware of his abnormal clearness of sight, can understand the

way that his craving for physical cleanliness is translated into the sphere of the spirit."

T.E. marked this with a cross, declaring that it was a pose—for a purpose. He also said that I over-estimated his passion for cleanliness—he didn't mind dirt. What he liked baths for was the pleasant sensation.

T. 390, B. 405 (329):
"He was intensely amused, however, by the comment of H. G. Wells, that it was a great human document without *pretentions* to be a work of art."

T.E. put a cross in the margin against the word here italicized and wrote above—"*Enormous pretentions*". He said that he was more amazed than amused by the comment.

T. 390, B. 405 (329):
"The message is there . . . In concluding the book he closed his life as T. E. Lawrence."

T.E. put a cross against this, and said that he had changed his name long before the book itself was finished—and that he might reassume the name of "Lawrence".

Chapter XXII ("Fulfilment")

T. 395, B. 407 (331):
"[He] had now the magnetic attraction of a legendary figure —for visitors to *Oxford*, *even* more than for members of the University."

T.E. underlined the words here italicized, wrote a *?* against "even"—and explained verbally that he did not think he had been any attraction for members of the University.

T. 396, B. 409 (332):
"Winston Churchill . . . was offered the Colonial Office . . . He consulted Lawrence /, who . . . frankly warned him . . ."

T.E. made a stroke as indicated and inserted:
on the problem of the M.E. [Middle Ear].

T. 397, B. 409 (333):
On his appointment as Political Adviser:
"He [T.E.] accepted the post on the understanding that the
wartime pledges *he had* made to the Arabs on Britain's behalf
would now be honoured . . ."
    T.E. crossed out the words here italicized.

T. 398, B. 410 (333):
"Lawrence had *long since* come to the conclusion that the
ultimate focus of Arab nationality, and its future lay in Mesopotamia, potentially richer and greater than Syria."
    T.E. put a cross against the words here italicized and in
the margin wrote: "*pre-war*".

T. 399, B. 411 (334):
On his sense of fulfilment when Feisal was placed on the
throne of Iraq:
"His satisfaction was not due to an anticipation of early perfection. He expected that the new-born Arab state would have
to suffer its growing pains. At the same time he foresaw possibilities that encouraged him in forwarding them."
    T.E. put a cross against the last sentence and wrote in the
margin: "*Promise to be kept*". He explained that he knew the
essential individualism of the Arab too well to have much
confidence, but it was essential to honour our promise. Even
from the point of view of policy we should run a greater risk
in failing to keep it.

T. 405, B. 416 (338):
"His dislike of the pomp of power is due not only to its waste
of time but to its hypocrisy . . .".

T.E. emphasised his agreement with this explanation by a marginal sign.

T. 405, B. 416 (338):
"Lawrence had the chance of filling one of the most important posts in the British Empire, and was *tempted* to accept."

T.E. put brackets round the word here italicized—and said that it did not seriously tempt him, although he did not turn down the suggestion outright.

N.B. The post, he had told me, was that of High Commissioner for Egypt.

T. 407, B. 418 (339):
On his hard experiences at the Uxbridge Depot of the R.A.F.:
"But it was at least the means of inspiring a book which T.E. considers his best writing, superior both in a literary and a philosophical sense to the *Seven Pillars of Wisdom*. He wrote the greater part while actually living the life he records, so that no lapse of time affects the photographic accuracy, but when he rejoined the Air Force in 1925 he added further chapters on life at Cranwell which form a happy contrast to the portrayal of Uxbridge. Artistically, T.E. considers that the addition tends to spoil the effect, but it is characteristic of his fairness that he should have made it. Whether the book will ever be published, only the future can tell. One difficulty, apart from T.E.'s indifference, is that it 'out-joyces' James Joyce in the fidelity of its record of barrack-room conversations."

T.E. crossed out this passage, and wrote in substitution:

, as he emphasised at the time in a diary which he maintained throughout the experience. These notes were added to later, at Cranwell where the atmosphere was happy; but they remained notes, without any attempt at formal composition. Incidentally in reproducing barrack-room conversation they out-joyce Joyce.

Mr. Jonathan Cape years later learnt of the existence of this manuscript diary (which T.E. prefers to the S.P. as writing), and suggested
that it might fulfil a clause in his contract for "Revolt in the Desert",
giving the firm an option on the next book. The author agreed instantly and submitted the notes for approval, with a statement that
his terms for them were a million pounds down in advance, and 75%
royalty! Mr. Cape was not able to raise the million pounds before his
option expired.

T. 407, B. 418 (340):
"an officer who had *penetrated his disguise* sold the news to the
press."

T.E. crossed out the words here italicized, and wrote in
substitution:

known him before the war.

(N.B. He subsequently altered this to: *"during the war."*)

T. 408, B. 418 (340):
On his job in the quartermaster's stores at Bovington Camp,
in Dorset:
"It was, on the whole, 'a cushy job' and had the advantage
of giving him the privacy of an office in which he could work
/ on the final revision of the *Seven Pillars*."

T.E. made a stroke as indicated and inserted:

at night

T. 409–10 B. (omitted):
"Much of the land in this part is owned by *kinsmen of his
father*, and from one of them T.E. *rented five acres* on which
stood the walls of a *two hundred year old* cottage. *Then* / he set
to work to slate the roof himself, and travelled round the
country on his motorcycle, making acquaintance with builders
from whom he "scrounged" slates—it surprised him that no
less than nine thousand were needed. The cottage has two
storeys and two rooms—a living room downstairs and a

bookroom upstairs. There is a bed but no bedroom. The bed is a concession to the needs of sundry friends or acquaintances, down on their luck, to whom he has lent the cottage. T.E. says that he will dispose of the bed when he goes into permanent residence, and instead have long-seated chairs—it is so much simpler to go to sleep where you are sitting. No water or drainage is laid on, but there is a spring in the garden. For his meals, T.E. usually runs into a nearby village, where, conveniently, there are several cheap cafés. One meal a day suffices, and any hour will serve. If the weather is bad, he can dine off bread and cheese, washed down by the water from his own well—T.E. neither drinks nor smokes, but he is an epicure in water."

T.E. underlined certain words here italicized. He also made a stroke as indicated and inserted:

The cottage was half a ruin and

Then, apparently changing his mind, he deleted the whole paragraph.

T. 411–12, B. 420 (342):

"*As it is, he has recently designed a black oilskin combination garment, with a zip-fastener, although he uses it only in really bad weather, because any such outer covering detracts from the sensuous appreciation of a swift passage through the atmosphere.* Air Force uniform, with its puttees for the calves and easily unhooked high collar, seems to him an ideal kit for motor-cycling under normal conditions, *and for this reason he almost always travels in uniform rather than in plain clothes.*"

T.E. deleted the words here italicized.

T. 426, B. 433 (352):

"Whether it be true as he suggests that '*genius* has gone out' of him."

T.E. deleted his own original word, here italicized, and wrote in the margin: "*virtue*".[1]

T. 427, B. 434 (353):
"With himself he found that happiness was intermittent—it came in *the doing of a job well-done, especially a job connected with mechanism.*"
    T.E. deleted the words here italicized and substituted: "*absorption*".

T. 429, B. 436:
"T.E. is rare among great men in adjusting . . ."
    T.E. underlined "great" and wrote "*?*" in the margin.

(N.B. I had obtained T.E.'s permission to quote from his letter to me of 26.vi.33 about his soldiership. But on seeing it in typescript he modified a number of phrases which, he thought, might sound boastful.)
"I was not an instinctive soldier, automatic with intuitions and happy ideas. When I took a decision or adopted an alternative it was after *studying* every relevant—and many an irrelevant—factor. Geography, tribal structure, religion, social customs, language, appetites, standards—*all* were at my finger-ends. The enemy I knew almost like my own side. I risked myself among them *a hundred times*, to learn."
    T.E. underlined the words here italicized, substituted, "*doing my best to study*"; deleted "all"; and substituted "*many times*".

"The same with tactics. If I used a weapon well it was because I could handle it. Rifles were easy. I put myself under instructors for Lewis, Vickers, and Hotchkiss. *If you look at my articles in The Pickaxe, you will see how much I* learned about

[1]See R.G., pp. 71, l. 22, and 150, l. 14.

explosives from my R.E. teachers, and *how far I* developed
their methods. To use aircraft *I learned to fly*. To use armoured
cars I learned to drive and fight them. I became a/gunner
at need, and could doctor and judge a camel."

T.E. deleted the words here italicized; substituted "*flew*"
for "*learned to fly*"; / and inserted "*bad*" before "gunner".
"The same with strategy. I have written only a few pages on
the art of war—but in these I levy contribution from my
predecessors of five languages. You . . . can see the allusions
and quotations, the conscious analogies, in all I say and do
militarily."

T.E. deleted this paragraph and substituted:

For my strategy, I could find no teachers in the field: but behind me
there were some years of military reading, and even in the little that
I have written about it, you may be able to trace the allusions and
quotations, the conscious analogies.

"Do make it clear that generalship, at least in my case, *came
of understanding, hard study*, and *brain-work and concentration*.
Had it come easy to me I should not have done it as well."

T.E. underlined the words here italicized and substituted:

came not by instinct, unsought, but by understanding, hard study,
and brain-concentration.

(Letter from L.H. to T.E.):

27.9.33

My dear T.E.,

I have taken the 27 articles as you suggested and taken a
condensed version to form with an introductory bit an "interlude" between Chapter VII and VIII. Here it is. I have been
hopefully waiting for the page I sent you on Friday.

All good wishes,

Yours,

B.H.L.H.

(Reply from T.E.):

I think this bit is quite interesting. I also return Page 2, amended, with apologies for tardiness. Life is fast here, just now. I am trying to think of too many things at once.

T.E.S.

(*Interlude*) (or as Chapter VIII)

T. 129a, B. 141 (107):
"Many of them [the Arab chiefs] behaved as if the British officers were their servants, and set an example of rudeness that was imitated by their followers, and even by their slaves."

"even their slaves"—but you are there socially wrong. Arabian slaves are privileged persons, and rank next to children. A slave, for instance, can eat with his master, and usually does. A servant never. A slave can sleep with his master—a servant must sleep outside the door. A slave can call his master by name—a servant not. T.E.S.

T. 129b, B. 141 (108):
"Nevertheless, there was a long way to go between this equality and the ascendancy which *one* among them later attained."

T.E. underlined the word here italicized and wrote in the margin:

? more than one.

T. 129b, B. 141 (108):
"Astonished at his unruffled manner when slaves brushed past him or spat in his presence, they were inclined to ascribe his capacity 'to eat humble pie' to his upbringing . . ."

Your reporter of this incident knew more about the manners of Egypt than of Arabia. The slave was only behaving before me as in his master's presence. Arab grandees habitually play with their slaves. I was *glad* to be accepted as natural.

T. 129b, B. 142 (108):

"When the campaign moved north, his [Lawrence's] method would change—and he would come out more into the open."

An Englishman was *somebody*, in pre-war Syria.

T. 129e, B. 144 (110):

"If you succeed, you will have . . . thousands of men under your orders . . ."

    T.E. crossed out "orders" and substituted "*control*".

T. 129g, B. 147 (112):

"Unnumbered generations of tribal raids have taught them more about some parts of the business than we will ever know".

    T.E. crossed out "will" and substituted "*shall*".

T. 129, B. 147 (113):

"In spite of Arab example, avoid too free talk about women . . . a remark, harmless in English, may appear as unrestrained to them, as some of their statements would look to us, if taken literally."

    T.E. crossed out "taken" and substituted "*translated*".

(N.B. The last four extracts were from Lawrence's "27 Articles" printed and distributed in 1917. That he should have revised the phrasing in view of their publication in my book is an interesting sidelight upon his way.)

At Amesbury, he had expressed a wish to make some small amendments in what he had originally written for Page 2 of my draft. I sent him the page for this purpose.

EXTRACTS FROM PAGE 2 OF DRAFT

T. 2, B. 14 (4):

"*Probably* my upbringing and adventures—and way of thinking—have bereft me of class. Only the leisured classes make me acutely uncomfortable. I cannot play or pass time. *Lots of people, especially women, go about saying they alone understand me. They do not see how little they see, each of them separately. My name is Legion!*"[1]

T.E. substituted "*Perhaps*" for "Probably"; deleted "classes" and "acutely"; changed the full stop after "uncomfortable" into a comma, and inserted "*as*"; he deleted the last three sentences here italicized. (N.B. These also had been his own words, as originally drafted.)

[1]See R.G., p. 80, bottom.

TALK WITH T.E.

(From Diary)

In evening (as it was my birthday) I took Jessie out to dinner, at Boulestin's. As car was turning in from Strand, someone rapped on nearside window—found it was T.E., who said he had rung me up ten minutes before. Had no time to warn me of his coming up. After some demur about his clothes, he came to dine with us at Boulestin's, and then back to the flat. We went through my new additions to the book, and he passed them, also maps.

Looking at the two photos of Augustus John sketches he gave Jessie, he said the one I liked best was now at the Fitzwilliam. Would have let me have it, but—would hardly let it out of his clutches. Promised me a large drawing of him by Eric Kennington now in cupboard at his Dorset cottage—if I would call there some time and collect it.

Said John was now doing another of him in a cap—looked like a field-marshal.

Had come up to town about contract for boats, with Scott-Paine who asked him to dine. T.E. had left him on pavement outside Waldorf, saying would be "barratry" to accept his invitation.

We asked T.E. to spend night, but he said he had left his things at the Union Jack Club—got cubicle there for 1/9ᵈ· a night. No one interfered or spoke. Last time he was up he went into the big Lyons at Tottenham Court Rd., and before long the "fellow in evening dress" came up and said the band was going to play "Lover in Damascus". T.E. said, "If it does I walk out".

Talked of Hogarth's imputation of T.E.'s callousness. T.E. thought it largely a matter of his manner. Emphasised his own *shyness*—dislike of giving himself away. I suggested it was surely a weakness in one so clearsighted.

Then spoke of H.'s suggestion that if T.E.'s will decided on an end, he had no morality about the means. I said I disagreed with H.'s view of him. T.E. said he agreed with me—he liked to appear careless of morality, but not really so. Agreed with my view that ill means distorted the end.

Told recent story of how, when Feisal died, someone from the Air Ministry rang him up to warn him that pressmen were on their way to interview him, and jokingly said, "I suppose you didn't kill him?" T.E. replied, "I haven't been doing any killing recently". Shocked the girl and increased his reputation for callousness. Gave reporters the slip by taking train for London, while they on their arrival at Southampton were taken to Cowes by skipper of boat, much to their indignation.

Led on to talk of Feisal and his family. When T.E. went out first to Hejaz, he saw that Abdulla was fundamentally indolent. Realised that Abdulla could not be made into a hero of revolt. Nor Ali. Feisal better—and he made the best of him.

Feisal a timid man, hated running into danger, yet would do anything for Arab freedom—his one passion, purely unselfish. Here, as later in Iraq, it made him face things and risks he hated. At original attack on Medina he had nerved himself to put on a bold front, and the effort had shaken him so that he never courted danger in battle again.

As for his statesmanship, his defect was that he always

listened to his momentary adviser, despite his own better judgment. All right so long as T.E. was his adviser! I asked T.E. why he portrayed Feisal as such a heroic leader in his reports. He replied it was the only way to get the British to support the Arabs—physical courage is essential demand of typical British officer.

I then asked why he did not tell me of Feisal's weakness earlier—he replied, while Feisal still alive, it might have injured his precarious position.

Negotiations between Feisal and Kemal in 1918 were separate from those with Jemal—began with correspondence between subordinates and then extended to principals.

I asked T.E. if his refusal of decorations was at a levee. No—at private meeting, no one else present at the time. T.E. had explained to Military Secretary . . . that he would not accept. M.S. startled and conventionally said, "You can't refuse," but T.E. assumed he would let the King know, instead of which he did nothing.[1]

Told us tale of how he sat next to a French duchess, who gushed about the East. T.E. unresponsive. Finally she raved about the marvellous nights. T.E.: "Sweaty, aren't they?" It crumpled her—barbarian English.

T.E.'s admiration for Eugene O'Neill: also for Compton Mackenzie's prose in *Water on the Brain*—and way he dealt with the old ladies; superb bit of farce.

How he spotted McMahon in railway train coming up from Southampton, when walking along the corridor. Went in and sat down, chatting during the rest of the journey. Another man in the carriage—who looked like a well-fed commercial traveller. Noticed him taking a great interest in the conversation. At last the man leaned across and said, "Aren't you Shaw?" It was H. G. Wells! Had forgotten him (?)

[1]See R.G., p. 106, tenth line from bottom.

Talk of Peace Conference.

He liked Clemenceau. Had great respect for House, "a world statesman", but found Wilson narrow and school-masterish, caring nothing for anything else so long as he could get his pet L. of N. project through. Found that House had lost all influence with Wilson, yet didn't know it. House promised, but Wilson ignored.

Talked of his second interview with the King. The King said to him, "Have you got any trophies?"—wanted them for his private museum. T.E. replied, "Would you like the wreath the Kaiser hung on Saladin's tomb?" The King exclaimed, "Nothing family, thank you!"

I asked him if it was true that he had cut notches in the rifle given him by Feisal (and now at Windsor Castle) when-ever he brought down a Turk. He said yes, but he gave it up after a while—it lost its zest. He did not carry the rifle itself any longer after he took to the use of an air-Lewis.

No one not descended from Mahomet could be a Sherif. The story that he was made a Sherif was a fiction. The only justification for it was that one day the Arabs were talking about giving themselves fancy titles, and one of them said to him, "What title will you choose?" He replied, "Emir Dynamite". The name stuck, for a time.

Discussing the part he played in securing air control in the Middle East, he said that he first talked to Scott and Winter-ton. Winterton was violently opposed, but Scott agreed, and he talked to Trenchard about the idea.

T.E. went on to remark to me that "air control was not so effective in 'narrow waters' as in 'wide waters' "—want room to manoeuvre in; aircraft want a wide turning circle. "Until they can hover it is not applicable to a crowded district". But went on to say, however, that it was "applicable to Waziristan, not to the Mohmand country, and becoming less and less effective as you approach Peshawar". "I'm a tremendous supporter of air but would have reservations about the N.W. frontier province; I would take over bits".— "Would evacuate Razmak tomorrow". He went on to say that he had spent 8 months flying and driving over every yard of this country.

1. Did you find out about Tafila machine-guns?

In collection, with Lionel Curtis.

2. Did you *yourself* print the Turkish Army Handbook?

I got three printers (Lowland Scots) from the Government Printing Office. Private Newton did the printing. I supervised—was connected with about 8 editions of it.

3. I am informed that you saw Nuri Shaalan in June 1917 after seeing Ali Riza, and arranged for Nuri's neutrality. Is this correct?[1]

I saw Nuri Shaalan in his tent near Azraq. Saw him on my way back from Damascus. Nuri was very nervous that he was going to be compromised. I said to him, "Send in to the Turks and say we are here". I wanted the Turks to think we were operating from the top of the Wadi Sirhan—in order to mask our coming move.

In checking the record of T.E.'s war career, I had sought information from Sir Coote Hedley, who was head of the Geographical Section of the General Staff when T.E. joined it in 1914. He replied:

17th May

". . . I lost several of my officers on the outbreak of war. Amongst other work we were engaged in finishing some

[1]This had reference to the Baalbek ride. See p. 69, l. 17.

1/250,000 maps of the Sinai Peninsula which connected the maps of Palestine (surveyed and published by the Palestine Exploration Fund) with those of the Sinai Peninsula prepared by the G.S.G.S. starting from the Egyptian end. When this area was actually being surveyed (by Capt. [now Colonel] S. F. Newcombe and others) Lawrence and Woolley (of 'Ur' fame) were attached to the survey party, to make an archeological survey. . . . I therefore knew about Lawrence although I had never met him and was only too glad to take him into my section in order to 'classify the roads on the new maps'. He came into my room . . . and said he had been rejected for the Army as being too small. He had on some grey flannels and wore no hat. He looked about 18. I said I would get him a commission and take him into my office to help to finish the Sinai Maps. . . . I knew that intelligence officers would be wanted in Egypt and told the D.M.I. I had the ideal officer for that work in my office. He stayed with me 2 or 3 months, perhaps more. I do not quite remember . . . He was very efficient and could I think have worked all through the night and hardly noticed what time it was".

In a further letter Sir Coote Hedley stated that he did not write to invite T.E. to come for interview—"He came on his own initiative". I incorporated the account in my draft, but T.E. marked it as incorrect and gave me a different version (see p. 90, bot.). In an endeavour to clear up the discrepancy I wrote to another man who might, from a third angle, be able to throw light on the sequence of events. He did not recall having played any part himself and so, of kind intention, wrote to Sir Coote Hedley; hearing that the latter had already given me an account, he was evidently puzzled why I had also applied to him—perhaps overlooking the need of cross-

checking historical evidence wherever possible. I sent his
letter on to T.E., who wrote back:

7.XI.33

The way of the seeker of truth is hard. Old Hincks sounds quite
stuffy. . . .

I can stick to it that Hogarth pulled the strings: that I went to
Col. Hedley by appointment: that I did not ask for a job (I have
never yet asked anybody for a job) and that my enlistment difficulty
was only due to that sudden September raising of the standard of
height to check the rush of recruits while hutments were preparing.
Also that I was weeks at the W.O. before getting into uniform.
Somebody in 1919 told me I was not properly commissioned. I do
not know or care what that means. Indeed I feel like Gallio just
now, having a cold. On Thursday I have to have an up-and-downer
with the British Legion H.Q. in London, they having apparently
published what purports to be an article from me in their Journal.
I hope to be in London only a few hours.

LETTER FROM L.H. TO T. E. SHAW, 4 NOVEMBER 1933
(*With answers*)

My dear T.E.,

1. I have been through the Imperial War Museum collection of photographs, as I want a number to illustrate the book.
Unfortunately I find they have very few, and they are very
bad. Do you know of any other sources, or of anyone who
took some good ones?

Lionel Curtis (Hales Croft, Kidlington, Oxon.) had about 1000—
all now burnt, I fancy.

2. I have been trying to trace on a map the Wadi Khalid
which you mentioned as the intermediate of the three alternative objectives in the Yarmuk Valley—between Tel-el-
Shehab and Um Keis. Can you give me any hint as to its
location?

W.K. is the name for a middle stretch of the Yarmuk Valley.

3. I got in touch with Hinks to try and clear up the point about how you came to go to the War Office in 1914. I enclose a letter from him for you to see. (Please return.) The mystery deepens!

Returned.

4. Did Augustus send an expedition to Wejh in 24 B.C.?

About then: Burton found some Roman pillars there, he says. See his Land of Midian: rotten book.

5. Was there a Roman stone dam across the Wadi Ithm at Khadra?

I suspect it of being post-Roman—400 A.D. perhaps.

6. Is there any specific foundation for the statement that Aqaba was King Solomon's port?

Ezion Geber is supposed to have lain on the N. shore of the Gulf, near Akaba town.

7. Did Allenby say in a report that you had made train-wrecking the national sport of Arabia?

I don't know!

8. Had Baldwin I built a wall round the crest of the hill, and were there remains of a castle within it?

8 beats me. Is Shobek meant? The castle of Monreale that was. Whether Baldwin I or not I forget. All the Trans-Jordan antiquities are well listed by Brunnow and Domadzewski. For Crusades read Stephenson.

· · ·

I wrote to let Sir Coote Hedley know how the further enquiry had arisen. He replied:

23.11.33

"Thank you very much for your explanation. It was not really necessary for you to bother to write to me again. I have no recollection whatever of receiving any warning about Lawrence's coming to see me from either Hogarth or Hinks. Hinks confirms this as far as he is concerned, and I well remember the pleasure and *surprise* with which I saw Lawrence, for I knew all about Lawrence and did not need a recommendation from anyone. It is very likely that Lawrence may have been advised by Hinks or Hogarth or by both to come and see me, but I am pretty certain that neither of them communicated with me on the matter. On this point my recollection is worth more than Lawrence's. On the point of whether they recommended him to come to me my word is worth nothing and his everything. I may say that if Lawrence had told me at our first interview that he had Hogarth's recommendation it would have made no impression on me, for I knew his value as well as Hogarth".

LETTER FROM L.H. TO T. E. SHAW, 29 NOVEMBER 1933

(*With answers as written*)

My dear T.E.,

A passion for historical accuracy is a very trying thing—as you must be thinking; but here are a number of fresh questions that have cropped up in my final correction of the proofs.

1. In Winterton's 1920 account in Blackwood's of the 16th September raid on the Jabir bridge I notice that he does not mention that enemy patrols were approaching after you had blown up the bridge. Were they close enough to worry you?

Not till we broke down.

2. His account also says that in the next phase on the way to Sheikh Sa'ad, Nuri Shalaan took Ghazale, while Auda took

Izra. Your account says Auda took Ghazale, and Tallal took Izra. Can you throw any further light on this?

I'm right.

3. You mentioned Demetrius Poliorcetes among your earlier reading. *Where* did you read about his sieges?

In some translation.

4. Did your reading embrace Vegetius

Perhaps.

and Frontinus?

No.

5. What book of Caemerrer did you read?

"?"

6. In one of your notes about your work at Carchemish you said, as far as I could read, that you "produced a complete stratification of types and rims" down to a certain level. As I am not an archaeological expert can you tell me if I read your handwriting correctly?

Pottery.

7. Was the name of the place you went to in the North "Birjik" or "Birijik"?

Birijik.

.   .   .

9. In *R. in D.*, regarding Buxton's raid you remarked that your camels, brought up to walk in Arab style, averaged more than 5 miles an hour compared with the 4 m.p.h. of Buxton's men's. I find by checking in Buxton's numerous timings that his camels' pace was almost exactly 3 m.p.h. Do you think that yours were more than a mile an hour faster?[1]

---

[1] In *Seven Pillars* Lawrence wrote: "Buxton's force marched nearly four". I found that on the northward march to which his remark referred, Buxton's pace averaged $3\frac{1}{4}$ m.p.h.

(T.E. did not answer this, but when we next met he said that Buxton's force had kept up the army custom of a ten-minute halt every hour, as well as halting for a longer rest every few hours. Deducting the hourly halts, the difference is largely explained.)

10. In one of your notes for me you remarked: "In the desert I shaved daily". Goslett queried this, and I seem to remember your telling me that you did not need to shave so frequently as this.

Regularly?[1]

I am also enclosing for you to glance at a few fresh additions and revisions which I have made as a result of your own* and other people's corrections. I should like you to look through them.

*(the night you were here)

P.S. I'm going down into the country this week-end, probably Friday, to see Adrian at Hindhead. Is there any chance of seeing you—either there or meeting you? I suppose there is no likelihood of your going to your cottage. I haven't forgotten your promise to give me the big drawing of yourself by Kennington if I would come and fetch it.

Aircraftman T. E. Shaw,
13 Birmingham Street,
Southampton.

When at T.E.'s cottage, Cloud's Hill, on December 3rd, I showed him a number of further insertions, which he approved. We also talked at length of the new armoured target-boats for the R.A.F. on which he had been working. The facts of this new development, rather garbled, had just been pub-

[1] See p. 154, l. 16.

lished in the American press, and copied in an English paper. I suggested that it would be a good thing to give a correct account, and T.E. was seized by the idea. We settled that I should give the facts in the *Daily Telegraph*. Rather than rely on memory, I sent him a detailed questionnaire, which he returned with answers and an accompanying note, as under:

In what you write refer to Bridlington in Yorkshire, and Felixstowe where the Bridlington detachment spend the winter. Also please mention Mr. Scott-Paine and the British Power-Boat Co.[1]

The origin of these boats was a request from D. of T. [raining]—Air-Commodore Mitchell, for the Boat Dept. to produce them a towed or W/T controlled target-boat. We said "Why not an armoured boat", and produced the required article in three or four months. Its design betrays the vices of haste, but they are cheap, safe, and afford wonderful practice. The finance people refuse the crews extra-pay, which we are pressing for—not that we think it dangerous, but damned uncomfortable! Hellish hot, smelly and noisy. They wear ear defenders, crash helmets, and gas masks! little else.

Picture postcards of these boats are on sale in the shops at Bridlington, and everybody there knows of them. They have also run in Christchurch Bay, off the Needles.

Robertson, the A.M. press lord, has had orders to prevent any publication of these boats. He can stop the D.T. but not U.S.A., of course! We have tried, for long enough, to get the ban removed. It is just silly.

The press has photos. of these boats, held up: and people like Sheppard [?], of the Times, know all about them.

As compared with the Centurion, the only other mobile marine target

(1) They cost only about £1 an hour in running expenses—and 3000–4000 pounds in capital charge. Centurion is a battleship + a destroyer, with crew of some 400 men.

(2) They can go any speed, whereas the Centurion can only go at 16 knots. They can turn fast or slow: the Centurion can only turn slowly.

[1]This was characteristic of his desire to see that credit should be given where it was deserved.

(3) They are too short—only 37½ feet long. So they are hard to hit, and do not mimic capital ships well in size or motion. An armoured capital ship would be better—if we could afford it.

I think the general opinion is that they have greatly improved the R.A.F. ship-bombing practice. In a few years aircraft will deal infallibly with ships.

Order not yet placed—but it is likely that several more target boats will be ordered for next summer.

(P.S.) Please keep me out of it as far as possible. Crews are all volunteers from regular R.A.F. marine section, and I have had no more to do with these boats than with the rest of the revised versions of boats with which the R.A.F. is being re-equipped. They are just part of my job—to consider design, to watch construction, and then to test, report on and tune the finished articles.

The sheet on which T.E. answered my technical questions bore the scribbled request that I would burn it after reading —with some remark, as far as I recall, that his handwriting must not be seen on it. As I was not ready to draft the article immediately, I made a note of the points for use in it, and at once burnt the paper. In writing him, I made some joking complaint at the trouble his request had caused me.

13 B'ham St.
S'ton
14.XII.33

Technique defective: procedure was to have called for secretary, dictated to her D.T. article from facts supplied, and *then destroyed memorandum.*

And if it comes to reckoning our times, you are yet in my debt. Consider how many hours & pages I have spent on your next-appearing book . . . and remember that each hour on that counts two, nothing so boring as one's own life rechauffed being imaginable!

I told the two necessary people of your likely-to-happen disclosure of the armoured boats. They laughed merrily. Each decided, on reflection, not to know anything about it beforehand. There'll be a perfect Hymn of Hate in the House that aspires towards the stars, roughly.

(Re "Spectator" article)[1]

This is better stuff. Your point about gas-defence is new to my idea. One thinks of it more often as a menace: as if Berlin could release enough muck today to devastate westward to the confines of Ireland—with us repaying the compliment as the wind changed. Those silly Portonites are always trying to make our flesh creep. Yet I'd rather be gassed than bombarded with 5.9 H.E.

As for aerial gas-attacks—they are not yet practicable—or rather, though practicable they would not be very lethal.

(P.S.) If I print "Burn this" on the heading of every sheet of note-paper I use, will I escape that posthumous "Life & Letters"?

Kennington is an exceedingly fine draughtsman, and a good psychologist. His portraits were excellent. Have you seen his sculptured "God of War"? A comic figure: reminded me of Milne + Plumer + Hereward the Wake.

Curtis has sent you the photos, I believe. Whew! what a job. Probably not a label in the lot.

I imagine he must have written this letter early on the 14th. For that same day I heard that he was on his way up to London; I met him at Waterloo and took him to the Savage Club. Here, besides further discussion of the target-boats, I showed him an additional page or so that I had just written for the Epilogue of my book. Discussing the final passage which ended, "He is the Spirit of Freedom come incarnate to a world in fetters", he contended that he did not respect others' freedom, so much as insisting on his own. He was the essential "anarch"—the very opposite of Socialist. I disputed his statement, argued that it could not be reconciled with his extraordinary understanding of others. He replied that this was easy for him because of the conditions in which he lived—

---

[1]This was an article I had contributed to the "Next Ten Years" series in the *Spectator* on "Warfare".

with most people such understanding was clogged by wealth, possessions, houses, families, conventions.

I remarked that the word "Spirit" was used of intent, his spirit being more consistent and truer than his mind. He suggested that I might add a footnote to the final passage and offered to draft one. Taking a sheet of notepaper he wrote:

This paragraph, seeming to me very personal was shown to the object of it who remarked that probably he more resembled a very agile pedestrian dodging the motor traffic along the main road.

We went on to talk of military things, and he surprised me by referring to General Grierson as if he had known him—for Grierson died in a train in France early in August 1914 on his way to the front. He told me he had met Grierson about 1909–10 when he (T.E.) was a cadet in the Oxford University O.T.C. and Grierson was commanding the 1st Division at Aldershot. Was sent over to him with papers, after a field day. Grierson asked him what he thought of the exercise. T.E. gave him strong criticisms. Grierson, evidently interested and not annoyed, asked T.E. over to his house and talked to him at length about war. Grierson was not at all patronising and far better read than most soldiers (knew lots of German writers). Yet his main idea was to concentrate mass at strongest point, and break through. He argued that one could not waste time in manoeuvre. Must go straight—head down. Overlooked the machine-gun.

As we came away, into the Strand, I happened to be talking of my desire to get at the root of things, and T.E., pointing to a match-seller, remarked, "If you let your passion for truth grow upon you like this, you'll finish by selling matches in the Strand".

Some months earlier I had questioned T.E.'s statement that he had captured twenty-seven Turkish machine-guns at

Tafileh, pointing out that the British Official History gave
the number as sixteen. T.E. had held to his statement and
told me that he had a photograph which would settle the point.
Then, in September, he told me that he thought his photographs had been burnt in a fire, back in the spring, at Mr.
Lionel Curtis's house near Oxford—Mr. Lionel Curtis had
taken charge of this collection as well as other things that
T.E. had abandoned when he walked out of All Souls. T.E.,
however, promised to make enquiries and, finding that the
collection had escaped, arranged for it to be sent up to
London. It arrived in a large suitcase, and I found that it
comprised over two thousand photographs, mainly of scenes
during the Arab campaign. Invaluable as historical records,
they were in mixed order and disorder, many of them un-
identified. After struggling to sort them, and carrying the
process as far as I could, I wrote to T.E. He replied:

[Postmark Southampton]
17.XII.33

Your article "took" very well, so far as I followed its fortunes.
My little department chortled for amusement at its hits. Bigsworth
(D. of E.) said "Splendidly done, if it had to be done. At last the
Air Ministry seems to be getting some favourable publicity"—the
mutt: they could have acres of favourable publicity, if they were not
too silly to allow it.

Robertson said "Well, I'm relieved. There is nothing but good in
it. Liddell Hart is one of the best military writers, and he has done
it better than anyone could do."

Some of the other papers, which had loyally pigeon-holed their
stories of the boats, for months, are a little peevish.

Photographs,—yes, I suppose it will not be easy to unravel the
mess. I made up two loose-leaf albums of them, titled and chrono-
logically arranged. Probably these are missing. Ha Ha.

I expect to be in London on Wed. after Christmas, probably the
27th and will try to find you.

Scott-Paine clucked over it like a broody hen! [Note in letter by T.E.L.]

(P.S.) I've just told Cape that I don't like "Lawrence" for the title, because of D.H.L.'s ownership of that name.[1]

I thought that comment of G.B.S. on your idea of my potential politicality was good—i.e. that I showed no mind to it: or rather that I showed a mind against it. As for the first chapters—I cannot judge. Everything in your book seems to me very good, except the part about me. I shall be glad when it's out (and therefore passed-by). We can then meet each other happily, as free men.

[1]See R.G., p. 183, ninth line from bottom.

TALK WITH T.E.

60 Gloucester Place, 27 December 1933

He arrived in the middle of the morning to help me sort out, and identify, his collection of war photographs.

In going through the set of Hejaz railway photos presented to him by Meissner Pasha, he came to one of the "first and biggest suspension (girder) bridges after entering the Yarmuk Valley" (No. 8 photo), and remarked that he had once tried to blow this up. When I remarked that I understood his target was the one at the other (top) end of the Yarmuk Valley, he said that his attempt was made on his *first ride* through Syria in *June 1917*—the ride that had been veiled in silence. The attempt was made with inadequate explosive and an inadequate party. He hoped to "necklace" the under-slung girder nearest the stone abutment (on right in photo), and cause collapse of the main span as a result.

The difficulty lay in the fact that a sentry was marching up and down. They had got along the bridge and reached the point intended, but were interrupted by the sentry's approach, and couldn't get the chance to smother him without causing an alarm. So had to give up the attempt.

13 Birmingham Street
Southampton.
16.1.34

I go for two weeks engine-hunting in the Midlands: so cannot consider London till that is over. The photos have waited so long that they can well wait two more weeks.

Today I met Admiral Boyle, of the Home Fleet (the S.N.O. of the Red Sea in 1916–1917). He told me how he read all your books, and carried many of them aboard the Nelson. He had just finished the Ghost of Napoleon, and enjoyed it mightily: but your Sherman was your best, etc. I told him of your forthcoming essay on me: explained that it said very little about him (he is sad that the official history says nothing about the great help he gave us on the shore, all the first stage of the Revolt) and that it would not be one of your best books, because of its fallible subject. I think he is bound to buy a copy. He tried to get you for the Senior Course at Greenwich, while he was there. A decent vigorous sailor.

I have been sent innumerable S. Chronicle[1] cuttings by indignant friends—and friends not indignant. Towards all I preserve a magistral silence. What a noble irritant silence can be.

Wolverhampton
28.1.34

As a journalist of many years' standing you ought to know better than to expect a leopard to change his spots. "His friend" conveys verisimilitude to the Sunday Chronicle mind!

Cheer up. Nobody files the S.C. It dies every week. (And there won't be many more instalments, anyway.)

If you have Stirling's address, do please send him a line to say that the seven twin-engined boats of this season's programme are finished. I am in Wolverhampton for passing the 15 engines for the 5 new target boats—but don't tell him that there are five—doing about one a day, with intervals for the works to refresh themselves.

I don't expect to get back to Hythe until the target boats are nearly ready for launching: March perhaps.

Southampton again
March 1, 1934

How late I am in answering your letters. The holiday will be over. I spent nearly three weeks in Wolverhampton, came here for a spell, went to Plymouth and London, back here; to Nottingham; here again. Next move is northward again; on Saturday. Duration of absence about a fortnight. I am sorry to be so vagrant.

[1]Extracts from my book had just begun serialisation in the *Sunday Chronicle*.

Those photographs. If they irk you, domestically, then please inflict them again on the long-suffering Lionel Curtis. He can hide them conveniently in that cabinet. To send them here, or to do the labelling any way but in a long evening of arrangement, seems to me not worth while. One evening would finish the job. Wait for it, if you can. After all, they have waited ten years like they are, and have twice been well arranged. Et sic ad infinitum, probably.

The book came to me as an advance copy. Very big and very solid, said I. Till now I have only run through the pictures and glanced at the maps, which seem to fill their purpose satisfactorily. I suppose reviews will begin to roll along next week. I shall be in Lincoln or Newcastle or Wolverhampton, out of sight and minding. For your sake I wish the book well (self-devoting of me!) but my judgement tells me that people will not want more yet about so hackneyed a subject. Now had you torn me to shreds in the Lytton-Strachey fashion: aha, that would have been a spectacle.

After these five target boats my seasonal activities end, and it seems to me that probably the Air Ministry will send me back to Felixstowe. If so, I shall ask for the leave (to accrue to me in 1934) in advance, to make sure of a holiday. After that we shall see. I confess myself very vague in mind about the next thing. Cottage, if I can afford it.

Did Cape arrange reproduction fee to Augustus John for the book's frontispiece? He owns the copyright of all his drawings of me. Beg them to fix it up promptly, if it has been overlooked. People so often take exhibited pictures for granted, quite wrongly.

Wavell told me he had read your book—to review it somewhere. So we must watch out for his sign-manual.

TALK WITH T.E., 60 GLOUCESTER PLACE, 6 MARCH 1934

(From Diary)

On returning to the flat T.E. came about 3 p.m.—he had rung up from Wren Howard's office in morning to ask if I was free later. We settled down to the task of classifying his war photographs. We worked steadily, partly on our knees, till 7.30, when I had to go out. He was still saying blithely that the book wouldn't sell. (It was published on the 5th.)

When I showed him a letter from a Miss Marguerite Johnston of Liverpool about her crippled young brother being "a hero-worshipper of Col. Lawrence", and finding that it helped him to "bite on the bullet"—T.E. said that you couldn't stop that sort of folly, it was a great mistake, etc. Yet when I said I had thought of sending the youth a copy of my book—it seemed such a genuine case—T.E. at once agreed to my tentative suggestion that he might sign it, and wrote a charming inscription for the boy.

TALK WITH T.E., 60 GLOUCESTER PLACE, 7 MARCH 1934

He had called to see Alan Dawnay at B.B.C. Very official doorkeeper—wanted to know why he wanted to see Dawnay. He had replied, "Oh, nothing in particular"—to the man's stupefaction. Remarked that B.B.C. had in four years acquired all the crusted traditions of an ancient Government institution.

Showed him Wavell's review of my book in the *Listener*, and the remark about my "girding" at professional soldiers. T.E. said he hadn't noticed anything of the sort, and added with a laugh that I was far more tolerant than he had been.

He remarked of regulars—"They do their best—not their fault it's such a rotten best". He went on to reflect on the force of military "trade-unionism"—"They are dreadfully dishonest to one another, yet rally as one man against outside criticism".

He drew my attention to Churchill's "deadly" sketch of Haig (in 1916 Vol. of *World Crisis*).

We talked of Conal O'Riordan's book, *Napoleon Passes*, which I defended on the whole against T.E.'s condemnation

of it as not only tediously written but all wrong in spirit—
"niggling". T.E. thought Napoleon a very great man—he
remade Europe. You could pick holes in every point, yet it
didn't diminish the greatness of the whole. N. like a structure
in which every brick was cracked, yet the effect was splendid
and the whole hung together. "How awful it must have been
for him at Waterloo—to be beaten by a Wellington".

At tea he surprised me by saying that he had once *stayed*
in Cambridge. Remarked that there were only two things of
architectural interest—Jesus Chapel and the tower of St.
Benet's. And a gateway somewhere. King's Chapel left him
cold—it was built when architecture "had become a game—
competitive—instead of an art". Was "exhibitionism" in
stone. He liked the Corpus Library, not only for its manu-
scripts but for its proportions. The "Backs" were fine as long
as one saw them "without preparation." Trinity was all
wrong.

I mentioned Oxford. T.E. first remarked that there was
nothing of architectural value there, then reflected and corrected himself—mentioned two things—the east end of St.
Peter's in the East and the Old Ashmolean—a superb bit.

I asked him if he had any views on religion. T.E. replied
that, although he had been brought up in conventional religion, he had discarded it, and did not notice its loss. Theological speculation and meditation were good as an intellectual exercise, but one could not get anywhere by such ab-
stractions. He felt that thought was as material as everything
else, within our human limitations. One couldn't conceive
thought as apart from our material being.

Talked about his journey from Wejh to the Sirhan. He took
compass bearings every half-hour, besides sketching all the
principal features. The map had been compiled from these
subsequently. Gertrude Bell had travelled over parts of the

same route, with a proper staff, so that had been a check—
yet he had only been 4 or 5 miles out.

He had done the same in his trip from Wejh to Wadi Ais,
despite his sickness. The ordinary Arabian explorer was too
much of a "professional" explorer—too much of a pedant.

Jessie picked up a print of Paul Nash's which had been
among his papers and said he had better take it away—surely
he wanted to keep it. T.E. promptly said, "No". When she
chid him for this recklessness, he said "I'd give everything
away—too much bother to keep—more free if you have no
possessions". And added, "Besides, I like giving".

(*Note by L.H.*) Talking with John Buchan at lunch on 7/3/34,
he told me that when Baldwin was Chancellor of St. Andrew's
he got them to offer an Hon. LL.D. to Lawrence—who took
it as a joke and did not even answer.

TALK WITH T.E., 60 GLOUCESTER PLACE, 13 MARCH 1934

He came while we were at dinner. Urged him to take
something, but he wouldn't—said he didn't mind in the least
watching us eat if we did not mind. Gave him the satisfaction
of feeling what a lot of bother—of eating—he was escaping.
He had never found it a pleasure. I remarked, "Yet your
senses are so acute, it's curious." He replied that his sensation
was mainly through the sight; not in taste.

Later I asked him whether there was any truth in Robert
Graves's statement that he (T.E.) had read all the books in the
Oxford Union Library. He said that Graves had misunderstood—what he really said was, "I had read *all I wanted to*"
—none of the large section of theological books, for example.[1]

In four years up to and during the time he was an under-

[1] See R.G., p. 64, l. 10. R.G.'s was an error in proof-reading.

graduate, he normally read one novel each afternoon, and 2–3 other books during the day. Sat in the Union and read, skimming through those that were not worth taking home.

Talked of memory—I contended that it was like a box-room, that as you accumulated more and more you had to be selective; you pushed unimportant stuff to the back, or discarded it altogether. T.E. disagreed—argued that it was photographic. Everything recorded there on the film, and you could call it up if you had the power. He could see every step of any journey, once he had got back into it. His memory had improved since thirty (?). A "collector of gargoyles".

We talked of Freud, of economics, of Guedalla. Of the first, he suggested that, as in all new developments, the style itself passes, but the thread remains—and thus produces a difference in all thinking henceforward. Instanced Cubism—now past, yet influence has permanently affected art. See a facet at a time.

Of the Arabs—how they had no "recollection", handed down, to make them visualise what a bow looked like.

In further talk of the Arabs, he expressed his real liking for the simple tribesmen, but not for the sheikhs.

Talk of the comprehensiveness of my index, led me to Doughty's, far more comprehensive.

Talked of Mussolini—T.E. said his intellect was nil: you had only to see his books and plays! Lot of practical sense, but no capacity for abstract thought. Lenin was the greatest man—only man who had evolved a theory, carried it out, and consolidated.

The work of classifying and identifying his war photographs was now complete. I had urged on him that the preservation of such records was a duty to history, and although he had expressed indifference as to what became of them, the help he gave me in the task was a better testimony. And now, with his agreement, I presented the collection to the Imperial War Museum.

Among the war collection I had found a large packet of negatives, which he identified as those he had taken of castles and churches in Syria and France during his youthful wanderings; they were in wonderfully good condition and, when printed off, were a proof not only of his skill but of his gift of choosing unusual angles. When I suggested that they ought to be published, he took to the idea, remarking that the American *National Geographic* magazine might be a suitable quarter, and that he might later find time to write some descriptive details. But the time never came.

Early in April I had a letter from the American publishers, Dodd, Mead & Company, saying that the examples of T.E.'s photographs published in my book had suggested to them the idea of a "Pictorial History of the Arab Revolt, with text by Lawrence", utilising his collection of photographs. I duly passed on their request to him, in the faint hope that he might relax his rule, of taking no profit from his part in the Arab Revolt, so far as to take some compensation for his photographic efforts—as these were no part of his duty.

13 Birmingham Street
Southampton
Sunday, 7 April '34

Yes, we blew and rolled about the sea, and made Devonport after some interesting days. Thence I returned here to the old job. "Here" is getting precarious, I fancy: a gent, describing himself as the French Consul, rang the bell this morning and then produced a News Chronicle card. If it develops I shall have to move.

I am dead against any further publication of the Arab Revolt, and would refuse to permit any of my photographs to be reproduced for the purpose—either here or in the States. So that hamstrings Dodd, Mead, I fancy! There has been far too much said already about the affair, which I devoutly wish had never happened: or do I wish that Newcombe, Joyce and Vickery had pushed it to a successful conclusion?

Anyway, I shall not move another turn towards ventilating it again.

I haven't seen the New Statesman for a long time, so missed Graves' letter—but it is rather amusing that apropos of yourself I told you how *he* was never able to let a reviewer alone. I like R.G.: but he is not wise.[1]

Nor have I seen Armstrong's book.[2] His Grey Wolf, about M. Kemal, made me feel ashamed of my countrymen: . . . so I feel disinclined to read anything more that Armstrong may (or rather inevitably will) write. Sensational books are up and out very quickly now-a-days; perhaps three months of life. Yours about me will probably survive Armstrong's latest.

Monday, Tuesday and Wednesday there are Air Ministry people down here. They may extend their stay, and so it looks as if I mightn't get up to London for a while. Not sorry, for I am rather short of money, and rather tired of gadding about, after three weeks in a suit-case. I'd like now to get to my cottage for a night or two. This is

---

[1]The writer in the *New Statesman*, while reviewing my book appreciatively, had contrasted it with its predecessors to their disparagement, referring to the "gossip column stuff provided by such writers as Robert Graves and Lowell Thomas". To class the former book with the latter was so obviously unfair that Robert Graves was, naturally, moved to protest. I called T.E.'s attention to the matter, thinking that he might feel disposed to make it clear directly or indirectly that Graves's book had been written with his authorisation and help—although I did not realise then the extent of that help.

T.E.'s remark "apropos of yourself" referred to my desire earlier to take up a historical point raised in the *Times Literary Supplement's* review of my own book. The reviewer, while endorsing my verdict on Lawrence's preponderating part in the Arab campaign, had raised the question whether he had intended his theory to have a wider application—to warfare as a whole. Quoting part of a passage from Lawrence's own story, the reviewer suggested that it showed that Lawrence was "sticking to the particular, whereas Captain Liddell Hart would apply his appreciation to the general". This point seemed to me of sufficient historical importance to require attention. In his letter of October 17, 1928, T.E. had explicitly told me, "I intended what I wrote to have the larger specious application which you have discovered", and he had since confirmed this in conversation. I therefore suggested that I might clear up the point by a letter to the *Literary Supplement*. But T.E. demurred; he was quite willing that I should quote his letter and emphasise his wider intention in some subsequent essay or book, but did not wish this to be done by a letter—because it was his principle never to answer a reviewer. I naturally complied with his wish, although feeling that the elucidation of history was in a different category from a personal complaint.

[2]This was H. C. Armstrong's book on Ibn Saud, *Lord of Arabia*.

weather for the country, and there is still something to do before I can settle in.

Please be firm about Dodd, Mead, and tell them there can be no picture-book.

> 13 Birmingham St.
> Southampton
> 11 May 1934

If your secretary could see my room here she would burst into tears. Opportunity of replying to so many letters missed!

It seems months since I wrote to you: and I feel obscurely that I owe you replies to three or four letters that I have received, read, and put aside. I am sorry. Perhaps everything has answered itself in the lapse of time. I have been busily and I hope usefully employed since I saw you last. I hope you can say the same. Also I hope you have made some money, whether out of the Daily Telegraph, or off your own bat. Money is useful to Mrs. L.H. and Adrian. How happy I can be with neither—or should I say none?

I am planning a visit to my cottage this Saturday, for the night; and at Whitsun for two nights. May the boats permit it! We are just beginning to test the second of this season's five target boats. No. 1 was a great success.

I remember that parcel which came from Gawsworth. He is a scribbler, like us, and has edited Ewart's diary of the war for Rich and Cowan. His letter was to ask if I would let an extract from a note I sent him (refusing to write an introduction) go on the dust-cover. Some footling remark about Ewart. Ah well!

This is the 7th letter I have written tonight: so don't feel upset if it has less poise and punch than average. The way to write good letters is to write few letters, and only letters-with-a-purpose. This is only from a sense of unfulfilled duty.

P.S. The poor author Lincoln Kirstein sent me this U.S.A. review. I hand it on wickedly, to show you how (like Boswell upon Johnson) you have withdrawn your individuality from your book upon me. The reviewer writes a dithyramb upon your subject, as he appears to him. The virtues and skill of your treatment are unrewarded. That is your reward for being too good an artist.

In May I was a guest at a dining club where one of the members present told me that he had recently met a man who was introduced to him as "Aircraftman Shaw, formerly Colonel Lawrence". Subsequent incidents had raised doubts in his mind, and as a business transaction was in prospect he had thought it worth while to take this chance of speaking to me about the man. A few questions, and a glance at a letter he had received, showed me that an impersonation was being attempted. I promptly wrote to tell T.E. about it.

13 Birmingham St.
Southampton
17 May 1934

Always I owe you two letters! Hard luck. I'm very sorry about the lunch with Ll.G. It struck me when I read it as a pleasant dream, and I should have liked to come: but then I forgot. These five new armoured boats fill the foreground, apparently; at least I am busy on them always. One is run-in, and waiting for the armour. The second has done the first 8 of its 20 hours, and all minor engine defects have been put right. In the last ten hours I do not expect anything to happen. Just one puts the polish on the pistons and bores. Then there are three more to do. They have not yet finished building.

Did you see a bad fake of an interview with me in the Daily Chronicle? Its local reporter fell into talk with me, promising not to repeat anything—and then spat out a travesty of what I said and he imagined. The Editor disowned him to the Air Ministry, and so averted trouble from my head!

Now about this other bloke—If you see the blighter do rub into him that I never have signed myself as Lawrence since 19 twenty something. He is years out of date. In fact he doesn't sound the right sort of man at all. Do you feel that I ought to do something? It is rather hard to catch him by post. However, there is Eliot; the Hon. E. Eliot . . . He is a very balanced solicitor, who looks after the legal interests of Revolt in the Desert. My trouble is that I cannot well risk legal expenses: but Eliot might feel able to assume that a "T. E. Lawrence" in being today was an infringement of his trust property, for the "Revolt" Trust owns the property in that name. If so, he could ask the bloke to stop his games, and charge his trouble to the fund. I'd pay a small bill, up to 3 or 4 pounds, but couldn't risk the promising of more. Will you send on the suggestion (or perhaps this note) to Eliot and see if he can square his conscience to the idea? I can conceive of its seeming to him as if he might legitimately be drawn in, if the affair developed—and to prevent that he might stall the fellow off now.

Failing Eliot, I can't think of anybody else who would do—unless you tell the Daily Express of the existence of a bogus Colonel L.! That would properly boil it—

.   .   .

This is very kind of you. There must be many impersonators, I think, judging by the number of letters I get from stranger-acquaintances, many of them women of whom I appear to have taken some advantage. Sometimes when they get too urgent I have got the police to help me out by asking them to make the correspondence cease. Only this chap hasn't written to me, so I can't well do that, now . . . can I?

Owing to absence from London, I could not follow up his suggestion until the following week, but then went to see Mr. Eliot, showed him T.E.'s letter, and told him such details as I knew. He promised to take up the matter—and did so most effectively.

Meantime a further matter had arisen about which I wanted to see T.E. For I had been approached to write the scenario for the authorised film of *Revolt in the Desert*. I was surprised to hear that such a film should have been sanctioned; after ascertaining that the trustees had agreed to its production, I intimated my provisional willingness to do the scenario, but said that I must first consult T.E., as I should only be willing to undertake the work if he approved.

13 Birmingham St.
Southampton
28.V.34

I sent your reply-wire to you tonight. Am just half-way through tuning the armoured boats: two done, one in hand, two to do: that is, the 20 hours running in for each. The first suit of armour is coming down by road from Sheffield tonight. It takes a few days to fit and finish off the boat: then official trials: then despatch.

I expect to stay here till about June 11, on this job: but late tonight arose a possibility of another few days in Wolverhampton. I'll let you know, if it comes to anything.

I shall be in Hythe all the daylight hours of every day, including Sunday, while the rush lasts. If you come down, try and warn me when—and you will probably have to come out on the boat with me for our talk. That is excellent, on a fine day.

13 Birmingham St.
Southampton
30.V.34

It is by return: I got your letter only 5 minutes ago.

On Saturday (the best day, I expect) I shall leave Southampton about 8.30 a.m. for Hythe: and shall be working in and out of the Power Boat Yard till further notice: till evening, I expect. Can you talk on the water? This always supposes the weather is fine, for these armoured boats are as yet uncovered, and in strong rain we dare not run them, lest the engines get wet.

If you can talk on the water, and will fix a time, then I can either bring the boat in to the Town Quay, Southampton (whence the Hythe Ferry runs) at any hour, morning or afternoon, which you prefer.

Or you can come to Hythe, to the Power Yard, and I'll come in there to meet you.

If, conversely, you want to talk on shore, then please fix a time (either a.m. or p.m. to suit you) and I'll arrange to fit it in to my day. I can meet you either at Hythe (the Lord Nelson Pub.) or in Southampton, anywhere.

Should Saturday fill itself more suitably with Adrian, then Sunday will suit me also. On Sunday I will leave for Hythe rather later, about 9.30, I expect: and follow much the same sort of routine. I can do on the Sunday exactly what I have outlined for the Saturday, to meet you, within reason anywhere at any time you fix.

I shall be as usually ill-dressed, and very commonly dirty.

Accordingly on June 2nd we drove down to Hythe: an American friend was with us. T.E. met us at the Power-Boat Yard, and we went out with him down Southampton Water in one of the new 30 m.p.h. R.A.F. "crash-boats": to show its ease of handling, T.E. handed over the wheel to my wife for a time on the outward run, and allowed me to bring it back to Hythe. Here T.E. explained the points of some of Scott-Paine's speed-boats, including the new armoured target-boats. During this look round he talked of his ideas on the future of sea warfare. We then drove to Otterbourne where we spent the evening.

As regards the film, he told me that the filming of *Revolt in the Desert* had been sanctioned as a means of avoiding something worse being perpetrated by Hollywood. By agreeing to Korda's proposal the trustees could keep control of it, ensure that it was reasonably correct, and prevent "sex-interest" and sensationalism being introduced. If it had to be done, this was the best way to avert distortion. And he approved of my doing the scenario. At the same time, he told me that at a later stage he intended to make a private effort to persuade Korda to postpone the film, so long as the Hollywood danger was averted.[1]

Having settled this matter, and discussed the impersonation affair, our talk became more general. I made notes of a few points later:

[1] See R.G., p. 181, l. 4.

TALK WITH T.E. AT HYTHE AND IN EVENING AT OTTERBOURNE,
2 JUNE 1934

Waiting for new bike from Nottingham—will develop 70 h.p. and do 110 m.p.h.

Future naval warfare—a fleet will loose off 300–400 (quantity counts) of wireless-controlled speed-boats like Miss Britain III (27 feet long) carrying one torpedo and almost flush with water—1 foot showing in front being splinter-proof. Only direct hit could stop, and no one could hit such a target at 60 m.p.h. except by a fluke. Cost perhaps £3,000—latest type 15-inch shell costs £7,500.

On care in driving—T.E. talked of way he will try to avoid running over even a hen, although to swerve is a risk. Said that only on a motorcycle was the driver compelled to take fair proportion of risk. In a big car can hit anything with impunity. On a motorcycle almost certain to be killed—quite right if careless. He would like to see cars fitted with a backward projection from bumper ending in a spearhead just in front of driver's chest, so that if he hit anything, point would pierce him.

Led T.E. on to say that in 1922 (?) at Farnborough a child suddenly jumped in front of his cycle, at 20 m.p.h.; he knocked her down but not hurt. Recently in Bournemouth he skidded on wet tramline, owing to motorist not leaving room, cycle fell over and a car, also skidding, ran over part of his cycle, smashing headlamp. He had jumped aside. Garage man, where he went for repair, said glad to return favour, as T.E. had promoted him corporal and sergeant in Egypt.

To Shiras: "You ought to see Adrian. He interests me. Makes me feel very young. He has the mind of 90 years of age and the manners of our great grandfathers—like a lot of the younger generation."

I said I was just beginning to read Robert Graves's *I, Claudius*, and thought it a very fine piece of work. T.E. admitted its skill but didn't like it—all the characters painted blackly, Graves too ready to believe the worst and to accept any scandalous rumour.[1] T.E. also went on to deprecate detective novels as "literary golf"—wasted brain concentration on imaginary problems.

13 B'ham St.
S'ton
14.VI.34

I was in London for a few hours yesterday: with Eliot and two Bow Street experts we interviewed Mr. . . . my imposure, and persuaded him that he was not me. To my relief, he agreed at once. Had he stuck to his statements I should have begun to question myself.

I owe you many thanks for putting me on his track. He was a little worm of a man. The game has been going on for some time, and has extended from the Zoo to Ward Locke, the publishers. Comically enough, he has been under observation as a case by the specialists of a mental institution, still under my former name. We arranged for him to write to his various victims, and explain that there had been a personation. I am not flattered at the thought that he got away with it successfully. An obviously feeble creature, with the wrinkling face of a chimpanzee.

I did not feel like London, so came back here at once afterwards. We start for Bridlington (four armoured boats) in a few days.

The photographs[2] are, as you say, excellent beyond the wont of such things. Mrs. L.H. is flattered. You and I get off about par. Very good. I am sending one to China as proof of my health!

I cannot think of aught else to tell you—oh yes: I haven't seen that angry review[3] of my Odyssey. Do send it; if it's amusing. About time somebody stood up for Homer. I've wanted to do it myself.

[1] See R.G., p. 174, bottom.

[2] The "photographs" were some snapshots taken at Hythe.

[3] The "angry review" of his Odyssey was by an Australian professor. A reprint of it had been sent to me.

On June 25th I went to a party given by the Newcombes to meet the Emir Abdulla, who was then visiting London. Most of those present had some connection with the Arab Revolt or with Middle East affairs. Soon after I arrived T.E. appeared, in uniform. He was, I think, too late to meet Lord Allenby—thus missing a chance of their first meeting for years. I left with T.E. and took him to catch the 7.30 train from Waterloo back to Southampton.

TALK WITH T.E., 25 JUNE 1934

T.E. came in soon after me, and I took him to catch the 7.30 from Waterloo. (He was in uniform.)

On the way I did a sharp bit of driving, which led him to compliment me on my "fine driving". "You are both snappy and safe. Scott-Paine is snappy, a brilliant driver, but always feels dangerous. I feel safe with you".

T.E. told me more about the exposure of his impersonator. Went along with Eliot and two Bow Street detectives to Janning's office where the man was. Eliot went up first and was introduced to "Colonel Lawrence", who interposed "now Aircraftman Shaw". Eliot: "That's curious—because he is just coming up the stairs". The man recovered himself well, and said this was the proudest honour of his life; and frankly said he was a complete fraud. (T.E. remarked to me, he was glad the man did not stick to his claim, or he [T.E.] would have begun to doubt himself.) The man said he had done it to get himself a position. He had been to the Zoo, and condemned the camels as mangy. Had tried to float a company, and to get Ward Locke to publish two of his poems. He had also been 6 months in a mental home—T.E. remarked that this was the unkindest cut of all!

T.E. said he was about the same build, but a little rat of

a man, with no forehead and thin on top. Not very flattering! As no money had actually passed, they let him off after making him write letters of apology to various people.

T.E. said he had come up this afternoon at cost of forgoing the first trip in the new R.A.F. "crash-boat" (Lion-engined) designed to do 50 m.p.h.—and T.E. aims to get 60 m.p.h. Disliked giving up duty for "social calls"—to see Abdulla, of whom T.E. said he was looking very well, though nothing in him.

Abdulla had asked him to go out to Trans-Jordan; Fethi Bey (Turkish Ambassador) was standing by; T.E. replied that he wouldn't be allowed through Turkey. Fethi Bey assured him he would—but T.E. told me that Philip Chetwode's son was recently out in Middle East, mistaken for T.E., and subjected to a close examination and questions.

T.E.'s new motorcycle (110 m.p.h.); he has not yet had time to collect it from Nottingham.

T.E. talked of publicity. I told him that if a man who had won a certain amount of fame refused the normal publicity attendant on it, he was bound to get much more. He laughed and said he might still want it—and more than he had. All right to accept normal publicity if one had finished—but his greatest activity might still lie ahead. Not yet sure.

I told him of the many people who were approaching me to seek him as "dictator". He said the Fascists had been after him. He had replied that he wouldn't help them to power, but if they gained it, he would agree to become "dictator of the press"—for a fortnight. That would suffice, to settle the press and him. Would stop all mention of anybody's name except public servants. I said that he was going against his own principle of freedom. He said it would do no harm to suppress the cheaper press, save the decent three. I questioned the wisdom of any suppression.

T.E. said there was no doubt there was a big call for a new
lead. Would cease to be Fascist when gained power. But said
Mosley was . . . and not likely to tolerate any really good chief
of staff. But his chance might come if somebody big took him
under their wing.

I put to T.E. the question—would he contemplate leading
any movement. He said "No"—still determined to try and
settle down in his cottage. But if he got tired of it, many things
he could do. (His attitude is certainly changing—more than
he is conscious of.)

Southampton
18.VIII.34

I've come up for breath, after a long period under the weather—
including two wasted voyages—to find myself probably too late for
the boat. Here is this, the Australian jest about my Odyssey, to return
to you. The delay in that was because I sent it to Bruce Rogers, the
printer, whose idea the O. was, and whose is half the responsibility,
at least.

I find that his withers are as little unwrung as mine. The version
was definitely made for non-scholars. I doubt whether this fellow
is a scholar (he betrays no knowledge of Greek, only of other translations: had he known or used the original, he could have sunk my
translation without trace. I slur over the difficult places, always) but
he is assuredly a pedant: and pedants are sure to dislike it. I'm glad
to have seen it, all the same. He gets quite hot, sometimes!

Here is the Viollet-le-Duc catalogue-entry, too. It isn't a book to
possess, but one to refer to. I call it a cheap price for what must be,
in England, a rarity. I expect it is common in Paris: but then there
is the franc exchange.

Also a letter from a woman to return.

As I said, I fear I have missed the boat, for lately a viking ship
came from you: so I place you in Norway. Those longships were very
finely built, and perfectly seaworthy. In a short sea they must have
been wet: but if one hove-to and waited for it to blow out, one would
be safe, if not comfortable. I don't think the Vikings were marvellous
seamen. They coasted, and came ashore whenever it seemed threaten-

ing. Had they had better ships, they would have gone to America long before the Spaniards.[1]

Southampton
31.VIII.34

Wolverhampton—here. Then Lympne. Thence Plymouth: and last night back from Nottingham. Tomorrow I start a week-end, and visit Malvern, to get a snatch of music at the Three Choirs. Some choral Elgar; that's the bill.

Thank you for "the War".[2] It seems radically unlike the first edition: you must have re-composed whole chapters. I have 22 books (about) to read and shall end by dumping them all into my cottage to wait till March 1: but when March comes I shall be so much in terror of the labours that face me at the cottage, as to avoid the cottage. And then who knows? Only I am very tired of working, and very disposed to sink into a quietude that might never end.

Don't, please, send these letters to me, c/o you, on.[3] They represent nothing I care for. Evoking the past is a weary business. Fling them back upon the postman, saying "Not known". I have nothing to give away, now; and no power or will to help.

The 5th and last target boat of this year was finished last Saturday. The programme nears its end. An interesting new Diesel is being installed for test. After that? Why, I may go back to Felixstowe for a spell of duty. I think I am tired of boats, and the camp-life (for a last brief time) appeals. Not yet, though. The Diesel first.

Letters knee-deep round my room. I need (but do not want) a Secretary.

13 Birmingham St.
Southampton
12.IX.34

I've been away for a fortnight—mixed business and pleasure. I note that you have been chasing soldiers about. Probably you are now near Bridlington!

---

[1] *Note by L.H.* I do not know T.E.'s reasons for rejecting the Leif Ericsson saga.

[2] This was the enlarged and revised edition of my *Real War*, now published under the title of *A History of the World War*.

[3] Since the publication of my book, a number of people had been treating me as a post office by which to get their letters readdressed to T.E. When they sent a covering letter and claimed old friendship with him, I felt bound to forward their letters.

As for my future—you have been misled by the description of me in a book called "T. E. Lawrence in Arabia and After". I'm really quite normal. Tired, very; and at the end of my motor-boat knowledge. Determined to work in these last six months to tie up all loose ends and so ensure my successor i/c Boats a fair start, without commitments—and after that six months no plans at all. What I feel like is a rest that should go on and on till I wanted no more of it—or wanted nothing else.

The last thing desirable is activity for the sake of activity. I hope I have enough mind for it to be quietly happy by itself. So I shall not do anything until it becomes necessary: or at least that is my hope. Not a plan in my head, not an ambition, not a want: but a doubt that my saved capital may not be enough to keep me in peace.

Enough or not enough, I'm going to have that rest, anyway!

> 13 Birmingham Street
> Southampton
> 19.X.34

Yes, I have been submerged for a long while, and am popping up my head now only to breathe, not to talk. There are three or four letters of yours on my "liability" side: and I would answer them herein, only that I cannot find them. There are about 80 other letters too.

In one of the chambers or galleries of my mind is a recollection that you asked me about something. I agree to it: if that is the way of inaction. I do not want to do anything (or anybody, or nothing) for quite a while.

We are, two of us, doing the first tests of a rather exciting new Diesel marine engine: and also some bomb-dinghies. Probably I shall spend the last four months of my RAF time at Bridlington, but nothing is settled yet. This address is the only one for the moment.

Clouds Hill, in the background, is the best part of the picture. How bored I'm going to be! Think of it: a really new experience, for hitherto I've never been bored.

In the autumn a Major Bray published a book, under the apt title of *Shifting Sands*. The publishers described it as "The

True Story of the Revolt". Predicting that it would be the sensation of the season, they announced it as being written by "the one man fully qualified to describe the operations in the Arabian peninsula of 1914–1918", and as showing "how Lawrence was totally incapable of leading the Arab Movement". On examination it appeared, however, that Major Bray had only been present during two brief spells in the early months of the Revolt, without going far into the interior. It became even clearer that he had made no adequate historical investigation into the facts of the subsequent campaign. His story of it was apparently based on reading *Revolt in the Desert*—but he had not even read this correctly. Passage after passage contained some absurd misstatement of fact. Yet upon this unstable foundation he built rhetorical charges against not only Lawrence's capacity but his motives—for example:

"Not till Deraa, did Lawrence, racing ahead of Nuri Bey and his men, enter the city alone, so that even the small credit of being the first to occupy the city was denied the Arab leaders. . . . From Suez to Aleppo, thousands of the Empire's sons sleep their last sleep—did they die so that Lawrence might ride alone into Deraa?"

If he had read *Revolt in the Desert* with any care he would have seen that an Arab force had already occupied Deraa when Lawrence rode thither, and that his haste was in order to join it, not to precede it, in order to check pillaging and establish order. I have never come upon a more curious case of consistent misreading and uncontrolled imagination.

When the book appeared a Sunday newspaper interviewed Lord Allenby and myself about it. Lord Allenby, after exposing the absurdity of its accusations against Lawrence, added a fresh tribute to the way that the latter had served him.

Knowing T.E.'s deep regard for Allenby, I told him of Allenby's action.

Ozone Hotel
Bridlington, Yorks.
23.XI.34

Here I am, for the balance of my RAF time, I expect, as the ten boats here for overhaul will not be finished before the end of February.

Mrs. Bernard Shaw sent me Bray's book—but it isn't much fun. If he was an enemy, I wouldn't detach more than a few light troops to push him back. However, I'm glad to have seen the book; I wonder why he didn't send me a copy?

I remember Bray quite well, now: a very honourable and conscientious Indian Army officer, who served under Wilson at Jeddah in the early days. I never heard what happened to him.

His book does its level best to be true, but isn't well informed—
. . . However—

I might get to my cottage (neighbour and tenant just died suddenly, rather complicating things) at Christmas for two or three days, but cannot say.

I didn't see much about Bray's book in the Press: but Allenby always was a great help to me, and I think I helped him in return: and we were always Lion and Mouse friends. A good old thing. Did he say anything new? I take kindness from him for granted.

Ozone Hotel
Bridlington, Yorks.
28.XI.34

I found this today, digging deep into the pile of slowly-rotting letters that await a reply: I fear it is yours, and should have gone back long ago.[1]

I've not anything to say about it. The "trace" of the Hejaz Railway was drawn by Meissner, a German Engineer. The technical staff (foremen and section men) were mostly Greek and Italian.

[1] An American historian, Professor Earle, had written to me in June, putting some questions bearing on Middle East affairs before and since the war. I had sent his letter on to T.E.

Mustapha Kemal was a great patriot, and anti-foreign from 1913 onwards. His Nationalism was founded to combat the pro-German tendency of Enver.

The Oil Company had (contrary to rumour) little or no influence in deciding our policy towards Mesopotamia. I can say this with complete assurance. I know foreigners are always smelling rats—but in practice if you tell a F.O. man that "Oil" wants this or that, his reaction is to go dead contrary to their wishes, in the name of honesty. I can truthfully say that neither Ll.G., nor Curzon, nor Bonar Law, nor Arnold Wilson nor myself paid any heed to the Anglo-Persian or the Imperial Petroleum Co. The British policy in Mesopotamia was decided on purely Imperial lines.

P.S. I think the German Bagdad-participation offers were more onerous than advantageous to us.

In early December the Imperial War Museum referred to me a request from a German woman for permission to reproduce a few of the photographs from Lawrence's war-collection. Enclosing a booklet on Lawrence which was in use as a school text-book in Germany, apparently for classes in English, she stated that a new edition was being issued and that it was desired to illustrate it. I forwarded her application to him, on December 4th, without expressing an opinion. He sent it back with the characteristic note:

I don't see any good in this project. Why should I help in a publicity that has no useful purpose? The poor German children had better read about something else. So please say NO to the lady.

Writing to T.E. at Christmas, I told him of my appointment, just arranged, as Military Correspondent of the *Times* and its adviser on defence in general.

Ozone Hotel
Bridlington

Returned to find your note, upon which warmest congratulations. . . . I am sure that you will be able to correlate the three Defences and Offences to the general benefit.

So I can only wind up by hoping that you are as pleased as myself. I implore you . . . to use your new enlargement for some unprofitable but worthy book. Give us some reflections upon the relations of density to type of war: working out the influences of much or little land-room upon tactics. . . .

For myself, I am going to taste the flavour of true leisure. For 46 years have I worked and been worked. Remaineth 23 years (of expectancy). May they be like Flecker's

"a great Sunday that goes on and on".

If I like this leisure when it comes, do me the favour of hoping that I may be able to afford its prolongation for ever and ever.

So these are our joint and separate wishes for 1935 and all that.

Early in February we went to Cornwall, and while there my wife had a letter from him, from Bridlington, dated the 25th, beginning "Tomorrow I leave here, and leave the R.A.F.". He went on to say that he was coming south by stages, that he would probably be looking in to see us, and that he could see nothing beyond the moment. Now that the prospect of leisured inactivity was at hand he seemed to like it less. We did not return to London until the middle of March. A few evenings later, when I came in I was told that a man had asked to see me, wanted to know when I should be back, but refused to give his name. His dress and demeanour had aroused the maid's suspicions. I naturally surmised that it was T.E., but the maid was new and so had not seen him before; and although there were portraits of T.E. in the flat, she did not think they tallied with the man who had called. However, this merely showed once again how easily he could escape recognition, for a few evenings later he came again. He said that he had come up to London to take refuge for a few days until the hubbub over his leaving the Air Force had quieted down. After he had managed to persuade the regular Pressmen to leave him in peace, some "free lance" photographers had refused to desist; they had even forced their way into his garden and had to be ejected by force. He told us that he had put his thumb out of joint in the struggle, which he recounted with a glee that sounded curiously youthful and "physical".[1] They seemed to have suffered worse. In revenge, he said, they had come back and thrown stones at his roof, smashing some of the slates. He told us also something of his ride down from Bridlington on a "push-bike". And I heaved a premature sigh of relief when he said that he had taken to this for good, having come to the conclusion that, on an income of two pounds a week, he could not afford to run a high-powered motorcycle.

TALK WITH T.E., 22 MARCH 1935

£20,000 instalment in this year's Air Estimates for new type of:

70 fast boats, 35–40 m.p.h. (perhaps raise to 50) with 3 Napier Lion engines of 500 h.p., and radius of 500 m. Easily fitted for torpedo tubes and depth charges.

If T.E. had stayed in service he would have taken the Air Council round the fleet in one at the Jubilee Review at full-speed, ensconced in armchairs!

Suggested I should write a book, "Fifteen Decisive British Defeats".

Said he had received approaches to become successor to Hankey, but had replied that he would only do so if the normal Cabinet side was removed from the C.I.D. side—(it is interesting to see him even contemplating the latter role).

· · ·

On Monday, May 13th, returning home about 7.30 p.m., I was told by my secretary that the Air Ministry, first, and

[1]But see R.G., p. 71, tenth line from bottom.

Alan Dawnay, later, had telephoned to say that T.E. had met with an accident when riding back, on his motor-cycle, to his cottage at Cloud's Hill from Bovington Camp, and that he was lying gravely injured with a fractured skull in the Military Hospital there. The Air Ministry had asked whether I knew the whereabouts of his next of kin. I got through to them at once, and gave them such information as I had. T.E.'s mother was in China, with his eldest brother, while his other surviving brother, the youngest of the five, who held a University appointment at Cambridge, was on holiday in Majorca. I was not able to get in touch with Alan Dawnay until later, but put a call through to the hospital and found that Lord Carlow, another friend of T.E., had arrived there; he had come on a visit to Cloud's Hill only to be greeted by the news of the accident, and was remaining on the spot to look after things. T.E. had pitched on his head after a violent swerve in trying to avoid a butcher's boy who was cycling along the road in company with another boy. Thinking that Newcombe ought to be informed, I sent him a message, and he arranged to go down to Bovington as soon as possible to relieve Carlow; these two kept vigil by turns until the end.

Days of anxiety followed, during which T.E.'s friends were concerned to obtain the best possible medical advice. All the time he lay unconscious, and it was clear that his head injuries were very severe. There seemed a glimmer of hope, as his vitality was astounding, but on the Saturday congestion of the lungs developed, and at about a quarter past eight on Sunday morning, the 19th, death came. A post-mortem examination showed that the brain was badly lacerated; even if he had survived he would have lost speech and memory, and been paralysed.

The funeral was arranged for Tuesday, May 21st. Most of those who came went direct to Moreton Church, but a few

gathered beforehand at the cottage. On the way there from
London one drove along the Salisbury-Blandford road, T.E.'s
favourite speed-stretch, where the switchback contour peculiarly gives the sensation which is described as that of
"moulding the hills and dales."

As for the funeral itself, here is part of a note which I jotted
down at the time, in recollection of it:

Shortly before 2 p.m. a light motor hearse passed the cottage
with T.E.'s plain unmarked coffin. We set off in cars and then
went ahead to the church at Moreton. The setting was perfect
in its pastoral charm—the church beside the banks of the
Frome, and the hall near by, at the end of the drive. May sunshine brought warmth, and the chilly wind that had cooled the
journey down had disappeared here. The path up to the
church and the wall was lined with spectators, but most
seemed to be from the near-by villages, and the only dis-
cordant note was the crowd of cameramen like a swarm of
black flies (there was a cloud of real flies at the graveside later,
like a delegation from the East). My urgency on Sunday
night to quench the idea of donning top-hats had succeeded,
and only one man present had disregarded the notification of
"no formal dress." . . . Only a few, even, wore black lounge
suits. Most of the friends went into the church, but I waited
until the hearse arrived, and then followed it in with Jack
Salmond and Scott-Paine. Augustus John trod on the heels
of the bearers—Newcombe, Eric Kennington, Ronald Storrs,
Pat Knowles, Aircraftman Bradbury, and ex-private Russell
of the Tank Corps. (They were chosen with the idea of representing six different phases of T.E.'s career.) The service was
simple and brief; the parson faltering as if overcome by the
occasion or emotion.

At the end the coffin was carried out, down the steps and
placed on a "trolley" which the bearers pushed along, the

rest of us following—out of the churchyard gates and along the wooded lane to the new cemetery. It had only a few graves. The coffin was lowered into the leaf-lined grave, the service continued, and then we took a last look at the small coffin before breaking away.

INDEX

Considerations of space make it impossible to give a descriptive entry to every reference. In order to make this index as comprehensive as possible, secondary or passing references are given by page number only after the abbreviation O.R. (i.e. other references).

I—Lawrence to Robert Graves   II—Lawrence to Liddell Hart